Page deliberately left blank

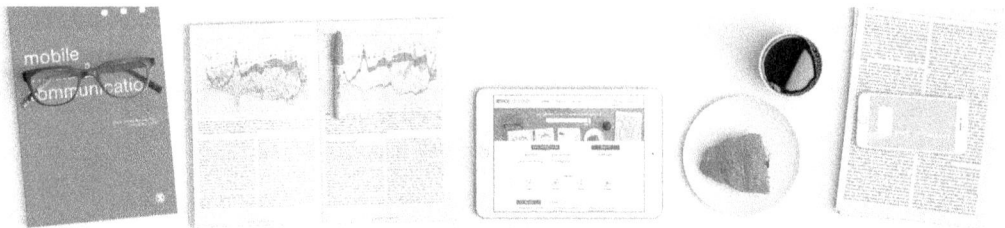

Sign up for FREE updates about the latest research!

journals.sagepub.com/action/registration

Register online at
SAGE Journals and
start receiving…

New Content Alerts

- Receive table of contents
  alerts when a new issue
  is published.

- Receive alerts when forthcoming
  articles are published online
  before they are scheduled to
  appear in print (OnlineFirst articles).

Announcements

- Receive need-to-know information about a journal such as calls for papers,
  special issue notices, and events.

Search Alerts

- Create custom search alerts based on recent search keywords or terms.

journals.sagepub.com   §SAGE journals

THE
ANNALS
of the American Academy of Political and Social Science

VOLUME 692 | NOVEMBER 2020

Toward a Better Approach to Preventing, Identifying, and Addressing Child Maltreatment

SPECIAL EDITORS:

Lawrence M. Berger
University of Wisconsin—Madison

Kristen S. Slack
University of Wisconsin—Madison

⑤SAGE

Los Angeles | London | New Delhi
Singapore | Washington DC | Melbourne

The American Academy of Political and Social Science

202 S. 36th Street, Annenberg School for Communication, University of Pennsylvania, Philadelphia, PA 19104-3806; (215) 746-6500; (215) 573-2667 (fax); www.aapss.org

---

Origin and Purpose. The Academy was organized December 14, 1889, to promote the progress of political and social science, especially through publications and meetings. The Academy does not take sides in controverted questions, but seeks to gather and present reliable information to assist the public in forming an intelligent and accurate judgment.

Meetings. The Academy occasionally holds a meeting in the spring extending over two days.

Publications. THE ANNALS of The American Academy of Political and Social Science is the bimonthly publication of the Academy. Each issue contains articles on some prominent social or political problem, written at the invitation of the editors. These volumes constitute important reference works on the topics with which they deal, and they are extensively cited by authorities throughout the United States and abroad.

Subscriptions. THE ANNALS of The American Academy of Political and Social Science (ISSN 0002-7162) (J295) is published bimonthly—in January, March, May, July, September, and November—by SAGE Publishing, 2455 Teller Road, Thousand Oaks, CA 91320. Periodicals postage paid at Thousand Oaks, California, and at additional mailing offices. POSTMASTER: Send address changes to The Annals of The American Academy of Political and Social Science, c/o SAGE Publishing, 2455 Teller Road, Thousand Oaks, CA 91320. Institutions may subscribe to THE ANNALS at the annual rate: $1257 (clothbound, $1419). Individuals may subscribe to the ANNALS at the annual rate: $134 (clothbound, $197). Single issues of THE ANNALS may be obtained by individuals for $41 each (clothbound, $58). Single issues of THE ANNALS have proven to be excellent supplementary texts for classroom use. Direct inquiries regarding adoptions to THE ANNALS c/o SAGE Publishing (address below).

All correspondence concerning membership in the Academy, dues renewals, inquiries about membership status, and/or purchase of single issues of THE ANNALS should be sent to THE ANNALS c/o SAGE Publishing, 2455 Teller Road, Thousand Oaks, CA 91320. Telephone: (800) 818-SAGE (7243) and (805) 499-0721; Fax/Order line: (805) 375-1700; e-mail: journals@sagepub.com. *Please note that orders under $30 must be prepaid.* For all customers outside the Americas, please visit http://www.sagepub.co.uk/customerCare.nav for information.

THE ANNALS

© 2020 by The American Academy of Political and Social Science

Editorial Office: 202 S. 36th Street, Philadelphia, PA 19104-3806
For information about individual and institutional subscriptions address:
SAGE Publishing
2455 Teller Road
Thousand Oaks, CA 91320

For SAGE Publishing: Peter Geraghty (Production)

From India and South Asia, write to:
SAGE PUBLICATIONS INDIA Pvt Ltd
B-42 Panchsheel Enclave, P.O. Box 4109
New Delhi 110 017
INDIA

From Europe, the Middle East, and Africa, write to:
SAGE PUBLICATIONS LTD
1 Oliver's Yard, 55 City Road
London EC1Y 1SP
UNITED KINGDOM

International Standard Serial Number ISSN 0002-7162
ISBN 978-1-0718-4862-3 (Vol. 692, 2020) paper
ISBN 978-1-0718-4863-0 (Vol. 692, 2020) cloth
First printing, November 2020

Information about membership rates, institutional subscriptions, and back issue prices may be found on the facing page.

Advertising. Current rates and specifications may be obtained by writing to The Annals Advertising and Promotion Manager at the Thousand Oaks office (address above). Acceptance of advertising in this journal in no way implies endorsement of the advertised product or service by SAGE or the journal's affiliated society(ies) or the journal editor(s). No endorsement is intended or implied. SAGE reserves the right to reject any advertising it deems as inappropriate for this journal.

Claims. Claims for undelivered copies must be made no later than six months following month of publication. The publisher will supply replacement issues when losses have been sustained in transit and when the reserve stock will permit.

Change of Address. Six weeks' advance notice must be given when notifying of change of address. Please send the old address label along with the new address to the SAGE office address above to ensure proper identification. Please specify the name of the journal.

THE
ANNALS
of the American Academy of
Political and Social Science

VOLUME 692 | NOVEMBER 2020

IN THIS ISSUE:

Toward a Better Approach to Preventing, Identifying, and Addressing Child Maltreatment

Special Editors: LAWRENCE M. BERGER and KRISTEN S. SLACK

The Contemporary U.S. Child Welfare System(s): Overview and
Key Challenges . . . .*Lawrence M. Berger and Kristen S. Slack*   7

The Scope, Nature, and Causes of Child Abuse
and Neglect. . . . . *Sarah A. Font and Kathryn Maguire-Jack*   26

Child Welfare Financing: What Do We Fund, How, and
What Could Be Improved? . . . . *Ron Haskins*   50

The Evolution of Federal Child Welfare Policy through the Family
First Prevention Services Act of 2018: Opportunities,
Barriers, and Unintended Consequences. . . . . *Mark F. Testa*   68
and David Kelly

The Child Maltreatment Prevention Landscape: Where Are We Now,
and Where Should We Go?. . . . . *Brenda Jones Harden, Cassandra Simons,*   97
Michelle Johnson-Motoyama, and Richard Barth

Leveraging Family and Community Strengths to Reduce Child
Maltreatment. . . . .*Debangshu Roygardner, Kelli N. Hughes,*   119
and Vincent J. Palusci

The Social Welfare Policy Landscape and Child Protective Services:
Opportunities for and Barriers to Creating
Systems Synergy . . . .*Megan Feely, Kerri M. Raissian,*   140
William Schneider, and Lindsey Rose Bullinger

A Practical Framework for Considering the Use of Predictive Risk Modeling
in Child Welfare . . . . *Brett Drake, Melissa Jonson-Reid,*   162
María Gandarilla Ocampo, Maria Morrison,
and Darejan (Daji) Dvalishvili

Who Is and Is Not Served by Child Protective Services Systems?
  Implications for a Prevention Infrastructure to Reduce
  Child Maltreatment . . . . *Kristen S. Slack and Lawrence M. Berger*   182

How Do Families Experience and Interact with
  CPS? . . . .*Darcey H. Merritt*   203

Foster Care in a Life Course Perspective. *Fred Wulczyn*   227

Racial Disproportionality and Disparities in the Child Welfare System:
  Why Do They Exist, and What Can Be Done
  to Address Them?. . . . . *Alan J. Dettlaff and Reiko Boyd*   253

FORTHCOMING

The Dynamics of Homelessness: Research and Policy
Special Editors: BARRETT A. LEE, MARYBETH SHIN, and DENNIS P. CULHANE

Legacies of Racial Violence
Special Editors: HEDWIG LEE, GEOFF WARD, and DAVID CUNNINGHAM

The Contemporary U.S. Child Welfare System(s): Overview and Key Challenges

By
LAWRENCE M. BERGER
and
KRISTEN S. SLACK

This volume of *The ANNALS* aims to increase awareness among scholars, policy-makers, and practitioners of the size, scope, and functions of child welfare services in the United States. We aim to promote a wider understanding of the broad impacts of child welfare policies and point to ways in which child welfare services can be better incorporated into cross-cutting social policy debates. The articles in this volume offer concrete recommendations for policies and practices that can reduce child maltreatment, and for systemic approaches—both within the purview of child welfare services and across the broader community and social policy landscape—that can better identify and respond to the needs of children and families in which maltreatment has already occurred or where there is a risk of abuse and neglect. This introduction sets a foundation for understanding the contents of the volume: we provide an overview of child welfare services in the United States and highlight current challenges that the U.S. child welfare systems face.

Keywords: child abuse and neglect; child maltreatment; child protective services; child welfare; child welfare system

Child welfare services in the United States are guided by a three-part federal mandate to promote safety, permanency (enduring residence in a stable and legally recognized family), and well-being for children experiencing or at risk of child maltreatment. Complying with this mandate requires that state and local governments first respond to alleged reports of suspected child abuse and neglect; investigate those reports when warranted; (often) make a

Lawrence M. Berger is Associate Vice Chancellor for Research in the Social Sciences, Vilas Distinguished Achievement Professor of Social Work, and former director of the Institute for Research on Poverty at the University of Wisconsin–Madison. His research focuses on the ways in which economic resources, sociodemographic characteristics, and public policies affect parental behaviors and child and family well-being.

Correspondence: lmberger@wisc.edu

DOI: 10.1177/0002716220969362

determination as to whether maltreatment has occurred; and, when appropriate, provide services to protect children from ongoing maltreatment. Second, it requires ensuring safe, stable, and permanent living arrangements for children either with their family of origin or by providing out-of-home care, either temporarily or permanently, for children who cannot safely live with their family of origin. Third, it requires intervening to promote the health; mental health; and educational, material, and social well-being of system-involved children and youth, particularly those who have been removed from their home. While these services fall under the purview of what is commonly referred to as "the" U.S. child welfare or child protective services "system," they are, in actuality, provided by a multitude of state-, county-, and territorial-administered systems that are characterized by considerable variation in policies and practices.

Child welfare services in the United States are far-reaching and expensive. A large proportion of American children and families—and particularly low-income children and families and children and families of color—are investigated for alleged maltreatment and, in many cases, subject to further intervention, including child removal (Kim et al. 2017; Wildeman and Emanuel 2014; Wildeman et al. 2014), at a cost of roughly $30 billion per year to federal, state, and local governments (Rosinsky and Williams 2018). Moreover, despite that the vast majority of child welfare–involved families are low-income and also involved in other social welfare programs, most commonly the Supplemental Nutrition Assistance Program (SNAP; formerly Food Stamps) and Medicaid/State Children's Health Insurance Program (SCHIP) (Cancian, Noyes, and Kim 2017; Feely et al., this volume; Slack and Berger, this volume), child welfare services typically receive limited attention in major social policy debates—a crucial omission given the substantial costs of child maltreatment to individuals, families, and society, as well as a growing body of evidence suggesting a causal link between income and child maltreatment, including that more generous social welfare transfers may result in lower rates of child abuse and neglect (Berger et al. 2017; D. Brown and De Cao 2020; E. Brown et al. 2019; Cancian, Yang, and Slack 2013; Pac 2019; Raissian and Bullinger 2017; Schneider, Waldfogel, and Brooks-Gunn 2017; Wildeman and Fallesen 2017).

This volume of *The ANNALS* brings together leading child maltreatment[1] and child welfare policy scholars to assess options and opportunities for better preventing, identifying, and addressing child abuse and neglect—through both child welfare services and through the wide range of other policies and programs with which populations at risk of child maltreatment and child welfare involvement regularly interact—bringing to bear the most rigorous existing research on child

Kristen S. Slack is professor and PhD program chair at the University of Wisconsin–Madison Sandra Rosenbaum School of Social Work. Her research focuses on understanding the role of poverty and economic hardship in the etiology of child maltreatment, caseload dynamics of child welfare systems in relation to other public benefit systems, and community-based programs designed to prevent child maltreatment.

NOTE: We are grateful to *The ANNALS*, Annie E. Casey Foundation, and Institute for Research on Poverty for generously supporting the authors' conference for this special issue.

maltreatment prevention and response. The volume is particularly timely for at least three reasons. First, after declining for more than a decade, foster care caseloads have risen substantially in recent years, which has largely been attributed to the opioid epidemic and its effects on families (Sepulveda and Williams 2019; Williams and Sepulveda 2019). Second, the school closures, lockdowns, and losses of employment and income that the COVID-19 pandemic has caused have created a context in which actual child abuse and neglect rates are likely rising, even as reports of child maltreatment are likely falling (Welch and Haskins 2020). This has raised concerns about both child safety and long-term system capacity. Third, recent federal legislation, the Family First Prevention and Services Act of 2018, has radically transformed child welfare financing by, for the first time, allowing federal Title IV-E funds—which have historically been available only for partial federal reimbursement of foster care, adoption assistance, and kinship guardian assistance—to be spent on evidence-based prevention efforts rather than solely on out-of-home care services. This has created an opportunity to substantially reform child welfare financing, policy, and practice (see articles by Haskins, this volume; Testa and Kelly, this volume).

This volume is intended to increase awareness among public policy scholars, policy-makers, and practitioners of the size, scope, and functions of child welfare services in the United States, with the aim of promoting a wider understanding of the potential implications of social policies and reforms thereof for child welfare services, as well as better incorporating child welfare services into cross-cutting social policy debates. To this end, the articles offer concrete recommendations for improving child maltreatment prevention as well as systemic approaches—both within the purview of child welfare services and across the broader community and social policy landscape—to identifying and responding to children and families at risk of abuse and neglect and those for which maltreatment has already occurred. In this article, we provide an overview of child welfare services in the United States, and highlight current challenges facing U.S. child welfare systems. Throughout, we point to the contributions to these areas that the articles included in the volume provide.

Why Do We Need a Child Welfare System?

A substantial number of American children experience abuse or neglect, which, in turn, is associated with adverse cognitive, emotional/behavioral, social, and economic outcomes throughout the life course. This incurs a high cost to both individuals and society. The extensive list of adverse outcomes associated with being maltreated in childhood spans mental health (depression, suicidality, anxiety, conduct disorder, aggression, post-traumatic stress disorder); drug and alcohol abuse; physical health (obesity, sexually transmitted diseases, diabetes, liver and kidney disfunction, vision problems); risky health behaviors; cognitive development (school performance, learning problems); difficulty relating to peers; educational achievement and attainment; delinquency, violence, and criminal behavior; and employment, employment stability, earnings, occupational status, and wealth accumulation (National Research Council 2014; Norman et al. 2012; Widom 2014). These outcomes may, at least in part, reflect that experiencing abuse and neglect during childhood can impact brain development and related biological processes, with consequences for executive functioning, stress response, emotion processing and regulation, and cognitive functioning and memory (Bernard, Lind, and Dozier 2014).

Moreover, evidence suggests a dose-response relation such that exposure to multiple forms of (Font and Maguire-Jack 2020), more frequent, and more severe abuse and neglect are associated with poorer development and life outcomes (Jackson et al. 2014; Jaffee and Maikovich-Fong 2011; Johnson-Reid, Kohl, and Drake 2012). Effects may also differ by the developmental stage(s) at which maltreatment occurs (Jaffee and Maikovich-Fong 2011). In addition, evidence points to high levels of intergenerational transmission of abuse and neglect such that children whose parents experienced childhood maltreatment are at substantial risk of experiencing maltreatment themselves at the hands of both their parents and others (Font et al. 2020). It is important to note, however, that there is an ongoing debate over the extent to which these associations are likely causal in nature versus reflecting other aspects of social and economic disadvantage that are associated both with experiencing childhood maltreatment and with poor outcomes throughout the life course. Nonetheless, child abuse and neglect are extremely costly to U.S. society: recent estimates suggest that the total cost of child abuse and neglect in the United States ranges from $428 billion to $2 trillion per year (Peterson, Florence, and Klevens 2018).

Recognition of both the consequences and costs of child maltreatment has led to a range of policies and programs in the United States, as in all industrialized countries, to prevent and respond to child abuse and neglect to minimize both their occurrence and their adverse consequences (Berger and Slack 2013; Berger and Waldfogel 2011). These efforts span public policies, laws, and regulations; federal, state, and local (e.g., county, territorial/tribal) funding allocations; and public and private agencies, programs, and services committed to intervening with children and families who are at risk of, suspected of, or have been identified as experiencing child abuse and/or neglect. Precise policies, services, and mechanisms differ substantially across (and within) countries, as well as by state/territory and county within the United States. Collectively, however, they are typically referred to as composing a country's child welfare or child protective services (CPS) system.

Although *child welfare system, child protection system, CPS system, CPS*, and similar terms are frequently interchangeably used, in this article, as in all of the articles in this volume, we use *child welfare system(s)* as the overarching term to indicate the full scope of systemic responses to child maltreatment, including both CPS and out-of-home (foster care) services. We use *CPS* to refer to "front-end" child welfare system activities, including report receipt, investigation, maltreatment determination, in-home services, child removal, and the like. We use *out-of-home care services* or *foster care services* to refer to child welfare system activities for children who have been removed from their home. Notably, we define the U.S. child welfare system as being responsible for identifying, responding to, and addressing alleged acts of maltreatment—we do not include child maltreatment prevention services to families who have not yet been reported to CPS as, in the U.S. case, such services are typically provided (and traditionally financed) by a range of government and private agencies and funding mechanisms outside of the formal child welfare system(s), which has been described as "reactionary by design" (Welch and Haskins 2020).[2] Finally, although we and the other authors in the volume refer to the U.S. child welfare, CPS, or foster care "system," it is important to recognize that child welfare policy and practice are predominantly determined and delivered at the state or county level (albeit under the guidance of federal mandates and funding mechanisms): thirty-eight states, Washington, D.C., and Puerto Rico operate state-administered systems, ten states operate county-administered but state-supervised systems, and two states operate hybrid systems in which some CPS functions are administered at the state level and others at the county level. Slack and Berger (this volume) provide a more detailed discussion of state and local variation in child welfare practice and policy.

The legitimacy of government-sanctioned child welfare systems as a mechanism for intervention in family life has been justified across the advanced industrialized countries by widespread agreement that child abuse and neglect are conditions that necessitate societal intervention both because children are not fully able to protect themselves from maltreatment at the hands of their parents and caregivers *and* because children are entitled to grow up in a home in which they are free from abuse and neglect (Waldfogel and Berger 2006). As such, child welfare systems have considerable coercive and legal power to intervene in (allegedly) abusive and neglectful families—if necessary, even against parents' wills (Freymond and Cameron 2006). That is, concerns for both equity and children's rights have meant that society's obligation to protect children from maltreatment is typically treated in law and policy as superseding society's obligation to ensure parental rights and family privacy once some legally defined threshold of abuse or neglect has *potentially* been crossed (Berger and Waldfogel 2011).[3] Berger and Waldfogel (2011) further assert that efficiency concerns also justify the need for child welfare systems. Specifically, given extensive evidence that experiencing abuse or neglect during childhood is associated with a wide range of adverse outcomes throughout the life course, which result in extensive short- and long-term costs to both individuals and society, they argue that cost-effective interventions for preventing and ameliorating the effects of abuse and neglect are warranted. At the same time, there are growing calls for reimagining the child welfare system and reducing or even eliminating foster care as a response to child abuse and neglect, replacing such policy responses with a more robust social and economic safety net and continuum of prevention services (Center for the Study of Social Policy 2020; Dettlaff and Boyd, this volume; Merritt, this volume; Feely et al., this volume; Ringel et al. 2017). As the field moves forward, innovations in policy are critically needed to both counteract the need for CPS and improve the experiences of families who come into contact with the child welfare system.

What Constitutes Child Maltreatment?

Child maltreatment is made up of acts of omission and acts of commission, usually on the part of a parent or primary caregiver, that have resulted in or *pose a threat of* potential harm to a child, typically regardless of parental or caregiver intent (Gilbert, Widom, et al. 2009). Many, but not all, U.S. state statutes include a clause indicating that the action or omission must have occurred *for reasons other than poverty* alone. Acts of commission—things parents or caregivers do that pose risk of or actual harm to children—are primarily categorized as child physical abuse, child sexual abuse, and child psychological or emotional abuse. Acts of omission—things parents or caregivers fail to do, so as to pose risk of or actual harm to children—are primarily categorized as child physical, medical, supervisory, educational, or emotional neglect.

Child neglect, the umbrella term for omissions in care, is characterized by inadequate provision of basic necessities such as food, clothing, shelter, supervision, education, and medical care and, in some cases, a failure to meet children's emotional or psychological needs. Neglect is by far the most common form of maltreatment in the United States and was indicated in 74.9 percent of all confirmed maltreatment cases in 2017 (U.S. Department of Health and Human Services [USDHHS] 2019a). In fact, child neglect is the most common form of maltreatment in all of the developed countries (Gilbert, Widom, et al. 2009). The second most common form of maltreatment, physical abuse, constitutes actions that put children at risk of, have the potential to cause, or have caused bodily harm; such actions are frequently undertaken for disciplinary or punitive purposes. Physical abuse was indicated in 18.3 percent of confirmed maltreatment cases in 2017 (USDHHS 2019a). Sexual abuse includes exposing a minor to or involving them in any form of direct sexual contact as well as exploitation or exhibitionism. It was indicated in 8.6 percent of confirmed maltreatment cases in 2017 (USDHHS 2019a). Finally, emotional or psychological abuse is broadly defined to encompass actions and omissions that are the cause of or have the potential to cause psychological/emotional harm to a child; this type of abuse was indicated in 5.7 percent of maltreatment victimizations in 2017 (USDHHS 2019a).[4] Notably, while precise definitions and thresholds of each form of abuse or neglect differ considerably by U.S. state (Rebbe 2018), as well as by country and, in many cases, by state, region, or province within a country, these overarching constructs are defined relatively similarly across the industrialized countries and the states and territories within them. Font and Maguire-Jack (this volume) provide a detailed discussion of various definitions of child abuse and neglect and the implications of identifying and measuring maltreatment.

How Does the Child Welfare System Identify Children and Families?

Alleged incidents of abuse and neglect come to the attention of the child welfare system when suspected maltreatment is reported by mandated or voluntary reporters. This initially requires that a parental or caregiver act of omission or commission is viewed by a potential (mandatory or voluntary) reporter who makes an assessment that the behavior may constitute child maltreatment and, in turn, a decision to make a report. This first stage of the process occurs outside of the child welfare system, itself.

Parameters for reporting suspected child maltreatment are governed by federal, state, and (sometimes) local laws and policies that dictate what conditions should be reported and to what agency. They also stipulate those categories of individuals that are legally obligated to report suspected maltreatment (mandated reporters), although all individuals may voluntarily do so. Mandated reporters typically include teachers, childcare providers, clergy, social workers, health care personnel, law enforcement, and other professionals with frequent contact with children; however, in some states and locales, all individuals are mandated to report suspected child maltreatment. Voluntary reporters include all other (nonmandated) individuals. However, most voluntary reports are made by relatives, the other parent, friends, and neighbors. Some reports are made anonymously. Roughly two-thirds of all reports are made by "professionals," such as educators, law enforcement, and social service personnel, who are likely mandated reporters. The remainder are from "nonprofessionals," who are much more likely to be voluntary reporters, or "unclassified" reporters (USDHHS 2020). Reports are typically submitted to a government or quasi-government agency via a telephone hotline.

What Happens after a Child or Family Is Reported?

Upon receiving a report, the child welfare agency engages in a screening process to first determine whether the information provided is substantial and precise enough to warrant further attention. Specifically, the information must enable the agency to identify and locate the family and must also contain evidence suggesting a reasonable likelihood that maltreatment may have occurred for a specifically identified child. If these conditions are not met, the case is screened-out and closed without further action. If they are met, it is screened-in, and the agency is mandated to contact and investigate or assess the family to determine whether there are child safety concerns, (often) whether maltreatment has occurred, and whether the family may benefit from additional voluntary or mandated services. Law enforcement may be contacted (and involved) in particularly severe cases of abuse or neglect and those that include illegal activities, such as prostitution and the manufacture and distribution of illicit substances, although law enforcement involvement is by no means the norm. If the agency determines that there is no, or insufficient, evidence that maltreatment has occurred, that there are no prevailing child safety issues, or that the family is not in need of additional services, the case is typically closed, although referrals to voluntary services may be made.

Families found to have engaged in abuse or neglect, or to be at considerable risk of maltreatment or related child safety concerns, as well as those deemed in need of additional (psychosocial) intervention, may be asked or required to collaborate with their child welfare worker to create a child protection or safety plan, offered voluntary short- or long-term services, or mandated to participate in such services. Services typically include parenting skills, mental health, substance use, and other related interventions for parents and/or children. They may be delivered in the family's home or in community agencies. In most states, the investigation concludes with a determination as to whether abuse or neglect has occurred, at least for families that are investigated after initially being deemed at considerable risk for abuse or neglect.[5] These determinations are referred to as "substantiations" or "indications" that maltreatment has occurred and may result in the perpetrator being placed on a child maltreatment registry.

When severe abuse or neglect has occurred, or substantial child safety concerns are identified, children may be removed from home and placed in relative or nonrelative foster homes, or in institutional settings (congregate care) if a suitable family foster home cannot be identified or if a foster home placement is deemed inappropriate (often because a child exhibits acute socioemotional problems). Once a removal has occurred, parents and children are typically offered or mandated to a range of services. Following a removal, most children are reunified with their family of origin (i.e., return to their home of origin) within a relatively short period of time and never reenter out-of-home care. However, there is considerable variation in children's placement experiences and trajectories with some experiencing multiple placement spells (removals and reunifications); multiple placements with various caregivers in a variety of settings within and across spells; eventual terminations of parental rights; and diverse (ultimate) exits from care into reunification, adoption, permanent (relative) guardianship or a similar arrangement; and emancipation from care (without a permanent placement) after reaching the age of majority (see Wulczyn, this volume).

Decision-making at each stage of the child welfare process—spanning reporting (which is external to the child welfare system), screening, investigating, case disposition, child removal, out-of-home care exit timing and type, and termination of parental rights—involves attempts by mandated and voluntary reporters, child welfare practitioners and, in some cases, judges to assess perceived risk in a context of incomplete information. These processes are, by their very nature, subjective. As such, they may reflect a variety of biases, misjudgments, errors, and the like. In response, a variety of risk assessment tools have been introduced to aid practitioner decision-making at multiple stages of the child welfare system. Most recently, some locales have implemented predictive analytics strategies, which harness large-scale longitudinal administrative data to generate family risk scores for practitioners to weigh in their decision-making. Their use has generated considerable controversy with respect to predictive accuracy, exacerbation of historical biases, and ethical use. At the same time, some evidence suggests that they result in improved safety for children without increasing racial and ethnic disparities. Drake and colleagues (this volume) provide a detailed analysis of the strengths and limitations of such approaches, including ethical concerns, within specific practice contexts.

In addition, a large research literature has documented that child welfare investigations—and, in particular, child removals—tend to be confrontational in nature and induce considerable stress, anger, and trauma for the children and families involved. Merritt (this volume) draws from both prior research and her own in-depth interviews with child welfare–involved families to highlight implications for policy and practice reforms to reduce conflict, improve information sharing and collaboration, and establish better family-agency partnerships to work toward common goals.

How Common Is Child Welfare System Involvement and for Whom?

High annual prevalence rates of CPS involvement and foster care placement have generated widespread concern among scholars, policy-makers, and practitioners. However, cumulative childhood incidence rates—particularly for children of color—are simply alarming. Figure 1 presents the annual (in 2018) and cumulative rate of investigation, substantiation, and out-of-home care that U.S. children experience, as well as the annual report rate (for which we are aware of no existing cumulative estimates). As shown in Figure 1, 5.9 percent of all U.S. children (7.8 million children) were reported, 4.8 percent were investigated, 0.92 percent were deemed victims of child maltreatment (USDHHS 2020); and 0.8 percent spent some time in out-of-home care (USDHHS 2019b).[6] Yet these prevalence rates are just the tip of the iceberg. Over the course of childhood, from birth to age 18, 37.4 percent of all U.S. children are investigated for (Kim et al., 2017) and 12.5 percent are determined to be victims of abuse or neglect (Wildeman et al. 2014); approximately 5.9 percent spend some time in foster care as a result of child welfare system involvement (Wildeman and Emanuel 2014).

Of particular concern, children and families of color—particularly Black and Native American children and families—are highly likely to be involved in the child welfare system at all levels. Figure 2 presents cumulative childhood investigation, substantiation, and out-of-home placement rates by race and ethnicity. These figures are striking. Whereas at some point during childhood, 28.2 percent, 10.7 percent, and 4.9 percent of white children are investigated, substantiated, and spend some time in out-of-home care, respectively; for Black and Native American children, these rates are 53.0 percent, 20.9 percent, and 11.0 percent; and 23.4 percent, 14.5 percent, and 15.4 percent, respectively. By comparison, for Hispanic and Asian/Pacific Islander children, they are 32.0 percent, 13.0 percent, and 5.4 percent; and 10.2 percent, 3.8 percent, and 2.1 percent, respectively (Kim et al. 2017; Wildeman et al. 2014; Wildeman and Emanuel 2014).

Additionally, child welfare–involved families tend to be highly economically disadvantaged—indeed, lack of economic resources is the strongest and most consistent predictor of child welfare system involvement in developed countries,

FIGURE 1
Annual and Lifetime (Birth–18) Rates of CPS Involvement in the United States

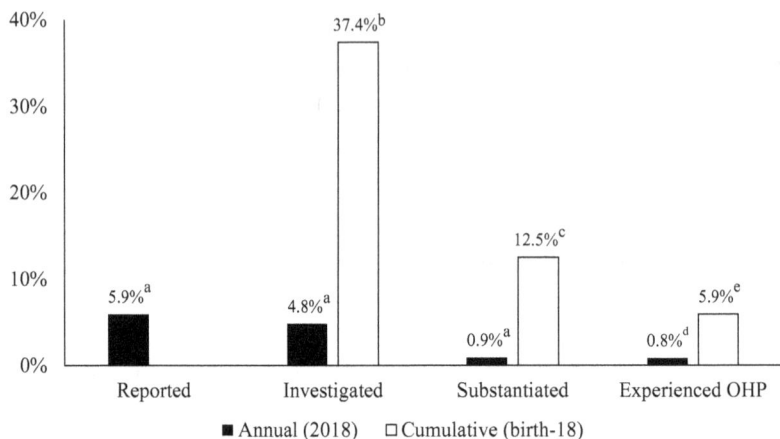

SOURCES: Authors' figures based on data from [a]USDHHS (2020); [b]Kim et al. (2017); [c]Wilde-man et al. (2014); [d]USDHHS (2019b); [e]Wildeman and Emanuel (2014).

FIGURE 2
Lifetime (Birth–18) Incidence of CPS Involvement in the United States by
Race/Ethnicity

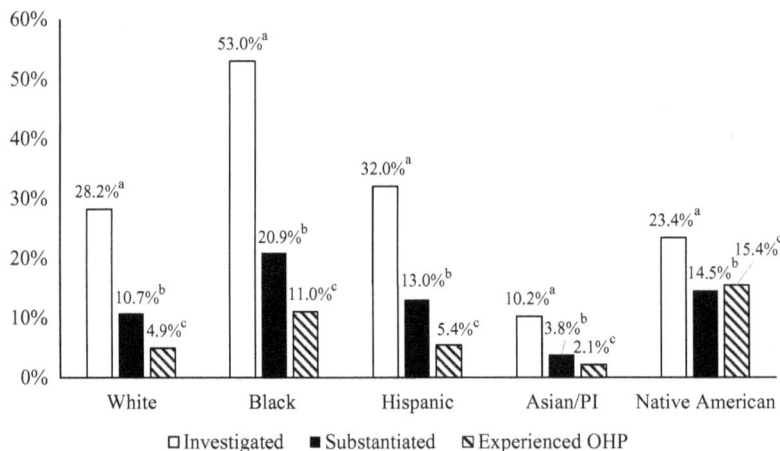

SOURCES: Authors' own figure based on data from [a]Kim et al. (2017); [b]Wildeman et al. (2014); [c]Wildeman and Emanuel (2014).

including in the United States (Cameron and Freymond 2006; National Research Council 2014; Pelton 2015).[7] On average, child welfare–involved families are characterized by considerable instability in employment and earnings, low incomes, and high levels of involvement in means-tested social welfare programs. While national estimates are not available, recent estimates from Wisconsin[8] indicate that, in the year prior to being investigated for child maltreatment, the vast majority of investigated families received benefits from one or more means-tested programs, including the SNAP (76 percent), Medicaid/SCHIP (71 percent), Temporary Assistance for Needy Families (TANF; 15 percent), child care subsidies (16 percent), child support enforcement (38 percent as a payee and 18 percent as a payer), and unemployment insurance (UI; 17 percent); moreover, roughly 40 percent had at least one-quarter with no reported earnings in the year before the investigation. This is particularly important in light of growing evidence that economic resources may be causally linked to child abuse and, in particular, neglect (Berger et al. 2017; Cancian, Yang, and Slack 2013; Raissian and Bullinger 2017; Schneider, Waldfogel, and Brooks-Gunn 2017; Wildeman and Fallesen 2017). Economic resources are thought to impact child maltreatment both directly and through several intermediary mechanisms (see Berger and Waldfogel 2011). First, when family resources are inadequate to provide the basic goods and services that children need for healthy development, the quality of the home environment may fall below legal thresholds for child neglect. As such, inadequate economic resources may have a direct and mechanical effect on child maltreatment risk, particularly child neglect. In addition, economic resources may affect child maltreatment through their influence on parental psychosocial functioning and family dynamics. Research has long established that inadequate economic resources are inversely linked to parental well-being, including being associated with greater stress, depression, and cognitive load, which, in turn, are linked to poorer quality parenting, including less parental warmth and responsiveness, and greater harsh, substandard, and neglectful parenting behaviors. More stringent resource constraints also suggest that lower-income parents have fewer disciplinary and behavioral control options than their higher-income counterparts and may, therefore, have fewer alternatives to physical discipline. Inadequate economic resources may indirectly influence risk of both child abuse and child neglect through these mechanisms. Yet existing child welfare services primarily focus on parental psychosocial functioning and parenting behaviors. Child welfare–involved families are not systematically offered services to increase their economic resources.

What Are the Key Challenges Facing the Contemporary U.S. Child Welfare System(s), and How Does this Volume Address Them?

Our overview of the contemporary U.S. child welfare system calls attention to several key issues. First, it is crucial that child welfare policy and practice be guided by the fact that *child neglect is by far the most common form of child maltreatment*. Moreover, child physical abuse and sexual abuse have declined to an unprecedented extent over the last three decades, whereas similar declines have not been observed for child neglect (Finkelhor, Saito, and Jones 2020)—such that child neglect is now driving child welfare caseloads even more than in the past. This simple fact is enormously important to understanding and reforming the U.S. child welfare system. To begin with, child neglect is closely linked to low incomes, poverty, and economic hardship. However, the child welfare system does not currently systematically attend to these issues. This begs the question of whether child welfare practice should continue to (almost exclusively) prioritize parenting skills and psychosocial interventions or should be expanded to consistently and systematically address economic struggles, through coordinated efforts both within and outside of the formal child welfare system (Feely et al., this volume; Slack and Berger, this volume).

Moreover, the current COVID-19 pandemic has triggered lockdown orders, school closures, and extensive losses of employment and income. Associated social isolation and economic hardship are highly likely to result in increased child maltreatment and, likely, child neglect, in particular. Although limited exposure to mandated reporters may result in decreased child welfare reporting while lockdowns and school closure orders are in effect (Welch and Haskins 2020), increases in underlying maltreatment have the potential to drive an influx of child welfare cases once such orders are lifted, particularly given dire predictions for a speedy economic recovery. Thus, we might expect substantial increases in child maltreatment and, perhaps, foster care placement, particularly for low-income families, in the wake of the adverse economic effects of the pandemic. At the same time, growing evidence indicates that generous and inclusionary social welfare programs have the potential to reduce abuse and neglect (Berger et al. 2017; Brown and De Cao 2020; Brown et al. 2019; Pac 2019; Raissian and Bullinger 2017; Wildeman and Fallesen 2017). The federal response to the epidemic represented an unprecedented expansion in the U.S. safety net via a wide range of policy initiatives, including income support expansions under the Coronavirus Aid, Relief and Economy Security Act (2020). The effects of these policy initiatives in the aftermath of the COVID-19 pandemic are ripe for analysis and evaluation; the results thereof may have widespread implications for informing future child maltreatment prevention efforts.

Second, *the formal child welfare system devotes very few resources to child maltreatment prevention*. Rather, prevention has traditionally fallen under the purview of other public and private systems, agencies, and funding mechanisms such that the formal system itself is characterized by a predominantly reactive, rather than proactive, mandate and approach (Welch and Haskins 2020). As noted above, the recent passage of the Family First Prevention and Services Act of 2018, for the first time, authorizes the use of federal (Title IV-E) funds to provide in-home prevention services to help families in crisis avoid (escalating) child welfare system involvement, including out-of-home placement, through the provision of specifically targeted interventions in the form of evidence-based substance use and mental health treatment, and in-home parenting services. These services can be provided to a wide range of families at risk of child removal, including those in informal kinship care arrangements and those who have reunified after a child was placed out-of-home. This flexibility allows child welfare agencies to begin serving families that have not (yet) been reported—a vast departure from traditional policy and practice—and to provide enhanced services to reunified families. This is particularly important in light of evidence that child abuse and neglect are, in general, underreported (Flaherty et al. 2008; Wood et al. 2017), coupled with recent evidence that underreporting (and thus underinclusion in the formal child welfare system of children and families for whom abuse or neglect has occurred) has increased in the context of the COVID-19 pandemic and associated lockdowns and school closures (Welch and Haskins 2020). It is also important given a paucity of resources targeted to reunified families, many of which will experience a subsequent child removal (Font, Sattler, and Gershoff 2019).

Several of the articles in this volume directly address the opportunities and challenges of the Family First Act, potential avenues to provide enhanced prevention efforts, both within and outside of the child welfare system, and the financing thereof. Haskins (this volume), for example, presents an in-depth analysis of child welfare financing, drawing out key implications for why the United States has not been more successful at preventing, identifying, and addressing child maltreatment and highlighting new opportunities for improvement given increased flexibility in use of federal funds under the Family First Act. Testa and Kelly (this volume) provide a framework for how states, counties, and child welfare agencies can best identify and evaluate initiatives to promote child safety and prevent maltreatment and child removal in a context of a limited range of demonstrated efficacious, evidence-based initiatives.

Other articles in the volume propose large-scale child maltreatment prevention initiatives. These span primary (prior to identification that risk of maltreatment has occurred), secondary (targeted at those identified as being at risk of abuse or neglect), and tertiary (targeted at those identified as already having been abused or neglected, and intended to prevent further maltreatment) prevention efforts, and may include universal (eligibility is not based on level of risk, nor income or assets) and targeted/categorical approaches (eligibility is based on level/category of risk or income/assets) (Merritt, Maguire-Jack, and Negash 2017). For example, Jones-Harden and colleagues (this volume) highlight key components necessary for creating an effective child maltreatment prevention landscape in the United States and recommend prioritizing a specific set of scalable evidence-based programs. Roygardner, Hughes, and Palusci (this volume) argue for better leveraging community strengths and resources to inform a universal "prevention zone" approach to a coordinated system of primary, secondary, and tertiary prevention of child abuse and neglect at the community level. Feely and colleagues (this volume) propose a "safe and consistent care of children" framework that would place child safety at the center of the full range of social welfare programs impacting children and families, with an emphasis on ensuring that families acquire adequate resources to ensure they are able to meet their children's needs, thereby reducing child maltreatment, particularly child neglect.

Third, *the child welfare system is far reaching such that involvement therein is a common experience for American children—particularly low-income children and children of color.* This begs the question of whether definitions may be too broad as to overinclude in the child welfare system children and families whose primary challenges are not related to parental actions or omissions but rather to, for instance, economic and material hardship. Font and Maguire-Jack (this volume), for example, highlight practical difficulties in determining whether parental omissions have occurred as a result of "poverty alone," and their implications for child welfare decisions regarding both whether and how to intervene. They further describe important definitional and measurement issues and their implications for estimates of the prevalence and incidence of maltreatment. Merritt's (this volume) description of the stress and trauma associated with children's and families' interactions with the child welfare system raises concerns about casting too wide a net vis-à-vis investigations and removals, given that unnecessary intervention in these areas may do more harm than good, and stresses the importance of a less confrontational approach. Dettlaff and Boyd (this volume) question whether child welfare system intervention is even necessary for many of the children and families of color involved in the system and whether, on average, child welfare involvement benefits or further disadvantages them. Other articles argue that appropriately resourced and implemented prevention efforts (Jones-Harden et al., this volume; Roygardner, Hughes, and Palusci, this volume) and comprehensive systems synergy–focused initiatives (Feely et al., this volume; Slack and Berger, this volume) have the potential to substantially reduce the proportion of low-income and minority children and families entering the formal child welfare system and advancing through the child welfare services continuum.

Fourth, *most children who are reported to the child welfare system are neither substantiated for maltreatment nor removed from home and, for those who are removed from home, most out-of-home care trajectories are relatively short-lived.* This, again, raises concerns about whether children and families are unnecessarily traumatized by (unnecessary) investigations (Merritt, this volume; Detlaff and Boyd, this volume) that ultimately do not result in receipt of services (Slack and Berger, this volume). It also raises key questions regarding the appropriate alignment of legal definitions and thresholds for maltreatment with services offered by the child welfare system (Font and Maguire-Jack, this volume), whether families may be better served by programs outside of the traditional child welfare system (Jones-Harden et al., this volume; Detlaff and Boyd, this volume; Feely et al., this volume; Roygardner, Hughes, and Palusci, this volume; Slack and Berger, this volume), and whether families may warrant services—and whether society should bear the responsibility to provide such services—even if their circumstances have not risen to legal thresholds for maltreatment (Slack and Berger, this volume). Indeed, Slack and Berger (this volume) argue on both equity and efficiency grounds that society has an obligation to serve the large number of children and families who are known to the child welfare system as a result of having been reported or investigated, but who have not (yet) been substantiated for maltreatment, because these children and families are documented to be at substantial risk for maltreatment and are highly likely to subsequently return to the child welfare system, often under exacerbated circumstances. They further argue that such intervention should be external to the child welfare system, where families can engage voluntarily.

Wulczyn's (this volume) analyses of out-of-home placement trajectories raise further concerns that foster care policies and practices do not reflect the reality of many children's out-of-home care placement experiences. This is of particular salience to the contemporary child welfare system, which has seen large increases in foster care caseloads; foster care caseloads consistently declined from 2002 to 2012, but have increased steadily thereafter (by 10 percent from 2012 to 2016 alone), reflecting both increased entries into care and longer placement spells (and, therefore, fewer exits); they are now at their highest level since 1999 (Child Trends Databank 2019). Moreover, in the context of the ongoing opioid epidemic and health, economic, and social impacts of the COVID-19 pandemic and its aftermath, it is likely that this upward trend will continue.

Finally, *decision-making at all stages of the child welfare system continuum is made in the context of incomplete information and is, frequently, subjective in nature*. While, to a considerable extent, this is unavoidable, it could perhaps be minimized in a variety of ways, including more precise, standardized, and easily operationalized legal definitions (Font and Maguire-Jack, this volume), as well as the implementation of efficacious and well-evaluated tools to aid practitioners in decision-making at specific junctures in the child welfare system continuum. To this end, Drake and colleagues (this volume) present a "practical framework" for considering the use of predictive analytics in the child welfare system that takes into account accuracy in optimal decision-making around specific decisions and potential outcomes both for the overall population of children and families that come to the attention of the child welfare system and for particular subgroups thereof; evaluating whether the use of predictive modeling results in better, worse, or equivalent decisions relative to status quo practice (or alternative risk-assessment/decision-making tools); and assessing whether a particular child welfare system has the capacity to successfully implement a predictive analytics approach. They also devote considerable attention to ethical debates surrounding use of predictive analytics, including its potential to exacerbate or reduce ongoing systemic biases. These are crucial considerations for policy and practice in the contemporary child welfare system given that decisions therein are extremely consequential to children and families, as well as to society. Reducing subjectivity in child welfare decisions has potentially widespread implications for the way families experience the child welfare system (Merritt, this volume), as well as for potential overinclusion and underinclusion at various levels of the system (albeit post reporting), both in general and based on factors such as race and ethnicity, economic disadvantage, and family and neighborhood characteristics.

Looking Forward: Toward a Better Approach to Preventing, Identifying, and Addressing Child Maltreatment

The articles in this volume tackle the challenge of recommending innovative approaches to better preventing, identifying, and addressing child abuse and neglect in the United States. These reforms span the child welfare system and the wide range of other policies and programs with which child welfare–involved children and families and those at risk of child maltreatment and child welfare involvement commonly interact. In doing so, the articles draw upon the most rigorous existing research to propose a wide range of approaches involving varying populations and domains of intervention, systems, and technologies. In the face of widespread child welfare system involvement, particularly for socially and economically disadvantaged groups, and growing out-of-home care caseloads, these articles are intended to seed a rich debate on social welfare policy reforms to improve the U.S. approach to child abuse and neglect.

Notes

1. We use the terms "child maltreatment" and "child abuse and neglect" interchangeably.

2. Efforts to prevent child abuse and neglect before they (or CPS involvement) have occurred include media campaigns, community-level interventions, school-based prevention programs, parenting resources and skills, home visiting, and other in-home or community-based services (Berger and Font 2015; MacMillan et al. 2009). In the United States, these efforts typically fall under the purview of health and mental health, family support/home visiting, childcare and education, economic support, juvenile justice, and related programs and systems, rather than that of the child welfare system(s). However, there is considerable international variation in the extent to which prevention efforts are internal or external to a country's child welfare system(s), largely reflecting differences in the extent to which the country's approach leans more toward a family-support focus or a child protection focus, as well as the degree to which the child welfare system is mandatory or voluntary, proactive or reactive, and integrated into or fragmented from the country's larger constellation of policies and practices for promoting child and family well-being (Berger and Slack 2013; Gilbert, Kemp, et al. 2009; Gilbert, Parton, and Skivenes 2011). Welch and Haskins (2020) describe the U.S. approach as lacking a clear overarching structure and system philosophy, as well as struggling to meet the dual mandate of, and therefore vacillating between, prioritizing family support (preservation) and child protection.

3. Notably, while each industrialized country—and each U.S. state and territory—has established such definitions and thresholds, they vary considerably by locale.

4. Additionally, whereas only one form of maltreatment was indicated to have occurred in 85.6 percent of confirmed cases in 2017, multiple forms of maltreatment were found to have occurred in 14.4 percent of confirmed cases. Among single-type maltreatment cases, 62.7 percent were for neglect, 11.0 percent for physical abuse, 6.7 percent for sexual abuse, and 2.3 percent for emotional or psychological abuse (USDHHS, 2019a).

5. As discussed by Slack and Berger (this volume), many states and counties have implemented "alternative response" or "differential response" approaches in which reports are essentially triaged by level of risk. Lower-risk reports then receive an "assessment," after which no determination is made as to whether abuse or neglect occurred; higher-risk reports receive a traditional "investigation," which results in such a determination.

6. Note that this figure includes all U.S. children who spent time in out-of-home care in 2018; it is not limited to those who were removed from home in 2018.

7. See Font and Maguire-Jack (this volume) for a complete discussion of risk factors for and causes of child abuse and neglect.

8. Calculated by the authors from linked longitudinal multisystem state administrative data available in the Wisconsin Administrative Data Core, housed at the Institute for Research on Poverty at the University of Wisconsin–Madison. Available upon request.

References

Berger, Lawrence M., and Sarah A. Font. 2015. The role of the family and family-centered programs and policies. *Future of Children* 25 (1): 155–76.

Berger, Lawrence M., Sarah A. Font, Kristen S. Slack, and Jane Waldfogel. 2017. Income and child maltreatment in unmarried families: evidence from the earned income tax credit. *Review of Economics of the Household* 15 (4): 1345–72.

Berger, Lawrence M., and Kristen Shook Slack. 2013. Child protection and child wellbeing. In *Handbook of child well-being: Theories, methods and policies in global perspective*, vol. 5, eds. Asher Ben-Arieh, Ferran Casas, Ivar Frones, and Jill E. Korbin, 2965–92. Dordrecht: Springer.

Berger, Lawrence M., and Jane Waldfogel. 2011. Economic determinants and consequences of child maltreatment. OECD Social, Employment and Migration Working Paper No. 111, Organization for Economic Cooperation and Development (OECD).

Bernard, Kristin, Teresa Lind, and Mary Dozier. 2014. Neurobiological consequences of neglect and abuse. In *Handbook of child maltreatment*, eds. E. Korbin and R. D. Krugman, 205–23. Dordrecht: Springer.

Brown, Dan, and Elisabetta De Cao. 2020. Child maltreatment, unemployment, and safety nets. Available from https://papers.ssrn.com/sol3/papers.cfm?abstract_id=3543987.

Brown, Emily C. B., Michelle M. Garrison, Hao Bao, Pingping Qu, Carole Jenny, and Ali Rowhani-Rahbar. 2019. Assessment of rates of child maltreatment in states with Medicaid expansion vs states without Medicaid expansion. *JAMA Network Open* 2 (6): e195529.

Cameron, Gary, and Nancy Freymond. 2006. Understanding international comparisons of child protection, family service, and community caring systems of child and family welfare. In *Towards positive systems of child and family welfare: International comparisons of child protection, family service, and community caring systems*, eds. Nancy Freymond and Gary Cameron, 3–25. Toronto: University of Toronto Press.

Cancian, Maria, Jennifer Noyes, and HeeJin Kim. 2017. Using linked administrative data to understand the dynamics of multiple program participation. Report to the Wisconsin Department of Children and Families.

Cancian, Maria, MiYoon Yang, and Kristen S. Slack. 2013. The effect of additional child support income on the risk of child maltreatment. *Social Service Review* 87 (3): 417–37.

Center for the Study of Social Policy. 2020. *The upEND Movement: All children deserve to be with their families*. Washington, DC: Center for the Study of Social Policy. Available from https://cssp.org/our-work/project/upend#story.

Child Trends Databank. 2019. *Foster care*. Available from https://www.childtrends.org/?indicators=foster-care.

Finkelhor, David, Kei Saito, and Lisa Jones. 2020. Updated trends in child maltreatment, 2018. Crimes Against Children Research Center, University of New Hampshire. Available from http://www.unh.edu/ccrc/pdf/CV203%20-%20Updated%20trends%202018_ks_df.pdf.

Flaherty, Emalee G., Robert D. Sege, John Griffith, Lori Lyn Price, Richard Wasserman, Eric Slora, Niramol Dhepyasuwan, Donna Harris, David Norton, Mary Lu Angelilli, Dianna Abney and Helen J. Binns. 2008. From suspicion of physical child abuse to reporting: Primary care clinician decision-making. *Pediatrics* 122 (3): 611–19.

Font, Sarah, Maria Cancian, Lawrence M. Berger, and Anna DiGiovanni. 2020. Patterns of intergenerational child protective services involvement. *Child Abuse and Neglect* 99:10427.

Font, Sarah, and Kathryn Maguire-Jack. 2020. It's not "just poverty": Educational, social, and economic functioning among young adults exposed to childhood neglect, abuse, and poverty. *Child Abuse & Neglect* 101:104356.

Font, S. A., K. Sattler, and E. Gershoff. 2019. When home is still unsafe: From reunification to foster care reentry. *Journal of Marriage and the Family* 80 (5): 1333–43.

Freymond, Nancy, and Gary Cameron. 2006. Learning from international comparisons of child protection, family service, and community caring systems of child and family welfare. In *Towards positive systems of child and family welfare: International comparisons of child protection, family service, and community caring systems*, eds. Nancy Freymond and Gary Cameron, 289–317. Toronto: University of Toronto Press.

Gilbert, Ruth, Alison Kemp, June Thoburn, Peter Sidebotham, Lorraine Radford, Danya Glaser, and Harriet L. MacMillan. 2009. Recognising and responding to child maltreatment. *Lancet* 373 (9658): 167–80.

Gilbert, Neil, Nigel Parton, and Marit Skivenes, eds. 2011. *Child protection systems: International trends and orientations.* New York, NY: Oxford University Press.

Gilbert, Ruth, Cathy Spatz Widom, Kevin Browne, David Fergusson, Elspeth Webb, and Staffan Janson. 2009. Burden and consequences of child maltreatment in high-income countries. *Lancet* 373 (9657): 68–81.

Jackson, Yo, Joy Gabrielli, Kandace Fleming, Angela M. Tunno, and P. Kalani Makanui. 2014. Untangling the relative contribution of maltreatment severity and frequency to type of behavioral outcome in foster youth. *Child Abuse & Neglect* 38 (7): 1147–59.

Jaffee, Sara R., and Andrea Kohn Maikovich-Fong. 2011. Effects of chronic maltreatment and maltreatment timing on children's behavior and cognitive abilities. *Journal of Child Psychology and Psychiatry* 52 (2): 184–94.

Jonson-Reid, Melissa, Patricia L. Kohl, and Brett Drake. 2012. Child and adult outcomes of chronic child maltreatment. *Pediatrics* 129 (5): 839–45.

Kim, Hyunil, Christopher Wildeman, Melissa Jonson-Reid, and Brett Drake. 2017. Lifetime prevalence of investigating child maltreatment among US children. *American Journal of Public Health* 107:274–80.

MacMillan, Harriet L., C. Nadine Wathen, Jane Barlow, David M. Fergusson, John M. Leventhal, and Heather N. Taussig. 2009. Interventions to prevent child maltreatment and associated impairment. *Lancet* 373 (9659): 250–66.

Merritt, Darcey, K. Maguire-Jack, and Tori Negash. 2017. Effective program models for the prevention of child maltreatment. In *The APSAC handbook on child maltreatment*, eds. J. Bart Klika and John R. Cont, 252–71. Thousand Oaks, CA: Sage Publications.

National Research Council. 2014. *New directions in child abuse and neglect research.* Washington, DC: National Academies Press.

Norman, Rosana E., Munkhtsetseg Byambaa, Rumna De, Alexander Butchart, James Scott, and Theo Vos. 2012. The long-term health consequences of child physical abuse, emotional abuse, and neglect: A systematic review and meta-analysis. *PLoS Medicine* 9 (11): e1001349.

Pac, Jessica. 2019. Three essays on child maltreatment. Dissertation, Columbia University. Available from https://academiccommons.columbia.edu/doi/10.7916/d8-y25b-cx13.

Pelton, Leroy H. 2015. The continuing role of material factors in child maltreatment and placement. *Child Abuse and Neglect* 41:30–39.

Peterson, Cora, Curtis Florence, and Joanne Klevens. 2018. The economic burden of child maltreatment in the United States, 2015. *Child Abuse & Neglect* 86:178–83.

Raissian, Kerri M., and Lindsey Rose Bullinger. 2017. Money matters: Does the minimum wage affect child maltreatment rates? *Children and Youth Services Review* 72:60–70.

Rebbe, Rebecca. 2018. What is neglect? State legal definitions in the United States. *Child Maltreatment* 23 (3): 303–15.

Ringel, Jeanne S., Dana Schultz, Joshua Mendelsohn, Stephanie Brooks Holliday, Katharine Sieck, Ifeanyi Edochie, and Lauren Davis. 2017. *Improving children's lives: Balancing investments in prevention and treatment in the child welfare system.* Santa Monica, CA: Rand Corporation. Available from https://www.rand.org/pubs/research_briefs/RB9949-1.html.

Rosinsky, Kristina, and Sarah Catherine Williams. 2018. Child welfare financing SFY 2016: A survey of federal, state, and local expenditures. Child Trends. Available at https://www.childtrends.org/wp-content/uploads/2018/12/CWFSReportSFY2016_ChildTrends_December2018.pdf.

Schneider, William, Jane Waldfogel, and Jeanne Brooks-Gunn. 2017. The Great Recession and risk for child abuse and neglect. *Children and Youth Services Review* 72:71–81.

Sepulveda, Kristin, and Sarah C. Williams. 2019. One in three children entered foster care in 2017 because of parental drug abuse. Child Trends. Available from https://www.childtrends.org/one-in-three-children-entered-foster-care-in-fy-2017-because-of-parental-drug-abuse.

U.S. Department of Health and Human Services, Administration for Children and Families, Administration on Children, Youth and Families, Children's Bureau. 2019a. *Child maltreatment 2017.* Washington,

DC: U.S. Department of Health and Human Services. Available from https://www.acf.hhs.gov/cb/research-data-technology/statistics-research/child-maltreatment.

U.S. Department of Health and Human Services. 2019b. *Trends in foster care and adoption: FY 2009 – FY 2018*. Washington, DC: U.S. Department of Health and Human Services. Available from https://www.acf.hhs.gov/sites/default/files/cb/trends_fostercare_adoption_09thru18.pdf.

U.S. Department of Health and Human Services, Administration for Children and Families, Administration on Children, Youth and Families, Children's Bureau. 2020. *Child maltreatment 2018*. Washington, DC: U.S. Department of Health and Human Services. Available from https://www.acf.hhs.gov/cb/research-data-technology/statistics-research/child-maltreatment.

Waldfogel, Jane, and Lawrence M. Berger. 2006. Child protection. In *International encyclopedia of social policy*, eds. T. Fitzpatrick, H. Kwon, N. Manning, J. Midgley, and G. Pascall, 137–38. New York, NY: Routledge.

Welch, Morgan, and Ron Haskins. 2020. What COVID-19 means for America's child welfare system. Washington, DC: Brookings Institution. Available from https://www.brookings.edu/research/what-covid-19-means-for-americas-child-welfare-system/?preview_id=799522.

Widom, Cathy Spatz. 2014. Longterm consequences of child maltreatment. In *Handbook of child maltreatment*, eds. J. E. Korbin, and R. D. Krugman, 225–47. Dordrecht: Springer.

Wildeman, Christopher, and Natalia Emanuel. 2014. Cumulative risks of foster care placement for American children, 2000–2011. *PLOS ONE* 9:e92785.

Wildeman, Christopher, Natalia Emanuel, John M. Leventhal, Emily Putnam-Hornstein, Jane Waldfogel, and Hedwig Lee. 2014. The prevalence of confirmed maltreatment among U.S. children, 2004–2011. *JAMA Pediatrics* 168:706–13.

Wildeman, Christopher, and Peter Fallesen. 2017. The effect of lowering welfare payment ceilings on children's risk of out-of-home placement. *Children and Youth Services Review* 72:82–90.

Williams, Sarah C., and Kristin Sepulveda. 2019. In 2017, the rate of children in foster care rose in 39 states. *Child Trends*. Available from https://www.childtrends.org/2017-the-number-of-children-in-foster-care-rose-in-39-states.

Wood, Joanne N., Heather M. Griffis, Christine M. Taylor, Douglas Strane, Gerlinde C. Harb, Lanyu Mi, Lihai Song, Kevin G. Lynch, and David M. Rubin. 2017. Under-ascertainment from healthcare settings of child abuse events among children of soldiers by the U.S. Army Family Advocacy Program. *Child Abuse & Neglect* 63:202–10.

The Scope, Nature, and Causes of Child Abuse and Neglect

By
SARAH A. FONT
and
KATHRYN MAGUIRE-JACK

Child maltreatment is a complex problem affecting millions of children in the United States every year. This article examines existing knowledge on the scope, nature, and causes of child abuse and neglect. First, we review the discordant definitions and conceptualizations of child maltreatment and consider the implications of broad and narrow definitions for the size and scope of the child welfare system and for child safety. Second, we provide an assessment of the quality and comprehensiveness of existing data for understanding the incidence rates and trends in child abuse and neglect. Third, we review theory and evidence on the causes of child maltreatment, with particular attention to whether and how social policy can reduce its prevalence. Last, we provide recommendations for improving the use of data and scientific evidence in child welfare policy and systems.

Keywords: child maltreatment; child welfare system; risk factors; measurement; data

Over the past several decades, states have developed and expanded their child welfare systems with growing federal oversight to effectively prevent and respond to child maltreatment. Over this same period, research and data to understand child maltreatment has proliferated. Yet core questions remain unanswered: How many children experience maltreatment today? How much have rates changed over time and why? How effective are existing systems in identifying children in need of protection?

Sarah A. Font is an assistant professor of sociology at the Pennsylvania State University. Her research focuses on the policies and practices of the child welfare system and the experiences and outcomes of system-involved children.

Kathryn Maguire-Jack is an associate professor of social work at the University of Michigan. She studies child maltreatment prevention with a focus on understanding contextual risk and protective factors. She has expertise in program evaluation and public policy.

Correspondence: Saf252@psu.edu

DOI: 10.1177/0002716220969642

What policies are most effective for reducing child maltreatment? These questions evoke important social values about the scope and size of government; roles of federal, state, and local governments; children's rights; and parental autonomy. In this article, we review these debates and, where possible, we draw on available research and data to make recommendations about how to move forward. We begin with a review of how child maltreatment is defined—in federal policy, in states' civil and criminal statutes, and in research—and explore the implications of broadening or narrowing definitions. Beyond definitions, we then describe the difficulties and limitations associated with estimating rates of child maltreatment. To this end, we draw on numerous population-level or nationally representative survey datasets to compare estimates of the incidence and prevalence of child maltreatment. These comparisons highlight the extent to which official statistics on victimization (based on confirmed reports to child protective services [CPS]) underestimate exposure to abuse and neglect among U.S. children. Underestimates of child maltreatment rates may lead to an underinvestment in resolving this problem. We then turn to a discussion of the causes of child maltreatment, with special emphasis on factors that may be malleable through social policy changes. Last, we provide recommendations about how investments in data and research can be leveraged to inform policy reforms, improve the child welfare system, and better protect children from abuse and neglect.

Scope and Nature of Child Maltreatment

This section reviews definitions of child maltreatment, describes approaches to measuring maltreatment, and reviews existing estimates of the incidence and prevalence of child maltreatment.

What is child maltreatment?

Child maltreatment has a range of definitions, with variability across and within countries; between civil and criminal statutes; and across legal, lay, and academic perspectives. Further, variability in measurement reflects differences in definitions, standards of evidence, and sources of information. In the United States, the Child Abuse Prevention and Treatment Act (CAPTA), originally passed in 1974 (P.L. 93-247), provides the federal definition of child maltreatment: "Any recent act or failure to act on the part of a parent or caretaker, which results in death, serious physical or emotional harm, sexual abuse, or exploitation, or an act or failure to act which presents an imminent risk of serious harm." This definition encapsulates a fairly broad range of actions and inactions that can be defined as child maltreatment but narrows the focus to perpetrators in caregiving roles. Typically, the child welfare system focuses on maltreatment perpetrated by individuals who are responsible for the child, consistent with the primary mandate of child safety. The child welfare system receives and investigates allegations of child maltreatment through CPS and provides in-home and foster care services to families at risk. When a child is abused by a person outside the family, the child's parents (or legal custodians) are expected to take protective action (e.g., by eliminating contact with the abuser), and law enforcement and the criminal justice system can act to protect society at large through criminal prosecution. This leaves no clear need for child welfare system intervention; in contrast, abuse or neglect by a parent may require child welfare system intervention, alone or in combination with law enforcement.

States provide more specific—and sometimes more expansive—definitions in their civil statutes (which guide child welfare system and family court actions) and criminal statutes (which guide decisions to prosecute forms of child maltreatment as a criminal offense). Consistent with a focus on child safety rather than parental culpability, statutory definitions of child maltreatment tend to emphasize harm or threat of harm to children that results from specific actions or inactions, with comparatively little emphasis on perpetrator intent. In research, definitions tend to be less restrictive with regard to perpetrators and may consider a range of exposures that pose a threat to children's safety or welfare, irrespective of whether they meet legal definitions. For example, survey-based measures of neglect tend to include so-called involuntary neglect, or situations in which a child experiences material deprivation but it is unknown whether the deprivation is solely due to poverty. The widely used Parent-Child Conflict Tactic Scales—a caregiver self-report survey instrument about the frequency of various parenting acts or omissions over the past 12 months in the domains of psychological aggression, physical assault, nonviolent discipline, and neglect (Straus et al. 1998)—include children lacking necessary medical care in the neglect subscale, which may occur for reasons of negligence, poverty, or (less commonly) malice.

Under many states' statutes, neglect that occurs solely due to poverty is not defined as child neglect (Rebbe 2018), regardless of harm incurred to the child. Nevertheless, definitions remain vague and subject to differential interpretation. In addition, low-income families compose a large majority of CPS reports and families receiving child welfare system interventions (Dolan et al. 2011), and child welfare agencies face persistent criticism about whether they accurately distinguish parental acts of neglect from poverty-driven material hardships (Eamon and Kopels 2004; Milner and Kelly 2020). Yet differentiating neglect from poverty is a rather difficult and subjective judgment. Consider a single parent who leaves her toddler home alone because she lacked childcare, and while alone, the child falls down the stairs. Injuries sustained in the fall were unintentional but were a foreseeable risk given the child's developmental stage. Whether the incident was mostly about poverty or mostly about parental negligence is not clear-cut. One approach is to consider whether a reasonable person might have made the same choice given the parent's constraints. For example, a parent who left her child home alone to avoid being fired from her job (which would risk homelessness and other forms of serious deprivation) arguably behaved more reasonably than a parent who left to attend a social event. However, to make such a determination about whether neglect was "involuntary," the circumstances must be investigated; as such, it is, to some extent, inevitable that impoverished families will be overrepresented in neglect reports to CPS. In addition, whereas the distinction between poverty and neglect can and should drive decisions about *how* to intervene—in-home services versus foster care, court-mandated services versus voluntary community supports—it is not clear such distinctions should determine *whether* to intervene. It would seem reckless for the child welfare system to ignore serious risk or harm to a child simply because the parent was not perceived to be "at fault," particularly in a society in which the child welfare system may be the best or only means of accessing services or resources.

Measurement of child maltreatment

There are numerous approaches to measuring maltreatment. The most prominent strategies and data sources are described in Table 1. Each data source or approach has significant limitations. Both the National Child Abuse and Neglect Data System (NCANDS; a federal database comprising extracts of state child welfare records) and the National Surveys of Child and Adolescent Well-Being (NSCAW; a federally sponsored longitudinal survey of CPS investigations) only contain information about families investigated by CPS, thus providing no information about the nature or extent of child maltreatment that does not reach the attention of CPS. Although NSCAW includes a variety of measures of child maltreatment, including parent-reported and child-reported, each measure is limited to a different subsample, thus inhibiting comparisons of measures. For example, the parent-reported measures are only asked for the primary parent and only if they retain custody of their children at the time of the interview, whereas the child-reported items that directly align with the parent-reported items are only asked of children ages 11 and older.

Outside of data collected on children and families already involved in the child welfare system (e.g., NCANDS, NSCAW), there is little prospective data collection on child maltreatment. Beginning in the 1980s, there have been four National Incidence Studies (NIS), which collected information about suspected child maltreatment from professionals who have regular contact with children. The value of these studies is that they captured child maltreatment that may not have been reported to CPS or that was reported but screened out (not investigated) by CPS. In addition, by relying on informants other than parents, these studies are, arguably, less biased by the limitations and biases of self-reported maltreatment. However, the last NIS was in 2005–2006, and we do not know when funding will be appropriated to conduct another round.

Many large-scale longitudinal surveys, such as the Fragile Families and Child Wellbeing Study (FFCWS; a longitudinal study that tracks a nationally representative birth cohort of children born in large U.S. cities between 1998 and 2000), do not collect explicit information on child maltreatment. Although there are a variety of reasons that surveys may include or exclude particular measures, of particular note, affirmative disclosures of child maltreatment victimization or perpetration introduce legal and ethical dilemmas about mandatory reporting to CPS and informed consent (Putnam, Liss, and Landsverk 2014). If disclosures would invoke mandatory reporting responsibilities, respondents may be unlikely to respond truthfully, which may limit the quality and utility of any data collected.

TABLE 1

Commonly Tracked Measures (and Proxies) of Child Maltreatment

Measure Type	Found In[a]	Examples of Measures	Utility as a Measure of Maltreatment
Child welfare involvement	NCANDS; NSCAW	Investigation, alternative response, and substantiation of maltreatment allegations, by type	**Benefits:** National coverage, annual collection, consistency of the variables included each year **Concerns:** Detection bias (Brown et al. 1998), ongoing debate regarding meaningfulness of substantiation (Font, Maguire-Jack, and Dillard 2020), state and temporal variation in statutory definitions and policies (Child Welfare Information Gateway 2016), variation in completeness and quality of state reports
Professional proxy-reports	NIS	Professional descriptions of scenarios coded by type and severity of maltreatment (Sedlak et al. 2010)	**Benefits:** Addresses some problems related to detection bias; accounts for degrees of severity **Concerns:** Small samples; concerns about methodology (proxy-reported estimation)
Parent-reported maltreatment	NSCAW, NSCEV	Parent-Child Conflict Tactic Scales (Straus et al. 1996); Juvenile Victimization Questionnaire (Finkelhor et al. 2005)	**Benefits:** Addresses some problems related to detection bias; includes more nuanced questions (e.g., frequency, severity) **Concerns:** Response bias due to social desirability and mandatory reporting requirements; low agreement between parent and child reports (Font and Cage 2018); inadequate measures of neglect
Child-reported maltreatment	NSCAW	Child version of Conflict Tactic Scales; Exposure to Violence Questionnaire (Fox and Leavitt 1995)	**Benefits:** May reduce detection and social desirability biases; allows for cross-comparisons of multiple sources of information (e.g., parent and child reports) **Concerns:** Ethical issues around reporting/risk to children who disclose; not available for young children; typically excludes neglect

(continued)

TABLE 1 (CONTINUED)

Measure Type	Found In[a]	Examples of Measures	Utility as a Measure of Maltreatment
Substandard parenting	Numerous population-based household surveys (e.g., FFCWS)	Commonly: physical punishment, severe material hardships, yelling/criticizing child, substance use and domestic violence in the household	**Benefits:** Parents may be more truthful about substandard parenting than maltreatment; responses do not trigger mandatory reporting duties; substandard parenting and maltreatment are similarly associated with child wellbeing; often combine parent reports and interviewer observations; relative measures of how far below "average" parenting quality a family is in a particular domain **Concerns:** Not exact measures of maltreatment (as legally defined); may still have underreporting due to social desirability bias; limited ability to track population-level change over time
Adult retrospective reports of maltreatment	BRFSS; Add-Health	Commonly: Adverse Childhood Experiences (ACEs) questionnaire (Felitti et al. 1998), which includes some maltreatment items	**Benefits:** By asking adults, there is no concern about mandatory reporting, which may allow for more truthful responses **Concerns:** Recall bias is likely significant, resulting in high rates of false negatives (Hardt and Rutter 2004); inadequate measures of neglect

NOTE: NCANDS: National Child Abuse and Neglect Data System (https://www.ndacan.acf.hhs.gov/datasets/datasets-list-ncands-child-file.cfm). NSCAW: National Survey of Child and Adolescent Wellbeing (https://www.ndacan.acf.hhs.gov/datasets/datasets-list-nscaw.cfm). NIS: National Incidence Studies (https://www.ndacan.acf.hhs.gov/datasets/datasets-list-nis.cfm). NSCEV: National Survey of Children's Exposure to Violence (https://www.icpsr.umich.edu/icpsrweb/NACJD/studies/36523). FFCWS: Fragile Families and Child Wellbeing Study (https://fragilefamilies.princeton.edu/documentation). BRFSS: Behavioral Risk Factor Surveillance System (https://www.cdc.gov/brfss/data_documentation/index.htm). Add-Health: National Longitudinal Study of Adolescent to Adult Health (https://www.cpc.unc.edu/projects/addhealth/documentation).

a. Not an exhaustive list.

31

Thus, some surveys may include measures of "substandard parenting" or "behaviorally-approximated" maltreatment measures—parenting behaviors or environments that post risks to child safety and well-being but are not considered to trigger mandatory reporting responsibilities. Such measures may include children's exposure to high-frequency or harsh physical discipline, domestic violence or parental substance use, or deprivation of basic needs (Font and Berger 2015; Schneider, Waldfogel, and Brooks-Gunn 2016; Berger et al. 2017).

Child victims may also underreport experiences of maltreatment for fear of the consequences to their parents or the unknown environment that may await them in foster care, or due to poor recall of early experiences or difficulty conceptualizing neglect. Moreover, interviews with young children require significant training to ensure quality, which may be cost-prohibitive in much survey research. Child-reported maltreatment is thus relatively uncommon in surveys, and when it is used, measures vary in depth and scope (Amaya-Jackson et al. 2000). Retrospective studies of child maltreatment are far more common, in part because they are used to examine long-term outcomes associated with early childhood experiences. However, such measures are prone to underreporting due to recall bias (Hardt and Rutter 2004), which may pose particular concerns for identifying less-severe maltreatment, maltreatment in early childhood (versus middle childhood or adolescence), and child neglect (versus physical, emotional, or sexual abuse).

More generally, existing data sources include inadequate and inconsistent measures of neglect. Child neglect can include a large number of domains, but commonly used scales tend to focus disproportionately on physical neglect (unmet basic needs). Such measures tend to conflate poverty-driven material deprivation with negligent parenting by sidestepping complex issues of parental capacity, intent, and culpability, and by excluding more difficult-to-measure experiences such as inappropriate supervision or failure to protect children from harm. In contrast, CPS records are, on the whole, likely to substantially undercapture emotional maltreatment and, by design, do not capture most physical or sexual abuse committed by noncaregivers. Moreover, low rates of substantiation for all forms of maltreatment are suggestive of substantial undercounting, and it is not possible to differentiate between genuinely false CPS reports and reports where CPS deemed the evidence insufficient or CPS did not consider the incident severe enough to warrant substantiation. Thus, researchers must use caution when using CPS records—and CPS victimization rates based on substantiated reports—to make claims about the incidence or prevalence of child maltreatment. In addition, substantial variability in the rate at which reports are screened-in for investigation or substantiated make cross-state or cross-year comparisons highly suspect. Notwithstanding, CPS investigation records are appropriate for studies of the causes or consequences of child maltreatment: CPS investigations are associated with short- and long-term adverse outcomes for children even when no intervention occurs, indicating that the adverse outcomes cannot be attributed solely to system intervention, but rather to the alleged maltreatment and related family circumstances (Hussey, Marshall, Knight, et al. 2005; Font and Maguire-Jack 2020). Moreover, children known to the child welfare system are

TABLE 2
Child Maltreatment Incidence Estimates (Annual Rate per 1,000 Children)

	National Incidence Study IV, 2005–2006		National Child Abuse and Neglect Data System, 2016		National Survey of Children's Exposure to Violence, 2013–2014
	Harm Standard	Endangerment Standard	Investigated Children	Confirmed Victims	
Any maltreatment	17.06	39.46	46.74	9.10	152
Neglect (composite)	10.48	30.58	29.78	7.01	51
Physical neglect	4.01	16.19		—	
Medical neglect			1.29	0.20	
Emotional neglect	2.63	15.94		—	
Educational neglect	4.9	4.9		—	
Physical abuse	4.39	6.47	11.83	1.66	50
Sexual abuse	1.84	2.45	3.68	0.78	1
Psychological maltreatment / emotional abuse	2.02	4.11	3.62	0.52	93

NOTE: NIS-IV estimates drawn from NIS-IV final report Appendices B and C (Sedlak et al. 2010); NCANDS estimates generated from the 2016 child file version 3; NSCEV estimates from Finkelhor et al. (2015).

those positioned to receive intervention, and thus studies of their circumstances and outcomes are necessary to inform policies and practices. Nevertheless, researchers should be diligent about explaining the limitations of such measures, including likely contamination of the comparison group (i.e., undetected maltreatment among those without CPS investigations). Ideally, however, questions of critical significance for social policy would be addressed with multiple measures of child maltreatment.

Estimating the incidence and prevalence of child maltreatment

The type of measure used has significant implications for estimating the incidence and prevalence of child maltreatment. Table 2 shows different estimates of child maltreatment incidence (annual rate per 1,000 children) from the NIS-4, NCANDS, and the National Survey of Children's Exposure to Violence (NSCEV). The estimates for NCANDS are based on the authors' analysis of the NCANDS child files, whereas the other estimates are pulled from published research or reports (Finkelhor et al. 2015; Sedlak et al. 2010). It is evident from Table 2 that CPS substantiations are likely to grossly understate all forms of child maltreatment, but especially physical abuse. The NIS-4 includes two measures: a harm

TABLE 3
Lifetime Prevalence Estimates by Source

Data Source	NCANDS		BRFSS	NSCEV
Measure	Substantiated CPS victims by age 18	Investigated as CPS victims by age 18	Adult retrospective self-report	Caregiver report for children ages 14–17
Data type	2014 population data		2011–2014; 23-state sample	2013–2014 nationally representative sample
(Source)	(Kim et al. 2017)		(Centers for Disease Control and Prevention 2019)	(Finkelhor et al. 2015)
Any maltreatment[a]	11.8%	37.4%	—	38.1%
Neglect	8.0%	25.2%	—	18.4%
Physical abuse	2.0%	11.5%	17.9%	18.1%
Sexual abuse (narrow perpetrator definition)	0.9%	4.1%	—	0.2%
Psychological maltreatment/ emotional abuse	0.6%	3.5%	34.4%	23.9%
Witness to family violence	—	—	17.5%	19.5%
Sexual abuse (broad perpetrator definition)	—	—	11.6%	3.2%

a. The types of maltreatment included in the composite "any maltreatment" measure vary by source.

standard and an endangerment standard. The harm standard is more stringent and requires evidence of specific harms to the child victim, whereas the endangerment standard includes any maltreatment that poses a significant risk to children.

Table 3 depicts estimates of lifetime prevalence (from birth to age 18) of child maltreatment for children in the United States, drawing from national population or nationally representative survey datasets. We show the overall estimate as well as subtypes due to lack of consistency across data source in types of maltreatment included. Unsurprisingly, estimated prevalence based on CPS-substantiated maltreatment is far lower than estimates based on CPS investigations or caregiver-reported maltreatment. For example, 2 percent of U.S. children have a CPS-substantiated allegation of physical abuse by age 18, whereas 18 percent of children are estimated to have experienced physical abuse based on retrospective reports of adults (Behavioral Risk Factor Surveillance System; BRFSS) or caregiver report (NSCEV).

Both CPS-substantiated and CPS-investigated maltreatment rates suggest emotional maltreatment is relatively rare, whereas emotional maltreatment is the most common form of maltreatment identified in the BRFSS and NSCEV. The differential findings related to emotional maltreatment may be driven by the fact that emotional maltreatment is difficult to demonstrate and "prove." However, forms of maltreatment most likely to have physical indicators, like physical abuse, also have very low rates of substantiation when investigated by CPS. Rather, low rates of CPS investigation for emotional maltreatment may indicate underreporting, which may reflect inadequate understanding of the signs or symptoms of emotional abuse among mandatory reporters, or reporters' ambivalence about the threshold at which harsh or withdrawn parenting becomes emotional maltreatment. Additionally, maltreatment subtypes commonly co-occur, but a single form of maltreatment is sufficient to justify intervention. Thus, CPS investigators may choose to pursue or focus on the allegations of abuse or neglect that are easiest to document. Scholars have long noted the difficulty in identifying and responding to emotional maltreatment, given the child welfare system's emphasis on physical safety (English et al. 2015). Moreover, in surveys, measures of emotional abuse tend to focus on the child's experiences of verbal abuse, whereas legal definitions (commonly, "mental injury") require evidence that the child suffered serious and observable injury to their psychological capacity or emotional stability (Child Welfare Information Gateway 2016) as a result of the experiences. (Of course, since researchers are often interested in the effects of maltreatment, defining maltreatment based on its effects would be tautological.)

Notably, CPS-substantiated sexual abuse is more prevalent than caregiver-reported sexual abuse by a parent or caregiver. This may reflect underreporting by caregivers, in addition to differences in what each measure captures. Depending on the state, CPS measures of sexual abuse may include a broader definition of perpetrator (e.g., not limited to parents or caregivers; may include figures such as babysitters, temporary household members, or siblings). Differences may also reflect some states' practice of designating "failure to protect from sexual abuse" in the same category as perpetration of sexual abuse.

Prior research on concordance across measures of child maltreatment

Prior research has also sought to compare estimates of child maltreatment using multiple sources or approaches to measurement. Overall, such research suggests low agreement between child and parent reports of children's experiences of abuse, neglect, and other adversities (Chan 2015; Font and Cage 2018; Schneider et al. 2014) and between child self-reports and CPS or court records (Pinto and Maia 2013; Swahn et al. 2006). Given lack of consensus about the definition and operationalization of neglect, it is perhaps unsurprising that agreement across reporting sources appears lowest for neglect (McGee et al. 1995).

The implications of low agreement across measures for scientific understanding of the antecedents and outcomes of child maltreatment are not fully apparent. Some research studies indicate that the correlates of victimization (both risk factors and outcomes) are similar irrespective of the source of information (Font and Berger 2015; Font and Cage 2018; Schneider et al. 2014). However, other research suggests that children's reports of their prior victimizations are more predictive of social-emotional functioning reports from social workers or information from child welfare case records, especially for child neglect and emotional maltreatment (McGee et al. 1995).

The discordance across measures of maltreatment raises critical questions about the extent to which child welfare agencies are providing services to the optimal number of families and whether families receiving services are those most in need. A large number of children are reported to CPS each year, and hundreds of thousands of children enter foster care (U.S. Department of Health and Human Services 2020), but are these numbers disproportionate to the size of the underlying problem of child maltreatment? It seems unavoidable that some number of nonmaltreated children will be reported to CPS if mandatory reporters are acting appropriately—suspicious events, such as unexplained injuries or a young child exhibiting inappropriate sexual behavior, should be reported but may ultimately have nonmaltreatment explanations. Some may point to the large proportion of "unsubstantiated" CPS investigations as an indication that too many investigations are occurring. However, there is little reason to believe that most unsubstantiated investigations are false allegations. Moreover, research has documented that there is little consistency across caseworkers or agencies in decision-making (Doyle 2007; English et al. 2002; Font, Maguire-Jack, and Dillard 2020), and there is substantial evidence that children with an unsubstantiated maltreatment report face heightened long-term risk of a host of negative outcomes (Font and Maguire-Jack 2020; Hussey, Marshall, English, et al. 2005), including future maltreatment (Kohl, Jonson-Reid, and Drake 2009) and death (Putnam-Hornstein 2011). In addition, annual and cumulative incidence rates of investigated maltreatment are not substantially greater than rates of child maltreatment reported in surveys (Tables 2–3). Another data point to consider is the approximately 2.7 million U.S. children informally raised by relatives (Annie E. Casey Foundation 2012) in what is referred to as the "hidden foster care system" (Gupta-Kagan 2020). This suggests that a rather large number of children require temporary or permanent substitute care, far exceeding the number of children placed in formal foster care. Collectively, these data points suggest that the number of children involved with the child welfare system may not be excessive relative to the number of children exposed to substantial risk in their familial environments.

However, these data also imply that the child welfare system may incorrectly identify which children are in need of intervention beyond the CPS investigation (i.e., in-home services or foster care). Certainly, not all children who experience maltreatment are in need of intervention, and part of the investigative process is to determine what, if anything, is needed to reduce future risk of harm. When a nonparent perpetrates maltreatment, and children have a parent or legal caregiver willing and able to protect them from future harm, intervention may unnecessarily usurp or undermine protective action taken by parents or caregivers. Similarly, in cases involving a single incident of nonsevere maltreatment, caregivers may be able to successfully address the precipitating factors (mental health, substance use, parenting skills) through voluntary community services. However, it would be a misstep for child welfare agencies to merely delay action until serious harm occurs—it is critical to identify (1) when a low-risk event is a signal of a deteriorating family environment or incipient crisis and (2) whether parents in need of support are able and willing to follow up on voluntary community services without oversight or court mandate. Unfortunately, there is relatively limited evidence to bring to bear on these issues, and subjective assessment of issues like parental cooperation raise concerns about implicit bias. Predictive risk modeling (discussed by Drake et al., this volume) may provide a path forward for more effective targeting of limited resources.

Are rates of child maltreatment increasing or decreasing?

Rates of child sexual abuse and child physical abuse appear to have declined substantially throughout the 1990s and early 2000s according to numerous data sources (victimization surveys, crime reports, CPS substantiations) and consistent with declines in violent crime broadly (Finkelhor and Jones 2006). However, in recent years, CPS-substantiated rates of sexual abuse have increased once again, and rates of physical abuse have stagnated (Finkelhor, Saito, and Jones 2020). Factors that may have contributed to declines in physical and sexual abuse specifically include increased public awareness and prevention efforts focused on physical abuse (e.g., shaken baby prevention campaigns) and sexual abuse (e.g., proliferation of "safe touch" training), increased treatment and medication options for child behavior problems, and more aggressive prosecution and sentencing of violent crimes (Jones, Finkelhor, and Halter 2006).

It is more difficult to ascertain whether neglect rates have changed during this period: CPS data suggest little net decline, with enormous variability across states (Finkelhor, Saito, and Jones 2020), and there are few other data sources to negate or confirm. Moreover, because neglect comprises a broad range of parental acts and omissions, it is possible that some forms of neglect have increased and others have declined. More detailed categorization of neglect in national data systems is essential for testing the impacts of various social, demographic, and governmental changes on rates of child neglect.

Moreover, critical questions about how and for whom maltreatment rates have changed remain unanswered. For example, has the cumulative incidence (prevalence) of perpetrators and victims declined? A decline in annual incidence of maltreatment coupled with no change in prevalence of victims or perpetrators may suggest effective interventions (success in reducing revictimization and reoffending) rather than effective prevention. Available data suggest slight declines in prevalence of substantiated maltreatment between 2004 and 2009, and little change between 2009 and 2016 (Wildeman et al. 2014; Yi, Edwards, and Wildeman 2020). Again, however, declines in the prevalence of substantiated maltreatment may reflect, in full or in part, changes to child welfare system policy and practice.

Risk Factors for Child Maltreatment

This section reviews theories surrounding the causes of child maltreatment, risk factors for maltreatment, and limitations of the current work.

Theories related to child maltreatment etiology

Several theories from a range of scientific disciplines help to explain differences in children's risk of experiencing maltreatment. These theories focus on child and parent characteristics, relationships within the family, and the environment surrounding the parent; some theories additionally emphasize the interplay among multiple factors. Although early frameworks for understanding child maltreatment focused largely on the pathologies of perpetrators, modern theories tend to emphasize a broader range of individual, family, environmental, and societal factors (Garbarino 1977; Gelles 1973).

A large body of research has focused on the intergenerational transmission of child maltreatment, or the processes through which individuals' experiences of maltreatment victimization increase the risk that their children experience maltreatment victimization (Schelbe and Geiger 2017). Attachment theory (Bowlby 1969) suggests that insecure attachment—or a phenomenon in which the parent-child relationship is contaminated with fear and distrust—explains intergenerational transmission of maltreatment. Parents who have not experienced secure attachments with their own caregivers have difficulty forming them with their own children (Morton and Browne 1998). Other research refers to social learning theory (Bandura 1978) to suggest that intergenerational transmission occurs because children learn how to be parents from their own parents (Muller, Hunter, and Stollak 1995). Both theories, as applied to maltreatment, suggest that the propensity to perpetrate child maltreatment is rooted in parents' own childhood relationships and experiences.

Looking beyond explanations related to prior parenting experiences, the family stress model of economic hardship (Conger and Elder 1994) was proposed to understand the pathway through which economic hardships, such as debt burden, income loss, or economic insecurity, negatively affect child and adolescent development. The model proposes that economic hardship may not only deprive children of critical material needs, but also adversely impact family dynamics. The model posits that difficulties in or inability to meet family economic needs results in economic pressure, which in turn produces psychological distress, relationship conflict, and changes in parental affect and behavior (Conger and Elder 1994). In these family environments, children may be subjected to harsh and inconsistent discipline practices, or parents may be withdrawn (Conger et al. 1994). In extreme cases, harsh or withdrawn parenting can escalate to child abuse or neglect.

Social disorganization theory was originally put forth to explain geographic variation in crime and delinquency (Shaw and McKay 1942), but it has since been widely applied to geographic variation in child maltreatment rates. The theory postulates that there is something unique about the communities in which individuals live that can increase the rates of crime and delinquency, and that by and large these differential rates are not driven by differences across individual people. Shaw and McKay (1942) referred to this phenomenon as social disorganization and proposed three community-level factors that they posited led to increased crime and delinquency: concentrated disadvantage, ethnic heterogeneity, and residential mobility. This theory has been adapted by child maltreatment researchers to understand geographic variation in maltreatment. These researchers have suggested that parents face multiple stressors, are unable to access resources, and do not have the necessary social norms to prevent maltreatment because of the neighborhood in which they live (Coulton et al. 2007; Coulton, Korbin, and Su 1999).

Theorists have also considered how child maltreatment is defined and the extent to which that reflects the norms of those in position to set and enforce parenting standards (Hutchinson 1990). Social deviance/labeling theory posits that there is no objective behavior that can be called "child abuse"; it is only through perceiving deviance from a socially accepted norm that it is labeled as such (Gelles 1975). Specifically, Gelles (1975) refers to child abuse as a social construction by which "a) a definition of abuse is constructed, b) certain judges or 'gatekeepers' are selected for applying the definition, and c) the definition is applied by designating the labels 'abuse' and 'abuser' to particular individuals and families" (p. 365). Thus, some argue that, although violence occurs in a range of family environments, it is predominantly labeled as "child abuse" when it occurs within lower-income or otherwise socially marginalized families (Newberger, Newberger, and Hampton 1983).

Last, ecological systems theory (Bronfenbrenner 1976) combines many of these theories, asserting that to truly understand individuals, one must consider all of the factors that occur at multiple levels of the social ecology, conceptualized as systems. Ecological systems theory is depicted as a series of concentric circles, with the child at the center of these circles surrounded by the microsystem (the child's most consistent and frequent connections: parents, siblings, peers, and school), mesosystem (relationships between the child's microsystems), exosystem (institutions and public policies), and macrosystem (social norms and cultural values). This theory posits that there is no single cause of maltreatment, but there are a range of independent and interactive factors that when combined may lead to abuse or neglect.

Although not originally created to explain child maltreatment, ecological systems theory is prolific in child maltreatment research and theory. An early adoption of this framework was Belsky's efforts to integrate child, family, and environmental influences into a holistic model of parenting and child maltreatment (Belsky 1980, 1984). Belsky theorized that a parent's own history of maltreatment as a child increases the likelihood that they will engage in abusive or neglectful parenting themselves. Within the microsystem, Belsky suggested that the family and child him/herself contributes to maltreatment—that children influence their parents' behavior, while simultaneously being influenced by it. At the exosystem level, Belsky pointed to places of employment and the neighborhood. Parents who are unemployed or have low job satisfaction may have a greater propensity to maltreat. Further, being socially isolated within one's neighborhood can both contribute to a greater level of stress/depression and increase the opportunity to maltreat because of a lack of oversight from others. Finally, at the macrosystem level, Belsky suggested that society's attitudes toward violence, corporal punishment, and the rights of children all contribute to maltreatment.

As the body of theoretical work proliferated, so too did empirical studies examining the extent to which data supported the theories. Applying attachment and social learning theories, studies have focused on factors about individual parents' own experiences of maltreatment in childhood (Muller, Hunter, and Stollak 1995). Applying the family stress model of economic hardship, researchers have focused on economic shocks in families and their relation to harsh parenting (Conger et al. 2002; Parke et al. 2004). Social disorganization theory has been applied by child maltreatment researchers to hone in on the impact of neighborhood characteristics on parenting (Coulton et al. 2007). Still other studies have relied on the more holistic ecological systems theory to focus on the array of characteristics at different levels of the social ecology that might contribute to maladaptive parenting behaviors (Mulder et al. 2018).

Taken together, these theories highlight that child maltreatment is a complex phenomenon with multiple conditions that must coalesce for abuse and neglect to occur. The theories range from unidimensional, focusing on specific factors of individual relationships (e.g., attachment theory) to the multidimensional, focusing on a broad array of factors (e.g., ecological systems theory). Theories that fall at different points on this continuum have complementary strengths and weaknesses, with those that are more narrowly focused being easier to examine and test, but possibly missing many other causes; and those that are broader being much more difficult to test, but more holistic in their consideration of the causes.

Prior reviews and meta-analyses on risk factors for child maltreatment

Four components are required to establish a causal effect of a presumed risk factor on an outcome: (1) there must be a logical relationship, (2) there must be an empirical association, (3) the temporal ordering must be accurate, and (4) the relationship must not be spurious or due to an omitted variable (National Research Council 2014). Most prior work has identified correlates of child maltreatment, as opposed to causal factors that meet all of the aforementioned requirements for causality. There has been a large focus on specific characteristics of the child, parents, and family that might contribute to abuse and neglect. Parent characteristics consistently associated with child maltreatment include parental experiences of childhood maltreatment (Assink et al. 2019; Mulder et al. 2018; Stith et al. 2009; van IJzendoorn et al. 2020); parental experiences of intimate partner violence (Assink et al. 2019; Korbin and Krugman 2014; van IJzendoorn et al. 2020); and parental behavioral health characteristics such as anger, depression, alcohol and drug abuse, and psychopathology (Mulder et al. 2018; Stith et al. 2009; van IJzendoorn et al. 2020). In addition, numerous studies indicate that parental and family socioeconomic status is associated with child abuse and neglect (Erickson, Labella, and Egeland 2018; Kolko and Berkout 2018; Korbin and Krugman 2014; National Research Council 2014; Stith et al. 2009) as well as family structure, with single-parenthood being associated with a greater risk for abuse and neglect (Mulder et al. 2018; Stith et al. 2009).

Research to identify the causal antecedents of child maltreatment has largely focused on factors that can be addressed through public policy. In particular, reforms and expansions of public benefit programs or economic policies provide bountiful opportunity for natural experiments. This body of research generally suggests that increased income (through the Earned Income Tax Credit, increased minimum wage, child care subsidy, welfare, and child support policies) reduces CPS reports, child neglect, and foster care caseloads (Berger et al. 2017; Biehl and Hill 2018; Cancian, Yang, and Slack 2013; Maguire-Jack et al. 2019; Raissian and Bullinger 2017; Yang et al. 2019), whereas reduced access to employment and public benefits may increase rates of CPS reports (Fein and Lee 2003; Paxson and Waldfogel 1999; Raissian 2015). Estimated effect sizes vary across studies and are difficult to compare due to differences in samples, methods, and measures. Broadly, however, studies of income changes suggest that relatively modest increases in income may reduce an individual's risk of a CPS report by about 10 percent (Berger et al. 2017; Cancian, Yang, and Slack 2013); state-level studies of policies that increase family income similarly suggest reductions in rates of CPS reports or foster care entries by 7 to 10 percent (Biehl and Hill 2018; Raissian and Bullinger 2017).

There is a related small but growing body of research that suggests that expansive social policies—particularly, those that increase access to income, child care, parental leave, and health care—may also have unintentional benefits vis-à-vis child maltreatment prevention, such as decreased child welfare reports, decreased self-reported maltreatment, and decreased foster care caseloads (Campbell 2019). This research is not conclusive, however, and the issues plaguing this body of research are complex and difficult to address. For example, policy impact studies often leverage differences in policies across states or changes in policy over time. As with other studies of the causes of maltreatment, many policy impact studies use CPS records to measure child maltreatment, and both temporal and geographic variability in child welfare systems practices and policies may confound policy variation. Thus, estimating the causal effect of a particular policy is challenging. Also, many studies rely on state-level data, making it difficult to identify the mechanisms through which policy changes impact rates of CPS-reported maltreatment. Because substantiation status is not a reliable means of distinguishing true versus false reports of child maltreatment, many studies focus on changes in the rate of CPS investigations (also referred to as "screened in reports"). Although there are plausible mechanisms through which such policies or programs could reduce child maltreatment (e.g., reducing parental stress, ensuring children's basic needs are met), it is also possible for CPS reports to decline with no true change in child maltreatment, given that some subset of children reported to CPS have not experienced maltreatment. Expanded economic benefits, for instance, may reduce low-risk CPS reports and those that are unlikely to be substantiated, in particular, by reducing suspicion of neglect among families for whom poverty is the sole or primary risk factor. Thus, claims about reducing the occurrence of child maltreatment on the basis of changes in CPS reports should be made and interpreted cautiously. Notwithstanding, if such policies or programs reduce the rate at which impoverished families are unnecessarily reported to CPS, that frees up resources to aid families where child maltreatment is occurring, which may ultimately improve the quality and functioning of the child welfare system.

Beyond income or antipoverty programs, few policy levers have been widely studied. There has been some effort by researchers to understand whether policy changes can reduce substance use, with results indicating that reductions in the supply of or access to illicit drugs and prescription drugs with high potential for dependence may reduce foster care caseloads (Cunningham and Finlay 2013; Gihleb, Giuntella, and Zhang 2019; Markowitz et al. 2011; Quast, Storch, and Yampolskaya 2018). Overall, the capacity of public policy to prevent and treat substance use and addiction is not altogether clear. However, substance use drives a substantial proportion of foster care entries and child maltreatment cases (Child Welfare Information Gateway 2014; U.S. General Accounting Office 1998), and its prevention and treatment should be a component of any comprehensive child maltreatment prevention strategy.

Another potential policy lever that has received little attention is expansion of health insurance coverage and affordable health care. Child welfare agencies have limited resources to spend on services for families, and there is little evidence that the services provided are effective at preventing and ameliorating the effects of maltreatment (Jonson-Reid et al. 2017). Yet many of the evidence-based services for reducing child maltreatment or associated risk factors are covered by health insurance, including various mental health and substance use services and home visiting programs. Child welfare agencies have limited resources and contract with a limited number of service providers, which may constrain the quality of services as well as the number of families to whom such services are offered (Child Welfare Information Gateway 2014). Insured parents are better positioned to seek treatment from providers outside of the narrow network of child welfare system contractors, which may allow parents to access effective treatments prior to the onset of child maltreatment and also increase the quality of services available to families in the child welfare system. However, approximately 11 million parents are uninsured (Karpman et al. 2016), and many more may be underinsured or face high out-of-pocket costs. Expansion of health care coverage and reduction of out-of-pocket health care costs may increase uptake and quality of services for at-risk parents.

Quality of data on risk factors for child maltreatment

The most common approaches to investigating risk factors for child maltreatment are to examine characteristics associated with child welfare system involvement, or to rely on parent self-report of maltreatment behavior or substandard parenting (i.e., concerning parent practices or environments that may not reach the legal threshold for reporting to CPS).

The only annual national data available on CPS cases, NCANDS, contain several variables related to risk factors for maltreatment, but there are significant limitations to the data. First, the dataset includes only those cases of maltreatment that are reported to CPS. As such, it is not possible to understand individual-level causal processes leading to maltreatment, because there is no counterfactual. Second, the quality of data is poor. Many states report no data on risk factors, whereas others report information that is highly suspect. Data on parental drug use illustrates these concerns (Seay 2015). In NCANDS in 2017, several states reported parental drug use as a risk factor in less than 5 percent of substantiated cases, despite strong indications that substance use is a major factor in child maltreatment and child welfare system involvement in particular (Berger et al. 2010; Brook and McDonald 2009; Child Welfare Information Gateway 2014; Murphy et al. 1991; Ross 1997). Although data quality problems are well known, states have little incentive to improve the quality of their NCANDS submissions. NCANDS submission is voluntary, and the Children's Bureau[1] indicates that the purpose of the data is "to examine trends in child abuse and neglect across the country"—a purpose that is of little direct value or consequence to the day-to-day operations of state agencies.

In addition, survey data may not provide reliable information on critical risk factors. Returning to the example of parental substance use, the accuracy of self-reported substance use is low in populations already involved with public systems (Garg et al. 2016; Peters, Kremling, and Hunt 2015; Rendon et al. 2017). In a review of different estimates of parental substance use among child welfare system–involved parents, parent self-report produced lower rates than caseworker report or case record reviews (Seay 2015).

In addition to underreporting, reliance on parent or caregiver reports, as is common in surveys, may produce findings that are driven or inflated by common method variance. Common method variance occurs when measures are produced using the same reporter: in survey data, the parent may be the source of information for both the risk factors and the maltreatment measures. It is difficult to ascertain how much of a problem this is; and for some constructs, alternative sources of measurement may be unavailable or unreliable. Recent meta-analyses of risk factors for neglect (Mulder et al. 2018) and sexual abuse (Assink et al. 2019) did not find that the source of information on neglect (child welfare records or self-report) explained heterogeneity in effects of various risk factors. Other meta-analyses of risk factors for child maltreatment have not addressed this question (Stith et al. 2009).

Conclusion

Child maltreatment is a complex problem with far-reaching consequences for victims. Decades of research from around the world has provided significant information about the ways in which maltreatment affects victims and the circumstances that increase the likelihood for maltreatment to occur. Despite this wealth of knowledge, significant issues with defining and measuring child abuse and neglect remain, which critically limit the knowledge to be gained. Official child abuse and neglect definitions vary by state, and these definitions are not necessarily consistent with those used in research, which also commonly vary from one study to the next.

We offer several recommendations for improving science, policy, and practice related to child maltreatment. First, we propose standardizing definitions of maltreatment within child welfare systems. Current variation in such definitions across states limits the utility of cross-state comparative studies and undermines national estimates of prevalence, incidence, and trends in child maltreatment. Further, although child abuse is commonly understood to have subtypes (e.g., sexual, physical, psychological), child neglect is not typically separated in this same way, despite the diverse array of parental acts and omissions that are captured by the overarching term "neglect" (e.g., supervisory neglect, emotional neglect, physical needs neglect). Though researchers have long urged the capture of this information (Slack et al. 2003), there has been no improvement to measures in NCANDS or other administrative datasets. Given that neglect is the most common form of maltreatment within the U.S. child welfare system, more nuanced information is needed on the causes and consequences of its various subtypes.

Second, we propose improving the measurement of child maltreatment, given the set of standardized definitions. All states are required to document child abuse and neglect through their systems, but submitting data to NCANDS is a voluntary process, and limited information is available. Notably, however, compulsory federal reporting (such as the Adoption and Foster Care Reporting and Analysis System) is also plagued with problems, which may in part reflect the dysfunctional and antiquated data systems used in many states (Font 2020). Current plans for the Comprehensive Child Welfare Information Systems (CCWIS) and corresponding data quality protocols (Federal Register 2016) should emphasize the quality and timeliness of NCANDS submissions and require complete and valid data on all NCANDS elements.

Third, social welfare programs within the United States gather a wealth of information about families. Commonly, such information is unable to be easily linked across systems, and concerns about privacy of individuals has hindered progress in making such linkages. If linked, such data would facilitate evaluation of state and federal policy or programmatic changes (e.g., expansions or retractions of public benefits). Advances in technology facilitate matching between systems and careful planning and security protocols can address concerns about privacy (Jonson-Reid and Drake 2008). Despite their limitations, administrative or systems data are an invaluable tool in understanding the experiences and outcomes of maltreated children who child welfare systems identify.

However, administrative data are insufficient to inform policy and practice, given that not all cases of child maltreatment reach the attention of the child welfare system. Thus, our final recommendation is that surveys include multiple-source measures of maltreatment to bound estimates of the prevalence, antecedents, and effects of child maltreatment. Further, there is a need for studies comparing maltreatment models across datasets that use the same measures, to ascertain the reliability of estimates across different sample parameters and time frames. Moreover, existing survey measures could be greatly improved. Slack and colleagues (2003) critique overreliance on studies that predict child welfare involvement or reinvolvement to understand the causes and correlates of child maltreatment, given limitations and potential biases of system involvement as a proxy for child maltreatment. To augment and validate current data focused on child welfare involvement, prospective survey designs, including birth cohorts, provide a viable option to track experiences and outcomes throughout childhood. To understand the causes of maltreatment, a universal sample of children, rather than focusing on children deemed to be "high risk" from prior research, is needed.

Note

1. See https://www.acf.hhs.gov/cb/research-data-technology/reporting-systems/ncands.

References

Amaya-Jackson, Lisa, Rebecca R. S. Socolar, Wanda Hunter, Desmond K. Runyan, and Rom Colindres. 2000. Directly questioning children and adolescents about maltreatment: A review of survey measures used. *Journal of Interpersonal Violence* 15 (7): 725–59.

Annie E. Casey Foundation. 2012. Stepping up for kids: What government and communities should do to support kinship families. Baltimore, MD: Annie E. Casey Foundation. Available from https://www.aecf .org/resources/stepping-up-for-kids/.

Assink, Mark, Claudia E. van der Put, Mandy W. C. M. Meeuwsen, Nynke M. de Jong, Frans J. Oort, Geert Jan J. M. Stams, and Machteld Hoeve. 2019. Risk factors for child sexual abuse victimization: A meta-analytic review. *Psychological Bulletin* 145 (5): 459–89.

Bandura, Albert. 1978. Social learning theory of aggression. *Journal of Communication* 28 (3): 12–29.

Belsky, Jay. 1980. Child maltreatment: An ecological integration. *American Psychologist* 35 (4): 320–35.

Belsky, Jay. 1984. The determinants of parenting: A process model. *Child Development* 55 (1): 83–96.

Berger, Lawrence M., Sarah A. Font, Kristen S. Slack, and Jane Waldfogel. 2017. Income and child maltreatment in unmarried families: Evidence from the Earned Income Tax Credit. *Review of Economics of the Household* 15 (4): 1345–72.

Berger, Lawrence M., Kristen S. Slack, Jane Waldfogel, and Sarah K. Bruch. 2010. Caseworker-perceived caregiver substance abuse and child protective services outcomes. *Child Maltreatment* 15 (3): 199–210.

Biehl, Amelia M., and Brian Hill. 2018. Foster care and the earned income tax credit. *Review of Economics of the Household* 16 (3): 661–80.

Bowlby, J. 1969. *Attachment and loss*. Vol. I: *Attachment*. London: Hogarth Press.

Bronfenbrenner, U. 1976. The ecology of human development: History and perspectives. *Psychologia Wychowawcza* 19 (5): 537–49.

Brook, Jody, and Tom McDonald. 2009. The impact of parental substance abuse on the stability of family reunifications from foster care. *Children and Youth Services Review* 31 (2): 193–98.

Brown, Jocelyn, Patricia Cohen, Jeffrey G Johnson, and Suzanne Salzinger. 1998. A longitudinal analysis of risk factors for child maltreatment: Findings of a 17-year prospective study of officially recorded and self-reported child abuse and neglect. *Child Abuse & Neglect* 22 (11): 1065–78.

Campbell, Kristine. 2019. Prevention of child maltreatment as an unexpected benefit of social policies. *JAMA Network Open* 2 (6): e195521.

Cancian, Maria, Mi-Youn Yang, and Kristen S. Slack. 2013. The effect of additional child support income on the risk of child maltreatment. *Social Service Review* 87 (3): 417–37.

Centers for Disease Control and Prevention. 2019. Behavioral risk factor surveillance system ACE data. Available from https://www.cdc.gov/violenceprevention/childabuseandneglect/acestudy/ace-brfss.html.

Chan, Ko Ling. 2015. Are parents reliable in reporting child victimization? Comparison of parental and adolescent reports in a matched Chinese household sample. *Child Abuse & Neglect* 44 (June): 170–83.

Child Welfare Information Gateway. 2014. Parental substance use and the child welfare system. Washington, DC: U.S. Department of Health and Human Services, Children's Bureau. Available from https://www.childwelfare.gov/pubpdfs/parentalsubabuse.pdf.

Child Welfare Information Gateway. 2016. Definitions of child abuse and neglect. State statutes. Washington DC: U.S. Department of Health and Human Services. Available from https://www.childwelfare.gov/pubpdfs/define.pdf.

Conger, Rand, and G. Elder. 1994. *Families in troubled times: Adapting to change in rural America.* New York, NY: de Gruyter.

Conger, Rand, X. Ge, G. Elder Jr., F. Lorenz, and R. Simons. 1994. Economic stress, coercive family process, and developmental problems of adolescents. *Child Development* 65 (2): 541–61.

Conger, Rand, L. Ebert Wallace, Y. Sun, R. Simons, V. McLoyd, and G. Brody. 2002. Economic pressure in African American families. *Developmental Psychology* 38 (2): 179–93.

Coulton, Claudia J., David S. Crampton, Molly Irwin, James C. Spilsbury, and Jill E. Korbin. 2007. How neighborhoods influence child maltreatment: A review of the literature and alternative pathways. *Child Abuse & Neglect* 31 (11–12): 1117–42.

Coulton, Claudia J., Jill E. Korbin, and Marilyn Su. 1999. Neighborhoods and child maltreatment: A multilevel study. *Child Abuse & Neglect* 23 (11): 1019–40.

Cunningham, Scott, and Keith Finlay. 2013. Parental substance use and foster care: Evidence from two methamphetamine supply shocks. *Economic Inquiry* 51 (1): 764–82.

Dolan, Melissa, Keith Smith, Cecilia Casanueva, and Heather Ringeisen. 2011. *NSCAW II baseline report: Introduction to NSCAW II final report.* Washington, DC: Office of Planning, Research and Evaluation, Administration for Children and Families, U.S. Department of Health and Human Services.

Doyle, Joseph J., Jr. 2007. Child protection and child outcomes: Measuring the effects of foster care. *American Economic Review* 97 (5): 1583–1610.

Eamon, Mary Keegan, and Sandra Kopels. 2004. "For reasons of poverty": Court challenges to child welfare practices and mandated programs. *Children and Youth Services Review* 26 (9): 821–36.

English, Diana J., Sherry C. Brummel, J. Christopher Graham, and Laura K. Coghlan. 2002. *Factors that influence the decision not to substantiate a CPS referral. Phase II: Mail and telephone surveys of child protective services social workers.* Olympia, VA: Department of Social and Health Services.

English, Diana J., Richard Thompson, Catherine Roller White, and Dee Wilson. 2015. Why should child welfare pay more attention to emotional maltreatment? *Children and Youth Services Review* 50 (March): 53–63.

Erickson, M. F., M. H. Labella, and B. Egeland. 2018. Child neglect. In *The APSAC handbook of child maltreatment,* eds. J. B. Klika and J. R. Conte, 127–44. Thousand Oaks, CA: Sage Publications.

Federal Register. 2016. Comprehensive child welfare information system. 81 (106). Washington, DC: U.S. Department of Health and Human Services, Administration for Children and Families, Administration on Children, Youth and Families. Available from https://www.govinfo.gov/content/pkg/FR-2016-06-02/pdf/2016-12509.pdf.

Fein, David J., and Wang S. Lee. 2003. The impacts of welfare reform on child maltreatment in Delaware. *Children and Youth Services Review* 25 (1–2): 83–111.

Felitti, M. D., J. Vincent, M. D. Anda, F. Robert, M. D. Nordenberg, M. S. Williamson, F. David, et al. 1998. Relationship of childhood abuse and household dysfunction to many of the leading causes of death in adults: The adverse childhood experiences (ACE) study. *American Journal of Preventive Medicine* 14 (4): 245–58.

Finkelhor, David, and Lisa Jones. 2006. Why have child maltreatment and child victimization declined? *Journal of Social Issues* 62 (4): 685–716.

Finkelhor, David, Kei Saito, and Lisa Jones. 2020. *Updated trends in child maltreatment 2018.* Durham, NH: Crimes Against Children Research Center.

Finkelhor, David, Heather A. Turner, Anne Shattuck, and Sherry L. Hamby. 2015. Prevalence of childhood exposure to violence, crime, and abuse: Results from the national survey of children's exposure to violence. *JAMA Pediatrics* 169 (8): 746–54.

Font, Sarah A. 2020. *Data challenges and opportunities in child welfare*. Washington, DC: American Enterprise Institute. Available from https://www.aei.org/research-products/report/data-challenges-and-opportunities-in-child-welfare/.

Font, Sarah A., and Lawrence M. Berger. 2015. Child maltreatment and children's developmental trajectories in early to middle childhood. *Child Development* 86 (2): 536–56.

Font, Sarah A., and Jamie Cage. 2018. Dimensions of physical punishment and their associations with children's cognitive performance and school adjustment. *Child Abuse & Neglect* 75:29–40.

Font, Sarah A., and Kathryn Maguire-Jack. 2020. It's not "just poverty": Educational, social, and economic functioning among young adults exposed to childhood neglect, abuse, and poverty. *Child Abuse & Neglect* 101 (March). Available from https://doi.org/10.1016/j.chiabu.2020.104356.

Font, Sarah A., Kathryn Maguire-Jack, and Rebecca Dillard. 2020. The decision to substantiate allegations of child maltreatment. In *Decision making and judgement in child welfare and protection: Theory, research, and practice*, eds. John D. Fluke, Monica Lopez, Rami Benbenishty, Erik J. Knorth, and Donald J. Baumann. New York, NY: Oxford University Press.

Fox, N. A., and L. A. Leavitt. 1995. The violence exposure scale for children-revised (VEX-R). College Park, MD: University of Maryland.

Garbarino, James. 1977. The human ecology of child maltreatment: A conceptual model for research. *Journal of Marriage and the Family* 39 (4): 721–35.

Garg, Mahek, Laura Garrison, Lawrence Leeman, Ajna Hamidovic, Matthew Borrego, William F. Rayburn, and Ludmila Bakhireva. 2016. Validity of self-reported drug use information among pregnant women. *Maternal and Child Health Journal* 20 (1): 41–47.

Gelles, Richard J. 1973. Child abuse as psychopathology: A sociological critique and reformulation. *American Journal of Orthopsychiatry* 43 (4): 611–21.

Gelles, Richard J. 1975. The social construction of child abuse. *American Journal of Orthopsychiatry* 45 (3): 363–71.

Gihleb, Rania, Osea Giuntella, and Ning Zhang. 2019. The effect of mandatory access prescription drug monitoring programs on foster care admissions. *Journal of Human Resources*. Available from https://doi.org/10.3368/jhr.57.1.0918-9729R2.

Gupta-Kagan, Josh. 2020. America's hidden foster care system. *Stanford Law Review* 72. Available from https://papers.ssrn.com/sol3/papers.cfm?abstract_id=3437849.

Hardt, Jochen, and Michael Rutter. 2004. Validity of adult retrospective reports of adverse childhood experiences: Review of the evidence. *Journal of Child Psychology and Psychiatry* 45 (2): 260–73.

Hussey, Jon M., Jane Marie Marshall, Diana J. English, Elizabeth Dawes Knight, Anna S. Lau, Howard Dubowitz, and Jonathan B. Kotch. 2005. Defining maltreatment according to substantiation: Distinction without a difference? *Child Abuse & Neglect* 29 (5): 479–92.

Hussey, Jon M., Jane Marie Marshall, Elizabeth Dawes Knight, Anna S. Lau, Howard Dubowitz, and Jonathan B. Kotch. 2005. Defining maltreatment according to substantiation: Distinction without a difference? *Child Abuse & Neglect* 29 (5): 479–92.

Hutchinson, Elizabeth D. 1990. Child maltreatment: Can it be defined? *Social Service Review* 64 (1): 60–78.

Jones, Lisa M., David Finkelhor, and Stephanie Halter. 2006. Child maltreatment trends in the 1990s: Why does neglect differ from sexual and physical abuse? *Child Maltreatment* 11 (2): 107–20.

Jonson-Reid, Melissa, and Brett Drake. 2008. Multisector longitudinal administrative databases: An indispensable tool for evidence-based policy for maltreated children and their families. *Child Maltreatment* 13 (4): 392–99.

Jonson-Reid, Melissa, Brett Drake, Patricia Kohl, Shenyang Guo, Derek Brown, Timothy McBride, Hyunil Kim, and Ericka Lewis. 2017. What do we really know about usual care child protective services? *Children and Youth Services Review* 82:222–29.

Karpman, Michael, Jason Gates, Stacey McMorrow, and Genevieve M. Kenney. 2016. *Uninsurance among parents, 1997–2014: Long-term trends and recent patterns*. Washington, DC: Urban Institute.

Kohl, Patricia L., Melissa Jonson-Reid, and Brett Drake. 2009. Time to leave substantiation behind: Findings from a national probability study. *Child Maltreatment* 14 (1): 17–26.

Kolko, D. J., and O. V. Berkout. 2018. Physical abuse of children. In *The APSAC handbook on child maltreatment*, eds. J. B. Klika and J. R. Conte, 111–26. Thousand Oaks, CA: Sage Publications.

Korbin, Jill E., and Richard D. Krugman. 2014. *Handbook of child maltreatment*. New York, NY: Springer.

Maguire-Jack, Kathryn, Kelly M. Purtell, Kathryn Showalter, Sheila Barnhart, and Mi-Youn Yang. 2019. Preventive benefits of U.S. childcare subsidies in supervisory child neglect. *Children & Society* 33 (2): 185–94.

Markowitz, Sara, Alison Evans Cuellar, Ryan M. Conrad, and Michael Grossman. 2011. *The effects of alcohol policies in reducing entry rates and time spent in foster care*. Cambridge, MA: National Bureau of Economic Research.

McGee, Robin A., David A. Wolfe, Sandra A. Yuen, Susan K. Wilson, and Jean Carnochan. 1995. The measurement of maltreatment: A comparison of approaches. *Child Abuse & Neglect* 19 (2): 233–49.

Milner, Jerry, and David Kelly. 17 January 2020. It's time to stop confusing poverty with neglect. Chronicle of Social Change. Available from https://chronicleofsocialchange.org.

Morton, Nicola, and Kevin D. Browne. 1998. Theory and observation of attachment and its relation to child maltreatment: A review. *Child Abuse & Neglect* 22 (11): 1093–1104.

Mulder, Tim M., Kimberly C. Kuiper, Claudia E. van der Put, Geert-Jan J. M. Stams, and Mark Assink. 2018. Risk factors for child neglect: A meta-analytic review. *Child Abuse & Neglect* 77 (March): 198–210.

Muller, Robert T., John E. Hunter, and Gary Stollak. 1995. The intergenerational transmission of corporal punishment: A comparison of social learning and temperament models. *Child Abuse & Neglect* 19 (11): 1323–35.

Murphy, J. Michael, Michael Jellinek, Dorothy Quinn, Gene Smith, Francis G. Poitrast, and Marilyn Goshko. 1991. Substance abuse and serious child mistreatment: Prevalence, risk, and outcome in a court sample. *Child Abuse & Neglect* 15 (3): 197–211.

National Research Council. 2014. *New directions in child abuse and neglect research*. Washington, DC: The National Academies Press. Available from https://doi.org/10.17226/18331.

Newberger, E. H., C. M. Newberger, and R. L. Hampton. 1983. Child abuse: The current theory base and future research needs. *Journal of the American Academy of Child Psychiatry* 22 (3): 262–68.

Parke, R., S. Coltrane, S. Duffy, R. Buriel, J. Dennis, Justina Powers, Sabine French, and Keith F. Widaman. 2004. Economic stress, parenting, and child adjustment in Mexican American and European American families. *Child Development* 75 (6): 1632–56.

Paxson, Christina, and Jane Waldfogel. 1999. Parental resources and child abuse and neglect. *American Economic Review* 89:239–244.

Peters, Roger H., Janine Kremling, and Elizabeth Hunt. 2015. Accuracy of self-reported drug use among offenders: Findings from the Arrestee Drug Abuse Monitoring–II program. *Criminal Justice and Behavior* 42 (6): 623–43.

Pinto, Ricardo J., and Ângela C. Maia. 2013. A comparison study between official records and self-reports of childhood adversity. *Child Abuse Review* 22 (5): 354–66.

Putnam, Frank W., Marsha B. Liss, and John Landsverk. 2014. Ethical issues in maltreatment research with children and adolescents. In *Ethical issues in mental health research with children and adolescents*, eds. Kimberly Hoagwood, Peter S. Jensen, and Celia B. Fisher, 113–29. New York, NY: Routledge.

Putnam-Hornstein, Emily. 2011. Report of maltreatment as a risk factor for injury death a prospective birth cohort study. *Child Maltreatment* 16 (3): 163–74.

Quast, Troy, Eric A. Storch, and Svetlana Yampolskaya. 2018. Opioid prescription rates and child removals: Evidence from Florida. *Health Affairs* 37 (1): 134–39.

Raissian, Kerri M. 2015. Does unemployment affect child abuse rates? Evidence from New York State. *Child Abuse & Neglect* 48 (October): 1–12.

Raissian, Kerri M., and Lindsey Rose Bullinger. 2017. Money matters: Does the minimum wage affect child maltreatment rates? *Economic Causes and Consequences of Child Maltreatment* 72 (January): 60–70.

Rebbe, Rebecca. 2018. What is neglect? State legal definitions in the United States. *Child Maltreatment* 23 (3): 303–15.

Rendon, Alexis, Melvin Livingston, Sumihiro Suzuki, Whitney Hill, and Scott Walters. 2017. What's the agreement between self-reported and biochemical verification of drug use? A look at permanent supportive housing residents. *Addictive Behaviors* 70 (July): 90–96.

Ross, Jane L. 1997. *Parental substance abuse: Implications for children, the child welfare system, and foster care outcomes.* Washington, DC: U.S. General Accounting Office.

Schelbe, L., and J. M. Geiger. 2017. *Intergenerational transmission of child maltreatment.* SpringerBriefs in Social Work. New York, NY: Springer.

Schneider, William, Michael MacKenzie, Jane Waldfogel, and Jeanne Brooks-Gunn. 2014. Parent and child reporting of corporal punishment: New evidence from the Fragile Families And Child Wellbeing study. *Child Indicators Research* 8 (2): 347–58.

Schneider, William, Jane Waldfogel, and Jeanne Brooks-Gunn. 2016. The Great Recession and risk for child abuse and neglect. *Children and Youth Services Review* 53:471–505.

Seay, Kristen. 2015. How many families in child welfare services are affected by parental substance use disorders? A common question that remains unanswered. *Child Welfare* 94 (4): 19–51.

Sedlak, Andrea J., Jane Mettenburg, Monica Basena, Ian Peta, Karla McPherson, Angela Greene, and Spencer Li. 2010. Fourth National Incidence Study of Child Abuse and Neglect (NIS-4). Washington, DC: U.S. Department of Health and Human Services.

Shaw, C., and H. McKay. 1942. *Juvenile delinquency in urban areas.* Chicago, IL: University of Chicago Press.

Slack, Kristen Shook, Jane Holl, Lisa Altenbernd, Marla McDaniel, and Amy Bush Stevens. 2003. Improving the measurement of child neglect for survey research: Issues and recommendations. *Child Maltreatment* 8 (2): 98–111.

Stith, Sandra M., Ting Liu, L. Christopher Davies, Esther L. Boykin, Meagan C. Alder, Jennifer M. Harris, Anurag Som, Mary McPherson, and J. E. M. E. G. Dees. 2009. Risk factors in child maltreatment: A meta-analytic review of the literature. *Aggression and Violent Behavior* 14 (1): 13–29.

Straus, Murray A., Sherry L. Hamby, David Finkelhor, David W. Moore, and Desmond Runyan. 1998. Identification of child maltreatment with the Parent-Child Conflict Tactics Scales: Development and psychometric data for a national sample of American parents. *Child Abuse & Neglect* 22 (4): 249–70.

Swahn, Monica H., Daniel J. Whitaker, Courtney B. Pippen, Rebecca T. Leeb, Linda A. Teplin, Karen M. Abram, and Gary M. McClelland. 2006. Concordance between self-reported maltreatment and court records of abuse or neglect among high-risk youths. *American Journal of Public Health* 96 (10): 1849–53.

U.S. Department of Health and Human Services. 2020. *Child maltreatment 2018.* Washington, DC. Available from https://www.acf.hhs.gov/cb/resource/child-maltreatment-2018.

U.S. General Accounting Office. 1998. *Foster care: Agencies face challenges securing stable homes for children of substance abusers.* GAO/HEHS-98-182. Washington, DC: U.S. General Accounting Office. Available from https://www.gao.gov/assets/230/226295.pdf.

van IJzendoorn, Marinus H., Marian J. Bakermans-Kranenburg, Barry Coughlan, and Sophie Reijman. 2020. Annual research review: Umbrella synthesis of meta-analyses on child maltreatment antecedents and interventions: Differential susceptibility perspective on risk and resilience. *Journal of Child Psychology and Psychiatry* 61 (3): 272–90.

Wildeman, Christopher, Natalia Emanuel, John M. Leventhal, Emily Putnam-Hornstein, Jane Waldfogel, and Hedwig Lee. 2014. The prevalence of confirmed maltreatment among US children, 2004 to 2011. *JAMA Pediatrics* 168 (8): 706–13.

Yang, Mi-Youn, Kathryn Maguire-Jack, Kathryn Showalter, Youn Kyoung Kim, and Kristen Shook Slack. 2019. Child care subsidy and child maltreatment. *Child & Family Social Work* 24 (4): 547–54.

Yi, Youngmin, Frank R. Edwards, and Christopher Wildeman. 2020. Cumulative prevalence of confirmed maltreatment and foster care placement for US children by race/ethnicity, 2011–2016. *American Journal of Public Health* 110 (5): 704–9.

Child Welfare Financing: What Do We Fund, How, and What Could Be Improved?

By
RON HASKINS

Government efforts toward the prevention, detection, and investigation of child abuse and neglect are carried out through the United States' child welfare system—a complex web of programs that provide family assistance and promote child safety. Most funding for these activities is split among federal, state, and local governments and comprises specific child welfare–related funding (such as Titles IV-E and IV-B of the Social Security Act) and non–child welfare funding that is spent on programs that support poor and disadvantaged families (Medicaid and TANF). I provide an overview of these funding streams that finance the child welfare system, review the federal legislation since 1970 that has led to the current funding structure, and end with a discussion of how the Family First Prevention Services Act of 2018 has the potential to create better outcomes for children and families by promoting prevention activities and program support with strong evidence of success.

Keywords: child welfare financing; child abuse and neglect; child protection; Title IV-E; Social Security Act; Medicaid; Family First Prevention Services Act

The United States has a long-standing problem with children who are abused and neglected by family members and a public policy response that has never proven adequate to solving the problem. Major progress against the problem is not for want of trying. Both federal and state governments have developed a host of programs to prevent abuse and neglect, to detect it when it occurs, and to deal with its aftermath. The goals of the nation's child

Ron Haskins was, until recently, a senior fellow in and held the Cabot Family Chair in Economic Studies at the Brookings Institution, where he codirected the Center on Children and Families. His research focuses on child and family policy, welfare reform, evidence-based policy, early childhood education, federal budget, marriage, child welfare, child support enforcement, poverty, inequality, and economic opportunity.

Correspondence: rhaskins@brookings.edu

DOI: 10.1177/0002716220970909

welfare system are to prevent child abuse and neglect and to provide assistance (including temporary and permanent homes for children) to families involved in or suspected of maltreatment. To achieve these ends, the child welfare system has developed as a complex series of programs that serve the purpose of prevention of maltreatment and detection, investigation, treatment, and removal and placement of children when prevention fails. The constituent programs of the child welfare system divide responsibilities between the federal government and the states. The system is financed by federal, state and (in most cases) local dollars; and in most states, local government plays a vital role in planning and conducting the programs.

Among the best sources of information about child protection programs, spending on the programs, and evidence about the programs' effects are the survey of state child welfare programs conducted by the independent, nonprofit organization Child Trends and various publications by foundations, like Casey Family Programs and the Annie E. Casey Foundation, that focus considerable attention and funding on child welfare. Government agencies, such as the Children's Bureau within the Administration for Children and Families at the U.S. Department of Health and Human Services (HHS; 2019) and the Congressional Research Service (CRS; 2019), also conduct important work to analyze data provided by state and federal agencies, as do researchers in the private sector. The Child Trends state survey, which has been conducted seven times since 2004, most recently in 2018 (providing results through 2016), is exceptionally valuable because it collects information on spending by federal, state, and local agencies. One of the most complete sources of financial information from CRS is a fifty-page report, issued in January 2018, that provides an overview of nearly twenty federal programs focused on child welfare and their current funding.

In 2018, 7.8 million children were subjects of the 4.3 million child maltreatment referrals received by the child welfare system. Of these, 2.4 million were screened, meaning that 3.3 percent of all U.S. children were subject to a child welfare investigation. Child victimization rates rose between 2016 and 2018, reaching a reported 678,000 children—or 0.9 percent of all children determined to be victims in 2018. In that year, about 85 percent of victims suffered a single type of maltreatment: 61 percent were neglected only, 11 percent suffered physical abuse only, and 7 percent suffered sexual abuse only. The other 15 percent of victims suffered two or more types of maltreatment (HHS 2020). Moreover, that the child welfare system is not more than moderately successful is suggested by annual data on the number of children in foster care. Although the number of children in foster care declined from around 493,000 to 441,100 between 2007 and 2017, the number increased every year between 2012 and 2017, rising from about 397,300 to 441,100. The number fell for the first time in 6 years in 2018, but by fewer than 4,000 children. The total cost of conducting the federal-state system involving all child welfare activities was around $30 billion nationwide, with states contributing somewhat more than half the funds and the federal government somewhat less than half (Rosinsky and Williams 2018).

TABLE 1
Federal Child Welfare Program Funding by Fiscal Year (FY)

Program	FY 2013	FY 2014	FY 2015	FY 2016	FY 2017
Title IV-E of the Social Security Act	7,072	7,784	7,681	7,913	8,041
Title IV-B of the Social Security Act	725	714	687	682	688
Other programs	190	199	197	192	189
Total	7,987	8,696	8,566	8,788	8,898

SOURCE: CRS (2018).
NOTE: Data in millions of real 2017 dollars.

Overview of Spending by Child Welfare Programs

Although there are a host of minor programs that contribute to this total of $30 billion, the child welfare system features six major sources of funding and a seventh program (the Family First Prevention Services Act) that is just getting started. I begin with an overview of these programs and the spending on each. The largest programs include Title IV-E and Title IV-B of the Social Security Act, the Child Abuse Prevention and Treatment Act (CAPTA) state grants, the Temporary Assistance for Needy Families (TANF) program, the Social Services Block Grant (SSBG), and Medicaid. Table 1 provides an overview of federal funding for these programs. A review of each of these programs provides a broad understanding of the financing of the child welfare system.

An important distinction is in order at the beginning of our inquiry. The programs reviewed in this section fall naturally into two groups: one group of programs is designed and funded exclusively to serve children and families involved with the child welfare system, and the other group serves children who qualify for services for reasons other than abuse or neglect. The former group of programs includes Title IV-B, Title IV-E (and associated programs), and CAPTA; the latter includes TANF, the SSBG, and Medicaid.

Title IV-E of the Social Security Act

Title IV-E is the biggest of the child welfare programs, both in terms of spending and the number of children and families receiving support. In 2017, the program, which primarily pays for out-of-home care, including both foster care and adoption, received about $8 billion from the federal government. Of this amount, $7.8 billion was for adoption, foster care, and guardianship payments to caretakers; $183 million was for payments in the Chafee Foster Care program for older youth, in large part to help them make the transition to adulthood; and $38 million was for adoption payments and legal guardianship incentive payments. The major share of this money is spent on monthly maintenance payments for the care and supervision of eligible children who have been removed from their homes, most of which goes to foster care or adoptive parents. The rest is spent on administrative costs, training of staff and foster parents and other providers, recruitment of foster and adoptive parents, and operation of an automated child welfare information system (called the Statewide Automated Child Welfare Information System or SACWIS),[1] which the federal government pays for if the states wish to use the system for improved case management and data tracking. To make these payments, IV-E is an open-ended entitlement program, meaning that states can qualify for open-ended federal funding as long as they meet all the program requirements and meet state matching payments.

The federal requirements for IV-E reimbursement are extensive. The most restrictive one is that the family must be considered "needy." The definition of poor or needy used in the program is eligibility for the now defunct Aid to Families with Dependent Children's (AFDC) program. Because that program was terminated by legislation in 1996, the poverty income required for qualification has remained the same since that time, and there has been no adjustment for inflation. As a result, only families with monthly incomes that range from $378 to $1,740 across the states are eligible. Not surprisingly, given these miserly family income requirements, the percentage of children in out-of-home care receiving IV-E fell from 60 percent in 2002 to 52 percent in 2012 and is almost certainly lower today, nearly a decade after 2010 (Child Trends 2014). Even so, the proportion of total child welfare spending from federal versus state and local sources held steady over the period from 2006 to 2016. Thus, the impact of the 1996 law has yet to have a major impact on federal versus state/local spending even though a lower percentage of children in foster care are receiving federal payments. It is easy enough to imagine that this surprising fact could change in the future, but so far it has not.

Additional and more complete information on child welfare spending is provided by remarkable reports from Child Trends (Rosinsky and Williams 2018; see also Stoltzfus 2019), which has, to date, produced eleven annual reports. These and similar reports by states and federal agencies provide the broadest picture of child welfare funding available, including spending by federal, state, and local government agencies. The most recent Child Trends report shows that total child welfare spending from all sources, as mentioned above, was $29.9 billion in 2016. The report also shows that spending within states across the years 2014 to 2016 varied widely: thirty states increased their spending, thirteen states decreased their spending, and seven states held steady.

Figure 1 shows the change in spending between 2006 and 2016 for twenty-nine states with comparable data. These data are not directly comparable with the data above because they include spending by only twenty-nine states rather than all states. The figure shows about a $0.5 billion decline in spending on child welfare across these twenty-nine states, although spending increased by almost $1 billion between 2014 and 2016 in inflation-adjusted 2016 dollars. The proportion of spending representing state and local funds compared with federal funds held steady over the 10-year period, with 56 percent of spending coming from state and local dollars and 44 percent coming from federal dollars.

FIGURE 1
Change in Total Child Welfare Agency Expenditures, State Fiscal Years (SFY) 2006–2016
(Twenty-Nine States with Comparable Data)

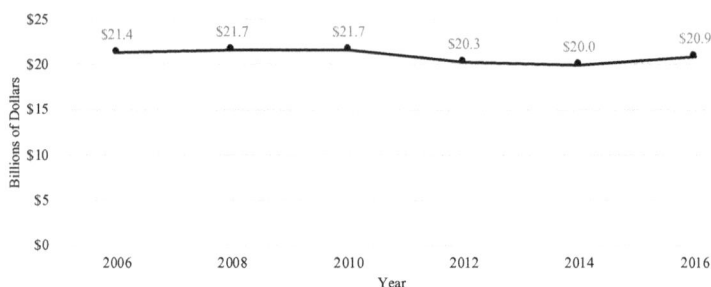

SOURCE: Figure re-created from Rosinsky and Williams (2018).
NOTE: All figures are adjusted for inflation and are shown in constant 2016 dollars.

Although IV-E funding plays the primary role in supporting child welfare spending, there are controversial features of the program that have led to serious reforms over the years, especially in 2018. As I pointed out, the most important limiting feature of the program is that only poor children and families can qualify for coverage. This feature was even more important after the welfare reform legislation of 1996 because fewer and fewer families are likely to meet this financial criterion because of the lack of an inflation adjustment in family income needed to qualify for eligibility. Although this unfortunate feature of IV-E can be expected to continue in the case of foster care payments, Congress has taken timely and wise action to stem the flow in the case of adoption payments. The offending "look back" feature resulting from the 1996 TANF legislation, stipulating that the family income defining needy or poor families that would be eligible for child welfare subsidies did not include an inflation adjustment, is being phased out in the case of adoption payments (but not foster care payments). Provisions in the Fostering Connections to Success and Increasing Adoptions Act of 2008 (National Conference of State Legislatures 2008) contained this reform.

In addition to Foster Care and Adoption Assistance, Title IV-E contains several smaller programs. These programs include Kinship Guardianship Assistance, the Chafee Foster Care Independence program, Chafee Educational and Training Vouchers, and Adoption and Legal Guardianship Incentive Payments (Stoltzfus 2018). The Kinship Guardianship program allows states to include payments to guardians under its IV-E plan. The program is optional, but in 2017 forty-four jurisdictions, including thirty-five states, the District of Columbia, and eight tribes, participated; and the caretakers of about twenty-five thousand children received maintenance payments. In a 2017 review, HHS estimated that the budget authority needed for this program for 2017 was $136 million.

Another IV-E program is the Chaffee Foster Care Independence Program. A special problem with foster care—and a major reason state programs work so hard to get children into a permanent placement (which usually means either back with their parents or in an adoptive placement)—is that research shows that youth who age out of foster care have worse outcomes than those with more permanent placements (Stott 2011). Thus, the Chaffee Independence program provides funds to states to identify children who remain in foster care until their 18th birthday and provides these children with services that prepare them for independence and living on their own. According to Stoltzfus (2018) of the CRS, these services can include financial assistance; help with housing, counseling, and education; and employment and mentoring. States are required to involve the youth in decisions about the services they receive. A total of $140 million is authorized for the Chaffee Independence program; this amount is scheduled to increase to $143 million in 2021. States also receive $43 million each year to support postsecondary education for children eligible for the Chaffee Independence program, which can be used for fees, books, room, and board at postsecondary institutions.

A final IV-E program is Adoption and Legal Guardianship Incentive Payments. The payments were originally established by the Adoption and Safe Families Act (ASFA) of 1997 and then revised slightly in the 2014 reauthorization bill. The long-standing goal of Congress, supported by nearly every child welfare expert, has been to increase adoptions because it is better for children to be in a permanent setting than in the temporary setting of foster care. Moreover, there has been a feeling among most experts that the adoption process in many states is too slow and cumbersome. For these reasons, the 1997 ASFA legislation introduced a financial incentive for states to increase adoptions and to perform them more efficiently. States were given cash payments for increasing the rate of adoptions of children in their state as compared with previous years. These incentive payments range from $5,000 to $10,000 per adoption depending primarily on the adopted child's age (states receive higher payments for older children). The incentive payments have been associated with more adoptions by states. Since enactment of ASFA in 1997, adoptions have increased from about thirty thousand to about fifty thousand per year. Moreover, the average time states took to complete adoption of children from foster care was reduced by about one year. More kids adopted; faster adoptions. A double victory.

The increase in adoptions underlines one of the most fundamental goals of the child welfare system. Of course, child safety is the single most important goal of the system, but not far behind, and not unrelated to safety, is the goal of minimizing congregate care and maximizing placements in families because achieving permanent placements is vital to the long-run well-being of children. As I mention several times in this article, most experts and administrators believe that the way to promote both safety and stability is to increase the share of children in relative care or adoption, as opposed to congregate care (Casey Family Programs 2018b). Permanent placement with kin, usually grandparents, is widely believed to be the next best arrangement. Reliance on permanent placements with kin, even without adoption, may have benefits such as fewer problems with visitation with parents, visits could be more frequent, kin foster parents are likely to be similar to biological parents in important respects (racial, ethnic, and cultural background), permanence for children could increase, sibling ties would be promoted, older youth would have support in making the transition to further education or adulthood, and involvement of the child welfare system could be minimized (Epstein 2017).

Title IV-B of the Social Security Act

Despite being much smaller than Title IV-E in terms of funding for child welfare, the Title IV-B program is also of primary importance. In 2017, Title IV-B provided states with $668 million for the Stephanie Tubbs Jones Child Welfare Services Program, the Promoting Safe and Stable Families Program, and child welfare research and demonstration programs. Unlike Title IV-E, all children and families, regardless of income, are eligible for IV-B services. In what follows, I briefly summarize each of the three parts of Title IV-B.

Stephanie Tubbs Jones Child Welfare Services. In 2017, the Child Welfare Services Act provided about $269 million in formula grant funds to states, territories, and tribes to pay for services designed to protect the welfare of all children, prevent child abuse and neglect, allow children to stay in their own homes, and similar purposes. There are no financial eligibility requirements for families, and the program is designed to ensure that all children in foster care, regardless of family income, receive permanency services (services aimed at helping children achieve a permanent placement). The money can be spent on a broad array of services but, in FY2019, states reported that they intended to spend nearly 48 percent of the funds on child protective services that include investigations of abuse and neglect, caseworker activities on behalf of both children in their homes and children who have been removed, counseling, and emergency services, among other uses. States planned to spend about 30 percent of the funds on family support, family preservation, and family reunification. The remaining approximately 7 percent of funds would be spent on foster care maintenance payments, program administration, and services to promote adoption and guardianship (see Children's Bureau 2019). The money is distributed to states in accord with a complicated formula that guarantees $70,000 to each state and distributes the rest in accord with the percentage of the national foster care caseload that is served by each state's foster care system.

Promoting Safe and Stable Families (PSSF). The PSSF program authorizes formula grant funds to states, territories, and tribes to help at-risk families by preventing maltreatment, preserving families, and ensuring children's safety by providing services that allow children to safely remain with their families. In FY2017, $59.8 million in discretionary funds (money that must be appropriated each year) and $321 million in mandatory funds (funds authorized by Congress, usually for several years; the authorized funding remains available until the years specified in the original legislation are reached or Congress changes the law) were devoted to the PSSF program. The funds can also be used to help families whose children are in foster care and to support families that have adopted a child. To qualify for these funds, states must be engaged in a Court Improvement Program[2] and related activities. PSSF funds are roughly apportioned by about 25 percent for family support services, 25 percent for family preservation services, 20 percent for adoption and promotion services, and 20 percent for time-limited family reunification services. The rest of the funds, around 10 percent, are to be expended for administration.

Child Abuse Prevention and Treatment Act (CAPTA). Created in 1974, CAPTA authorizes formula grant funding to states to provide social services to families that have abused or neglected their children. Under CAPTA, states receive funds to improve their Child Protective Services system. In the last several years, CAPTA state grants have remained almost fixed and provide a total of about $25 million per year for all the states. Compared with Title IV-B and especially Title IV-E, this is a small amount of funding. CAPTA also has a section for discretionary activities and for community-based grants to prevent abuse and neglect; but taken together, these two additional sections of the CAPTA law provide less than an additional $75 million.

Child welfare research, training, or demonstration projects. The Social Security Act authorizes HHS to sign contracts and other agreements to support research or demonstration projects that could have positive impacts on child welfare, encourage research-based experiments or special child welfare services, or advance training for child welfare workers. Although the funding of child welfare research, training, and demonstration under Title IV-B has been reduced since 2014, it was $18 million in both 2017 and 2018.

Each year since 2015, Congress has used funds from this source to support the National Survey of Child and Adolescent Well-Being (NSCAW), an important longitudinal survey that collects data on several aspects of foster care, adoption, and child well-being. NSCAW is a representative survey of families that have been investigated for child abuse and neglect. Two cohorts of children and families have been enrolled in NSCAW. By ignoring whether the report of maltreatment was confirmed, the survey provides a complete spectrum of information about families that come to the attention of child welfare agencies. In addition, by collecting information from parents, teachers, and caseworkers, the second round of NSCAW, which is being conducted by Abt Associates, a respected international research firm, is examining the education, health status, and socioemotional condition of children reported as potentially abused or neglected.

This brief overview of the programs in Title IV-B shows that states are authorized to spend funds on a broad range of services, although much of the spending is restricted by federal requirements. In addition, the Title IV-B provisions overlap to a large extent, causing those who plan the use of program funds to see that they are not at all mutually exclusive and some to wonder why it is necessary to have programs with overlapping purposes. Still, states have enough flexibility in the use of the IV-B funding to make nonoverlapping funding decisions in their state plans for child welfare spending. Here, as elsewhere, it is states that must provide the direction in child welfare spending and to plan sophisticated uses of their federal and state funds to get the most out of their resources.

Non–child welfare programs supporting child welfare services

Some social programs provide states with flexibility in deciding who is eligible for program benefits, usually under the broad guidance of federal eligibility requirements. These programs make benefits available to a wide range of children, not just a group of children with specific problems. The programs discussed above are available only to children who are in foster care, adoption, or related programs. But the nation has very large social programs that provide benefits to a broad range of children and families. Many of these programs, such as Medicaid, SSBG, and TANF, provide their benefits to low-income children and families who are similar in many respects to children involved with child welfare programs. In fact, many children receive services from one or more of these programs before becoming eligible for benefits from the various child welfare programs. But regardless of previous participation in the programs, benefits from Medicaid, SSBG, and TANF play a vital role in child welfare financing.

Medicaid. Perhaps the most important of these programs is Medicaid, not only because of the value of medical and related benefits it provides to families and children, but because of the high cost of these benefits if families had to pay for them out of pocket. In fact, if poor families had to pay for these benefits, it is reasonable to assume that they would be forced to go without them, with especially serious consequences for children. The typical benefits provided to families by Medicaid are emergency and rehabilitative medical services, targeted case management, and various treatments or even therapeutic foster care home settings. Each of these services is likely to cost thousands of dollars per year, much more than poor families can afford. This and the information about Medicaid presented here is based on state surveys of spending on Medicaid. In 2016, the thirty-seven states that reported data for the Child Trends survey of spending on child welfare and related programs (Rosinsky and Williams 2018) spent $867 million on Medicaid benefits for children in child protection programs. Spending data collected by Child Trends for the years between 2006 and 2016 showed that Medicaid spending on child welfare services declined from $1.6 billion to $0.8 billion (adjusted for inflation). Even so, based on Medicaid spending data reported by all states for the years between 2014 and 2016, twenty-three states increased their spending on Medicaid for child welfare and only sixteen states deceased their spending; ten states did not change; and one state did not submit data. The decline in state spending on Medicaid might not represent actual declines in spending on Medicaid services. Rather, the declines could be caused by the way states administer the program (Rosinsky and Williams 2018, 2). A report from the CRS, for example, found that in 2014, total Medicaid spending on children involved with child welfare did not change significantly between 2005 and 2010 but that, while total spending remained relatively constant, spending on specific services, such as rehabilitative services and case management, did change substantially (Stoltzfus et al. 2019).

SSBG. Another source of federal funding for children and families involved with child welfare is the SSBG. Although the SSBG is a program of modest size—about $1.8 billion in 2018—it provides states with great flexibility in how the money is spent. The SSBG statute defines twenty-eight categories of spending that are allowed; many of them, such as preventing or remedying abuse or neglect, preventing inappropriate institutional care, and providing care to individuals in institutions, could be used for children and families involved with the child welfare system.

Thus, it is no surprise that a sizable portion of SSBG funds are spent on child welfare. According to the Child Trends 2018 survey, in 2016 states reported spending $1.5 billion of SSBG funds on child welfare activities (Rosinsky and Williams 2018). Although the $1.5 billion represents a 5 percent increase compared with 2014, it was a decline from the all-time high of $1.8 billion in 2010 (all figures adjusted for inflation to 2016 dollars). The five top services and activities funded in 2016 were foster care (twenty-seven states), child protection (twenty-one states), case management (fourteen states), administrative costs (thirteen states), and prevention and intervention services (twelve states).[3] The 5 percent increase in spending in 2016 compared with 2014 is in line with the 4.8 percent increase in the foster care caseload between those two years.

TANF. The third of the non–child welfare programs that are commonly used for child welfare services is TANF. Enacted in 1996, TANF is a $16.5 billion block grant that provides funding to help needy families to end their dependence on government benefits, to prevent and reduce out-of-wedlock pregnancies, and to encourage the formation of two-parent families. The funding is designed to be flexible, as is the case with most block grants, so states have dramatic leeway in the use of TANF funds. This flexibility is strengthened by the fact that the Aid to Families with Dependent Children program that TANF replaced allowed funds to be spent on purposes related to foster care and by the TANF provision that allows states to transfer up to 10 percent of their annual TANF funds (around $1.65 billion each year) into the SSBG where spending flexibility is optimum.

To demonstrate the importance of TANF funds to the financing of child welfare, in 2016 states reported spending $2.7 billion in TANF funds on child welfare services. The TANF spending trend line for the decade between 2006 and 2016 shows that spending on child welfare was less than $2.5 billion only in 2014 and was as high as $3.2 billion in 2010. The four leading service categories related to child welfare for which these funds were used by states were family preservation (eighteen states), child welfare services (thirteen states), foster care payments (ten states), and emergency assistance (nine states).[4]

Major Federal Child Welfare Legislation, 1974–2018

As shown in Table 2, the basic laws and programs designed to form the nation's response to abuse and neglect have been reformed many times. Table 2 provides

TABLE 2
Major Federal Reforms Bills Since 1970

Date	Title of Bill	Brief Description
1974	Child Abuse Prevention and Treatment Act (CAPTA) (Originally enacted in Public Law 93-247)	CAPTA was originally enacted in 1974 but has been amended several times. CAPTA provides federal funds to states to use on child abuse and neglect prevention and treatment activities. The act also defined the role for the federal government in providing guidance and assisting state in research, technical assistance, and capacity building.
1978	Indian Child Welfare Act (ICWA) (Public Law 95-608)	ICWA was enacted in 1978 after Native American and Alaska Native children were entering into the child welfare system at disproportionate rates. The Act provides guidance for states on the placement of Native American and Alaska native children in foster care or adoptive homes, with special attention given to the preservation of these families
1980	Adoption Assistance and Child Welfare Act of 1980 (Public Law 96-272)	The Adoption Assistance and Child Welfare Act of 1980 amended Titles IV-B and XX (grants to states for services) of the Social Security Act to establish a program and authorize spending for adoption and foster care assistance and created the new Title IV-E program, which required states to make reasonable efforts to prevent placement in foster care and find a permanent placement for a child in foster care.
1986	Independent Living Program as part of the Consolidated Omnibus Budget Reconciliation Act (Public Law 99-272)	The Consolidated Omnibus Budget Reconciliation Act of 1985, through the addition of Section 477 to Title IV-E of the Social Security Act, authorizes funds to States for service programs and activities to assist eligible children (age 16 and over) in Title IV-E foster care to make the transition from foster care to independent living.
1993	Family Preservation and Family Support Services Program, as part of the Omnibus Budget Reconciliation Act (Public Law 103-66)	The Family Preservation and Family Support Services Program aims to promote family strength and stability, enhance parental functioning, and protect children through funding a capped entitlement to states to provide family support and family preservation services, which the law defines broadly.
1994	The Multi-Ethnic Placement Act (MEPA) (Public Law 103-382)	MEPA was enacted in 1994 with a goal to promote permanency by prohibiting states from delaying or denying a child's foster care or adoptive placement on the basis of the child's or the prospective parent's race, color, or national origin
1997	The Adoption and Safe Families Act (ASFA) (Public Law 105-89)	ASFA was enacted in 1997 in response to concerns that many children were remaining in foster care for long periods or experiencing multiple placements. The act addressed this issue by requiring timely permanency planning for children and emphasizes that the child's safety is the paramount concern.

(continued)

TABLE 2 (CONTINUED)

Date	Title of Bill	Brief Description
1999	The Foster Care Independence Act of 1999 (Public Law 106-169)	The Foster Care Independence Act amends Title IV part E (Foster Care and Adoption Assistance) of the Social Security Act to revise the program of grants to states for independent living programs providing education, training, employment services, and financial support for individuals between ages 16 and 18 leaving foster care for independent living.
2018	The Family First Prevention Services Act (FFPSA) as part of the Bipartisan Budget Act of 2018 (Public Law 115–123)	This groundbreaking legislation gives states the option to use Title IV-E funds for the purpose of preventative services (which include mental health services, substance abuse prevention and treatment services, and in-home parent skill-based programs) for children who are "candidates for foster care."

SOURCES: Stoltzfus (2018); Committee on Ways and Means (2004); HHS (2019).

a brief summary of nine major reforms enacted between 1974 and 2018. The themes of these reforms were providing more flexibility for states, keeping children at home if possible and promoting permanency, increasing equality of racial and ethnic treatment, allowing federal payments to youngsters after age 18, and emphasizing the importance of evidence-based programs and of program evaluation both of child removal and out-of-home placement and of child welfare issues more generally. The Family First Prevention Services Act (FFPSA) of 2018 is a kind of capstone of all these reforms, as it allows IV-E dollars to be used for prevention programs (for a more extensive treatment of the FFPSA, see Testa and Kelly, this volume). Beginning in October 2019, FFPSA made it possible for states to use federal funds from the Title IV-E program to provide prevention services (which include mental health services, substance abuse prevention and treatment services, and in-home parenting skill-based programs) for children who are "candidates for foster care." At one stroke, the FFPSA allowed states to flexibly use several billion dollars for prevention, an approach that many, if not most, scholars, administrators, and policy-makers believe is superior since it addresses the needs of families before child abuse and neglect occur and can prevent the removal of children from their families. Historically, federal policy required that children be removed from their homes before IV-E funds could be used. Thus, the new legislation designed to promote prevention represents a major change in both IV-E policy and, given the prominence and the funding value of IV-E, in the direction of the nation's child welfare system as a whole.

Congress has been aware for many years of the financial incentive to remove children from their homes created by the IV-E programs. In response to this flaw, legislation was enacted in 1994 that allowed states to apply for waivers that would permit IV-E funds to support prevention activities if the states met several requirements. The original legislation was extended so that by the time the

FFPSA was enacted in 2018, the waiver legislation was supporting waiver programs in thirty jurisdictions. Because these waivers would be difficult to administer under the FFPSA law, they constituted a barrier to implementation of the new law. For this reason, Congress examined ways to neutralize the waiver law. Under the terms of the waiver legislation, waivers were set to expire on September 30, 2019. This date became a deadline for Congress, signaling that something had to be done on or before September 30, 2019.

While the new use of funds envisioned by the FFPSA has the potential to fundamentally change the way child welfare agencies operate, some states had already been moving in the direction of keeping more children with their families rather than removing them and placing them in foster care—this reflected the growing notion that it is better to provide families with services and keep them together longer than to prematurely remove children. As the field came increasingly to appreciate, removing children from their families often has negative effects on the child's well-being and can leave children in settings that are less than ideal (Doyle 2007; Casey Family Programs 2018a, 2018b, 2018c). Thanks in part to the California Evidence-Based Clearinghouse (CEBC), and to other clearinghouses as well, states have a host of good programs based on quality evidence that they can use to help families improve their child rearing and avoid abuse and neglect. The FFPSA was enacted precisely for this purpose.[5]

Transition to FFPSA

This review shows that there are at least six major problems with the child welfare system about which there has long been widespread agreement among program operators and researchers:

- Before FFPSA, IV-E funds were tied to removing children from their homes and were not available for prevention.
- Too many children were being removed from their homes and placed in settings that often were questionable.
- Among these questionable settings was congregate care, which is widely seen as inferior to family and family-like settings.
- Before children were removed from their homes, child welfare agencies should have effective ways to identify relatives available to provide a loving home for children, a principle of good practice that was often ignored.
- Before removal, children and families should have the opportunity to participate in programs that high quality evidence shows to have produced positive impacts in previous evaluation studies.
- If foster care becomes necessary, state and local child welfare agencies should have the experience and resources to recruit and train effective foster parents; a small amount of money was included in the FFPSA legislation for this purpose.

The FFPSA was, in part, designed to address these problems, and Congress—realizing the implementation challenges of FFPSA and the still-active waiver programs—enacted legislation that could ease the transition from the then-current law to the FFPSA. This action was necessary because, according to Emilee Stoltzfus of the Congressional Research Service, FFPSA amended almost every provision of Title IV-E and Title IV-B (Stoltzfus 2018). A good example of the changes is that the FFPSA required that at least 50 percent of the programs used by states be "well supported," "supported," or "promising" as indicated by rigorous research. The Transition bill delays the implementation of this requirement, which would be difficult to meet for many states, for two years (through FY2021). As a result, states can temporarily use programs that do not meet the high standard of being evidence-based required by FFPSA during the transition period.

A second provision of the FFPSA that helps with the transition is that the law provides states with $500 million in flexible funding to support their implementation of the legislation and to handle adverse effects that may occur due to startup costs, the waiver transition, and improving foster care safety and quality. Of the $500 million, 3 percent is set aside for tribes and the rest is distributed to states, with no requirement for state matching payments, in accord with the same formula used to distribute funds in the Stephanie Tubbs Jones Child Welfare services funding.

The Transition bill also provides funding to jurisdictions with expiring waivers that face loss of funds as they transition away from their waiver. In 2020, states will have received roughly 90 percent of the amount that they were guaranteed under their waiver for 2019; for 2021, they will receive not less than 75 percent of the amount they were guaranteed under their waiver for 2019. This funding is in addition to the regular transition funding provided to all states under the Transition Act, as I described.

In exchange for the much greater flexibility in designing and delivering prevention services to families and having greater flexibility in spending federal funds under the FFPSA, states must meet several conditions. They must first have a plan for their program approved by HHS. Second, their program must feature evidence-based interventions that have evidence they can succeed with families. The intervention program must feature a manual that details the program and how it should be implemented. Many such successful programs are surveyed in the CEBC.

A few programs have already been evaluated by HHS as part of the clearinghouse mandated by the FFPSA (evidence-based programs are reviewed by Testa and Kelly, this volume). This clearinghouse, called the Title IV-E Prevention Services Clearinghouse, would operate much like the CEBC. It would be sponsored by HHS, and HHS has already hired Abt Associates to run the clearinghouse.[6] The child welfare intervention programs approved by the clearinghouse would be approved for state use and for IV-E reimbursement. The clearinghouse, which is just now getting started, has already identified several programs that have been shown by high-quality studies to have impacts on parenting or on families (see also Testa and Kelly, this volume). The Family Connects program has also been shown to have impacts on families in multiple settings (Dodge et al. 2013), as have several home visiting programs that have been implemented in multiple sites in one or more communities and appear to have maintained their impacts on children or families for a year or more. These and similar programs are now under review and many seem certain to be approved because the CEBC for Child Welfare has many parenting programs that have been rated as "well supported," "supported," or "promising." Thus, any organization or community that wants to select and use evidence-based programs for parents would be likely to have little trouble finding a good program that suits their needs. In the months and years ahead, HHS will likely approve many additional evidence-based programs for use by state programs eligible for FFPSA funds. Evidence-based programs are expanding rapidly and can be expected to present many more options to states for effective interventions in the future.

FFPSA and the future of evidence-based programs

Arguably the most important innovation of the FFPSA, and the one that holds the greatest promise for strengthening the child welfare system over the long term, is the requirement that states use evidence-based programs and evaluate their outcomes. The FFPSA requires that only programs with evidence of success in previous studies can be reimbursed by IV-E dollars. Moreover, the statute provides a detailed definition of how to define an evidence-based program. Anyone who has followed state policy over the years knows that states can often overcome federal rules in qualifying to spend federal dollars, but the definitions and procedures outlined in the FFPSA statute seem much stronger than previous attempts to get states to follow federal guidelines. It is difficult to overstate the importance of these provisions because the advantages of states' use of evidence-based programs depend on tight implementation of the new federal provisions. The field of child welfare will not benefit from use of evidence-based programs unless the use of these programs is actually increased, well implemented, and carefully evaluated.

Casey Family Programs (2018a) has conducted notable work in determining which child welfare programs seem well qualified to received FFPSA funding. Because it will take a year or two before the federal government can evaluate the programs adequately (as I mentioned, only thirteen programs have been evaluated so far), Casey Family Programs' work could have a big impact in getting states' use of evidence-based programs rolling. Under the terms of FFPSA, the federal government can reimburse only for evidence-based programs. Table 3 presents a summary of Casey's extensive work in summarizing evidence from the CEBC on the effectiveness of programs that would be useful in child welfare activities. These programs fall into the three categories created by the legislation, namely, mental health services, substance use prevention and treatment, and in-home programs for parenting skills and education. There is a certain level of risk that states that use the programs in Table 3 will be left holding the bag if the programs are not included on the HHS list of evidence-based programs when it is finally determined. If it turns out that the programs Casey determines are evidence based do not pass the eventual federal evaluation, the states might not be able to claim funding for use of the programs. However, this outcome seems

TABLE 3
Ratings of Intervention Programs by Casey Family Programs

Intervention Program Type	Number of Programs per Rating Category		
	Well-Supported	Supported	Promising
Mental Health Services for Children and Parents	29	22	19
Substance Abuse Prevention and Treatment for Children and Parents	4	15	7
In-Home Parent Skill-Based Programs: Parenting Skills Training and Parent Education	5	5	7
In-Home Parent Skill-Based Programs: Individual and Family Counseling	2	7	14

SOURCE: Casey Family Programs (2018a).

unlikely because of the care with which the CEBC and Casey analyses were conducted and because the strength of the definitions of evidence-based policy used in the FFPSA statute.

Casey Family Programs reviewed 136 programs across the three categories of programs defined in the statute. The programs had been scored as "well-supported," "supported," or "promising,"[7] by the CEBC. Programs that fall into these three categories could be eligible for funding under the FFPSA statute if the evidence of impacts is strong enough. The Casey work demonstrated, as does the CEBC website itself, that states have an abundance of evidence-based programs with which to work. It seems certain that the future will bring many more evidence-based programs that will play a role in improving child welfare services, thanks to the requirement in the FFPSA that states use evidence-based programs.

Concluding Comment

Given the history of implementation of innovative federal policies, it would be foolish to label the FFPSA as "can't miss legislation." On the other hand, this review makes it clear that the development of federal and state child welfare policy and the funding now available point to the likely improvement of child welfare policy and outcomes in the years ahead. To a considerable degree, the FFPSA is constructed on the accumulated wisdom of previous child welfare policy and experience. Notable are the emphasis on evidence-based programs, the requirement for evaluation by states of its new programs, the emphasis on keeping children at home and providing services to families rather than removing children at the first sign of abuse or neglect, the requirement to avoid placing children in institutions unless they require treatment, and the emphasis on placing children who must be removed from their homes with relatives. Perhaps the most notable and fortunate feature of the FFPSA is the emphasis on program evaluation that will allow the field to know whether the extent to which the new legislation is having its intended impacts in protecting children and reducing the number of children in out-of-home care.

Notes

1. For more information on SACWIS, see https://www.childwelfare.gov/topics/management/practice-improvement/reviews/external/federal-monitoring/sacwis/.

2. For more information on the Court Improvement Program (CPI), see https://www.childwelfare.gov/topics/systemwide/courts/reform/cip/.

3. See https://www.childtrends.org/wp-content/uploads/2018/12/SSBGSFY2016_ChildTrends_December 2018.pdf.

4. See https://www.childtrends.org/wp-content/uploads/2018/12/TANFSFY2016_ChildTrends_December 2018.pdf.

5. In anticipation of enactment of the FFPSA, Casey Family Programs performed an exceptionally useful service by surveying evidence-based programs related to the "safety, well-being, or permanence of the child or to prevent the child from entering foster care." See Casey Family Programs (2018a).

6. Sandra Wilson is the project director and Erin Bumgarner is the deputy project director; Suzanne Kerns at the University of Denver is the principal investigator. The federal project officers at the Administration for Children and Families are Christine Fortunato, Laura Nerenberg, and Jenessa Malin.

7. Casey Family Programs did not count programs that lacked enough evidence to be scored as "well-supported," "supported," or "promising" (2018a, p. iv).

References

Casey Family Programs. 2018a. *Interventions with a special relevance for the Family First Prevention Services Act (FFPSA)*. Seattle, WA: Casey Family Programs. Available from https://caseyfamilypro-wpengine.netdna-ssl.com/media/Family-First-Interventions-Catalog.pdf.

Casey Family Programs. 2018b. *What are the outcomes for youth placed in congregate care settings?* Seattle, WA: Casey Family. Programs. Available from https://caseyfamilypro-wpengine.netdna-ssl.com/media/SF_CC-Outcomes-Resource.pdf.

Casey Family Programs. 2018c. *What impacts placement stability?* Seattle, WA: Casey Family Programs. Available from https://www.casey.org/placement-stability-impacts/.

Child Trends. 2014. *Federal, state, and local spending to address child abuse and neglect in SFY 2012*. Bethesda, MD: Child Trends. Available from https://www.childtrends.org/wp-content/uploads/2014/09/SFY-2012-Report-for-Posting-July2015.pdf.

Children's Bureau. 2019. *Report to Congress on state child welfare expenditures*. Washington, DC: Children's Bureau.

Committee on Ways and Means. 2004. 2004 Green Book: Background Material and Data on the Programs within the Jurisdiction of the Committee on Ways and Means (WMCP 108-6). Washington, DC: U.S. House of Representatives. Available from https://greenbook-waysandmeans.house.gov/.

Congressional Research Service. 2018. *Child welfare: An overview of federal programs and their current funding*. Washington, DC: Congressional Research Service Available from https://www.everycrsreport.com/files/20180102_R43458_9a7c2ce137b5409661780 3ba8c171c543c4575b0.pdf.

Congressional Research Service. 2019. *Child welfare: Purposes, federal programs, and funding*. Washington, DC: Congressional Research Service. Available from https://crsreports.congress.gov.

Dodge, Kenneth A., W. Benjamin Goodman, Robert A. Murphy, Karen O'Donnell, and Jeannine Sato. 2013. Randomized controlled trail of universal postnatal nurse home visiting: Impact on emergency care. *Pediatrics* 132 (Suppl. 2): S140–46.

Doyle, Joseph J., Jr. 2007. Child protection and child outcomes: Measuring the effects of foster care. *American Economic Review* 97 (5): 1583–1610.

Epstein, Heidi Redlich. 2017. *Kinship care is better for children and families*. Washington, DC: American Bar Association. Available from https:// www.americanbar.org.

National Conference of State Legislatures. 2008. Fostering Connections to Success and Increasing Adoptions Act of 2008. Denver, CO: National Conference of State Legislatures. Available from https:// www.ncsl.org/documents/cyf/FosteringConnectionsSummary.pdf.

Rosinsky, Kristina, and Sarah Catherine Williams. 2018. *Child welfare financing SFY 2016: A survey of federal, state, and local, expenditures*. Bethesda, MD: Child Trends. Available from https://www.childtrends.org/wp-content/uploads/2018/12/CWFSReportSFY2016_ChildTrends_December2018.pdf.

Stoltzfus, E. 2018. *Family first prevention services act (FFPSA)*. Washington, DC: Congressional Research Service. Available from https://fas.org/sgp/crs/misc/IN10858.pdf.

Stoltzfus, E. 2019. *Child welfare: Purposes, federal programs, and funding*. Washington, DC: Congressional Research Service. Available from https://fas.org/sgp/crs/misc/IF10590.pdf.

Stott, Tonia. 2011. Placement instability and risky behaviors of youth aging out of foster care. *Child and Adolescent Social Work Journal* 29:61–83.

U.S. Department of Health & Human Services. 2020. *Child maltreatment 2018*. Washington, DC: U.S. Department of Health & Human Services Administration for Children and Families, Administration on Children, Youth and Families, Children's Bureau. Available from https://www.acf.hhs.gov/cb/research-data-technology/statistics-research/child-maltreatment.

U.S. Department of Health and Human Services, Administration for Children and Families, Children's Bureau. 2019. *Major federal legislation concerned with child protection, child welfare, and adoption*. Washington DC: Child Welfare Information Gateway, Children's Bureau. Available from https://www.childwelfare.gov/pubPDFs/majorfedlegis.pdf.

The Evolution of Federal Child Welfare Policy through the Family First Prevention Services Act of 2018: Opportunities, Barriers, and Unintended Consequences

By
MARK F. TESTA
and
DAVID KELLY

The Family First Prevention Services Act of 2018 affords child welfare agencies a new opportunity to fund evidence-supported interventions to prevent children's removal into public foster care and ensure that youth in care receive appropriate treatment in the least restrictive (most family-like) setting. The new law has been generally heralded as a much-needed improvement over prior funding constraints, but there are concerns among a growing number of child welfare leaders, researchers, professional membership organizations, and advocacy groups that its focus on the families of children who are at immanent risk of removal because of maltreatment is too limiting and that overreliance on strict evidence standards may contribute to racial disparity. This article considers how child welfare agencies can best leverage the opportunities presented by Family First while addressing potential barriers posed by the paucity of evidence-supported prevention programs and avoiding the unintended consequences of limiting reimbursement to only selective prevention services that meet rigorous evidence standards of effectiveness.

Keywords: child welfare history; prevention of foster care; evidence-supported interventions; primary prevention of child maltreatment

The Family First Prevention Services Act (Family First) of 2018 affords child welfare agencies a new opportunity to fund evidence-supported interventions to prevent children's removal from their homes and placement into public foster care and to ensure that youth in care receive appropriate treatment in the least restrictive (most family-like) setting. There is general agreement among the child welfare community that the expansion of the federal Title IV-E entitlement program beyond reimbursement for

Mark F. Testa is a distinguished professor emeritus at the University of North Carolina School of Social Work at Chapel Hill. He is an elected fellow of the American Academy of Social Work and Social Welfare and is nationally recognized for his scholarship and public engagement in child welfare reform.

Correspondence: mtesta@unc.edu

DOI: 10.1177/0002716220976528

ANNALS, *AAPSS*, 692, November 2020

child placement services and foster care maintenance payments is a much-needed improvement over prior funding constraints (Children's Defense Fund 2018). At the same time, there is growing concern among child welfare professionals and advocacy groups that Family First's focus on clinical interventions that are targeted at families of children who are at immanent risk of removal because of reported maltreatment is too limiting. Given the role that poverty plays in child welfare, the lack of recognition of poverty as an impediment to family stability in the law and its failure to allow for basic supports to help prevent or ameliorate poverty related challenges and address selective needs for income support and concrete services may hamper the efficacy of clinical interventions (see Slack and Berger, this volume; Feely et al., this volume). The fact that very few of the interventions rated as evidence supported by the Title IV-E Prevention Services Clearinghouse (Clearinghouse) have been demonstrated to be effective with minority populations, especially Black and American Indian/Native Alaska (AI/NA) populations that are overrepresented in the child welfare system, also warrants careful consideration. That there is so little current evidence for which services work specifically with Black and AI/NA populations may prevent the law from achieving its stated purpose and contribute to the presence or growth of racial disparity by failing to offer Black and AI/NA families equal access to prevention services. Relying on existing evidence-supported interventions without adequately testing their generalizability to minority populations may actually end up perpetuating racial disparities (for a discussion of racial disparities in the child welfare system, see Dettlaff and Boyd, this volume).

Other unintended consequences include a possible disincentive for child welfare agencies to fund community-based, primary prevention services and supports, which can help to strengthen parental protective capacities prior to severe need or instability, in favor of selective mental health services and substance use treatment rated as reimbursable by the Clearinghouse.

In this respect, Family First could discourage upstream efforts to prevent deeper-end needs from developing. Mindful of Family First's potential risks and benefits, this article considers how child welfare agencies can best leverage the opportunities presented by the law to address potential barriers posed by the paucity of evidence-supported, universal prevention programs and avoid the unintended consequences of limiting reimbursement to only selective prevention services that meet evidence standards.

Universal, Selective, and Indicated Prevention Programs

Family First became operative on October 1, 2019. The new law rededicates Title IV of the Social Security Act to its original purpose of maintaining children

David Kelly is special assistant to the associate commissioner of the Children's Bureau (CB). He has overseen CB's work with courts and the legal community and advised CB and ACF leadership for more than a decade. He has served as an attorney representing parents and youth in child welfare proceedings, as senior assistant child advocate for the State of New Jersey, and in leadership positions with child and family advocacy organizations.

in the home of a parent or relative as an alternative to institutional or foster family care. A major difference, however, is that the 1935 Aid to Dependent Children (ADC) program—renamed Aid to Families with Dependent Children (AFDC) in 1962—sought to achieve this aim through a selective prevention strategy of income support by targeting children who were deprived of breadwinner support because of death, continued absence, or incapacity. Family First seeks to achieve this same goal of maintaining children in the home of a parent or relative through an indicated prevention strategy of social services, which offers evidence-supported mental health, substance use treatment, and parent training to families with children who are at imminent risk of removal from their home and place-ment into institutional or family foster care.

It is important to note that "prevention services" in the law's title applies to only a subset of evidence-supported programs that are targeted on one or more subpopulations of children who have *already come to the attention of child wel-fare agencies* because of reported neglect, abuse, or exploitation. Only those reported cases that have been indicated for child maltreatment and assessed to be at imminent risk of removal into institutional or foster family care are unam-biguously eligible for Title IV-E prevention services. It should also be noted that Family First requires detailed individualized prevention plans and individualized data tracking for all recipients of services, which is one way it is distinct from public health models of prevention that take population-based approaches. As Jones Harden and colleagues (this volume) describe, indicated and selective pre-vention programs are distinguishable from universal prevention programs in that the latter encompasses measures designed for the general population without regard to specific risk or protective factors. In this respect, Family First is not intended to prevent child abuse, neglect, and exploitation before they happen. Rather, its aim is to reduce the secondary harms associated with these problems by funding evidence-supported mental health, substance use treatment, and par-ent training, which are targeted on the parents or kin caregivers of "candidates for foster care." The premise is that the secondary harms of child maltreatment can be successfully ameliorated without removing children from their home and further compounding their trauma. Because similar behavioral health services are available to the parents and kin caregivers of children already in public foster care, the law excludes them from eligibility for Title IV-E prevention services. It does, however, extend eligibility to the adoptive parents and legal guardians of former foster children whose permanent placement is assessed to be at risk of disruption or dissolution.

Candidates for foster care are children who have been identified in a formal service plan as being at imminent risk of removal but who can remain safely in the home of a parent or relative if Title IV-E fundable prevention services are deemed sufficient to prevent their entry into public foster care. Other than in these general terms, the statute does not further define "candidates for foster care" or "imminent risk." States and tribes have broad discretion to define which specific children may be assessed as at imminent risk of entering foster care. Unfortunately, Family First misses an opportunity to provide significant support to tribal communities by limiting the ability to tap into these funds to tribes that directly operate IV-E programs as opposed to the much larger number of tribes that have IV-E agreements with state child welfare agencies.

How broadly state-specific definitions may be interpreted to accommodate selective subpopulations of children who have not been indicated for maltreatment but are nonetheless assessed to be at higher than usual risk of removal remains an open question. The statute does identify two selective populations of children—pregnant and parenting foster youth and children under the care of relatives—for whom states and tribes can claim Title IV-E reimbursement for prevention services. In addition, relative caregivers are eligible for qualified Title IV-E kinship navigator programs. These are family support programs targeted at children who are under the full-time care of relatives irrespective of whether the relatives are public kinship caregivers or voluntary kinship caregivers caring for children diverted from the formal foster care system. Their purpose is to assist public and voluntary caregivers in learning about, finding, and using existing support services and programs, such as Temporary Assistance for Needy Families (TANF), Supplemental Nutrition Assistance Program (SNAP), child care, and foster home licensing, to meet their own needs and the needs of the children and youth they are raising. Support services may include any combination of financial supports; training or education; support groups; referrals to other social, behavioral, or health services; and assistance with navigating government and other types of assistance, financial or otherwise.

Current estimates are that between 2.3 and 2.7 million children reside apart from their parents in the homes of relatives (U.S. Census Bureau 2019; Stoltzfus and Boyle 2019). Based on the 2013 National Survey of Children in Nonparental Care (NSCNC), less than 10 percent of alternative kinship care arrangements fall under the supervision of the formal foster care system. An estimated 39 percent of children in kinship homes are arranged privately among family members without the mediating help or intervention of a court or child welfare agency (Testa, Hill, and Ingram 2020). Another 32 percent reside in kinship homes that are arranged with the help and support of a child welfare agency but without the agency's taking legal custody of the child. Somewhere in the vicinity of 20 percent of children in kinship care are living in legally permanent homes with relatives who adopted them. Children who are living in legally permanent homes with relatives who assume private guardianship of them are usually counted in other kinship categories. The proportion of children in permanent kinship homes would rise above 20 percent in adoptive homes if children in legal guardianship arrangements were redistributed from other categories into the category of permanent kinship care.

Even though child welfare prevention services are usually equated only with the preservation of the parental care of dependent, neglected, abused, and exploited children, the preservation of private, voluntary, and permanent kinship care has long been a special focus of federal prevention efforts ever since the federal government first assumed partial responsibility in 1935 for the income support of dependent and neglected children. Prior to the abolition of AFDC in 1996, a key practice question was whether an income-support strategy alone was sufficient to prevent unnecessary family disruption or whether to be genuinely effective it needed to be integrated with a social-service strategy that addressed the underlying social problems that contributed to family instability.

The passage of Family First brings this long-standing practice question and its accompanying value propositions full circle, but with the order of prevention strategies reversed: is a social services strategy alone sufficient to prevent unnecessary family disruption, or does it need to be integrated with an income-support strategy to be genuinely effective (see, e.g., Feely et al., this volume)? The question remains as poignant today as ever given recent federal data that make clear the high incidence of poverty in the lives of families making contact with the child welfare system and the very high percentage of neglect cases that constitute the primary reason for child removals in the United States (see Slack and Berger, this volume). As reflected in the history of child welfare funding that we provide here, Family First is the most recent chapter in an ongoing debate over how much the federal government should invest in the health and well-being of families in the United States, particularly poor families and families of color. Limitations on who can be served, in what ways, for how long, and under what circumstances can legitimately be understood to be cost control measures, service rationing, or a judgment of certain populations' worth.

Changing Definitions of Work and Family in the Twentieth Century

Policy-makers have debated periodically the fundamental practice question of whether to integrate social services with income support or separate them since the creation of ADC in 1935. Answers varied depending on the different goals that policy-makers set for federal, state, and tribal child welfare programs and the changing definitions of "work" and "family" that framed these debates. As evidenced from the legislative history, such decisions are often deeply ideological, reflect implicit or explicit biases, and result from politically negotiated compromises as opposed to what families actually need.

The 1935 ADC program built on the "maternalist" assumptions (Gordon 1994) of state mothers' pensions programs, which acknowledged that parental care of children was "work" and "family" care was less costly to preserve than out-of-home care of children. The Report of the Committee on Economic Security, which was transmitted to the president in January 1935, outlined the assumptions of state mothers' pensions, which the ADC program federalized, as follows:

> [Mothers' pensions] are not primarily aids to mothers but defense measures for children. They are designed to release from the wage-earning role the person whose natural function is to give her children the physical and affectionate guardianship necessary not alone to keep them from falling into social misfortune, but more affirmatively to rear them into citizens capable of contributing to society. (Committee on Economic Security 1935)[1]

ADC's selective prevention strategy of releasing mothers from the wage-earning role so that dependent children could be raised in their own homes also applied to the survivor provisions of the Social Security Act. Child welfare leaders, researchers, and professional groups initially judged the prevention strategy to be a grand success (Kadushin 1978). The percentage of children with no parent in the home declined from 5 percent in 1940 to 3 percent in 1970 (Hernandez 1993). Proponents of the income-support strategy attributed the program's success to meeting children's maintenance needs for food, clothing, and shelter as well as relieving the stresses of chronic poverty, which can aggravate the risk of child abuse and increase the dangerousness of parental neglect (Pelton 1978). As AFDC and survivor insurance coverage expanded from 1962 to 1973, the number of poor children in the United States plummeted from seventeen million to under nine million.

The complementary trends of declining child poverty and rising AFDC participation rates lifted the AFDC-to-child-poverty ratio from 16 to 83 per 100 children in poverty. The subsequent plateauing of AFDC caseloads during the 1970s, which continued through the economic recessions of the early 1980s despite the rebound in child poverty rates, coincided with a shift in public attitudes. The acceptability of releasing single mothers from the wage-earning role and the suitability of the families this policy preserved became topics of concern. The sympathetic reception that ADC initially received for easing the stresses of poverty and preserving the care of children in their own home turned increasingly hostile as the stratified system of provision built into the Social Security Act came more prominently into view. The system had intentionally cast the support of widows and children through social insurance as superior both in payment and reputation to the support of unmarried mothers and children through public assistance (Gordon 1994). As participation in the AFDC program expanded and the social insurance provisions siphoned off the support of widows and children, a competing narrative gained a foothold, which Glazer (1988) summarized as follows:

> By the early 1960s something that was increasingly being called a "crisis in welfare" was being analyzed. The number of mothers and children on welfare was increasing, not declining, as the social insurance system matured. And there was a second reason for the crisis: the composition of those on welfare was changing. The miner's widow was less and less in evidence. The women on welfare were those who had been divorced or deserted by living spouses, or, increasingly, had never been married at all and were the mothers of one or more illegitimate children. (Glazer 1988, 23)

Framing the expansion of AFDC coverage as subsidizing failed marriages rather than preserving fragile families helped to reinforce long-standing misgivings about the problems of child dependency and neglect. Instead of viewing the problems as offshoots of limited opportunities and discriminatory practices in the marketplace, the welfare crisis was blamed on the "pathological behavior" of the poor. From 1960 to 1979, the percentage of children being raised in single-parent families doubled from 9 percent to 18 percent. Critics argued that these families were becoming "broken" because selective subpopulations of the poor were failing to abide by the dominant norms of work and marriage, which supported conventional family life. They pointed to the dwindling presence of wage-earning fathers, the spread of matriarchal family structures, and inadequate child-rearing practices in lower-class and minority communities as creating a self-perpetuating "culture of poverty," which income assistance alone was impotent to change (Geary 2015).

Habilitating Poor Parents for Stable Marriages and Paid Work

To help address the perceived crisis in welfare, the 1956 and 1962 amendments to the Social Security Act integrated social services into the act's income-support provisions. The intention was "to help maintain and strengthen family life and to help such parents or relatives to attain the maximum self-support and personal independence consistent with the maintenance of continuing parental care and protection" (Social Security Act 1956). By social services, the proponents of integration meant intensive counseling by highly skilled social workers with small caseloads ("soft services"). Also included were homemaker services, emergency assistance, transportation help, and other tangible goods ("hard services"). To encourage states to invest in social services, the 1962 amendments increased the Title IV-A match from 50 to 75 percent.

The Report of the Ad Hoc Committee on Public Welfare to the Secretary of Health, Education, and Welfare (U.S. Department of Health, Education, and Welfare 1961) articulated the theory of change underlying the enhanced funding of social services as follows:

> Information is already available, and has been tested, on measures of treatment for families in which the incidence of multiple problems has created a pattern of dependency. With enough trained workers available, these patterns could be broken by application of this knowledge. As the proportion of individuals and families who are in need because of severe disturbances in their pattern of life increases, the demand for skilled services increases. These positions are critical ones demanding trained understanding of human behavior and of human needs. (U.S. Department of Health, Education, and Welfare 1961, 40–41)

According to the Ad Hoc Committee, less than 1 percent of welfare workers in 1960 held a masters' degree in social work. To make headway toward delivering the intensity of casework services envisioned, it promoted a goal that within 10 years, one-third of all persons engaged in social work capacities in public welfare should hold a masters' degree in social work. Even though legislation offered federal support to accredited schools of social work, hardly any time was extended to schools to rise to the challenge. Within just five years of enacting the amendments, Congress was ready to turn from social services to "stronger remedies for the welfare crisis" (Handler 1973).

The reasons for the shift reflected a variety of misgivings. Congress became impatient with the social-service strategy because of the lack of immediate returns on the promise that lower-class and minority families would become more stable and economically self-sufficient. Instead of declining, as Glazer noted, the AFDC caseload continued to rise from 2.8 million child beneficiaries in 1962 to 3.6 million in 1967. In a stunning about face, which Daniel Patrick Moynihan characterized as the "first purposively punitive welfare legislation in the history of the American national government" (Moynihan 1968), Congress effectively abandoned the family-preservation strategy in favor of a work-incentive strategy to push single mothers into doubling-up on the parenting and wage-earning roles. The racial resentment that helped to fuel the reaction also was not lost on Moynihan, which he characterized as the "first deliberate anti–civil rights measure of the present era" (Moynihan 1968).

The 1967 amendments offered earnings exemptions ($30 and 1/3 rule), which raised the limits on the combined earnings and AFDC payments that recipients could retain before losing income eligibility. The amendments also threatened the loss of categorical eligibility if recipients failed "without good cause" to work or participate in work training. To clamp down on any further proportionate growth in father-absent families, the amendments capped AFDC reimbursements for children of absent parents at the same proportion of children in absent-father families as in the child population as a whole.

Separating Income Support from Social Services

Welfare rights advocates joined the call for separating income support from social services. They hoped that separation would finally clear the way for procedural regularity to supplant what they perceived to be arbitrary and often punitive discretionary power of caseworkers to reduce income benefits to otherwise eligible parents or relatives. Social work professionals held on a little longer to the hope that the social services strategy would eventually pay off in incremental dividends if not massive social reform. However, as the AFDC program ballooned from 3.6 million children in 1967 to 8.0 million children in 1973 despite the unprecedented rise in federal social services spending from $354 million in 1969 to $1.7 billion in 1972 (Derthick 1975), professional leaders also began distancing themselves from the integration of social services and income support.

Many trained social workers had grown resentful of the voluminous paperwork demanded of them to process cash payments. They also chaffed at the connections that the public was beginning to draw between social casework and the stigma of welfare. The emerging problem-solving approach (Perlman 1957) struggled to live up to the unrealistic expectations that politicians were demanding. The editor-in-chief of *Social Work*, Gordon Hamilton, cautioned as early as 1962 that social casework can be no stronger than the economy, culture, and government within which these programs operate (Hamilton 1962). Accepting the necessity of more comprehensive economic and social reforms before social casework could deliver on its promises, the majority of social work leaders eventually joined the call for separating social services and income support. In the end, there was barely a dissenting voice when the U.S. Department of Health,

Education, and Welfare issued instructions that required all states to separate income support from social services by 1973.

Extending AFDC to the Coverage of Foster-Care Maintenance Payments

The seeds of discontent with the integration of social services and income support were earlier sown by the widespread misuse of state discretion to deny AFDC payments to otherwise eligible homes that welfare workers deemed "unsuitable" because of out-of-wedlock births, nonmarital cohabitation, or failure to comply with service plans (Bell 1965). The 1962 Social Security amendments mandated a halt to the practice by prohibiting states from terminating AFDC payments while any children remained in the home. Instead, states were instructed to use the enhanced federal match to fund casework services to rehabilitate parents and remedy the underlying problems that made the home unsuitable. If the severity of problems threatened the safety of the children, the new law authorized states to tap into the Title IV-A entitlement to claim 50 percent reimbursement to cover the costs of removing AFDC-eligible children from parental or relative custody and maintain them in foster family care. Subsequent amendments added institutional care to the mix of reimbursable costs and broadened the definition of child welfare services fundable under Title V to include social services that supplement or substitute for parental care to address the problems that contribute to the neglect, abuse, exploitation, or delinquency of children.

The 1967 Social Security amendments further expanded eligibility for Title IV-A foster care beyond those children who were actually receiving AFDC benefits to include those additional children who would have been eligible had their parents or relatives applied for benefits during the month of removal. The amendments also moved child welfare services from its original location under Title V to a new Title IV-B. The new law added a state-plan stipulation that required the same state agency, which administered the AFDC program, to administer the Title IV-B program. Because Title IV-B spending was capped at $110 million, the program was spared the recriminations that the subsequent growth in social-services spending under Title IV-A later provoked.

Clamping Down on Uncontrollable Social Services Spending

We should note that the unprecedented rise in federal social services spending under Title IV-A had little to do with the goal that the Ad Hoc Committee had set in 1961 for one-third of the public welfare workforce to hold a masters' degree in social work. Rather, the growth resulted from a "loophole" that state budget examiners and politicians were able to exploit, which used the AFDC entitlement to purchase and refinance state-funded social services from other state human-services agencies (Derthick 1975). How much of the increased spending was directed toward new services as opposed to refinancing existing services may never be known. Nonetheless, the co-occurrence of increased spending on social services with double-digit annual rates of growth in the number of AFDC child beneficiaries between 1962 and 1972 undermined legislative faith in the efficacy of social services to deliver on the promises of marital stability and economic self-sufficiency. Further, the lack of any reduction in the number of children in public foster care despite the rise in AFDC participation sowed additional doubts about the critical importance of in-home financial assistance for the prevention of the out-of-home care of dependent, neglected, and abused children.

The 1974 Social Services amendments clamped down on uncontrollable social services spending by separating the social services funding stream from the AFDC entitlement. The law moved it to a new Title XX, which Congress capped at $2.5 billion. One of the purposes of the new title was "preventing or remedying neglect, abuse, or exploitation of children and adults unable to protect their own interest, or preserving, rehabilitating or reuniting families." Because these purposes overlapped with Title IV-B, child welfare agencies could tap into two capped funding streams to provide child welfare services either directly or indirectly by purchasing them from private or other public agencies to prevent children's removal into foster care and facilitate their return to parents.

The basic lessons drawn from the federal government's brief foray into the integration of social services and income support affected federal allocations for decades to come. As summarized by Martha Derthick (1975), the plain lesson was that federal grants-in-aid laws either should fix a spending limit by capping social services spending or precisely defining the kinds and purposes of the services to be funded. Because the individualistic-orientation of social casework at the time did not readily lend itself to precise definitions, the other constraint of capped spending limits was the path chosen, at least until the passage of Family First. Title IV-B funding for child and family services peaked at $672 million in 2003. Congress converted Title XX into a Social Services Block Grant (SSBG) in 1981, which states could use flexibly without regard to income eligibility to achieve a wide range of policy goals. Appropriations for SSBG have not increased since being capped in 2002 at $1.7 billion (for a detailed discussion of child welfare services spending, see Haskins, this volume).

Separating Child Welfare Programs from Income Support

The Adoption Assistance and Child Welfare Act (AACWA) of 1980 further distanced child welfare programs from income support by moving the IV-A foster care program to a new title IV-E. The new program retained many of the same rules and procedures that had earlier been established under the AFDC foster care program. AACWA encouraged IV-B spending on preplacement prevention services by limiting states' use of these funds for foster care maintenance payments made on behalf of non–IV-E eligible children.

The separation of foster care maintenance payments from IV-A helped to move down the chain of policy priorities the original purpose of AFDC as providing income support to maintain children in the home of a parent or relative as an alternative to institutional or foster family care. The 1956 Social Security amendments had already added a second purpose of helping caregivers attain financial self-sufficiency. Two additional purposes were added in 1996 to address the "unsuitable home" conditions that the 1962 social services and AFDC foster care provisions were intended to remediate. These included the reduction of out-of-wedlock pregnancy and the formation and maintenance of two-parent families. Most significant, the 1996 legislation applied the lesson drawn from the brief era of uncontrollable social services spending by converting the open-ended AFDC entitlement into a capped block grant, which Congress entitled, Temporary Assistance to Needy Families (TANF).

The End of the AFDC Entitlement

The creation of TANF reflected a major shift in the gendered division of family labor and attitudes toward the unequal wage-earning capabilities of men and women. The new assumption was that mothers, even with young children, were expected to join men in the paid labor force. If families were to hold onto the same middle-class standard of living that they had previously enjoyed based on the "family-wage" earnings of the male breadwinner alone, both parents would need to join the paid labor force. It soon became clear, however, that the work incentives that the 1967 amendments incorporated into Title IV-A, which Moynihan had derided as punitive and racist, did no better than social services in reducing AFDC caseloads. Rather than second guess the theory of change underlying its definition of the problem, Congress doubled down on even stronger remedies to solve the welfare crisis.

Ironically, it was the report that Moynihan authored in 1965 as Assistant Secretary of the U.S. Department of Labor, *The Negro Family: The Case for National Action* (U.S. Department of Labor 1965), that sowed the seeds of a neoconservative reaction that culminated 30 years later in the "ending of welfare" as we knew it. Moynihan shared the same maternalist assumptions of Progressive Era reformers, which accepted that marriage, female domesticity, and male breadwinner support were family arrangements best adapted to the conditions of modern urban society (Parsons 1955). He believed that the weakest link in the normative order of middle-class family life was male unemployment, which he documented was most severe among African Americans. Above all, he argued, male joblessness prevented African American families from attaining equal status to whites. His solution was to increase the supply of jobs for Black men.

Moynihan's push for a national jobs program was overshadowed, however, by the alarms he sounded about the spread of matriarchal family structures. Seeing a weakening correlation between rising male employment and declining AFDC caseloads, Moynihan imagined the emergence of a self-perpetuating "tangle of pathology" that could become resistant to "repair" even if white racism ceased (Geary 2015). Even though Moynihan did not completely retreat from the speculation that the welfare system itself might be undermining marital stability among the poor, he ultimately settled on a guaranteed minimum income for every family with children as the preferred solution to the crisis in welfare (Moynihan 1973). It was Charles Murray who later fueled the fires of neoconservative reaction by stoking resentments about rising illegitimacy rates and a growing "underclass" of fatherless children (Murray 1993). His solution was not to create jobs for fathers but to end income support altogether for single mothers. In an influential opinion piece that appeared in the *Wall Street Journal* (1993), he wrote,

> To restore the rewards and penalties of marriage does not require social engineering. Rather, it requires that the state stop interfering with the natural forces that have done the job quite effectively for millennia. . . . Restoring economic penalties translates into the first and central policy prescription: to end all economic support for single mothers. The AFDC payment goes to zero. Single mothers are not eligible for subsidized housing or for food stamps. An assortment of other subsidies and in-kind benefits disappear. . . . From society's perspective, to have a baby that you cannot care for yourself is profoundly irresponsible, and the government will no longer subsidize it. (Murray 1993, 3)

Even though Congress did not heed all of Murray's admonishments, it did replace the open-ended AFDC entitlement with a block grant in 1996. The TANF program terminates federal cash assistance to most needy families after the head of household reaches a lifetime cumulative maximum of 60 months of public assistance.

What the federal government was unable to accomplish with its social services and work-incentive strategies, it was able to accomplish quickly with time-limited, income support for poor children and mothers. From 1996 to 2012, the number of TANF child beneficiaries declined from 8.7 million to 3.1 million. Murray's prediction that ending the entitlement would regenerate the stigma of out-of-wedlock births, however, did not pan out exactly as projected. The percentage of births to unmarried women continued to climb until 2008, at which time they leveled off at 53 percent among Hispanic women and 29 percent for white women. Black out-of-wedlock births did level off at 70 percent after the repeal of AFDC in 1996. It is impossible to know, however, whether the proportion of out-of-wedlock births would have continued to rise among African Americans had the AFDC entitlement not been abolished.

Surprising to both proponents and critics of TANF alike was the absence of any spike in the number of children who were placed into institutional or foster family care after their removal from homes that were deprived of open-ended income assistance. During the period that TANF child beneficiaries declined to 3.1 million in 2012, the U.S. foster care population also declined from 507,000 in 1996 to 396,000 in 2012. The loss of the AFDC entitlement did not precipitate a

FIGURE 1
Child Welfare Trends: 1962–2018

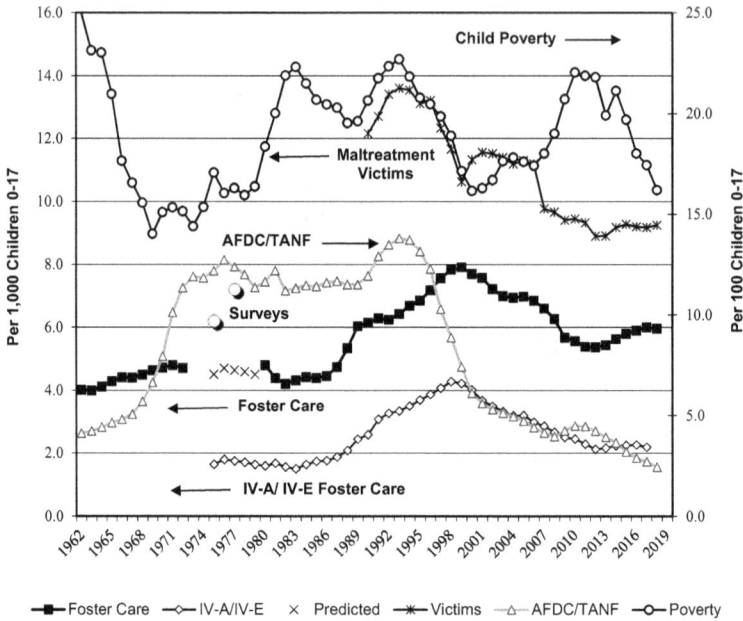

sharp rise in the U.S. foster care population as feared by many child welfare experts (Matthews 1999).

Child Poverty, AFDC/TANF Receipt, Child Maltreatment, and Foster Care

Figure 1 summarizes the statistical trends discussed in previous sections. An interesting feature is the relative constancy of foster care caseloads (scaled per 1,000 children on the left axis) during the decades when official child poverty rates declined to record lows in the late 1960s (scaled per 100 children on the right axis) before rising again during the economic recessions of the early 1980s. We should note that this claim of constancy differs from the story once told about a purported spike in foster care caseloads during the 1970s following the passage of mandatory child maltreatment reporting laws in most states (Pelton 1989; Curtis, Dale, and Kendell 1999). The alleged increase was suggested by prevalence surveys (marked with circles in the chart) conducted after the federal government temporarily ceased collecting foster care statistics directly from the states. Inspection of administrative data from the states of California, Illinois, and New York, however, shows no such roller coaster–like change in foster care caseloads (Testa 2009). The relative constancy of foster care in these three states, which accounted for one-quarter of national counts, makes it highly unlikely that the rest of the country was solely responsible for the inferred spike at the nationwide level. A more plausible time series may be generated from predictions (marked with Xs in the chart) based on the regression of aggregate foster care counts on Title IV-A/IV-E reimbursement claims submitted by the states. The correlation between national counts and reimbursement claims between 1980 and 2000 is .98. Filling in the missing time series suggests that a relatively constant fraction of children was involved at any one time in the foster care system throughout the entire period from 1962 to 1987.

One of the possible explanations for the constancy of foster care in the face of declining and rising child poverty rates was the expanded AFDC coverage of poor children during the late 1960s as detailed previously. Even though AFDC payments lifted few families above the official poverty line, it is possible that, in combination with other benefits such as food stamps and Medicaid, the increased participation of families in the AFDC program protected all but the most vulnerable of children from the dangers of maltreatment and the risks of removal. The connection between child poverty and child maltreatment is suggested by victimization data that became available after 1990. The victimization time series prior to 2006 are unduplicated child counts based on the 2006 to 2010 ratio of 1.08 substantiated reports per unique child.

Figure 1 shows that unique counts of children with substantiated reports of abuse and neglect (scaled per 1,000 children on the left axis) tracked closely changes in child poverty rates until the start of the 2008 to 2009 economic recession. Considering the strong association between economic deprivation and physical neglect, the fact that child maltreatment victimization rates did not rise with the rebound in child poverty rates during the subprime mortgage crisis of the late 2000s has puzzled many longtime observers of victimization trends (Finkelhor, Saito, and Jones 2019). Instead, victimization rates dropped along with the decreases in the per-capita rate of foster care during this period.

A possible explanation for the recent divergence of child poverty and victimization rates is that official poverty measures are incomplete indicators of economic deprivation because they overlook in-kind benefits and tax policies, such as the Supplemental Nutrition Assistance Program (SNAP) and the earned income tax credit (EITC), which have increasingly become the backbone of the U.S. social safety net. Supplemental poverty measures that take into account such programs showed much greater alleviation of financial hardships than suggested by official poverty measures (Moffitt 2013).

An alternative explanation for the decline in child victimization rates is that vulnerable children are less likely to be reported to child welfare authorities because of the contraction of the safety net under TANF, which puts a dwindling proportion of poor families under the routine surveillance of mandated reporters. The sharp fall-off in maltreatment reports following the closing of schools during the COVID-19 pandemic, for example, illustrates the importance of mandated reporters in bringing vulnerable children to the attention of child welfare authorities (see Slack and Berger, this volume). While this explanation fits well with recent changes in TANF coverage, child victimization, and foster care rates (see

Figure 1), public assistance workers have had only limited opportunity to observe parent-child interactions in the home ever since the separation of social services from income assistance in the early 1970s (Courtney et al. 2005). Social service professionals have historically accounted for a smaller proportion of maltreatment reports (<12%) than educators and law enforcement personnel (>30%).

The recent decline and plateauing of child victimization and foster care rates despite the spikes in child poverty suggests that the wider community has been able to hold the line against child removal even in the absence of a federal entitlement to minimum family assistance. U.S. Census data show that the percentage of children who reside with one or both of their parents has remained approximately constant between 95 to 97 percent since the 1960s. For the remaining 3 to 5 percent who reside apart from their parents, more than 70 percent of the need for alternative care has been absorbed privately or voluntarily by kin. Extended kin and other informal networks have long protected fragile families from experiencing the full brunt of economic-related stressors that contribute to physical neglect. Even though these informal networks have long functioned on their own as buffers against economic deprivation and child maltreatment, it is important to understand how the additional support and assistance available from formal systems can best reinforce the strengths of informal networks.

To some extent, the spike in national foster care counts, which gained momentum during the mid-1980s (see Figure 1), may be interpreted as an outgrowth of the blurring of the boundaries between the voluntary care of dependent children by relatives and the public foster care of neglected children. As urban child welfare systems struggled within the context of a spreading cocaine epidemic to comply with the Supreme Court decision in *Miller v. Youakim* (1979), which ruled that relatives could not be denied federal foster care benefits for reasons of kinship alone, a segment of kinship care arrangements that states had previously supported under the AFDC program became incorporated into the public foster care system (Testa 1997). It was not until these systems accepted the appropriateness of kinship adoption assistance and developed supplementary permanency options, such as subsidized guardianship, that foster care rates began to decline in the late 1990s as states discharged children from long-term foster care to permanent homes with relatives and former foster parents.

Another trend, which can be glimpsed from Figure 1, is the widening divergence between national foster care counts and the number of children whose foster care is reimbursable to states under the federal IV-E entitlement. Whereas 55 percent of foster children qualified for federal foster care benefits in 1998, IV-E coverage has steadily eroded over the last two decades to 36 percent in 2018. This erosion is attributable to a "look-back" provision, which requires states to determine whether the home from which the child is removed would have qualified for AFDC based on the income limits that were in effect when the program was still in operation in 1996. Because these income limits have not been adjusted for cost-of-living increases, a growing fraction of foster children lose IV-E eligibility each year because of inflation. Even though there are calls for "de-linking" foster care reimbursements from the look-back provision as was done for adoption assistance (see Haskins, this volume), an alternative solution for preserving federal resources is Family First's policy of reimbursing all quali-fied services regardless of family income. Retaining the look-back for foster care while delinking reimbursements for prevention services and permanency sti-pends, including guardianship assistance, would allow for the gradual realign-ment of federal financial incentives in favor of family preservation and permanence rather than child removal and long-term foster care. Further, by limiting reimbursements for congregate care that fails to qualify as an intensive, time-limited intervention, Family First promotes placing children in the least-restrictive, most family-like setting appropriate to their needs.

Family First's Reintegration of Child Welfare Services into the Title IV Entitlement

To reintegrate child welfare services into the open-ended Title IV entitlement, Family First had to address a fundamental weakness that Derthick (1975) identi-fied as contributing to uncontrollable social services spending in the 1970s. At the time of the 1967 social services amendments, the individualist orientation of social casework did not lend itself to clear and specific definitions of services or the outcomes they were supposed to achieve. Family First deals with this limita-tion by grounding preventive services in the "average-effects" framework of evidence-based practice (EBP; Gambrill 2001).

EBP differs from the "individual-effects" framework of problem-solving practice (PSP; Perlman 1957). EBP starts with manualized practices that rigorous evaluation has demonstrated worked effectively, on average, in the past. By contrast, PSP attempts to assess what might work in the future for a particular individual based on practice wisdom and conformity with a diagnostic school of thought. Because it is harder to ascertain at an individual level than at the group level whether an outcome is causally attributable to preventive measures, it is difficult to counter the charge that PSP is more "authority-based" than "evidence-based" (Gambrill 2001). Even though EBP overlaps with PSP by factoring in practitioner expertise and client preferences when offering empiri-cally supported services to an individual client, grounding service definitions and expected outcomes in the EBP "average-effects" framework allows for lifting the spending cap and delinking eligibility from the AFDC "look-back" provision. By incorporating an EBP constraint on social services spending, Family First controls social services spending by limiting reimbursements to only those interventions that meet scientific evidence standards of promising, supported, or well-supported practices (Wilson et al. 2019).

Family First requires precise definitions of service delivery based on a book, manual, or other available writings, which specify the components of the practice protocol and describe how to implement it. It further specifies outcome measures, which are reliable and valid, and administered consistently and accurately across all beneficiaries receiving the intervention. To qualify as a "promising" intervention, the service or program, in addition to meeting the above minimum requirements, must be rated by an independent systematic review that attests to the quality of the study design and execution. It expects the design to have utilized some form of control (such as an untreated group, a placebo group, or a wait list). The observed contrasts in outcomes must be superior to an appropriate comparison practice in terms of both practical importance and statistical significance.

To receive the rating of "supported," the service or program, in addition to meeting the minimum criteria for promising, must also be supported by at least one randomized controlled trial (RCT) that was carried out in a usual care or practice setting. If an RCT is not available, a study using a rigorous quasi-experimental design may also satisfy the requirement if it adequately approximates the desired "counterfactual" (i.e., what might have happened if the treatment group instead received the comparison condition). The RCT or quasi-experimental study must also establish that the treatment has a sustained effect, when compared to the comparison condition, for at least six months beyond the end of treatment.

Finally to qualify for the highest rating of "well-supported," the service or program must be supported by still another rigorous RCT (or, if not available, a study using a rigorous quasi-experimental research design), which replicates the findings of the first summative evaluation in a usual care or practice setting. At least one of the studies must have established that the intervention had a sustained effect for at least 12 months beyond the end of treatment.

As of June 2020, twenty-five programs have been reviewed by the Title IV-E Prevention Services Clearinghouse (see Table 1). Of these, the Clearinghouse determined three to be promising, two to be supported, and nine to be well-supported. Eleven programs were rated as not currently meeting criteria. Table 1 groups each program under one or more of the four service areas specified in Family First: mental health, substance use treatment, parent training services, or kinship navigator services. The last category includes services that assist kinship caregivers in learning about, finding, and using supportive services, such as TANF, SNAP, and child care, to meet the needs of the children they are raising. Previously funded in fourteen states and several tribes with Family Connections Grants authorized under the Fostering Connections to Success and Increasing Adoptions Act of 2008, there are no kinship navigator programs that currently qualify for reimbursement under Family First.

To increase the output of the rating process, the Children's Bureau provided states with a transitional payment option, which allows them to conduct their own systematic reviews. The Family First Transition Act, which passed in 2019 with bipartisan support, allows additional time before the funding requirement kicks in that 50 percent of total prevention dollars must be spent on well-supported, mental health, substance use treatment, or parent training services. The new law postpones this requirement until federal fiscal year (FFY) 2024. Kinship navigator services were already exempt from the 50 percent rule.

There are several ways that states and tribes can accommodate the requirement that half of prevention dollars eventually be spent on well-supported programs. They can invest half of their expenditures on one or more of the well-supported programs and devote the remainder of dollars to promising and supported services. Alternatively, they can press for additional delays or request

TABLE 1
Evidence Ratings of Programs Reviewed by the Title IV-E Prevention Services Clearinghouse by Service Area, as of June 2020

Program Rating	Service Area	Program Name
Well-supported	Mental health	Brief strategic family therapy[a,b] Functional family therapy Multisystemic therapy[a] Parent-child interaction therapy
	Substance abuse	Motivational interviewing
	Parent training	Health families America Homebuilders- Intensive family preservation and reunification services Nurse-family partnership Parents as teachers
Supported	Substance abuse	Families facing the future SafeCare
	Parent training	

Program Rating	Service Area	Program Name
Promising	Mental health	Child-parent psychotherapy Trauma-focused cognitive behavioral therapy
	Substance abuse	Methadone maintenance therapy
Does not currently meet criteria	Mental health	Multisystemic therapy for child abuse and neglect
	Substance abuse	Family behavior therapy – adolescent Family behavior therapy – adult Family behavior therapy – adult with child welfare supplement Seeking safety
	Parent training	Nurturing parenting program for parents and their infants, toddlers, and preschoolers Nurturing parenting program for parents and their school-age children 5 to 11 years Solution-based casework
	Kinship navigator	Children's Home Society of New Jersey kinship navigator model Kinship interdisciplinary navigation technologically-advance model (KIN-Tech) Ohio's kinship supports intervention / ProtectOHIO

SOURCE: Title IV-E Prevention Services Clearinghouse, https://preventionservices.abtsites.com/.

a. Also substance use.

b. Also parent training.

further relaxation of the evidence standards. More in the spirit of evidence-based policymaking, they can take advantage of the ability to claim 50 percent reimbursement for the costs of conducting rigorous evaluations under section 471 of the act to elevate promising and supported programs to the highest tier of well-supported programs.

Increasing the supply of well-supported programs will require state and tribal champions to demonstrate "moral courage" (Arnold Ventures 2020) in risking disconfirmation of hoped-for effects by subjecting cherished programs to rigorous evaluations. The hallmarks of rigor include allocating subjects to intervention and comparison groups in an unbiased fashion, minimizing or adjusting for measurement attrition, and preregistering study designs and the primary expected outcomes. Family First can support the field testing of rigorous replications and generalizable adaptations of promising and supported programs to foster accountability and improve child welfare policy and service delivery. It is increasingly being acknowledged by child welfare practitioners and administrators that "uncontrolled experimentation" on vulnerable children by well-intentioned child welfare agents is no more ethical than randomized controlled trials that seek to test the validity of knowledge and improve the efficacy of child welfare policy and practice (Testa 2010).

On the other hand, there are potential unintended consequences in limiting reimbursable child welfare services to a restricted set of indicated preventive interventions. There is danger that the restrictions will divert attention and resources away from the larger challenge of universal primary prevention of child maltreatment and family disruption, which the general public understands to be the true meaning of preventive services. Unless there is continuous tracking of improvements in outcomes, there is always the risk that too many prevention dollars will be misspent on downstream interventions that occur too late to make meaningful differences in the lives of children and families. To fulfill the broader purposes of primary prevention requires getting to the root causes of child maltreatment. This involves exploring and testing innovative solutions that address both the underlying social problems that contribute to child maltreatment and the harsh realities of poverty that amplify the risk of child abuse and increase the dangerousness of parental neglect. The fact that this path has been traveled before with limited success should not dissuade child welfare leaders from rejoining the journey with the newer knowledge gained about brain development, the adverse effects of childhood trauma, and the restorative power of nurturing and responsive attachment relationships between a child and at least one permanent caregiver. Further, with the technical expertise acquired from conducting rigorous trials with IV-E waivers and using automated allocation procedures and administrative data to reduce study costs, administrators and evaluators are better able to partner together to test many promising practices in the hopes of enlarging the supply of well-supported interventions with meaningful positive effects (Arnold Ventures 2020).

Routine testing is especially critical given the 4 to 1 odds against successfully transitioning promising service innovations through all levels of evidence building from exploration through formative and summative evaluation to broad-scale rollout (Testa et al. 2019). In other words, most promising innovations, when properly evaluated, lead to dead ends (Rossi 1978). Even though moral intuition may incline the child welfare field toward funding universal approaches to the prevention of child maltreatment and family disruption, the absence of consensus on whether "prevention is always better than cure" (Dunt, Crowley, and Day 1995) can make the public funding of universal approaches politically challenging. Perhaps a more practicable first step is to test prevention services on a smaller selective population, such as kinship caregivers, where issues of personal responsibility and self-sufficiency are less contentious, before evaluating their generalizability to all caregivers.

The Promise of Kinship Navigator Programs

Family First offers new dollars to invest in the prevention of child maltreatment and preservation of family relationships through the support of private, voluntary, and permanent kinship care arrangements. Less than 10 percent of children in kinship care are removed from parental custody and placed in public foster care with kin. Because removal has already occurred, these children and their caregivers are ineligible for Title IV-E mental health, drug treatment, and parent-training services. They do remain eligible, however, for kinship navigator services. An additional 32 percent of children in kinship care, whose living arrangements are facilitated by the child welfare agency, may be eligible for both Title IV-E clinical and navigator services because the agency has not taken the children into public custody. They may qualify as foster care candidates if the agency determines that without voluntary kinship care as part of a short-term safety plan, they would need to be taken into the public foster care system. A large percentage of these children may also be targets of selective prevention of child maltreatment. Even though the child welfare agency has investigated their families for possible maltreatment, many children are subsequently determined not to be victims of abuse, neglect, or exploitation under prevailing evidence standards (U.S. Department of Health and Human Services 2020).

The largest segment of kinship care—the 39 percent of children whose care was arranged privately among family members without the mediating help or intervention of a court or child welfare agency—are selective targets for the prevention of the occurrence of child maltreatment. Because of the private intercession of kin, children are often protected from the trauma of maltreatment. Kinship navigator services are selectively available to private kinship caregivers because the children remain at higher than usual risks of parental maltreatment and removal into foster care. Therefore, navigator programs provide fertile ground for testing whether the integration of social services, legal services, and income support can prevent vulnerable children from experiencing the trauma of maltreatment at the hands of birth parents or other caregivers.

The reason that kinship care provides a fertile testing ground is because TANF does not deprive kinship caregivers of stable income assistance. Except for a few states, relative caregivers are exempted from the time limits and means testing, which TANF imposes on birth parents. Because relatives are not legally liable for the support of their kin's children, most are permanently eligible for TANF "child-only" assistance regardless of their own family assets and income. This provision continues an AFDC policy enacted during the 1960s in response to states' repeal of "relative responsibility" laws that previously held extended kin legally liable for the support of needy relatives who applied for public assistance (Bell 1965). Despite the continued entitlement to income support, however, receipt of child-only grants still remains very low across the country, with only 12 percent of eligible kinship families receiving them (Mauldon et al. 2012). This is one of the eligibility-receipt gaps that kinship navigator services are intended to close.

Family First offers a special opportunity to engage extended families in selective prevention services by funding promising and evidence-supported kinship navigator services. These services help kinship caregivers to learn about, find, and use existing programs and services, such as TANF, SNAP, and child care, to meet the needs of the children they are raising and address the parents' problems that necessitated relative's voluntarily taking the children into their home. According to the *Title IV-E Prevention Services Clearinghouse Handbook of Standards and Procedures* (Wilson et al. 2019), kinship navigator services may include any combination of financial supports; training or education; support groups; referrals to other social, behavioral, or health services; and assistance with navigating government and other types of assistance, financial or otherwise. Such programs may be housed either within the IV-E agency or at another social service agency that has a purchase-of-service contract with the IV-E agency to operate the program.

Prior to the separation of social services from income support in 1973, child welfare workers had the opportunity to visit with AFDC recipients, at which time they not only redetermined the need for continued financial aid but could also offer social services to address selective family risks before they escalated to indicated abuse and neglect. After separation, child welfare workers typically had little to no direct contact with needy families until after they came to the attention of the child welfare system in response to formal reports of child maltreatment. Through kinship navigator programs, child welfare agencies can broaden their outreach to vulnerable families before child maltreatment occurs. Kinship navigator programs allow child welfare agencies to rely on voluntary kinship care as a prevention resource rather than simply a deflection option from public foster care.

Even though the balance of costs still tilts in favor of deflection to voluntary kinship care and avoidance of removal into public kinship care, the law's allowance for children to retain Title IV-E eligibility at the end of a maximum 12-month service period opens up new opportunities for parents and relatives of children in voluntary kinship care to receive the services they need without formally removing children from their parents' custody. If, toward the end of the 12-month service period, the child and family team decides that adoption or guardianship is the best permanency plan for the child, the family can enter into a voluntary placement agreement to qualify the kinship caregivers for licensed foster care benefits and permanent guardianship or adoption assistance.

The fact that at the time of this writing, not a single kinship navigator program meets the criteria for even the lowest-evidence tier of "promising" heightens the urgency for building credible evidence of the program's effectiveness. It is possible under existing evidence standards for navigator programs to be rated as promising based on improvements in what the United States Health Resources and Services Administration (HRSA) defines as "enabling services." These are largely nonclinical services that help recipients to improve their likelihood of accessing supports, services, and treatment by increasing knowledge, and removing barriers that may stand in the way of access and participation. Enabling services and supports can be provided by professionals, paraprofessionals, peers with lived experience, and others. According to the evidence standards promulgated by the Title IV-E Prevention Services Clearinghouse (Wilson et al. 2019), the efficacy of navigator services can be rated as promising based on improvements in the delivery of enabling services, such as referrals, access to treatment, and satisfaction with program delivery. Once a promising program is identified, the availability of federal reimbursement for rigorous evaluations can help to shore up the evidence base for these enabling services. Rigorous evaluations of the effects of coordinating navigator programs with clinical interventions holds much promise for assessing the generalized benefits of integrating income support with parenting skills training to strengthen the stability of extended family care.

Universal Primary Prevention of Child Maltreatment

There is general acknowledgment in the field of child welfare by leaders, researchers, membership organizations, advocates, and families and young people with lived experience that the current child welfare system in the United States is reactive. It is designed almost exclusively to respond to reports of child maltreatment rather than prevent maltreatment (see Slack and Berger, this volume). Such an indicated prevention strategy is inadequate to the broader goals of universal prevention and the promotion of child and family well-being. Responding skillfully to situations that place children in danger is a critical feature that must always be present in universal prevention services. Addressing trauma and promoting healing for those children and families where maltreatment has already occurred will always be a necessary function of indicated prevention services. Nevertheless, national discourse is increasingly questioning what child welfare can and should be in the United States and there is an emerging consensus among child welfare leaders, practitioners, researchers, and advocacy groups that a wider array of supports and a full continuum of prevention services that promote overall family well-being are needed (Milner and Kelly 2020). This discourse is informed by research on the social determinants of health, which identifies the importance of community protective factors and parental protective capacities in child and family health and well-being. A useful model is a framework adapted from the Institute of Medicine (1994), which recognizes the promotion of child well-being as an important component of the child welfare intervention spectrum. The full spectrum includes the upstream interventions of child well-being promotion and prevention of maltreatment as well as the downstream interventions of treatment in the least restrictive, most family-like setting, and maintenance in a safe and stable permanent home (see also the articles in this volume by Jones Harden et al.; Feely et al.; Roygardner, Hughes, and Palusci; Slack and Berger).

Family First adds an important new type of response that a child welfare agency may employ to remediate risk and keep children safely with their families. By reimbursing states for qualified, evidence-supported interventions, state and local child welfare systems can engage in a wider variety of harm-reduction strategies that lessen the likelihood of removal for children assessed to be at imminent risk of entering foster care. The act also contains an often-overlooked provision that allows for IV-E foster care maintenance payments to be made on behalf of children placed with a parent or parents in residential substance use treatment programs. If maximized, these programs may help many families affected by substance use to remain healthy and intact. These elements are an important acknowledgment that families are critical to child well-being and that there is value in strengthening families; but even with these additions, child welfare in the United States remains remedial. In focusing exclusively on clinical needs and parenting skills, Family First fails to acknowledge or address the contextual factors present in the lives of families that become involved with the child welfare system, such as employment instability; inadequate income; and insufficient access to health care, food insecurity, housing instability, and homelessness; and lack of reliable transportation and lack of childcare. Any one of these issues may contribute to stress that contributes to potential mental health issues or substance misuse, and anyone of these issues could prove a sizable barrier to a parent or caregiver accessing services available through Family First. In the larger picture of federal funding for vulnerable families, Family First's focus on clinical and reparative needs apart from family and community context and basic needs may portend a significant challenge to achieving its stated goals.

To move toward a system that is proactive and prioritizes child well-being and universal primary prevention of maltreatment, we must draw upon lessons from public health and medicine and population-based approaches. It requires the field to seek to understand and address the root causes of family vulnerability. It demands that the field and elected officials acknowledge that child welfare and the need for child welfare services exists in the space where poverty, public health, and civil rights intersect. It will obligate the field to apply, with rigor and completeness, research findings on the trauma of parent-child separation, brain science, the social determinants of health, and parental protective factors. Moving toward a family strengthening and well-being system requires policy-makers, agency administrators, and providers to think beyond clinical silos. There is a need to consider the effectiveness of how service needs are identified and what we choose to make available, with particular attention to the stresses associated with poverty and the ways those stressors may manifest in harmful toxicities. There is also a need to begin looking at child welfare from a perspective of justice.

Beginning in 2017, the Children's Bureau began vigorously promoting a new vision for child welfare in the United States. The vision calls upon child welfare agencies to work together with a wide array of stakeholders from the public, private, and philanthropic sectors to create and support robust community-based, primary prevention networks to strengthen families in their communities to prevent child maltreatment and the need for foster care. The vision is a clear statement that child welfare should strive to do more than child protection alone and that, as a country, we should do all that is possible to reduce the need for child protection in the first place. The vision requires leaders, officials, professional, and communities to work together to convert the traditional concept of child protection and child welfare to a child and family well-being system. While safety must always be paramount, we must take care not to pursue it at the expense of child well-being and family integrity or permanence. The responsibility to achieve positive outcomes for children and families that make contact with child welfare must be understood as a joint venture and shared responsibility across agencies and community actors.

To accomplish this aspiration, the U.S. Children's Bureau seeks to reduce the need of families to come into contact with the formal child welfare system through the creation and support of robust networks of community-based services (Administration for Children and Families 2018). The Children's Bureau believes that such services should be available universally to all families that might benefit, located in easily accessible places within communities, and offered in trusted places by trusted people in culturally appropriate, responsive, and stigma-free ways. Such approaches are supported by research that examines the importance of supports being attuned to the local ecology of risk and protective factors that influence the likelihood of child abuse and the dangerousness of child neglect (Pelton 1978; Testa 1992). There is a need to recognize the role that perceptions of financial hardship and requests for public assistance play in child welfare, especially physical neglect cases (Courtney et al. 2005; Turner et al. 2019). This need is reinforced by recent child maltreatment data that indicate that 60 percent of victims of maltreatment have a finding of neglect only. Given the associations between financial hardship and neglect and the disproportionate presence of poverty in communities of color, it is crucial to be mindful of how the types of services and supports that are offered may contribute to disparity and disproportionate representation.

In thinking about the services that are most likely to benefit families, we must also be aware of the circumstances that may make it challenging for families to access those services and the conditions that may help or hinder the probability that those services will achieve their intended result. There is cause for consideration of how homelessness or housing insecurity, inadequate income or income insecurity, food insecurity, lack of transportation and social isolation impact parents' and other relatives' abilities to access, participate in, and benefit from certain services. As we have witnessed during the ongoing pandemic, clinical services and interventions are not always available and often not what families may need to remain safely together in difficult times.

Perhaps more than any other step, moving toward a system that strengthens the family and promotes child well-being requires all stakeholders and decision-makers to reexamine core values and confront implicit and explicit biases about how we feel about and perceive vulnerable families. It also calls upon all in the field to closely consider the weight we afford to what families tell us they need, if asked, and how their responses impact what we choose to provide (see Merritt, this volume). It is critical to remain mindful of the dark history of child welfare in the United States, which led to the creation and use of orphan trains and off-reservation boarding schools. In retrospect, we can now clearly see the gravity of the injustice and trauma that was inflicted by such practices on poor children, children of immigrants, and American Indian and Alaska Native children, their families, and their communities. That racial disproportionality and disparities continue to exist at the magnitude they do today in child welfare is living proof of the destructive legacy of such practices and evidence of how biases against poor families and families of color continue to shape thinking about child welfare and become manifest in policy and practice (see Dettlaff and Boyd, this volume). While such thinking and biases may be less overt than it has been at certain points in history, it is always there, just below the surface in insidious ways. It is also important to remain mindful that evaluation work with tribes and other minority populations must be thoughtfully conceived, approached, and con-ducted and to be sensitive to and account for historic trauma and tragically mis-guided and harmful research efforts with tribes and minority populations. Failure to act on what we now know about the trauma associated with parent-child sepa-ration, the conflation and entanglement of poverty and neglect, and the impor-tance of natural familial support will leave us in a similar position of remorse and reflection when future generations look back to judge how well today's leaders responded to the challenge.

Conclusion

Family First takes an important step toward rededicating Title IV of the Social Security Act to its original purpose of maintaining children in the home of a par-ent or relative as an alternative to institutional or foster family care. While Family First does not fundamentally reorient child welfare toward prevention and family preservation, or take a public health approach to preventing maltreatment from occurring, it begins to open the door to what could become a more balanced federal funding structure. Should more states elect to operate IV-E prevention programs and as the Family First Clearinghouse continues to grow incrementally, the dollars available for tertiary and some secondary prevention services and programs will increase.

Absent thoughtful changes or additions, however, Family First will remain largely focused on the symptoms of family vulnerability as opposed to root causes and wait for some level of trauma to occur prior to offering families services as opposed to actively working to prevent trauma through proactive supports to enhance family resiliency and parental protective capacities.

There is a growing consensus in the field that a far more proactive approach is necessary and that families are inherently worthy of such investments. This value premise has gathered considerable scientific support since the 1909 White House Conference on the Care of Dependent Child first proclaimed that "home life is the highest and finest product of civilization. . . . Children should not be deprived of it except for urgent and compelling reasons. . . . Except in unusual circumstances, the home should not be broken up for reasons of poverty" (White House Conference on the Care of Dependent Children 1909).

Research findings have since bolstered confidence in this belief by demonstrating the critical importance of nurturing relationships and mutually responsive interactions between young children and at least one adult caregiver. A variety of evidence-supported interventions have shown favorable impacts on well-being outcomes for young children raised under conditions of significant economic and social hardship (Heckman 2006; Karoly, Kilburn, and Cannon 2005; Phillips and Shonkoff 2000). These scientific breakthroughs help to point the way toward realizing Title IV's original purpose of securing for children the physical and affectionate care necessary to raise them to become productive and responsible citizens.

The expansion of the federal Title IV-E entitlement beyond reimbursement for child placement services and foster care maintenance payments is a much-welcomed improvement over prior spending constraints. There is still the concern that Family First's focus on a small subset of indicated clinical interventions, which are far downstream on the prevention spectrum, will continue to limit the extent to which implementation will actually reduce the need for family separation and foster care. To minimize these potential barriers and unintended consequences, the Children's Bureau has taken important steps to maximize areas of the law where flexibilities can be located. Three such examples include (1) not further defining imminent risk, which is intended to encourage IV-E agencies to think more broadly than the traditional definition of candidacy under IV-E; (2) not requiring that "in home parent skill building services" actually be provided in the homes of families, but rather require application of skills learned within the home; and (3) providing flexibility to tribes to utilize traditional healing and well-being practices without the need to meet the evidence standards.

Kinship navigator programs also offer an underutilized opportunity to enrich our understanding of the optimal combination of social services and income supports to strengthen family life and counteract the role that financial hardship plays in destabilizing the family care of children. The original Title IV program focused on the prevention of family disruption among both children who lived with single mothers and dependent children who resided apart from their parents in the homes of relatives. Family First circles back to this original aim of family preservation but with a wider focus on all family forms. Equipped with fresh scientific insights on the developmental importance of stable child-caregiver attachments, the child welfare field can leverage the new investment dollars to build credible evidence in support of more effective service delivery.

Although the initial focus on kinship care may fall short of the desire to build a comprehensive, universal preventive services system, it is an accessible place to start because funding already exists, and political disagreements are less contentious. Small incremental successes in preserving extended family care through the integration of social services and income support may help to open the door one day to offering these same evidence-supported programs to all children and families.

Note

1. See https://www.ssa.gov/history/reports/ces5.html.

References

Administration for Children and Families. 2018. *Reshaping child welfare in the United States to focus on strengthening families through primary prevention of child maltreatment and unnecessary parent-child separation*. Children's Bureau. ACYF-CB-IM-18-05. Washington, DC: U.S. Department of Health and Human Services. Available from https://www.acf.hhs.gov/sites/default/files/cb/im1805.pdf.

Arnold Ventures. 29 January 2020. Disappointing findings and moral courage – The Camden Health Care "Hotspotting" randomized trial. *Straight Talk on Evidence*. Available from https://www.straighttalkonevidence.org.

Bell, Winifred. 1965. *Aid to dependent children*. New York, NY: Columbia University Press.

Children's Defense Fund. 2018. *The Family First Prevention Services Act: Historic reforms to the Child Welfare System will improve outcomes for vulnerable children*. Washington, DC: Children's Defense Fund. Available from https://www.childrensdefense.org/wp-content/uploads/2018/08/family-first-detailed-summary.pdf.

Committee on Economic Security. 1935. *The report to the President of the Committee on Economic Security*. Available from https://www.ssa.gov/history/reports/ces5.html.

Courtney, Mark E., Amy Dworsky, Irving Piliavin, and Andrew Zinn. 2005. Involvement of TANF applicant families with child welfare services. *Social Service Review* 79 (1): 119–57.

Curtis, Patrick A., Grady Dale, and Joshua C. Kendall. 1999. *The foster care crisis: Translating research into policy and practice*. Lincoln, NE: University of Nebraska Press, in association with the Child Welfare League of America.

Derthick, Martha. 1975. *Uncontrollable spending for social services grants*. Washington, DC: Brookings Institution Press.

Detalff, Alan J., and Reiko Boyd. 2021. Racial disproportionality and disparities in the child welfare system: Why do they exist and what can be done to address them? *The ANNALS of the American Academy of Political and Social Science* (this volume).

Dunt, David R., Seven Crowley, and Neil A Day. 1995. Is prevention really better than cure? Parameters of the debate and implications for program evaluation design. *Health Promotion International* 10 (4): 325–34.

Feely, Megan, Kerri M. Raissian, William Schneider, and Lindsey Rose Bullinger. 2020. The social welfare policy landscape and child protective services: Opportunities for and barriers to creating systems synergy. *The ANNALS of the American Academy of Political and Social Science* (this volume).

Finkelhor, David, Kei Saito, and Lisa Jones. 2019. *Updated trends in child maltreatment, 2017*. Durham, NH: Crimes against Children Research Center. Available from http://unh.edu/ccrc/pdf/Updated%20trends%202017_ks.pdf.

Gambrill, Eileen. 2001. Social work: An authority-based profession. *Research on Social Work Practice* 11 (2): 166–75.

Geary, Daniel. 2015. *Beyond civil rights: The Moynihan Report and its legacy*. Philadelphia, PA: University of Pennsylvania Press.

Glazer, Nathan. 1988. *The limits of social policy*. Cambridge, MA: Harvard University Press.

Gordon, Linda. 1994. *Pitied but not entitled: Single mothers and the history of welfare, 1890–1935*. New York, NY: Free Press.

Hamilton, Gordon. 1962. Editor's page. *Social Work* 7 (1): 2, 128.

Handler, Joel F. 1973. *The coercive social worker: British lessons for American social services*. Chicago, IL: Rand McNally College Publishing Co.

Haskins, Ron. 2020. Child welfare financing: What do we fund, how, and what could be improved? *The ANNALS of the American Academy of Political and Social Science* (this volume).

Heckman, James J. 2006. Skill formation and the economics of investing in disadvantaged children. *Science* 312 (5782): 1900–1902.

Hernandez, Donald J. 1993. *America's children: Resources from family, government and the economy*. New York, NY: Russell Sage Foundation.

Institute of Medicine. 1994. *Reducing risks for mental disorders: Frontiers for preventive intervention research*, eds. Patricia J. Mrazek, and Robert J. Haggerty. Washington, DC: National Academy Press.

Jones Harden, Brenda, Cassandra Simons, Michelle Johnson-Motoyama, and Richard Barth. 2021. The child maltreatment landscape: Where we are now and where should we go? *The ANNALS of the American Academy of Political and Social Science* (this volume).

Kadushin, Alfred. 1978. Children in foster families and group homes. In *Social service research: Reviews of studies*, ed. Henry S. Maas, 90–148. Washington, DC: National Association of Social Workers, Inc.

Karoly, Lynn A., M. Rebecca Kilburn, and Jill S. Cannon. 2005. *Early childhood interventions: Proven results, future promises*. Santa Monica, CA: RAND Corporation.

Matthews, Martha. 1999. Assessing the effect of welfare reform on child welfare. *Clearinghouse Review* 32 (9–10): 395–407.

Mauldon, Jane, Richard Speiglman, Christina Sogar, and Matt Stagner. 2012. *TANF child only cases: Who are they? What polices affect them? What is being done?* Report to the Office of Planning, Research and Evaluation, U.S. Department of Health and Human Services. Chicago, IL: Chapin Hall.

Merritt, Darcey. 2021. How do families experience and interact with CPS? *The ANNALS of the American Academy of Political and Social Science* (this volume).

Miller v. Youakim, 440 U.S. 125 (1979).

Milner, Jerry, and David Kelly. 2020. Continuum or continuation? A choice of conscience. *Children's Bureau Express* 21 (1). Available from https://cbexpress.acf.hhs.gov/index.cfm?event=website.viewArticles&issueid=213&sectionid=2&articleid=5499.

Moffitt, Robert A. 2013. The Great Recession and the social safety net. *The ANNALS of the American Academy of Political and Social Science* 650:143–66.

Moynihan, Daniel P. 1968. The crises in welfare. *Public Interest* 1:3–29. Available from https://www.nationalaffairs.com/public_interest/detail/the-crises-in-welfare.

Moynihan, Daniel P. 1973. *The politics of a guaranteed income: The Nixon administration and the family assistance plan*. New York, NY: Random House.

Murray, Charles. 29 October 1993. The coming white underclass. *Wall Street Journal*, A14.

Parsons, Talcott. 1955. The American family: Its relations to personality and social structure. In *Family, socialization and interaction process*, eds. Talcott Parsons and Robert F. Bales, 3–33. Glencoe, IL: The Free Press.

Pelton, Leroy H. 1978. Child abuse and neglect: The myth of classlessness. *American Journal of Orthopsychiatry* 48 (4): 608–17.

Pelton, Leroy H. 1989. *For reasons of poverty: A critical analysis of the public child welfare system in the United States*. New York, NY: Praeger.

Perlman, Helen Harris. 1957. *Social casework: A problem-solving process*. Chicago, IL: University of Chicago Press.

Phillips, Deborah, and Jack P. Shonkoff. 2000. *From neurons to neighborhoods: The science of early child development*. Washington, DC: National Academy Press.

Rossi, Peter H. 1978. Issues in the evaluation of human services delivery. *Evaluation Quarterly* 2 (4): 573–99.

Roygardner, Debangshu, Kelli N. Hughes, and Vincent J. Palusci. 2021. Leveraging family and community strengths to reduce child maltreatment. *The ANNALS of the American Academy of Political and Social Science* (this volume).

Slack, Kristen S., and Lawrence Berger. 2021. Who is and is not served by child protective services systems? Implications for a prevention infrastructure to reduce child maltreatment. *The ANNALS of the American Academy of Political and Social Science* (this volume).

Social Security Act, P.L. 880, 84th Cong., Sec. 312 (a) (1956).

Stoltzfus, Emilie, and Conor Boyle. 2019. *2.7 million children in the United States live in kinship care.* Washington, DC: Congressional Research Service. Available from https://crsreports.congress.gov/product/pdf/IG/IG10016.

Testa, Mark. 1992. Conditions of risk for substitute care. *Children and Youth Services Review* 14 (1–2): 27–36.

Testa, Mark. 1997. Kinship foster care in Illinois. In *Child welfare research review*, vol. 2, eds. Jill Duerr Berrick, Richard Barth, and Neil Gilbert, 101–29. New York, NY: Columbia University Press.

Testa, Mark. 2009. How the bear evolved into a whale: A rejoinder to Leroy Pelton's note contesting Mark Testa's version of national foster care population trends. *Children and Youth Services Review* 31 (4): 491–94.

Testa, Mark. 2010. Evaluation of child welfare interventions. In *Fostering accountability: Using evidence to guide and improve child welfare policy*, eds. Mark Testa and John Poertner, 195–230. Oxford: Oxford University Press.

Testa, Mark, Robert Hill, and Charlene Ingram. 2020. New directions for supporting kinship care under Family First. In *Reflections on kinship care: Learnings from the past, implications for the future*, eds. Mark Testa, Robert Hill, and Charlene Ingram, 203–22. Washington, DC: Child Welfare League of America.

Testa, Mark, Kirsten Woodruff, Rosanna Bess, Jerry Milner, and Maria Woolverton. 2019. Every child deserves a permanent home: The permanency innovations initiative. *The Future of Children* 29 (1): 145–62.

Turner, Heather A., Jennifer Vanderminden, David Finkelhor, and Sherry Hamby. 2019. Child neglect and the broader context of child victimization. *Child Maltreatment* 24 (3): 265–74.

U.S. Census Bureau. 2019. *Current Population Survey, March and annual social and economic supplements.* Available from https://www.census.gov/data/tables/time-series/demo/families/children.html (accessed June 1, 2020).

U.S. Department of Health and Human Services, Administration for Children and Families, Administration on Children, Youth and Families, Children's Bureau. 2020. *Child maltreatment 2018.* Available from https://www.acf.hhs.gov/cb/research-data-technology/statistics-research/child-maltreatment (accessed June 1, 2020).

U.S. Department of Health, Education, and Welfare. 1961. *Report of Ad Hoc Committee on Public Welfare to the Secretary of Health, Education, and Welfare.* Washington, DC: U.S. Department of Health, Education, and Welfare. Available from https://www.hathitrust.org/.

U.S. Department of Labor. 1965. *The Negro family: The case for national action.* Washington, DC: Office of Policy, Planning and Research, U.S. Department of Labor.

White House Conference on the Care of Dependent Children. 1909. *Proceedings of the White House Conference on the Care of Dependent Children.* Washington, DC: Government Printing Office.

Wilson, Sandra Jo, Cristofer Price, Suzanne Kerns, Samuel Dastrup, and Scott Brown. 2019. *Title IV-E Prevention Services Clearinghouse handbook of standards and procedures, version 1.0.* OPRE Report # 2019-56. Washington, DC: Office of Planning, Research, and Evaluation, Administration for Children and Families, U.S. Department of Health and Human Services. Available from https://preventionservices.abtsites.com/themes/ffc_theme/pdf/psc_handbook_v1_final_508_compliant.pdf (accessed June 1, 2020).

The Child Maltreatment Prevention Landscape: Where Are We Now, and Where Should We Go?

By
BRENDA JONES HARDEN,
CASSANDRA SIMONS,
MICHELLE JOHNSON-
MOTOYAMA,
and
RICHARD BARTH

Child maltreatment calls for a broad range of preventative policies and practices, but limited governmental funding and leadership has been devoted to the problem. Effective strategies to prevent maltreatment exist, but they have had limited uptake in the child welfare system. In this article, we trace how government responsibility for the prevention of child maltreatment became centered within the nation's child protection response. Further, we discuss developments in prevention science, review the existing literature on the effectiveness of a range of prevention strategies, and present a public health approach to prevention. The article concludes with a set of recommendations to inform future efforts to prevent child maltreatment through approaches that seek to expand capacity for the implementation of evidence-based prevention programs, while addressing the adverse community experiences that exacerbate risk for child maltreatment.

Keywords: maltreatment prevention; prevention science; prevention programs; child maltreatment; child welfare

C hild maltreatment arises from highly varied influences on children and families, such as parental mental health, intimate partner relationships, intergenerational caregiving experiences, community characteristics, and socioeconomic status. The prevention of child maltreatment requires an equally broad view and response. From the inception of the child protection system in the United States, child welfare policies have laid the blueprint for a largely reactive child protection response. Meanwhile, interdisciplinary research and development occurring outside of

Brenda Jones Harden is Alison Richman Professor of Children and Families at the University of Maryland School of Social Work. She is a scientist-practitioner who conducts research on the effects of interventions to prevent maltreatment of young children, including home visiting, early childhood education, and parenting interventions.

Correspondence: Brenda.Jones-Harden@ssw .umaryland.edu

DOI: 10.1177/0002716220978361

the child welfare policy framework in fields such as behavioral science, early care and education, pediatric primary care, child development, child psychology, and others have produced an array of programs with demonstrated effectiveness in preventing child maltreatment, such as early childhood education and parenting interventions. However, widespread implementation of effective child maltreatment prevention strategies has been slow and uneven.

In this article, we trace how governmental responsibility for child maltreatment prevention became centered within the nation's child welfare system, initially created to ensure the protection of children who were at risk for or had experienced abuse or neglect. We also discuss developments in prevention science, present a public health approach to prevention, and review the existing literature on the effectiveness of a range of prevention strategies. The article concludes with a set of recommendations to inform future efforts to prevent child maltreatment through approaches that seek to expand capacity for the adoption and implementation of evidence-based prevention programs, while addressing the adverse community experiences that exacerbate risk for a host of adverse childhood experiences, of which child maltreatment is one of the most deleterious.

Child Protection and Child Maltreatment Prevention: A Brief History

In 1912, Congress established a broad role for the federal government in the welfare of children with the creation of the U.S. Children's Bureau. In the wake of the Great Depression, the Social Security Act of 1935 furthered the government's role in ensuring children's welfare by creating the Aid to Dependent Children (ADC) cash assistance program and expanding the role of the Children's Bureau in its implementation through cooperation with state public welfare agencies. Public assistance in the form of ADC, and later Aid to Families with Dependent Children (AFDC) in 1962, continued as a single federal response to child and family need

Cassandra Simons is a postdoctoral research associate in the Center for Early Childhood Education and Intervention at the University of Maryland, College Park. Her research investigates the academic socialization beliefs of low-income and underserved families as well as the effectiveness of early childhood preventative interventions.

Michelle Johnson-Motoyama is an associate professor at The Ohio State University College of Social Work and faculty affiliate of the Institute for Population Research. Her research examines the effects of social policies and programs in preventing child maltreatment and reducing social disparities in child and family health and well-being.

Richard Barth is a professor at the University of Maryland School of Social Work. He has designed interventions and conducted evaluations addressing child abuse prevention, parent training, child fatalities, and evidence-based practices in child welfare. He is past-president of the American Academy of Social Work and Social Welfare and chairs the Executive Committee of the Grand Challenges for Social Work.

NOTE: The authors would like to acknowledge the contributions of Patricia Kohl, Washington University, to the conceptualization of this article.

and might be thought of as one of the earliest strategies in the primary prevention of child maltreatment (Berrick and Heimpel 2019). However, in time, the behavior of parents came to be viewed as separate from their financial needs through a series of key developments in the 1960s that would emphasize legal, cultural, medical, and technological perspectives for responding to maltreatment. The passage of the 1974 Child Abuse Prevention and Treatment Act (CAPTA) formalized a narrow role of the federal government in family life and squarely placed prevention within the federal response to child maltreatment but emphasized reporting of victims and perpetrators rather than family-focused services. Despite the breadth of new activity under CAPTA and the inception of modest financial opportunities for states to develop child abuse and neglect identification and prevention programs, CAPTA's narrow approach failed to address the depth and complexity of concerns facing families with limited resources. In its early years, CAPTA authorized research into child abuse prevention and treatment and created the National Center on Child Abuse and Neglect (2014). Primary prevention would not, however, become a major focus of the field for at least two more decades.

The 1990s ushered in a series of developments that culminated in the federal prevention policies and programs in place today. Community-Based Child Abuse Prevention (CBCAP) funds were provided through a small formula grant (still only at $39 million as of fiscal year [FY] 2019) to state-designated lead agencies for the primary prevention of child maltreatment through family strengthening and support services, interagency collaboration, and the development of prevention networks. The Family Preservation and Support Services Act (FPSSA) of 1993 revised Title IV-B of the Social Security Act to support states in creating a continuum of services to promote family strengths, enhance parental functioning, and preserve families in crisis. The act required states, for the first time, to engage in a comprehensive planning process with broad community input across programs and funding streams to develop more responsive prevention strategies. However, these funds, later reauthorized as the Promoting Safe and Stable Families program, are largely designated to address the prevention of placement into foster care.

The next 20 years of federal child welfare policy observed a number of significant changes focused on reducing foster care impermanence, improving outcomes for youth emancipating from foster care, and reducing the use of residential treatment (Child Welfare Information Gateway 2019). Most recently, the Family First Prevention Services Act of 2018 authorized a shift in child welfare financing to support states' use of evidence-based programs to prevent foster care entry (see Haskins, this volume; Testa and Kelly, this volume). However, beyond CBCAP, few policies have focused explicitly on preventing child maltreatment before it occurs.

Prevention Science

At the turn of the twenty-first century, scientific breakthroughs in early brain development drove renewed interest in primary prevention and efforts to increase coordination across child serving systems, particularly in the early childhood arena. Additionally, advances in the field of prevention science precipitated the implementation and evaluation of prevention strategies across multiple service sectors. The prevention science approach integrates many strands of research, including life course development, community epidemiology, etiology of disorders, intervention efficacy and effectiveness trials, and dissemination research (Hawkins 2006). Consistent with its overarching goal to prevent the manifestation of disorders or dysfunctions, research in prevention science is designed to inform policy-makers and practitioners about the best strategies to mitigate the causes of dysfunction. As such, prevention science is grounded in the conceptualization that adverse health, developmental, mental health, and life course outcomes are attributable to a variety of empirically based risk and protective factors. Thus, to be effective, prevention strategies should be designed to reduce risk factors and enhance protective factors among individuals, families, and their social ecologies.

Risk for child abuse and neglect perpetration and victimization is influenced by a number of factors that interact to increase or decrease risk over time and within specific contexts. Factors that protect or buffer children from being abused or neglected are known as protective factors. Although risk factors provide information about who is most at risk for being a victim or a perpetrator of child maltreatment, it is important to note that they are not direct causes and cannot predict who will be a victim or a perpetrator (for additional discussion, see Font and Maguire-Jack, this volume). The Centers for Disease Control and Prevention (CDC; 2016) has adopted a four-level social-ecological model that considers the interplay between risk and protective factors at the (1) individual, (2) relationship, (3) community, and (4) societal levels to inform violence prevention strategies (Fortson et al. 2016). Although the forces that contribute to the most commonly studied forms of child maltreatment (i.e., neglect, physical abuse, sexual abuse, and emotional maltreatment) differ, we argue that the factors are layered and, in the main, commonly shared.

The determinants of child maltreatment are typically understood as involving the interaction of social-ecological and transactional factors (Cicchetti and Toth 2005). At the first level of the CDC (2016) framework, key individual factors associated with neglect perpetration or victimization include parent anger/hyperreactivity, depression, substance use, low levels of social support, young parental age, unemployment, single parenting, large family size, and low family socioeconomic status (Stith et al. 2009; Slack et al. 2011). At the CDC's second level of relationships, parent-child dynamics are inextricably part of physical abuse, sexual abuse, emotional maltreatment, and, even, child neglect (Stith et al. 2009).

A growing number of studies have identified risks for child maltreatment at the *third level* of community including neighborhood characteristics, conditions, and social processes (e.g., Marco et al. 2020). Neighborhood collective efficacy (i.e., the degree to which communities exhibit social cohesion, informal social control, and mutual trust) and social organization have been found to enhance or weaken the ability of parents to care for their children (e.g., Freisthler and Maguire-Jack 2015). Neighborhoods and other social institutions almost certainly interact with child and family characteristics. For example, supportive neighborhoods appear

protective for African American girls insofar as they are associated with less exposure to adverse childhood experiences (Melton-Fant 2019).

At the *fourth level* are societal factors, including social norms about the acceptability of child maltreatment and social benefit programs that strengthen household financial security. Analyses of American social norms find a general rejection
of the acceptability of child maltreatment, that prevention frameworks need to be
strengthened, and that prevention is possible (Klika, Haboush-Deloye, and
Linkenbach 2019). Also operating at this level are local, state, and federal programs that support basic human needs and that monitor and respond to shortcom-
ings in the provision of inadequate care at the family or community levels. For
example, a recent series of experimental and quasi-experimental studies that
evaluated the effects of providing economic assistance to families with limited
resources attests to the role of income in child maltreatment dynamics. Specifically,
rigorous evaluations demonstrate that increases in income via state-level Earned
Income Tax Credit programs reduce abusive head trauma hospitalizations
(Klevens et al. 2017) and family involvement with child protective services (Berger
et al. 2017). State restrictions on access to Temporary Aid to Needy Families
(TANF) are significantly associated with increases in the number of child protection reports, victims of child maltreatment, as well as foster care placements, even
after controlling for changes in incarceration and the nation's opioid epidemic
(Ginther and Johnson-Motoyama 2017). Participation in nutrition assistance programs (e.g., Lee and Mackey-Bilaver 2007), the expansion of Medicaid (e.g.,
Brown et al. 2019), and supportive housing experiments (e.g., Farrell et al. 2018)
have also been associated with child maltreatment prevention as well as a range of
other positive child and family outcomes. Yet the U.S. child maltreatment prevention landscape, which emphasizes specific prevention programs, does not significantly build upon the more universal social and health programming available in
other Western countries.

Beyond the CDC's model, Ellis and Dietz (2017) have conceptualized, in their
discussion of health disparities, two broad clusters of problematic influences that
are co-occurring with child maltreatment. They frame the general influences as
the "two ACEs": adverse childhood experiences (commonly referred to as ACEs)
and adverse community environments (see Figure 1). Child maltreatment is a
specific adverse childhood experience that often occurs in the context of, and in
combination with, multiple adverse childhood experiences and is more likely to
be activated for children living in adverse community environments (Friesthler
and McGuire-Jack 2015). *More broadly, adverse childhood experiences have a
significant antagonistic relationship to individuals' short- and long-term health*
(Jones, Merrick, and Houry 2020).

Adverse Childhood Experiences

The likelihood and impact of child maltreatment is also aligned with a critical
body of research on poly-victimization (the increased likelihood of victims to

FIGURE 1
Lack of Opportunity, Economic Mobility, and Social Capital

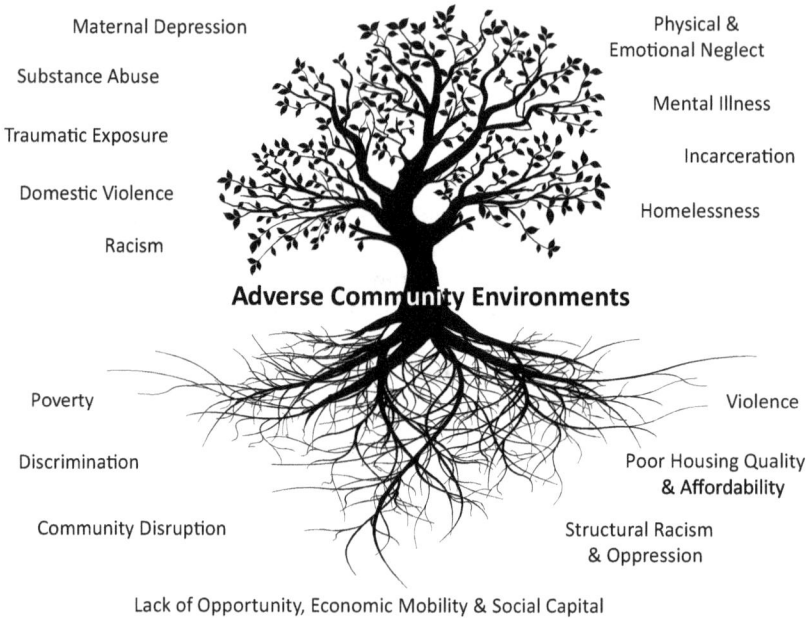

Maternal Depression

Substance Abuse

Traumatic Exposure

Domestic Violence

Racism

Physical &
Emotional Neglect

Mental Illness

Incarceration

Homelessness

Adverse Community Environments

Poverty

Discrimination

Community Disruption

Violence

Poor Housing Quality
& Affordability

Structural Racism
& Oppression

Lack of Opportunity, Economic Mobility & Social Capital

experience multiple forms of violence) (Turner, Finkelhor, and Ormrod 2010), poly-perpetration (the increased likelihood of those who commit violence in one context to commit violence in other contexts), common consequences of different forms of violence, and the common risk and protective factors for different forms of violence over the life course (Wilkins et al. 2014). Further, the number of types of maltreatment experienced (e.g., physical, sexual, emotional) is associated with the likelihood of perpetrating violent delinquency in adolescence (Wolfe 2018).

This body of research is moving the field away from looking for single causes or antidotes to child maltreatment and toward common causes that suggest interventions that reduce exposure to adverse acts and environments that are cumulative, ubiquitous, and toxic risks for children (Wolfe 2018). Notably, economic conditions feature heavily across the multilevel axis of risk for multiple forms of violence (Wilkins et al. 2014). A consistent body of research demonstrates the relationship between economic hardship and child maltreatment (e.g., Berger and Waldfogel 2011) and its disproportionate impact on children of color (see Dettlaff and Boyd, this volume).

Reinforcing our understanding of the array of adverse family and community factors associated with the likelihood, and outcome, of child maltreatment is the recognition that child maltreatment is not necessarily a singularly influential risk factor for later behavioral problems. Maltreated children are likely to have many other vulnerabilities and untoward influences. Thus, maltreatment can be conceptualized as a signal of more general problems in the environments of our most vulnerable children, rather than the problem itself (MacKenzie et al. 2011).

To address the breadth and magnitude of human dysfunction, prevention science has evolved as an interdisciplinary field that incorporates many scientific frameworks. More recently, prevention science has integrated knowledge from developmental science. In this vein, scholars advocate for a developmental approach to prevention design (Wulczyn et al. 2005). They postulate that the effects of risks vary depending on the developmental phase of the individual. For example, very young children may be more susceptible to the effects of risks, as well as more amenable to the benefits of preventive intervention, as a result of the rapid brain and behavioral maturation that occurs during this developmental period (Shonkoff 2010).

A developmental approach to the design of prevention strategies also emanates from two conceptualizations of the impact of adversity on children's functioning. First, Toth and Cicchetti (2013) argue for the use of a developmental psychopathology framework to address child maltreatment, which employs a developmental perspective to understand children's adaptation and maladaptation in the face of maltreatment and the varying outcomes of maltreatment. A second perspective emanates from Shonkoff's (2010) biodevelopmental framework, in which maltreatment can be understood as an experience of toxic stress that potentially disrupts brain architecture, compromises physiological and psychological responses to future stressors, limits development, and increases lifelong vulnerability to stress-related illnesses. Taken together, these conceptualizations underscore the import of positive caregiving to attenuate risks for maltreatment and promote resilience in maltreated children.

From an epidemiologic standpoint, Wulczyn et al. (2005) have asserted that interventions for maltreated children should be designed using a developmental perspective because children are more vulnerable to child welfare involvement at distinct periods (i.e., the beginning of life, during the transition to formal schooling, and in adolescence). They have argued for a developmental approach to linking families with appropriate programs in the child welfare system. Thus, preventive interventions should employ strategies that are aligned with the age of the target child and account for the distinct outcomes for children of different ages when they experience child welfare involvement.

A Public Health Approach to Prevention

Addressing the complexity of maltreatment through a prevention science lens, scholars have also advocated for using a public health approach in the design of strategies to prevent maltreatment (Prinz 2016; Whitaker, Lutzker, and Shelley 2005). Specifically, a public health approach would entail research that examines rates of maltreatment in the general population, studies on the risk and protective factors pertinent to maltreatment, the design and evaluation of interventions to address maltreatment, and the dissemination of evidence-based interventions to prevent maltreatment (Whitaker, Lutzker, and Shelley 2005). With respect to maltreatment prevention, a public health framework would entail a three-tiered approach that addresses (1) the point in the trajectory of maltreatment that an intervention occurs (i.e., primary, secondary, and tertiary) and (2) the maltreatment intervention's target population (i.e., universal, selected, and indicated) (Institute of Medicine and National Research Council 2009, 2014; see also Roygardner, Hughes, and Palusci, this volume).

The first tier of prevention strategies includes primary and universal approaches to prevent maltreatment. Primary strategies are designed to prevent the onset of maltreatment; universal strategies are geared to entire populations or vulnerable subgroups of a population (e.g., low-income families with no evidence of maltreatment). Thus, primary/universal prevention approaches aim to reduce the incidence of maltreatment and related outcomes through the implementation of population-based programs. These strategies may ameliorate risk factors for child maltreatment, such as poverty and violence in communities, and promote positive outcomes in vulnerable subgroups of families and children (e.g., families living in poverty).

In the second tier are secondary and selective intervention strategies to prevent maltreatment. The purpose of secondary preventive interventions is to reduce harm from the experience of risk factors associated with maltreatment. Selective interventions are targeted to individuals who have demonstrated elevated risk for maltreatment. Thus, secondary/selective interventions are designed to ameliorate the effects of maltreatment risks, such as parental physical and mental illness, parental lack of knowledge and skill about parenting and how to promote child development, family social isolation, child physical and psychological disabilities, and inadequate concrete resources (Institute of Medicine and National Research Council 2014), as well as the double ACEs that we mentioned earlier in this article.

Finally, the third tier of maltreatment prevention programs includes tertiary and indicated preventive interventions. Tertiary prevention approaches aim to prevent the recurrence of maltreatment and its adverse outcomes or mitigate the outcomes of maltreatment. Indicated preventive interventions are targeted to individuals who display symptoms emanating from exposure to maltreatment. As such, tertiary/indicated preventive interventions are designed to counteract the effects of abuse and/or neglect on maltreated children and their families and may have family preservation or placement prevention as a goal. Although programs at this level may entail involuntary services (i.e., court-mandated) or therapeutic treatment, they are beyond the scope of this article.

Services and Programs to Prevent Maltreatment

Despite the relatively low level of child welfare financing targeted to prevention services, policy-makers, practitioners, and researchers have brought attention to these services and their relation to child welfare outcomes. Studies that have examined the effectiveness of prevention services financed through federal child welfare financing mechanisms such as CBCAP have typically lacked rigorous evaluation, leaving considerable gaps in our knowledge about the programs' effectiveness in the primary prevention of child maltreatment (Institute of Medicine and National Research Council 2014). Services funded through Title IV-B of the Social Security Act have historically focused on secondary or tertiary prevention by preventing the recurrence of child maltreatment and foster care entry through "usual care" services: the screening of hotline calls, assessment or investigation of a number of accepted reports (which varies by jurisdiction), and the provision of services ranging from brief family visits and resource referrals to longer-term case management and intensive family preservation services (Jonson-Reid et al. 2017). Well-designed studies that have examined the extent to which usual care services have been successful in achieving child protection's tertiary prevention goals have yielded inconsistent and often disappointing findings that have raised questions about the capacity of such services to ameliorate the often complex and chronic needs of the families served (Jonson-Reid et al. 2017).

Further, there have been many evaluations (with comparison groups) of differential response (DR) programs, which provide a modicum of services in lieu of formal court-ordered services. Results have demonstrated that child safety, typically measured by report recurrence, substantiated rereport, or removal of a child from the home, is not significantly different than it is for those involved with more formal child welfare services (e.g., Fluke et al. 2019; Fuller and Zhang 2017). Although many questions about DR remain, including the threshold of risk and level of utilization at which child safety can be maintained without court supervised services (Fluke et al. 2019), a recent quasi-experiment in economics found states using DR experienced fewer victims and foster care entries over time when compared to states without the program (Johnson-Motoyama et al. 2020). The reductions in victims and foster care entries were causally related to the implementation of DR, suggesting DR may have an important role in secondary and tertiary prevention.

Despite the small number of policy-level studies on prevention services, a proliferation of programs to prevent child maltreatment has emerged from prevention science research. Further, the wide-ranging research on risk and protective factors for maltreatment has facilitated the design and evaluation of prevention programs that address influences on and features of maltreatment. In this section, employing a public health approach, we describe the strategies found to be effective in preventing maltreatment at the primary, secondary, and tertiary levels. Although maltreatment can occur in the context of other perpetrators (e.g., peers, school personnel, other adults), we focus herein on the prevention of maltreatment by birth parents.

Because we cannot discuss every program documented to prevent maltreatment, we also include two tables that delineate a broader range of programs found to be effective in reducing maltreatment (see Table A1 in the online appendix) and enhancing parenting outcomes related to maltreatment (see Table A2 in online appendix). Only programs that have been evaluated using rigorous designs (i.e., experimental or quasi-experimental), or are delineated in evidence-based clearinghouses are included. These tables offer a brief description of the programs, the developmental phase of the target population of children, the designs used to evaluate the programs, and information pertinent to program effectiveness (i.e., formal designation as effective, magnitude of effects). Our delineation of programs is presented with an understanding that other prevention programs that are more community-driven and socio-culturally grounded may not appear in designations of evidence-based programs but may nevertheless be effective for specific populations (Tawa 2020).

Primary prevention of maltreatment

Primary prevention strategies aim to prevent maltreatment by promoting protective factors for optimal family functioning. They are often universal programs (i.e., geared to an entire population of families) but may also be targeted to families at risk (e.g., low-income families) who do not necessarily display risk for maltreatment. Strategies for the primary prevention of maltreatment include early care and education, home visitation, clinic-based programs, school-based programs, and community education and mobilization initiatives.

Early childhood education programs. Robust evidence exists for the positive effects for young children and their families of participation in early care and education programs. These programs tend to serve low-income families with children under the age of five and have enhanced child development as a major goal. Many of these programs are comprehensive and two-generational (i.e., targeting the development of the parent and child), with an explicit focus on promoting positive parenting and parent-child interaction. The programs may include center-based services (i.e., provide full-time childcare for young children) as well as home-based services. Typically, these programs provide supportive services to parents on a global or an as-needed basis (e.g., general parenting education, self-sufficiency services, case management and referral to public income supports and other concrete services), but do not necessarily provide family-specific, intensive interventions to improve parenting. However, the family support provided by these programs may be the mechanism by which they reduce maltreatment. Early care and education programs have been documented to prevent maltreatment, including reduced child protection reports (Early Head Start: Green et al. 2014; Chicago Child-Parent Centers: Reynolds and Robertson 2003).

Home visitation. High-quality home visiting programs represent another primary preventive strategy found to enhance child and family functioning, as well as to reduce the incidence of child maltreatment (Donelan-McCall, Eckenrode, and Olds 2009). These programs tend to recruit parents during the prenatal or early postnatal period and provide preventive services to families during infancy and early childhood. Depending on the program, home visits may be offered weekly or the dosage may be determined based on specific family characteristics. Many of these programs use nurses as the service providers; others employ developmental specialists or social workers to deliver the home-based services. Fueled to a great extent by the recent Maternal, Infant, and Early Childhood Home Visiting legislation (MIECHV; Administration for Children and Families 2020), research has documented the positive impact of several high-quality home visiting programs on global parenting and maltreatment-specific outcomes (see Sama-Miller et al. [2017] for a review; Nurse Family Partnership: Olds et al. 2014; Family Connects: Dodge et al. 2014; Family Check-up; Dishion et al. 2015).

Clinic-based programs. There has been recent growth in the delivery of primary prevention programs during early childhood (i.e., zero to five years), which are situated in pediatric care clinics. These models supplement conventional preventive medical services with a child development specialist or social worker, who provides developmental and parenting guidance to parents, as well as case management services, during children's pediatric visits. Additionally, health care personnel may be trained to understand early childhood development and mental health. Clinic-based models of primary prevention show promise with respect to preventing maltreatment and promoting positive parenting practices in the context of pediatric care (SEEK: Dubowitz et al. 2009; Healthy Steps: Minkovitz et al. 2003).

School-based programs. Many programs aimed at preventing sexual abuse are based in schools. Schools are an excellent context in which to share information about abuse prevention because teachers can reach a wide audience of children before they are affected by maltreatment. Almost all school-based programs involve discussions, and many involve modeling and interactive learning with role-play or behavioral skills rehearsal (Topping and Barron 2009; Walsh et al. 2018). Meta-analyses have concluded that school-based programs can have positive effects on self-protection, personal safety knowledge, awareness of others' behavioral intentions, and knowledge about abuse behaviors (Topping and Barron 2009; Walsh et al. 2018). However, findings regarding disclosure of abuse, a key outcome, have been inconclusive in most studies (Walsh et al. 2018). Longer programs (i.e., four or more sessions) and programs that had an experiential component for children seemed to be more effective (Davis and Gidycz 2000).

Community education and mobilization. Representing a distal primary prevention approach, community education and mobilization have been employed to prevent maltreatment at a population or community level. These strategies include media campaigns, global parenting education provided in community settings, and community mobilization efforts. For example, public education campaigns have been mounted in many states to address a specific form of infant maltreatment—abusive head trauma (also known as Shaken Baby Syndrome)—but they have yielded varying and inconclusive results (Zolotor et al. 2015). Leventhal, Asnes, and Bechtel (2017) have advocated for integrating these strategies into other primary prevention programs (e.g., home visiting), addressing parental affect, and targeting male caregivers who are often perpetrators of this form of maltreatment as a means to strengthen program effectiveness.

Media campaigns for the primary prevention of other forms of maltreatment have also been launched by scholars and practitioners in the field of child abuse and neglect. In a systematic review of universal campaigns to reduce physical abuse, Poole, Seal, and Taylor (2014) documented enhanced parental self-efficacy and knowledge of concepts and actions relevant to preventing child abuse, but more variability in outcomes regarding reductions in physical abuse. Similarly, findings from evaluations of media campaigns to prevent child sexual abuse are somewhat mixed (e.g., Rheingold et al. 2007).

Community mobilization efforts to prevent child maltreatment often enlist volunteers and community members to support families at risk for maltreatment. Although there are many examples of these community mobilization strategies, many of these initiatives have not been subject to rigorous evaluation. A rare example is Strong Communities for Children (SCC), designed to prevent the maltreatment of children from birth through adolescence, which yielded many benefits for families including decreased parental stress, substantiated child mal-treatment, and childhood injuries related to maltreatment, as well as enhanced social support, collective efficacy, child safety, and parenting practices (McDonnell, Ben-Arieh, and Melton 2015).

Secondary prevention of maltreatment

Secondary prevention strategies focus on families that have been identified as at risk for maltreatment. Programs in the secondary prevention arena are designed to promote the parenting skills of individuals at risk of maltreating their children, may concentrate on risk factors for maltreatment, or may be adapted from theoretically and evidence-based parenting interventions.

Home visitation. Home visiting programs in the secondary tier address the functioning of families who have displayed risk for maltreatment. Similar to pro-grams in the primary tier, these programs may be comprehensive in nature, geared toward improving family, parenting, and child outcomes, and longer in duration (e.g., two to five years). An exemplar of this approach is Healthy Families America (HFA), which uses an eligibility screener for families to deter-mine risks of maltreatment. HFA evaluations have documented reductions in child maltreatment (e.g., DuMont et al. 2011; Lee et al. 2018), more positive parenting practices (e.g., LeCroy and Krysik 2011), improved home environ-ments, and decreased violence in the home (LeCroy and Lopez 2020).

Other home visiting programs in the secondary tier are intensive in terms of content (e.g., specific set of parenting skills) and format (e.g., parent-child interaction), and tend to be brief in duration (e.g., 10–20 weeks). Many have a foundation in attachment theory, underscoring attachment as a critical devel-opmental milestone, and a focus on promoting positive parent-child interac-tion. Others are grounded in social-cognitive theory, with a focus on parent management. Regardless of theoretical orientation, these programs tend to be very experiential, employing active coaching to promote improved parenting behaviors. More recently, some have been integrating video feedback as a method of facilitating participants' observation, awareness, and change relative to their parenting practices. Burgeoning research demonstrates the benefits of several high-quality home visiting models with respect to maltreatment risk, specifically increased sensitive and responsive parenting (e.g., Attachment and Bio-behavioral Catchup: Dozier and Bernard 2019; Promoting First Relationships: Oxford et al. 2016), less physical punishment (Cognitively-Enhanced Home Visiting: Bugental and Schwartz 2009), improved child safety (Family Connections: Collins et al. 2011), and reduced child abuse recidivism (Safe Care: Chaffin et al. 2012).

Interventions to address parental risks. Because secondary prevention programs address risk factors for maltreatment, it is important to identify specific caregiver risks for maltreatment when designing preventive interventions. Interventions designed to explicitly address these risks in the context of parenting have been found to affect maltreatment risk. For example, substance using mothers participating in parenting interventions displayed more sensitive and responsive caregiving (Mothers and Toddlers Program: Suchman et al. 2010) and reported reductions in their child abuse potential (Parents under Pressure Program: Dawe 2009). Mothers affected by intimate partner violence who participated in a risk-specific parenting intervention were more likely to show a decrease in their use of corporal punishment over the course of the intervention than those who did not participate in the intervention (Moms' Empowerment Program; Grogan-Kaylor et al. 2019).

Parent management interventions. Parent management interventions are grounded in social-cognitive theory and aim to reduce maltreatment by increasing parental skill at managing child behavior. Such interventions may be delivered in multiple settings, including the home, early childhood center, school, or mental health clinic. Because children and adolescents who exhibit behavior problems are more likely to have experienced maltreatment (Mills et al. 2013), parent management interventions assist parents to alter their cognitions and behaviors in response to children's and adolescents' negative behaviors.

Parent management programs appear to be an effective method of treating externalizing behaviors and disorders and reducing harsh parenting behaviors (Dretzke et al. 2005; Weber et al. 2018). These programs typically follow two approaches: behavior change (e.g., teach specific parenting skills to reduce problem behaviors) or relationship building (e.g., facilitate responsive parent-child interaction). Programs are typically short (several weeks), conducted in individual or group format, and administered by therapists or other qualified individuals (e.g., social workers, psychologists). Many of these programs are geared toward children from 2 to 12 years of age. Research has found such interventions to be effective in preventing new reports of physical abuse and reducing child welfare recidivism (Parent Child Interaction Therapy: Chaffin et al. 2011; Batzer et al.

2018), as well as increasing the use of appropriate discipline and praise/incentives among families at risk of neglect and improving parents' nurturance and positive affect in families with a history of maltreatment (The Incredible Years; Webster-Stratton and Reid 2010).

Tertiary prevention of maltreatment

Tertiary-level prevention programs have a goal of preventing the recurrence of maltreatment or maladaptive outcomes associated with maltreatment. Due to their focus on preventing maltreatment among families with the most intensive needs, these programs often have an intensive, therapeutic component that seeks to reduce maltreating parents' negative parenting behaviors. They may have a relationship-based approach in which providers intervene with nurturance and reflection, or may have a parent management orientation, in which providers actively coach parents to alter negative interaction patterns with their children.

Evaluations of relationship-based programs have shown benefits for participant families with regard to maltreatment risk, including increases in secure attachment and decreases in disorganized attachment among maltreated children (Child Parent Psychotherapy [CPP]: Stronach et al. 2013); reductions in behavior problems and trauma-related symptoms (CPP: Lieberman, Ippen, and Van Horn 2006); and decreases in parenting stress, maternal psychopathology, and family involvement with the child protection system (Child First: Lowell et al. 2011). Parents who participated in a parent management intervention showed reductions in disruptive child behavior, dysfunctional parenting, parental distress and relationship conflict, negative parental attribution for children's misbehavior, potential for child abuse, unrealistic parental expectations, rates of child protection systems reports, foster care placement, and abuse/neglect related medical injuries (Triple P; Prinz et al. 2009; Sanders et al. 2014).

Summary and Recommendations

Contemporary approaches to the prevention of child maltreatment in public health typically entail a four-step process of establishing the prevalence of maltreatment in general and specialized populations, building knowledge of the risk and protective factors for maltreatment, designing and testing strategies to prevent and address maltreatment, and widely disseminating evidence-based strategies to prevent maltreatment (Hanson et al. 2012). As other articles in this volume note, progress has been made toward the first two steps of this model through periodic national child maltreatment incidence surveys in the general population, ongoing surveillance data for the population of children reported to child protection agencies, etiological research regarding risk and protective factors, and research on the consequences of child maltreatment.

Further, as outlined in this article, a growing number of studies have contributed to the third step of developing and testing effective interventions. Several meta-analyses and reviews have documented the impacts of maltreatment prevention programs (e.g., Chen and Chan 2016; Euser et al. 2015; Gubbels, van der Put, and Assink 2019). In general, these reviews have suggested that parent training programs, no matter at which level of prevention or theoretical orientation, tend to be effective in preventing child maltreatment. Programs with moderate dose and duration have more consistently favorable outcomes than very short or very long programs. Maltreatment prevention programs such as high-quality home visiting and parent training programs have small to moderate effects on maltreatment and related risk factors (Chen and Chan 2016; Euser et al. 2015; Gubbels, van der Put, and Assink 2019). However, when the outcomes are narrowed to direct measures of child maltreatment, effects are generally small (Euser et al. 2015).

Despite evidence of positive impacts, critical questions remain about prevention programs' capacity to reduce maltreatment, which should be prioritized for research investment. First, many of the evidence-based programs have not been taken to scale and implemented and evaluated in "real-world" community contexts and have not been tested with a broad range of sociocultural groups. In addition, many of these programs have not been tested with child welfare–involved families, or families that display extreme risk for maltreatment. Many evaluations of prevention programs have not included outcome measures of child maltreatment, such as substantiated CPS reports, child injuries, or out-of-home placements. Instead, evaluations have tended to focus on outcomes related to risk and protective factors for maltreatment, which are difficult to compare across studies. Additionally, the magnitude of the effects of the programs are variable; thus, there may be limited "clinical and practical significance" with respect to the differences between program participants and those who did not experience the program. Effect size information is not available for many evaluations at the population level because exact sample sizes are unknown. Further, many interventions are only effective for certain subgroups and cannot be compared to programs created for the entire population. Finally, many studies of the effectiveness of programs for the reduction of maltreatment are not methodologically rigorous and do not use "gold standard" designs such as randomized control trials or high-quality quasi-experimental designs.

These caveats notwithstanding, extant evidence underscores that child and family service entities should integrate evidence-based, developmentally appropriate preventive interventions into their ongoing work with vulnerable families. However, scholars have suggested that these interventions are not broadly utilized by clinicians or child welfare systems, a necessary fourth step in the public health process that requires dedicated investments (Toth and Manly 2011; Saul et al. 2008). The lack of widespread adoption and implementation can be partly attributed to a range of key system-level factors, including leadership, organizational capacities and resources, and relationships between stakeholders across multiple sectors that must be addressed to advance prevention (Smith, Wilkins, and McClure 2020).

First and perhaps foremost, national leadership to coordinate and deliver effective child maltreatment prevention strategies has not been well organized or funded. Roughly a quarter century after CAPTA was originally funded and managed under the Children's Bureau to provide a modest and decentralized source of support for case finding, the CDC has been given a greater role in reframing child maltreatment as a public health concern in the United States. The CDC's vision has been expressed through national objectives conveyed in the Healthy People's 2020 initiative (U.S. Department of Health and Human Services 2020); technical packages for policy, norm, and programmatic activities that cut across multiple health and social welfare policies; funding streams and governmental activities (Fortson et al. 2016); and a strategic vision for addressing the overlap among multiple forms of violence (CDC 2016).

The CDC's (2016) vision focuses attention on four areas: "(1) the developmental periods of childhood and adolescence, where prevention efforts are likely to achieve the greatest long-term impact; (2) the populations and communities that disproportionately bear the burden of violence in society; (3) the shared risk and protective factors that are most likely to influence multiple forms of violence; and (4) priority to the programs, practices, and policies that are most likely to impact multiple forms of violence." Connecting child maltreatment to the health sector is long overdue but is still not accomplished at the state level, where child abuse prevention continues to be excluded from the main strategic efforts of health departments (see, also, Roygardner, Hughes, and Palusci, this volume).

Our broader understanding of how child maltreatment occurs also demands an expanded response to child maltreatment prevention that incorporates a developmental perspective in its interplay with levels of family adversity. Singular efforts such as increasing parent skills training or relationship enhancement—although helpful in their singular way at certain points in a child's development—do not satisfactorily match up with the dynamic and multiply determined phenomena of child maltreatment. Therefore, population-level reductions to child maltreatment are unlikely to be achieved solely through scaling up particular evidence-based programs but rather through comprehensive national and local efforts that combine the dissemination of evidence-based strategies with approaches that address social, economic, health, education, and policy-system levers. Preventing exposure to the dual ACEs associated with child maltreatment requires a strong and sustained social and public health strategy that is integrated across child and family serving systems and sectors (for a detailed discussion, see Feely et al., this volume).

The CDC, in its technical manual, has identified seven necessities: (1) *strengthen economic supports for families*, (2) *promote social norms that protect against violence and adversity*, (3) *ensure a strong start for children*, (4) *enhance parenting skills to promote healthy child development*, (5) *intervene to lessen harms and prevent future risk*, (6) *engage and connect services across sectors, and* (7) *monitor, evaluate, and improve*. Notably, only the last requires the central role that we often assign to child welfare services and to medical and legal specialists in child abuse and neglect. All the other elements can be steered by designated leaders and implemented by an array of other organizations that need not have specialty training. Thus, efforts by child maltreatment specialists can be pursued in tandem with comprehensive community-based ACE prevention strategies and evidence-based approaches that ensure a strong start for children, enhance the coping skills of parents and youth, connect youth to caring adults and activities, promote social norms that protect against violence and adversity, and strengthen economic supports for families (Jones, Merrick, and Houry 2020).

At the same time, when young children are at the highest levels of risk, their families are repeatedly engaged with CWS, and children are experiencing poly-victimization, there is a need for intensive, coordinated, and longitudinal care (National Academies of Sciences 2016). There is evidence that a call to a child protection hotline, regardless of the disposition, is the best predictor of a later child abuse or neglect fatality (Commission to Eliminate Child Abuse and Neglect Fatalities 2016). Further, research shows that CWS involvement as a child is related to CWS involvement when the child becomes a parent, although there is considerable variation in outcomes that requires flexibility in response (Eastman and Putnam-Hornstein 2019). Taken together, the accumulating information on the risks of subsequent child maltreatment among those who have ever been reported to CWS and ever been involved with CWS requires developing an approach with more sustained engagement and support provided to families.

We also have an ongoing need for linked data and collaboration across multiple programs for multiple purposes including surveillance, evaluation of existing and new policies, planning and implementation of community-level violence prevention and child maltreatment prevention strategies, and evaluation of services. The CDC could certainly better leverage funding to states for the accumulation of birth records—under the National Vital Records Program—by asking states to link those data to CWS data to generate intervention opportunities to assist CWS-involved families who are having newborns (Shaw et al. 2013). We could also learn much more about service needs, usual care in child welfare, and preventive services through investments in cross-systems data exchanges such as the Comprehensive Child Welfare Information System (CCWIS) and efforts to enhance and modernize existing data systems to support research, business, practice, and client data needs (Harrison et al. 2018). Additional investments are also needed to rigorously evaluate and potentially expand CBCAP's role in primary prevention.

In sum, child maltreatment is a complex phenomenon that requires a broad range of strategies to prevent its incidence and recurrence. These strategies should be evidence based, developmentally informed, specific to family need, grounded in a prevention science approach, and address the adverse community experiences that render families susceptible to child maltreatment. Hawkins (2006) states, "As a result of the progress of prevention science, we now have an opportunity to help communities reinvent themselves as protective environments for the positive development of all children" (p. 149). For children in the United States, this requires a marked shift from the reactive responses of the child welfare system to a set of prevention strategies that crosses disciplines, service sectors, policies, and funding streams to build the safe, stable, and supportive environments that all children deserve.

References

Administration for Children and Families. 2020. The Maternal, Infant, and Early Childhood Home Visiting Program. Available from https://mchb.hrsa.gov/sites/default/files/mchb/MaternalChild-HealthInitiatives/HomeVisiting/pdf/programbrief.pdf.

Batzer, Stephanie, Teresa Berg, Meripa T. Godinet, and Rebecca L. Stotzer. 2018. Efficacy or chaos? Parent–child interaction therapy in maltreating populations: A review of research. *Trauma, Violence, & Abuse* 19 (1): 3–19.

Berger, Lawrence M., Sarah A. Font, Kristen S. Slack, and Jane Waldfogel. 2017. Income and child maltreatment in unmarried families: Evidence from the Earned Income Tax Credit. *Review of Economics of the Household* 15 (4): 1345–72.

Berger, Lawrence M., and Jane Waldfogel. 2011. Economic determinants and consequences of child maltreatment. OECD Social, Employment and Migration Working Paper.

Berrick, Jill Duerr, and Daniel Heimpel. 2019. How federal laws pertaining to foster care financing shape child welfare services. In *The Oxford handbook of children & the law*, ed. James D. Dwyer. New York, NY: Oxford University Press.

Brown, Emily C.B., Michelle M. Garrison, Hao Bao, Pingping Qu, Carole Jenny, and Ali Rowhani-Rahbar. 2019. Assessment of rates of child maltreatment in states with Medicaid expansion vs states without Medicaid expansion. *JAMA Network Open* 2 (6): e195529.

Bugental, Daphne Blunt, and Alex Schwartz. 2009. A cognitive approach to child mistreatment prevention among medically at-risk infants. *Developmental Psychology* 45 (1): 284–88.

Centers for Disease Control and Prevention. 2016. Preventing multiple forms of violence: A strategic vision for connecting the dots. Atlanta, GA: U.S. Department of Health and Human Services, Centers for Disease Control and Prevention. Available from http://http://www.cdc.gov/violenceprevention/overview/strategicvisionhtml.

Chaffin, Mark, Beverly Funderburk, David Bard, Linda Anne Valle, and Robin Gurwitch. 2011. A combined motivation and parent–child interaction therapy package reduces child welfare recidivism in a randomized dismantling field trial. *Journal of Consulting and Clinical Psychology* 79 (1): 84–95.

Chaffin, Mark, Debra Hecht, David Bard, Jane F. Silovsky, and William Howard Beasley. 2012. A statewide trial of the SafeCare home-based services model with parents in child protective services. *Pediatrics* 129 (3): 509–15.

Chen, Mengtong, and Ko Ling Chan. 2016. Effects of parenting programs on child maltreatment prevention: A meta-analysis. *Trauma, Violence, & Abuse* 17 (1): 88–104.

Child Welfare Information Gateway (US). 2019. *Major federal legislation concerned with child protection, child welfare, and adoption*. Washington, DC: U.S. Department of Health and Human Services, Children's Bureau.

Cicchetti, Dante, and Sheree L. Toth. 2005. Child maltreatment. *Annual Review of Clinical Psychology* 1:409–38.

Collins, K. S., F. H. Strieder, D. DePanfilis, M. Tabor, P. A. Clarkson-Freeman, L. Linde, and P. Greenberg. 2011. Trauma adapted family connections: Reducing developmental and complex trauma symptomatology to prevent child abuse and neglect. *Child Welfare* 90 (6): 29–47.

Commission to Eliminate Child Abuse and Neglect Fatalities. 2016. *Within our reach: A national strategy to eliminate child abuse and neglect fatalities*. Washington, DC: Government Printing Office.

Davis, M. Katherine, and Christine A. Gidycz. 2000. Child sexual abuse prevention programs: A meta-analysis. *Journal of Clinical Child Psychology* 29 (2): 257–65.

Dawe, Sharon. 2009. Improving family functioning and child outcome in methadone maintained families: The Parents under Pressure Programme. *Drug and Alcohol Review* 22 (3): 299–307.

Dettlaff, Alan J., and Reiko Boyd. 2021. Racial disproportionality and disparities in the child welfare system: Why do they exist, and what can be done to address them? *The ANNALS of the American Academy of Political and Social Science* (this volume).

Dishion, Thomas J., Chung Jung Mun, Emily C. Drake, Jenn-Yun Tein, Daniel S. Shaw, and Melvin Wilson. 2015. A transactional approach to preventing early childhood neglect: The family check-up as a public health strategy. *Development and Psychopathology* 27 (4, pt. 2): 1647–60.

Dodge, Kenneth A., W. Benjamin Goodman, Robert A. Murphy, Karen O'Donnell, Jeannine Sato, and Susan Guptill. 2014. Implementation and randomized controlled trial evaluation of universal postnatal nurse home visiting. *American Journal of Public Health* 104 (S1): S136–43.

Donelan-McCall, N., J. Eckenrode, and D. L. Olds. 2009. Home visiting for the prevention of child maltreatment: Lessons learned during the past 20 years. *Pediatric Clinics of North America* 56 (2): 389–403.

Dozier, M., and K. Bernard. 2019. *Coaching parents of vulnerable infants: The attachment and biobehavioral catch-up approach*. New York, NY: Guilford.

Dretzke, J., E. Frew, C. Davenport, J. Barlow, S. Stewart-Brown, J. Sandercock, S. Bayliss, J. Raftery, C. Hyde, and R. Taylor. 2005. The effectiveness and cost-effectiveness of parent training/education programmes for the treatment of conduct disorder, including oppositional defiant disorder, in children. *Health Technology* 9 (50): iii, ix–x, 1–233.

Dubowitz, H., S. Feigelman, W. Lane, and J. Kim. 2009. Pediatric primary care to help prevent child maltreatment: The Safe Environment for Every Kid (SEEK) model. *Pediatrics* 123 (3): 858–64.

DuMont, Kimberly, Kristen Kirkland, Susan Mitchell-Herzfeld, Susan Ehrhard-Dietzel, Monica L. Rodriguez, Eunju Lee, China Layne, and Rose Greene. 2011. A Randomized Trial of Healthy Families New York (HFNY): Does home visiting prevent child maltreatment? American Psychological Association. Available from https://doi.org/10.1037/e529652011-001.

Eastman, A. L., and E. Putnam-Hornstein. 2019. An examination of child protective service involvement among children born to mothers in foster care. *Child Abuse & Neglect* 88:317–25.

Ellis, Wendy R., and William H. Dietz. 2017. A new framework for addressing adverse childhood and community experiences: The building community resilience model. *Academic Pediatrics* 17 (7): S86–S93.

Euser, Saskia, Lenneke R. A. Alink, Marije Stoltenborgh, Marian J. Bakermans-Kranenburg, and Marinus H. van IJzendoorn. 2015. A gloomy picture: A meta-analysis of randomized controlled trials reveals disappointing effectiveness of programs aiming at preventing child maltreatment. *BMC Public Health* 15(1). Available from https://doi.org/10.1186/s12889-015-2387-9.

Farrell, Anne F., Preston A. Britner, Melissa A. Kull, Debra L. Struzinski, Kim Somaroo-Rodriguez, Kathryn Parr, Lindsay Westberg, Betsy Cronin, and Chelsea Humphrey. 2018. Connecticut's Intensive Supportive Housing for Families Program. Chicago, IL: Chapin Hall at the University of Chicago.

Fluke, John D., Nicole Harlaar, Brett Brown, Kurt Heisler, Lisa Merkel-Holguin, and Adam Darnell. 2019. Differential response and children re-reported to child protective services: County data from the National Child Abuse and Neglect Data System (NCANDS). *Child Maltreatment* 24 (2): 127–36.

Font, Sarah A., and Kathryn Maguire-Jack. 2021. The scope, nature, and causes of child abuse and neglect. *The ANNALS of the American Academy of Political and Social Science* (this volume).

Fortson, Beverly L., Joanne Klevens, Melissa T. Merrick, Leah K. Gilbert, and Sandra P. Alexander. 2016. *Preventing child abuse and neglect: A technical package for policy, norm, and programmatic activities*. Washington, DC: CDC.

Freisthler, Bridget, and Kathryn Maguire-Jack. 2015. Understanding the interplay between neighborhood structural factors, social processes, and alcohol outlets on child physical abuse. *Child Maltreatment* 20 (4): 268–77.

Fuller, Tamara, and Saijun Zhang. 2017. The impact of family engagement and child welfare services on maltreatment re-reports and substantiated re-reports. *Child Maltreatment* 22 (3): 183–93.

Ginther, Donna K., and Michelle Johnson-Motoyama. 2017. Do state TANF policies affect child abuse and neglect? Paper presented at the APPAM 39th Annual Fall Research Conference.

Green, Beth L., Catherine Ayoub, Jessica Dym Bartlett, Adam Von Ende, Carrie Furrer, Rachel Chazan-Cohen, Claire Vallotton, and Joanne Klevens. 2014. The effect of Early Head Start on child welfare system involvement: A first look at longitudinal child maltreatment outcomes. *Children and Youth Services Review* 42:127–35.

Grogan-Kaylor, Andrew, Maria M. Galano, Kathryn H. Howell, Laura Miller-Graff, and Sandra A. Graham-Bermann. 2019. Reductions in parental use of corporal punishment on pre-school children following participation in the Moms' Empowerment Program. *Journal of Interpersonal Violence* 34 (8): 1563–82.

Gubbels, Jeanne, Claudia E. van der Put, and Mark Assink. 2019. The effectiveness of parent training programs for child maltreatment and their components: A meta-analysis. *International*

Journal of Environmental Research and Public Health 16 (13). Available from https://doi.org/10.3390/ijerph16132404.

Hanson, Dale W., Caroline F. Finch, John P. Allegrante, and David Sleet. 2012. Closing the gap between injury prevention research and community safety promotion practice: Revisiting the public health model. *Public Health Reports* 127 (2): 147–55.

Harrison, Teresa M., Donna Canestraro, Theresa Pardo, Martha Avila-Marilla, Nicolas Soto, Megan Sutherland, Brian Burke, and Mila Gasco. 2018. A tale of two information systems: Transitioning to a data-centric information system for child welfare. In *Proceedings of the 19th Annual International Conference on Digital Government Research: Governance in the data age*, 1–2. New York, NY: Association for Computing Machinery.

Hawkins, J. David. 2006. Science, social work, prevention: Finding the intersections. *Social Work Research* 30 (3): 137–52.

Institute of Medicine and National Research Council. 2009. *Preventing mental, emotional, and behavioral disorders among young people: Progress and possibilities*. Washington, DC: The National Academies Press. Available from https://doi.org/10.17226/12480.

Institute of Medicine and National Research Council. 2014. *New directions in child abuse and neglect research*. Washington, DC: The National Academies Press. Available from https://doi.org/10.17226/18331.

Johnson-Motoyama, Michelle, Donna Ginther, John Fluke, and Rebecca Phillips. 2020. Did differential response systems reduce child neglect and foster care entries in the U.S.? Results from a national study. Presented at the Society for Social Work & Research 24th Annual Conference, Washington, DC, January 15–19, 2020.

Jones, Christopher M., Melissa T. Merrick, and Debra E. Houry. 2020. Identifying and preventing adverse childhood experiences: Implications for clinical practice. *JAMA* 323 (1): 25–26.

Jonson-Reid, Melissa, Brett Drake, Patricia Kohl, Shenyang Guo, Derek Brown, Timothy McBride, Hyunil Kim, and Ericka Lewis. 2017. What do we really know about usual care child protective services? *Children and Youth Services Review* 82:222–29.

Klevens, Joanne, Brian Schmidt, Feijun Luo, Likang Xu, Katie A. Ports, and Rosalyn D. Lee. 2017. Effect of the earned income tax credit on hospital admissions for pediatric abusive head trauma, 1995–2013. *Public Health Reports* 132 (4): 505–11.

Klika, J. Bart, Amanda Haboush-Deloye, and Jeff Linkenbach. 2019. Hidden protections: Identifying social norms associated with child abuse, sexual abuse, and neglect. *Child and Adolescent Social Work Journal* 36 (1): 5–14.

LeCroy, Craig, and Judy Krysik. 2011. Randomized trial of the Healthy Families Arizona home visiting program. *Children and Youth Services Review* 33 (10): 1761–66.

LeCroy, Craig, and Darlene Lopez. 2020. A randomized controlled trial of healthy families: 6-month and 1-year follow-up. *Prevention Science* 21 (1): 25–35.

Lee, Bong Joo, and Lucy Mackey-Bilaver. 2007. Effects of WIC and food stamp program participation on child outcomes. *Children and Youth Services Review* 29 (4): 501–17.

Lee, Eunju, Kristen Kirkland, Claudia Miranda-Julian, and Rose Greene. 2018. Reducing maltreatment recurrence through home visitation: A promising intervention for child welfare involved families. *Child Abuse & Neglect* 86:55–66.

Leventhal, John M., Andrea G. Asnes, and Kirsten Bechtel. 2017. Prevention of pediatric abusive head trauma: Time to rethink interventions and reframe messages. *JAMA Pediatrics* 171 (3): 218–20.

Lieberman, Alicia F., Chandra Ghosh Ippen, and Patricia Van Horn. 2006. Child-parent psychotherapy: 6-month follow-up of a randomized controlled trial. *Journal of the American Academy of Child & Adolescent Psychiatry* 45 (8): 913–18.

Lowell, Darcy I., Alice S. Carter, Leandra Godoy, Belinda Paulicin, and Margaret J. Briggs-Gowan. 2011. A randomized controlled trial of Child FIRST: A comprehensive home-based intervention translating research into early childhood practice. *Child Development* 82 (1): 193–208.

MacKenzie, Michael J., Jonathan B. Kotch, Lee-Ching Lee, Astraea Augsberger, and Nathan Hutto. 2011. A cumulative ecological–transactional risk model of child maltreatment and behavioral outcomes: Reconceptualizing early maltreatment report as risk factor. *Children and Youth Services Review* 33 (11): 2392–98.

Marco, Miriam, Kathryn Maguire-Jack, Enrique Gracia, and Antonio López-Quílez. 2020. Disadvantaged neighborhoods and the spatial overlap of substantiated and unsubstantiated child maltreatment referrals. *Child Abuse & Neglect* 104:104477.

McDonell, James R., Asher Ben-Arieh, and Gary B. Melton. 2015. Strong communities for children: Results of a multi-year community-based initiative to protect children from harm. *Child Abuse & Neglect* 41:79–96.

Melton-Fant, Courtnee. 2019. Childhood adversity among Black children: The role of supportive neighborhoods. *Children and Youth Services Review* 105. Available from https://doi.org/10.1016/j.childyouth.2019.104419.

Mills, Ryan, James Scott, Rosa Alati, Michael O'Callaghan, Jake M. Najman, and Lane Stratheam. 2013. Child maltreatment and adolescent mental health problems in a large birth cohort. *Child Abuse & Neglect* 37 (5): 292–302.

Minkovitz, Cynthia S., Nancy Hughart, Donna Strobino, Dan Scharfstein, Holly Grason, William Hou, and Tess Miller. 2003. A practice-based intervention to enhance quality of care in the first 3 years of life: The Healthy Steps for Young Children Program. *JAMA* 290 (23): 3081–91.

National Academies of Sciences, Engineering, and Medicine. 2016. *Parenting matters: Supporting parents of children ages 0-8.* Washington, DC: The National Academies Press.

Olds, David L., Harriet Kitzman, Michael D. Knudtson, Elizabeth Anson, Joyce A. Smith, and Robert Cole. 2014. Effect of home visiting by nurses on maternal and child mortality: Results of a 2-decade follow-up of a randomized clinical trial. *JAMA Pediatrics* 168 (9). Available from https://doi.org/10.1001/jamapediatrics.2014.472.

Oxford, Monica L., Susan J. Spieker, Mary Jane Lohr, and Charles B. Fleming. 2016. Promoting First Relationships®: Randomized trial of a 10-week home visiting program with families referred to child protective services. *Child Maltreatment* 21 (4): 267–77.

Poole, M. K., D. W. Seal, and C. A. Taylor. 2014. A systematic review of universal campaigns targeting child physical abuse prevention. *Health Education Research* 29 (3): 388–432.

Prinz, Ronald J. 2016. Parenting and family support within a broad child abuse prevention strategy. *Child Abuse & Neglect* 51:400–406.

Prinz, Ronald J., Matthew R. Sanders, Cheri J. Shapiro, Daniel J. Whitaker, and John R. Lutzker. 2009. Population-based prevention of child maltreatment: The U.S. Triple P System Population Trial. *Prevention Science* 10 (1): 1–12.

Reynolds, Arthur J., and Dylan L. Robertson. 2003. School-based early intervention and later child maltreatment in the Chicago Longitudinal Study. *Child Development* 74 (1): 3–26.

Rheingold, Alyssa A., Carole Campbell, Shannon Self-Brown, Michael de Arellano, Heidi Resnick, and Dean Kilpatrick. 2007. Prevention of child sexual abuse: Evaluation of a community media campaign. *Child Maltreatment* 12 (4): 352–63.

Roygardner, Debangshu, Kelli N. Hughes, and Vincent J. Palusci. 2021. Leveraging family and community strengths to reduce child maltreatment. *The ANNALS of the American Academy of Political and Social Science* (this volume).

Sama-Miller, E., L. Akers, A. Mraz-Esposito, M. Zukiewicz, S. Avellar, D. Paulsell, and P. D. Grosso. 2017. *Home visiting evidence of effectiveness review: Executive summary.* Cambridge, MA: Mathematica Policy Research.

Sanders, Matthew R., James N. Kirby, Cassandra L. Tellegen, and Jamin J. Day. 2014. The Triple P-Positive Parenting Program: A systematic review and meta-analysis of a multi-level system of parenting support. *Clinical Psychology Review* 34 (4): 337–57.

Saul, Janet, Jennifer Duffy, Rita Noonan, Keri Lubell, Abraham Wandersman, Paul Flaspohler, Lindsey Stillman, Morris Blachman, and Richard Dunville. 2008. Bridging science and practice in violence prevention: Addressing Ten Key Challenges. *American Journal of Community Psychology* 41 (3–4): 197–205.

Shaw, T. V., R. P. Barth, J. Mattingly, D. Ayer, and S. Berry. 2013. Child welfare birth match: The timely use of child welfare administrative data to protect newborns. *Journal of Public Child Welfare* 7:217–34.

Shonkoff, Jack P. 2010. Building a new biodevelopmental framework to guide the future of early childhood policy. *Child Development* 81 (1): 357–67.

Slack, Kristen Shook, Lawrence M. Berger, Kimberly DuMont, Mi-Youn Yang, Bomi Kim, Susan Ehrhard-Dietzel, and Jane L. Holl. 2011. Risk and protective factors for child neglect during early childhood: A cross-study comparison. *Children and Youth Services Review* 33 (8): 1354–63.

Smith, L. Shakiyla, Natalie J. Wilkins, and Roderick J. McClure. 2020. A systemic approach to achieving population-level impact in injury and violence prevention. *Systems Research and Behavioral Science*. Available from https://doi.org/10.1002/sres.2668.

Stith, Sandra M., Ting Liu, L. Christopher Davies, Esther L. Boykin, Meagan C. Alder, Jennifer M. Harris, Anurag Som, Mary McPherson, and J. E. M. E. G. Dees. 2009. Risk factors in child maltreatment: A meta-analytic review of the literature. *Aggression and Violent Behavior* 14 (1): 13–29.

Stronach, Erin Pickreign, Sheree L. Toth, Fred Rogosch, and Dante Cicchetti. 2013. Preventive interventions and sustained attachment security in maltreated children. *Development and Psychopathology* 25 (4, pt. 1): 919–30.

Suchman, Nancy E., Cindy DeCoste, Nicole Castiglioni, Thomas J. McMahon, Bruce Rounsaville, and Linda Mayes. 2010. The Mothers and Toddlers Program, an attachment-based parenting intervention for substance using women: Post-treatment results from a randomized clinical pilot. *Attachment & Human Development* 12 (5): 483–504.

Tawa, Kayla. 2020. Redefining evidence-based practices: Expanding our view of evidence. Brief. Washington, DC: CLASP.

Testa, Mark F., and David Kelly. 2021. The evolution of federal child welfare policy through the Family First Prevention Services Act of 2018: Opportunities, barriers, and unintended consequences. *The ANNALS of the American Academy of Political and Social Science* (this volume).

Topping, Keith J., and Ian G. Barron. 2009. School-based child sexual abuse prevention programs: A review of effectiveness. *Review of Educational Research* 79 (1): 431–63.

Toth, Sheree L., and Dante Cicchetti. 2013. A developmental psychopathology perspective on child maltreatment. *Child Maltreatment* 18 (3): 135–39.

Toth, Sheree L., and Jody Todd Manly. 2011. Bridging research and practice: Challenges and successes in implementing evidence-based preventive intervention strategies for child maltreatment. *Child Abuse & Neglect* 35 (8): 633–36.

Turner, Heather A., David Finkelhor, and Richard Ormrod. 2010. Poly-victimization in a national sample of children and youth. *American Journal of Preventive Medicine* 38 (3): 323–30.

U.S. Department of Health and Human Services. 2020. Healthy People. Available from healthypeople.gov.

Walsh, Kerryann, Karen Zwi, Susan Woolfenden, and Aron Shlonsky. 2018. School-based education programs for the prevention of child sexual abuse: A Cochrane systematic review and meta-analysis. *Research on Social Work Practice* 28 (1): 33–55.

Weber, Linda, Inge Kamp-Becker, Hanna Christiansen, and Tanja Mingebach. 2018. Treatment of child externalizing behavior problems: A comprehensive review and meta–meta-analysis on effects of parent-based interventions on parental characteristics. *European Child & Adolescent Psychiatry* 28:1025–36.

Webster-Stratton, Carolyn, and M. Reid. 2010. Adapting the Incredible Years, an evidence-based parenting programme, for families involved in the child welfare system. *Journal of Children's Services* 5 (1): 25–42.

Whitaker, Daniel J., John R. Lutzker, and Gene A. Shelley. 2005. Child maltreatment prevention priorities at the Centers for Disease Control and Prevention. *Child Maltreatment* 10 (3): 245–59.

Wilkins, Natalie, Benita Tsao, Marci F. Hertz, Rachel Davis, and Joanne Klevens. 2014. *Connecting the dots: An overview of the links among multiple forms of violence*. Washington, DC: CDC.

Wolfe, David A. 2018. Why polyvictimization matters. *Journal of Interpersonal Violence* 33 (5): 832–37.

Wulczyn, F., R. Barth, Y. Yuang, B. Jones Harden, and J. Landsverk. 2005. *Beyond common sense: Child welfare, child well-being, and the evidence for policy reform*. Piscataway, NJ: Transaction/Aldine de Gruyter.

Zolotor, Adam J., Desmond K. Runyan, Meghan Shanahan, Christine Piette Durrance, Maryalice Nocera, Kelly Sullivan, Joanne Klevens, Robert Murphy, Marilyn Barr, and Ronald G. Barr. 2015. Effectiveness of a statewide abusive head trauma prevention program in North Carolina. *JAMA Pediatrics* 169 (12): 1126–31.

Leveraging Family and Community Strengths to Reduce Child Maltreatment

This article reviews and analyzes extant literature on the prevention of child maltreatment. We give an overview of protective factors that research finds to be efficacious in maltreatment prevention and pay particular attention to research that shows how health-based models and community-based models can leverage family and community strengths to that end. We go on to offer recommendations for potential future prevention programming, including an approach with untapped potential—the *Prevention Zones* framework. Finally, we discuss policy considerations and implications specific to the goal of increasing programming and services that leverage family and community strengths.

Keywords: prevention; strengths-based; child maltreatment policy

By
DEBANGSHU
ROYGARDNER,
KELLI N. HUGHES,
and
VINCENT J. PALUSCI

Supports for children and families in the United States are, generally speaking, carried out through community service programming and through the criminal and legal systems. Child maltreatment, though, is seen as a criminal or legal issue and is addressed primarily by the child welfare system and in the courts (Dias, Mooren, and Kleber 2018; Krugman 1995; Palusci 2017; U.S. Advisory Board on Child Abuse and Neglect 1991, 1993). We know that child maltreatment is more than the physical and mental health traumas borne by individual children and families: it is a public health problem. If society truly wants to promote the developmental needs of children, that goal is not likely to be achieved through the legal or child welfare systems alone (Emery, Trung, and Wu 2015; Klicka, Lee, and

Debangshu Roygardner is the director of evaluation for mental health services at New York Foundling, an affiliate of the Vincent J. Fontana Center for Child Protection, and consortial faculty of psychology at the CUNY School of Professional Studies.

Correspondence: Debangshu.Roygardner@sps.cuny.edu

DOI: 10.1177/0002716220978402

Lee 2018). Rather, community-based prevention strategies need to be ready and able to respond to and alleviate family and community risk factors, as well as to leverage and support family and community strengths and protective factors.

Recognizing the need to work toward a prevention-based strategy for at-risk children and families, the federal government assembled the U.S. Advisory Board on Child Abuse and Neglect in 1993. According to U.S. Advisory Board member Richard Krugman (1995, 25), "caring is not enough"; and despite well-intentioned efforts to make a difference or concern for the well-being of children, we need system-wide, cross-disciplinary approaches. The U.S. Advisory Board outlined a multi-disciplinary community-based approach for preventing child abuse and neglect that invokes policy, implementation, and research and evaluation.

Since then, an increased understanding of primary, secondary, and tertiary prevention has allowed for more accuracy in medical diagnosis, better treatment, and better understanding of the epidemiology of and strategies for preventing maltreatment (Palusci and Perfetto 2018). Despite the advances in knowledge, only a small amount of the research on child maltreatment prevention has been performed with sophisticated designs (U.S. Commission 2016; Levey et al. 2017). However, the field is driven to expand the prevention research portfolio by integrating clinical trials and well-evaluated multimodal interventions to progress the level of rigorous research beyond an overabundance of correlative studies on the issue (Berthelot, Lemieux, and Maziade 2019).

In this article, we focus on child maltreatment prevention programs and strategies that leverage family and community strengths and protective factors—collectively referred to herein as a resilience approach. We review family-based, health-based, and community-based prevention programs as well as discuss overarching child maltreatment prevention strategies and frameworks. Our overarching goal is to examine best practices and evidence-based literature and integrate the findings into a multilevel, community-based, resilience-focused approach to child abuse prevention—one that not only alleviates risk factors, but one that also leverages the strengths of, and promotes protective factors within, families and communities.

To achieve this approach, we advocate adopting dual frameworks/strategies: (1) the 1993 U.S. Advisory Board on Child Abuse and Neglect's concept for *Prevention Zones*, articulated in their report *Neighbors Helping Neighbors: A New National Strategy for the Protection of Children*[1] and (2) the *Strong and Thriving Families Resource Guide* (U.S. Children's Bureau 2019).[2] The 1993 U.S. Advisory Board on Child Abuse and Neglect's *Neighbors Helping Neighbors* strategy is our preferred strategy or framework due to extensive research

Kelli N. Hughes is an attorney and serves as the program director of the American Professional Society on the Abuse of Children's (APSAC's) Center for Child Policy.

Vincent J. Palusci is a professor of pediatrics at New York University Grossman School of Medicine. He is a general and child abuse pediatrician at Bellevue Hospital in New York City and chairs the Hassenfeld Children's Hospital Child Protection Committee at NYU Langone Health.

evidence to support its promise and logic model, and because it is targeted to communities with identified risks for child maltreatment. The *Strong and Thriving Families Resource Guide*, which represents a culmination of research invoking family and community strengths and protective factors, provides practical parenting and community-based strategies, informed by decades of research, to engage parents and communities in child abuse prevention from a primary lens of resilience, rather than risk.

Stated another way, the 1993 report called for a new national strategy to prevent child abuse that was neighborhood-based, and child- and family-centered, with a focus on strengthening families and communities. *Prevention Zones* is meant to be implemented in communities with identifiable risk factors. However, coupled with the *Strong and Thriving Families Resource Guide*, the two frameworks collectively espouse an approach to prevention that focuses on risk factors to identify communities where services should be allocated (secondary prevention), and a primary prevention strategy that focuses on entire communities, with an emphasis on community strengths, allowing for a greater degree of universality.

The result of this integration holds promise as an empirically grounded, theoretically rich resilience approach for stakeholders wishing to implement child maltreatment programming within family, health care, and community settings. We hope that this discussion illustrates the richness and utility of a resilience orientation for prevention programming and that policy-makers and practitioners consider such robust, comprehensive strategies when setting future policy agendas or making practice recommendations.

First, we outline key concepts and definitions used in the article. We then review the literature on efficacious community and family-based child maltreatment prevention programs as well as prevention strategies and frameworks that leverage community and family strengths. Finally, we draw from this literature to recommend an approach that adopts elements of two different strategies and frameworks for prevention—*Prevention Zones* and the *Strong and Thriving Families Resource Guide*—and discuss why the approach of integrating these strategies promotes child safety more comprehensively and holistically by focusing intervention on promoting strengths and increasing resiliency.

Key Concepts and Definitions

Levels of prevention

Over time, multiple, sometimes contradictory, terminologies around prevention have developed.[3] Our discussion of community-based prevention will employ Caplan's terminology of primary, secondary, and tertiary prevention because it affords an approach involving comprehensive cross-sector collaboration. Achieving prevention of child maltreatment will take cross-systems collaboration involving many entities, one of the most important being child protective services (CPS) systems (Klicka, Lee, and Lee 2018).

Preventing programs/models versus strategies/frameworks

We make a distinction between child maltreatment prevention programs/ models and strategies/frameworks. A program or model is a specific intervention designed to prevent child maltreatment. Alternatively, a child maltreatment prevention strategy is a more generalized plan for preventing maltreatment. Strategies tell more about the who, what, where, and when, while programs/ models are meant to explain the "how" (Klicka, Lee, and Lee 2018).

Risk factors for child maltreatment

Risk factors for child maltreatment are factors that are thought to increase the probability that child maltreatment will occur. They exist at the individual, family, and community levels, and different types of child maltreatment can have different risk factors across levels (Merritt, McGuire-Jack, and Negash 2018). Font and Maguire-Jack (this volume) discuss the definitions and mechanisms of risk factors more thoroughly than we do here. For the current article, the most important concept is that risk factors may interact in ways that influence child maltreatment. For example, a child who cries often and also has a parent who is highly reactive to adverse stimuli may experience a multiplying effect on overall risk of maltreatment (Bronfenbrenner 1979). How a child's caregivers interact with the child is a function not only of their own experiences, but also of the environment in which they are situated. Grounded in Bronfenbrenner's ecological theory of child maltreatment, which emphasizes the interconnectedness of the environment and family functioning on child development, research continues to support the idea that environmental risk factors can influence and multiply risk factors present in both the family system and the individual (Bronfenbrenner 1979). To best prevent child maltreatment, any strategy must address the multifaceted nature of risk, addressing risk factors across all levels of social ecology (Klicka, Lee, and Lee 2018).

Protective factors for child maltreatment

Protective factors are conditions or attributes (skills, strengths, resources, supports, or coping strategies) in individuals, families, communities, or the larger society that help people to deal more effectively with stressful events and mitigate or eliminate risk of child maltreatment in families and communities. Some moderate the effects of various risk factors such as intimate partner violence (IPV) and depression (Ridings, Beasley, and Silovsky 2016) as a "counterweight" in that they buffer the impact of their effects such as toxic stress (U.S. Children's Bureau 2019).

There are many approaches in development and use by various agencies, programs, and practitioners that incorporate protective factors in their efforts to prevent child abuse and neglect and promote child well-being. While some approaches are more grounded in research than others, there is no single "right way" to categorize protective factors (Table 1). For example, the Center for the

TABLE 1
Various Approaches to Protective Factors

1) Strengthening Families (CSSP):
- Concrete Supports in Times of Need
- Knowledge of Parenting and Child Development
- Parental Resilience
- Social Connections
- Social and Emotional Competency of Children

2) The ACYF Protective Factors:
- Caring Adults
- Positive Peers
- Positive Community
- Positive School Environment
- Economic Opportunities
- Self-Regulation
- Relational Skills
- Problem-Solving Skills
- Involvement in Positive Activities
- Parenting Competencies

3) The Essentials for Childhood:
- Promote the community norm that we all share responsibility for the well-being of children
- Raise awareness and commitment to support safe, stable, nurturing relationships and environments
- Create the context for healthy children and families through norms change and programs
- Create the context for healthy children and families through policies

SOURCE: CSSP (2020); ACYF Protective Factors: https://www.childwelfare.gov/topics/preven ting/?hasBeenRedirected=1; Essentials for Childhood: http://www.cdc.gov/violenceprevention/ childmaltreatment/essentials.html.

Study of Social Policy (CSSP) developed Strengthening Families™ and Youth Thrive™. Essentials for Childhood is an approach that the Centers for Disease Control and Prevention (CDC) developed. The Administration on Children, Youth and Families (ACYF), Administration for Children and Families, U.S. Department of Health and Human Services (HHS) is currently working on an approach that identifies protective factors specifically relevant to the populations that ACYF serves (Child Welfare Information Gateway 2020). However, protective factors that promote resilience among children and families, despite profound adversities, remain incompletely studied.

Various Approaches to Protective Factors

Protective factors fall along the lines of both intrapersonal and sociological factors (Ridings, Beasley, and Silovsky 2016), with one of the most profound protective factors being individual resilience. Resilience can be defined as an intrapersonal characteristic, such as perseverance or self-reliance, that allows an individual to adapt in the face of adversity (Tlapek et al. 2017). Higher resiliency is associated with fewer depression symptoms, fewer post-traumatic stress disorder symptoms, and lower rates of revictimization (Tlapek et al. 2017). Other intrapersonal protective factors include higher level of self-regulation as well as individual child temperament, with easier temperaments being associated with higher levels of receiving nurturance (Font, Sattler, and Gershoff 2018). According to the *Strong and Thriving Families Resource Guide*, the Youth Thrive Protective and Promotive Factors include youth resilience, social connections, knowledge of adolescent development, concrete support in times of need as well as cognitive and social emotional competence in youth.

Protective factors also exist at the family level and can be defined as sensitive and stimulating caregiving behaviors, cognitive stimulation, and emotional support (Font, Sattler, and Gershoff 2018). To provide these positive experiences to children, families need to have their basic needs met, and have the sorts of social supports that encourage positive parenting techniques irrespective of stressful situations (Tlapek et al. 2017). According to the *Strong and Thriving Families Resource Guide*, the Strengthening Families Protective Factors include parental resilience, social connections, knowledge of parenting and child development, concrete support in times of need, and social emotional competence of children.

At the community and systems levels, protective factors are often tied to neighborhood socioeconomic status (SES). With child maltreatment rates, neighborhood effects have been consistently reported (Coulton et al. 2018), with low neighborhood SES being associated with higher levels of abusive head trauma (AHT) and neglect (Coulton et al. 2018). Indeed, in many countries, health and injury-related outcomes proportionately improve as people's social status increases (Orpana and Lemyre 2004). Safety net systems can also have a major impact on children's risk of exposure to child abuse and neglect by influencing family income (Cancian, Slack, and Yang 2010; Slack, Lee, and Berger 2007). For example, increased child support payments are linked to a reduced risk for child maltreatment (Cancian, Slack, and Yang 2010), whereas reducing public welfare benefits has been associated with increased CPS reports (Slack, Lee, and Berger 2007). At the macro level, public policies, such as those associated with Earned Income Tax Credit (EITC), have the possibility of reducing the stressors associated with financial insecurity that provides parents with more psychological "room" to engage in the types of nurturing and positive parenting behaviors that link to positive outcomes for children (Arno et al. 2009). And access to safe, affordable housing, and high-quality childcare are associated with less child abuse and neglect (Runyan 2018).

Attempts to explicitly measure the effects of protective factors on child abuse and neglect are, however, still needed. Recently, a team of researchers generated items informed by the literature on child maltreatment protective factors. Sprague-Jones and colleagues (2019) conducted focus groups with caregivers and practitioners to review these items, and then fielded revised items using survey panel data from caregivers and practitioners. They conducted exploratory factor analyses of these panel data, finding a five-factor solution for protective factors, consisting of family functioning and resilience, nurturing and attachment, social supports, and concrete supports. A fifth factor emerged, consisting of items intended to capture social supports. Their findings were, in turn, used to develop the Protective Factors Survey, 2nd edition.

Prevention of child maltreatment requires programs to systematically and comprehensively address multiple risk and protective factors, including the family and community (Herrenkohl, Kim, and Anderson 2018). While we recommend that future research target multiple levels of influence on maltreatment, so too should policy-makers address the implications of multiple system interactions. While ensuring the safety of children is paramount, policies can help to strengthen communities to support families and to reduce prevalence of child maltreatment (Coulton et al. 2018; Feely et al., this volume). Community social support, which may include neighborhood characteristics and resources as well as system factors, appears to be an especially important protective factor that warrants further research to identify mechanisms for building this capacity to decrease child maltreatment risk. A more collaborative cross-systems approach will enable a more comprehensive response to children who have experienced maltreatment. States and communities need to invest in efforts to more fully understand the size, scope, and extent of the needs and issues that families that are involved in multiple systems in their jurisdictions face, as these factors may vary depending on geographic locations and neighborhood characteristics.

Programs/Models That Leverage Family and Community Strengths to Prevent Child Maltreatment

Health care–based programs/models

Empirical evidence demonstrates that community- and neighborhood-based prevention methods are effective at reducing a variety of harms to children, including serious physical abuse and AHT. Health care providers were early advocates for identifying and responding to child abuse and neglect through prevention strategies delivered in health care settings (Palusci 2017). These interventions tend to begin at birth and are provided in community and medical settings rather than by child welfare systems, which can be stigmatizing (Helfer 1987; Dias et al. 2005; Showers 2001; Merritt, this volume; Molnar et al. 2016; van Dijken, Stams, and de Winter 2016; Muñoz, Olmos, and García 2018). Health care–based approaches emphasize protective factors (in addition to risk factors) and are multigenerational, teaching family planning and diverse parenting skills in the prenatal and postnatal period. Roygardner, Hughes, and Palusci (forthcoming) highlight promising strategies such as health-based education programs, and efforts to increase professional awareness, to enhance case management, and implement wider training delivery.

Early health-based strategies focused on providing parents with tools for appropriately responding to infant crying. Lopes and colleagues (2016) provide a comprehensive review of 20 AHT initiatives—five initiatives with the main objective of reducing infant crying in the first months of life, three aimed at caregiver emotional regulation and twelve aimed at raising parents' and caregivers' awareness of infant crying behavior at the time of the child's birth. Among them, parental education about infant crying and risks of shaking a baby stands out for its empirical evidence. Stolz and colleagues (2017), for example, found that Shaken Baby Syndrome training provided in both the home and hospital setting was effective and well received among parents. Dias et al. (2005) created a hospital-based prevention program where medical staff were asked to provide mothers and fathers information describing the dangers of infant shaking, including alternative parenting strategies. A rigorous evaluation showed that the incidence of child maltreatment after the introduction of the prevention program decreased by 47 percent. The program has since been replicated and further evaluated (Altman et al. 2011; Kelly et al. 2016; Palusci et al. 2006). Kelly et al. (2016) found that 85 percent of respondents remembered one key message from the intervention and that 92 percent made a plan of what to do when frustrated. Palusci et al. (2006) found a 25 percent reduction in AHT cases in their hospital in Michigan after they provided the program to 15,850 families. However, other replications failed to show the same results as these earlier studies. In response, Leventhal, Asnes, and Bechtel (2017) suggest that the postpartum timing for delivering interventions may not be ideal and may not reach the intended audience; they offer recommendations such as providing multiple sources for the intervention, focusing on parents' feelings rather than infant behaviors, combining them with other types of interventions and population approaches such as home visiting and targeting male caregivers.

Integrating some of these recommendations, Barr and colleagues created Period of Purple Crying® for families with infants (Barr et al. 2009; Reese et al. 2014). The intervention was associated with statistically significant improvements in knowledge and self-reports of "walking away" when a child is inconsolable. A replication in Japan showed knowledge scores that were significantly higher in the intervention group and self-reported walking away behavior that was significantly higher in the intervention group (Fujiwara et al. 2012).

Beyond the newborn period, health-based strategies focus on using pediatric primary care visits to support families in engaging in positive parenting behaviors (Kairys 2020). The Medical Home (or Patient or Family Centered Medical Home) model, for example, aims to provide comprehensive primary care that facilitates partnerships among patients, clinicians, medical staff, and families (Medical Home Initiatives for Children With Special Needs Project Advisory Committee 2002). Specifically, health care providers are tasked with family focused and child-centered care using practices that promote their patients having a relationship with a personal physician, and with a practice-based care team that takes collective responsibility for the patient's ongoing care. Care is coordinated across settings and disciplines with enhanced access and communication. The medical home provides the majority of the care but also works collaboratively with other providers in the community. Numerous reports have documented improvements in quality and efficiency when patients have a usual source of care through a primary care practice. This can be achieved through changes in workflow, health care delivery design, and professional education of practitioners.

Groups for children and parenting programs sponsored by health care institutions have also showed promise for child maltreatment reductions (Palusci, Bliss, and Crum 2007; Palusci et al. 2008). For example, SEEK (Safe Environment for Every Kid) is an intervention to identify and address prevalent psychosocial risk factors for child maltreatment (Dubowitz et al. 2012). The model offers health care providers a small group training conducted by an interdisciplinary team of pediatricians, social workers, and psychologists. The training focuses on the impact of parental risk factors (parental depression, substance use, major stress, and intimate partner violence) on children's health, development, and safety; how to briefly assess for such factors; and how to initially address them, including principles of motivational interviewing. SEEK has been associated with reduced maternal aggression and minor physical assaults that, while not always reported to CPS, can pose serious potential harm to children (Dubowitz et al. 2012).

Other programs have utilized partnerships between families and health care providers. Donelan-McCall, Eckenrode, and Olds (2009) assert that over the past 20 years, one of the most effective means of preventing child maltreatment has come from health services and parenting education within the home setting through high-quality home visiting. Several programs have shown empirical promise, including the Nurse Family Partnership and Healthy Families America (Donelan-McCall, Eckenrode, and Olds 2009). Unfortunately, while there is a large and growing body of research regarding the wider array of home-visiting programs, research has found few reductions in abuse and CPS reports (Donelan-McCall, Eckenrode, and Olds 2009; DuMont et al. 2010).

Beyond health care providers and pediatric practices, health care institutions also have a potential role in addressing the social conditions contributing to child maltreatment by serving as community centers for social programs and professional hubs for a public health approach to child maltreatment prevention that does not stigmatize families for participating (Herrenkohl, Leeb, and Higgins 2016). Given that public health has the goal of protecting and improving the health of people and their communities, steps should be taken to promote healthy lifestyles and protective factors to reduce child maltreatment. In the public health model, professionals try to prevent problems from happening or recurring through implementing educational programs, recommending policies, administering services, and conducting research. A large part of public health is promoting health care equity, quality, and accessibility. For example, Kelleher, Reece, and Sandel (2018) evaluated a case study of a hospital treating its adjacent impoverished neighborhood as a "patient" to address social determinants of health. Community partners assessed and treated the community with a multifaceted housing intervention, accelerating neighborhood development after 80 years of redlining and institutional racism. Although the long-term child benefits remain uncertain, prior experience suggests the potential to decrease child maltreatment.

Community-based programs/models

Community-based models consider individual-family behavior as embedded within broader neighborhood, community, and cultural contexts (Bronfenbrenner and Morris 2006). Taking this broad view, the U.S. Centers for Disease Control and Prevention (Fortson et al. 2016) recommends forming community-level strategies to modify negative influences and change cultural norms regarding the prenatal, perinatal, and postnatal periods, and to address the social and economic contexts.

How parents interact with children is a function of not only their own formative experiences and levels of preparation for parenting, but also how well they are supported by their surrounding environments (Herrenkohl, Kim, and Anderson 2018). Depending on their composition and quality, neighborhoods can either foster children's healthy development or place them at significant risk for physical, psychological, or developmental harm (Daro and Dodge 2009). Research reviewing prevention programs targeting neighborhood processes has found strong theoretical evidence to indicate that activities aimed at changing contexts surrounding the family, including neighborhood and schools, are necessary for stable behavior change; in other words, strong communities prevent child maltreatment (van Dijken, Stams, and de Winter 2016). Factors such as community stability, number of adults per child, concentrated disadvantage, and density have been associated with child maltreatment, and protective factors, such as reciprocal exchange, collective efficacy, intergenerational closure, and high social networks, have been associated with lower proportions of abuse and neglect (Molnar et al. 2016).

Research has also identified important aspects for community-based programming: (1) the diversity of social support needs of at-risk families and their association with child endangerment, (2) the need to supplement the emotionally affirmative aspects of social support with efforts to socialize parenting practices and monitor child well-being, (3) the desirability of integrating formal and informal sources of social support for recipients, and (4) the importance of considering complex recipient reactions to receiving support from others (Thompson 2015).

Given strong and consistent associations of both individual and neighborhood economic disadvantage with child maltreatment (Gustavsson and MacEachron 2010), community-based economic programming and macro-level economic support policies may be particularly important (Cancian, Slack, and Yang 2010; Klevens et al. 2016, 2017; National Research Council 1993; Raissian and Bullinger 2017; Runyan 2018; Slack, Lee, and Berger 2007).

Strategies/Frameworks That Leverage Family and Community Strengths to Prevent Child Maltreatment

In contrast to models/programs of child maltreatment prevention, we now look to the larger, more general considerations that different strategies/frameworks for child maltreatment prevention propose. We argue for considering *Prevention Zones* as the premier community-based strategy for child maltreatment prevention, but also that we must consider it in conjunction with, or as modified by, key aspects of design and implementation of primary prevention-focused strategies/frameworks. Our preferred modifying strategy is articulated by the *Strong and Thriving Families Resource Guide*.[4]

Prevention Zones

The *Prevention Zones* approach was first recommended in the 1993 U.S. Advisory Board on Child Abuse and Neglect report, which emphasized that neighborhoods with higher levels of child maltreatment had multiple levels of fragmentation, including isolation and perceived low desirability for residence (Roygardner, Palusci, and Hughes 2019). The U.S. Advisory Board recommended implementing *Prevention Zones* where diverse population makeup and density is met with enhanced law enforcement, development efforts, social services, employment, and social and emotional supports for families (U.S. Advisory Board on Child Abuse and Neglect 1993).

We prioritize the *Prevention Zones* framework because the model is oriented toward reducing abuse and neglect, is nonmanualized (to allow for community flexibility in design and implementation), effectively integrates medical and community models, and is grounded in empirical evidence. Effective implementation of the framework should include (1) the identification of key stakeholders in the community, to communicate with families; (2) public education in neighborhoods on child maltreatment and positive parenting; (3) implementation of healthy-family activities including in home health assessments, financial literacy, community babysitting, and volunteer play groups; and (4) institutionalizing sustainability practices by developing steering and strategic innovations committees (Roygardner, Palusci, and Hughes 2019). Active ingredients should focus on addressing the family and community contexts in which maltreatment occurs, the stimulation of supportive community relationships, flexibility of implementation, and the use of assets already present within the community (Kimbrough-Melton and Melton 2015).

Strong and Thriving Families Resource Guide

While the *Prevention Zones* framework is strengths-focused, implementation is guided by building strengths in areas where there are higher levels of risk factors for child maltreatment. As an example of this intentionality, the framework was designed to allow programs to be implemented to take advantage of community block grants. In this way, the *Prevention Zones* framework is organized as a secondary level approach to prevention—one that is more targeted toward groups/locations that exhibit identifiable risk factors for child maltreatment.

The *Prevention Zones* framework is explicitly committed to building community and family strengths and resilience, and, in the almost 30 years since its conception, research has demonstrated the efficiency and effectiveness of more universal approaches to prevention. As outcomes for children, families, and neighborhoods begin to improve, fewer and fewer specialized targeted program approaches are necessary. Therefore, we recommend also adopting a solid theoretical approach to primary prevention in order to facilitate a smooth transition into primary prevention level programming: the *Strong and Thriving Families Resource Guide*, which includes both *Youth Thrive Protective and Promotive Factors* and the *Strengthening Families Protective Factors*.

The *Strong and Thriving Families Resource Guide* is a strength-based approach focused on promoting protective capacities (at the individual level) and protective factors (at the individual, family, and community levels) to increase child safety and family well-being. It also incorporates crucial issues of social oppression and policy consequences for disadvantaged and oppressed groups, including youth and families of color, LGBTQ+ youth and families, and pregnant youth and young mothers.

Strong Communities for Children (Kimbrough-Melton and Melton 2015)[5] is an informative contemporary example of a program that could fit the guidelines of both the *Prevention Zones* framework and the *Strong and Thriving Families Resource Guide*. The initiative was implemented in the early 2000s in a region spanning urban, suburban, and rural South Carolina, with the goal of changing community norms by organizing communities to "keep kids safe" and support "strong families" through promoting mutual assistance among families. The program intended to change community norms toward parenting and to encourage parents to believe they can improve theirs and other parent's quality of life. *Strong Communities* was not tied to a particular set of techniques but rather, drew on a set of principles, including (1) integrating support in settings where children and families are naturally found, (2) strengthening community norms for protecting children, (3) mobilizing community residents and leaders to become involved, (4) strengthening organizational capacity in primary community institutions, (5) assisting parents, and (6) providing support to children and families in a nonstigmatizing manner (McDonnel, Ben-Arieh, and Melton 2015). Implementation includes the phases of spreading the word, mobilizing the community, increasing resources for families, and institutionalizing resources (Kimbrough-Melton and Melton 2015). In terms of what this looked like in practice and on the ground, *Strong Communities* used a three-pronged entry approach toward enrolling and interfacing with families. The aim was for all families that had children under the age of six to have access to someone who would "watch out for them" (Melton and McLeigh 2020).

The first point of entry included a nurse employed by *Strong Communities* to engage pediatric and obstetric physicians to enroll families and to provide anticipatory guidance to expectant moms and infants (Melton and McLeigh 2020). Physicians were also provided with the opportunity to contact a family advocate for home- and community-based supports to parents (Melton and McLeigh 2020). Over the course of the initiative, *Strong Communities* employed twelve outreach workers with diverse professional experiences (McLeigh et al. 2020). Each community was assigned an outreach worker with the task of mobilizing the community to provide direct and indirect support to families with young children (McLeigh et al. 2020).

The second point of entry was in partnership with local schools that enrolled four- to five-year-olds to receive home visits, offer parent child activities, provide mental health support, and provide informal support that helps families to get information about organizations and activities in the community (Melton and McLeigh 2020).

The third point of entry was community organizations, which included such diverse institutions as fire departments, churches, law enforcement agencies, and apartment complexes, to enroll families (Melton and McLeigh 2020). Organizations also worked with outreach workers to develop Family Activity Centers (FACs), which included play groups, parent-child activities, childcare, financial education, counseling, and chat time with family advocates (McLeigh et al. 2020). FACs also developed their own councils comprising individuals from diverse professional backgrounds who had interest in child safety; one such council activity included the revitalization of an underutilized building that had been an active community center (McLeigh et al. 2020). More than three thousand families participated (defined as being enrolled through the three points of entry listed above) in *Strong Communities* between 2002 and 2008, and thirteen hundred activities occurred from 2006 to 2008. Empirical results showed that *Strong Communities* samples showed significant changes in social support, collective efficacy, child safety, and parental stress; and showed lower rates of substantiated child maltreatment (McDonnell, Ben-Arieh, and Melton 2015), even when controlling for socioeconomic status differences. The initiative was evaluated via a rigorous randomized control trial, which indicated that the program produced statistically significant decreases in child abuse and neglect reports and in childhood injuries (assessed via ICD-9 codes) of substantial magnitude.

Prevention Zones and *Strong and Thriving Families Resource Guide*: From Strategy to Implementation

By adopting the strategies of child maltreatment prevention articulated in *Prevention Zones* and the *Strong and Thriving Families Resource Guide*, the integrated strategy is targeted, yet universal, allowing us to increase our focus on leveraging strengths and building resilience without sacrificing our focus on specialized interventions. Our review suggests that promising models of effective, health-based and community-based prevention initiatives could be integrated into place-based *Prevention Zones*, leading to a universal, comprehensive, community-level approach that leverages local strengths and resources to prevent child maltreatment (Roygardner, Palusci, and Hughes 2019). This public health–oriented strategy (Dias, Mooren, and Kleiber 2018; Herrenkohl, Leeb, and Higgins 2016; Kelleher, Reece, and Sandel 2018; Fortson et al. 2016) tasks community members to move beyond mere reporting to CPS and, instead, to engage in explicit actions to prevent maltreatment through a coordinated, multidisciplinary infrastructure of evidence-based primary prevention interventions for reducing risk factors and enhancing protective factors before maltreatment occurs (Palusci and

Vandervort 2014; Herrenkohl, Leeb, and Higgins 2016). This infrastructure integrates social service, legal, law enforcement, health, mental health, and education systems in a collaborative approach to promoting child safety by addressing risk factors in their domain and connecting families to other systems to address those outside of their domain. As such, the success of any specific application of the *Prevention Zones* strategy/framework is likely to heavily depend on the extent to which a community is successful in (1) service integration; (2) providing comprehensive services addressing a range of risk factors; and (3) facilitating adoption of protective social attitudes, behaviors, and networks (Institute of Medicine and National Research Council 1998, 260).[6]

Theoretically, if implemented successfully, this targeted, yet universal, approach is a unique strategy for child maltreatment prevention in that it allows for the development of universalized goals or values (as are articulated through strategies), and also for adherence to a more secondary level, targeted application by choosing communities for participation based also on identified risks. The elements articulated by both *Prevention Zones* and *Strong and Thriving Families Resource Guide* overlap and allow for dual layers of prevention to be implemented simultaneously.[7]

Some proponents of adopting a strictly universal strategy to child maltreatment prevention may question our position that universal approaches show promise as the most effective type of prevention strategy, while at the same time, we recommend that targeted approaches be adopted. There are several reasons for focusing on targeted services—at least initially, with the goal to transition to more primary prevention programs eventually. First, current research shows our understanding of intergenerational child maltreatment to be more nuanced than previously thought. While not all parents who were victimized end up being perpetrators themselves, research shows that if a parent experiences maltreatment as a child, it is more likely that they will have children who are also exposed to abuse or neglect, regardless of whether the parent is the eventual perpetrator (Child Welfare Information Gateway 2016a). Given this higher risk, targeted prevention remains an important stopgap for reducing intergenerational maltreatment.

Second, certain populations may need targeted services, because they are unable to take full advantage of universal services. Consider a hypothetical situation of Jessica and Sybil. Jessica is a young, single white mother who lives in an impoverished, dilapidated suburban neighborhood. Sybil is a young, single Black mother who lives in an urban neighborhood. Both mothers work and need childcare, and paying for it themselves is not an option. To remedy the problem, a universal program providing free childcare to mothers is implemented statewide. However, due to their locations relative to the childcare centers, to make use of this program, Sybil also needs safe and reliable transportation to and from the childcare center. Without it, she will not be able to take advantage of the service, and her situation will not improve. Jessica, on the other hand, lives close to a center, and even without a car, she could safely walk back and forth between the center and her home. She takes advantage of the services, and her situation improves. This hypothetical illustrates two of the potential problems that could arise if we are to focus only on universal services. First, due to factors not inherent in the program design, needed, effectual services might not always be accessible or useful for the entire population. Second, if services are not having an expected effect on a particular group, this can lead to unfair stereotyping of a particular group as not worthy as a focus of prevention efforts. Finally, while there is growing evidence suggesting less targeted community-based approaches to child maltreatment prevention merit consideration, research has yet to establish that such approaches will reduce maltreatment with certainty (van Dijken, Stams, and de Winter 2016). Of critical note is that both risk and protective factors can be understood as mediators of success in the measurement and evaluation of our proposed framework; specifically, we hypothesize that programming will increase protective factors (i.e., community- and health-based programming, effective mental health programs) and will promote positive outcomes not through eradicating risk factors altogether, but by providing a counterbalance to risk factors that promote child safety.

Considering this last point, it is also important to recognize that whereas *Prevention Zones* is intended to prevent maltreatment and, therefore, subsequent CPS involvement, it is not a substitute for CPS itself. Indeed, reporting and investigation will still be necessary for families that potentially cross the legal threshold for abuse or neglect, despite having access to a broad array of community prevention services. Courts will still be needed to adjudicate the most serious offenses (Palusci, Hicks, and Vandervort 2001). However, in the *Prevention Zones* framework, CPS agencies would coordinate closely with the prevention network to ensure that families who come to their attention also receive any necessary social and economic supports.

As such, the overall service-delivery structure for child and family services writ large could be twofold, much resembling the structure of the current system of health care in the United States. In the health care system, the emergency room and primary care practice are two integral, yet programmatically separate, services. They share the same vision: to ensure the health and well-being of the populations they serve. At the same time, each has a specific mission and distinct sets of goals, responsibilities, and processes. The emergency room provides urgent and critical treatment in the midst of a health crisis; it is not meant to be a person's primary, or even secondary, option to ensure their long-term health. Primary care, on the other hand, exists to help prevent, diagnose, and treat illnesses and support individuals in achieving and sustaining long-term health. Although comprising separate programs serving distinct purposes, the two interact frequently and engender a high level of codependency. For example, primary care likely helps to reduce need for emergency care, whereas emergency rooms triage care and resources to patients who are in greatest crisis and refer nonacute patients to primary care. Similar to health care, child maltreatment prevention and treatment is appropriately approached from programmatically separate, yet unified, systems. Like emergency and primary care in the medical sphere, child maltreatment prevention and CPS would be complementary, yet distinct, parts of a larger system with a unified underlying mandate—to ensure safety, permanency, and well-being for children.

If we were to build a system based on this health care system analogy, one potential future avenue of inquiry would be the intake process, or the mechanisms for screening in and screening out reports of potential abuse or neglect. In most jurisdictions in the United States, reports are received by an individual or department with the job of screening in or screening out reports based on potential for abuse. To develop an effective child maltreatment prevention system, researchers and policy-makers might consider how the intake process and the screening process could be designed to accurately direct children and families to the services they need. One potential avenue for exploration could be the development and coordination of multitiered screening tools to assess risks and protective factors related to the community, the family, and the child.

Successful implementation of any prevention strategy/framework, including *Prevention Zones* and the *Strong and Thriving Families Resource Guide*, will also require careful balancing of prevention and CPS funding allocations (Klicka, Lee, and Lee 2018). As Haskins (this volume) and Testa and Kelly (this volume) discuss in detail, the Family First Prevention and Services Act of 2018 has provided new funding streams that can be earmarked specifically for evidence-based prevention services. We caution, however, that it is also crucial that adequate funding be provided for CPS as failing to do so could have devastating consequences for some of the most vulnerable children. Thus, it remains important to advocate for adequate funding of both child protection and maltreatment prevention programming, and to avoid placing child welfare system program dollars in competition with prevention dollars (Klicka, Lee, and Lee 2018; McGowan and Walsh 2000).

Advocates and policy-makers should also consider less conventional sources for child maltreatment prevention funding. With the current political and social unrest over the treatment of Black Americans by law enforcement across the country, protesters and reformers have echoed calls to "defund the police" and to reallocate funds to social welfare programs and policies that would help to rectify inequalities and injustices experienced by Black Americans resulting from years of exploitation and systematic racism. Should this occur, though, it is imperative that child maltreatment stakeholders both be part of the discussion for developing new programs and to ensure that child maltreatment programs are considered eligible to receive reallocated funding.

Finally, on a related note, any effort to reform or develop policy that requires making recommendations related to social welfare also carries with it the obligation to explicitly consider the potential influence of, and influence on, systemic racism (see Dettlaff and Boyd, this volume). The systems, strategies, programs, and research—even the stories that we tell about child maltreatment—are largely biased toward the experiences and benefits of white America (Child Welfare Information Gateway 2016b; Smedley and Smedley 2005). During the decision-making processes in child maltreatment policy, this perspective bias has helped to create and perpetuate systemic discrimination, which is a major factor contributing to the disparate representation of Black children in the child maltreatment system (Hill 2004). As discussed earlier with the hypothetical situation of Jessica and Sybil, white bias could lead to programs that fail to adequately address the needs of individuals who are situated differently, eventually culminating in negative group stereotyping, implicit bias, and, cyclically, more systemic racism. If child maltreatment policy-makers adopt strategies that communicate universal goals or values as well as a targeted approach to implementation, not only will their efforts be effective, it may help to ensure that policies do not have the unintended effect of creating or reinforcing systemic racism. Ultimately, this type of "targeted universalism," which is also reflected in our recommendation for a mixed or dual application of *Prevention Zones* and *Strong and Thriving Families Resource Guide*, has the potential to aid our country in building a stronger sense of community belonging, responsibility, and pride, by reinforcing that we are all a part of the same social fabric (powell, Menendian, and Ake 2019).

Notes

1. For ease of reference, we refer to this strategy as *Prevention Zones* for the remainder of the article.

2. Hereafter referred to as *Strong and Thriving Families Resource Guide*.

3. The original conceptualization of the levels of prevention was proposed by Caplan in 1964. He laid out three different levels: primary, secondary, and tertiary (Caplan 1964). Decades later, Gordon (1983) laid out another set of terminology, also with three levels, including universal prevention, selective prevention, and indicated prevention (Gordon 1983).

4. There are other quality strategies/frameworks with similarly structured design and implementation, including Essentials for Childhood (Centers for Disease Control and Prevention 2019) and Strengthening Families (Center for Study of Social Policy 2020). Our focus on the *Strong and Thriving Families Resource Guide* is, in large part, due to the successful related *Strong Communities for Children* program, also discussed in this article (McDonell, Ben-Arieh, and Melton 2015).

5. Hereafter referred to as *Strong Communities*.

6. Several organizations and agencies have developed resource guides and technical packages to assist organizations and communities in implementing such strategies. These include the CDC's *Essentials for Childhood Framework*; the Children's Bureau's *Building Communities, Building Hope*; and the Center for the Study of Social Policy's *Strengthening Families Framework* (Klicka, Lee, and Lee 2018).

7. It also could allow them to be implemented without distinction, which may have implications for how services are perceived by individuals receiving them.

References

Altman, Robin L., Jennifer Canter, Patricia A. Patrick, Nancy Daley, Neelofar K. Butt, and Donald A. Brand. 2011. Parent education by maternity nurses and prevention of abusive head trauma. *Pediatrics* 128 (5): 1164–72.

Arno, Peter S., Nancy Sohler, Deborah Viola, and Clyde Schechter. 2009. Bringing health and social policy together: The case of the earned income tax credit. *Journal of Public Health Policy* 30 (2): 198–207.

Barr, Ronald G., Marilyn Barr, Takeo Fujiwara, Jocelyn Conway, Nicole Catherine, and Rollin Brant. 2009. Do educational materials change knowledge and behaviour about crying and shaken baby syndrome? A randomized controlled trial. *Canadian Medical Association Journal* 180 (7): 727–33.

Berthelot, Nicolas, Roxanne Lemieux, and Michel Maziade. 2019. Shortfall of intervention research over correlational research in childhood maltreatment: An impasse to be overcome. *JAMA Pediatrics* 173 (11): 1009–10.

Brofenbrenner, Urie. 1979. *The ecology of human development: Experiments by nature and design*. Cambridge, MA: Harvard University Press.

Bronfenbrenner, Urie, and Pamela A. Morris. 2006. The bioecological model of human development. In *Handbook of child psychology*, vol. 1: *Theoretical models of human development*, ed. Richard M. Lerner, 793–828. Hoboken, NJ: Wiley.

Cancian, Maria, Kristen S. Slack, and Mi Youn Yang. 2010. *The effect of family income on risk of child maltreatment*. Madison, WI: Institute for Research on Poverty, University of Wisconsin–Madison.

Caplan, Gerald. 1964. *Principles of preventive psychiatry*. New York, NY: Basic Books.

Center for Study of Social Policy. 2020. Strengthening families. Washington, DC: Center for Study of Social Policy. Available from https://cssp.org/our-work/project/strengthening-families.

Centers for Disease Control and Prevention. 2019. *Essentials for childhood: Creating safe, stable, nurturing relationships and environments for all children*. Washington, DC: Centers for Disease Control and Prevention. Available from https://www.cdc.gov/violenceprevention/pdf/essentials-for-childhood-framework508.pdf.

Child Welfare Information Gateway. 2016a. *Intergenerational patterns of child maltreatment: What the evidence shows*. Washington, DC: U.S. Department of Health and Human Services, Children's Bureau. Available from https://www.childwelfare.gov/pubs/issue-briefs/intergenerational.

Child Welfare Information Gateway. 2016b. *Racial disproportionality and disparity in child welfare*. Washington, DC: U.S. Department of Health and Human Services, Children's Bureau. Available from https://www.childwelfare.gov/pubs/issue-briefs/racial-disproportionality.

Child Welfare Information Gateway. 2020. *Protective factors approaches in child welfare*. Washington, DC: U.S. Department of Health and Human Services, Children's Bureau. Available from https://www.childwelfare.gov/pubs/issue-briefs/protective-factors/.

Coulton, Claudia J., Francisca G. Richter, Jill Korbin, David Crampton, and James C. Spilsbury. 2018. Understanding trends in neighborhood child maltreatment rates: A three-wave panel study 1990–2010. *Child Abuse and Neglect* 84:170–81.

Daro, Deborah, and Kenneth A. Dodge. 2009. Creating community responsibility for child protection: Possibilities and challenges. *The Future of Children* 19 (2): 67–93.

Dettlaff, Alan J., and Reiko Boyd. 2021. Racial disproportionality and disparities in the child welfare system: Why do they exist, and what can be done to address them? *The ANNALS of the American Academy of Political and Social Science* (this volume).

Dias, Aida, Trudy Mooren, and Rolf J. Kleber. 2018. Public health actions to mitigate long-term consequences of child maltreatment. *Journal of Public Health Policy* 39 (3): 294–303.

Dias, Mark S., Kim Smith, Kathy DeGuehery, Paula Mazur, Veetai Li, and Michele L. Shaffer. 2005. Preventing abusive head trauma among infants and young children: A hospital-based, parent education program. *Pediatrics* 115 (4): 470–77.

Donelan-McCall, Nancy, John Eckenrode, and David L. Olds. 2009. Home visiting for the prevention of child maltreatment: Lessons learned during the past 20 years. *Pediatric Clinics of North America* 56 (2): 389–403.

Dubowitz, Howard, Wendy G. Lane, Joshua N. Semiatin, and Laurence S. Magder. 2012. The SEEK model of pediatric primary care: Can child maltreatment be prevented in a low-risk population? *Academic Pediatrics* 12 (4): 259–68.

DuMont, Kimberly, Kristen Kirkland, Susan Mitchell-Herzfeld, Susan Ehrhard-Dietzel, Monica L. Rodriguez, Eunju Lee, China Layne, and Rose Greene. 2010. *A randomized trial of Healthy Families New York (HFNY): Does home visiting prevent child maltreatment?* Washington, DC: National Institute of Justice.

Emery, Clifton R., Hai Nguyen N. Trung, and Shali Wu. 2015. Neighborhood informal social control and child maltreatment: A comparison of protective and punitive approaches. *Child Abuse and Neglect* 41:158–69.

Feely, Megan, Kerri M. Raissian, William Schneider, and Lindsey Rose Bullinger. 2021. The social welfare policy landscape and child protective services: Opportunities for and barriers to creating systems synergy. *The ANNALS of the American Academy of Political and Social Science* (this volume).

Font, Sarah A., and Kathryn Maguire-Jack. 2021. The scope, nature, and causes of child abuse and neglect. *The ANNALS of the American Academy of Political and Social Science* (this volume).

Font, Sarah A., Kierra M. P. Sattler, and Elizabeth T. Gershoff. 2018. Measurement and correlates of foster care placement moves. *Children and Youth Services Review* 91:248–58.

Fortson, Beverly L., Joanne Klevens, Melissa T. Merrick, Leah K. Gilbert, and Sandra P. Alexander. 2016. *Preventing child abuse and neglect: A technical package for policy, norm, and programmatic activities*. Atlanta, GA: National Center for Injury Prevention and Control, Centers for Disease Control and Prevention.

Fujiwara, Takeo, Fujiko Yamada, Makiko Okuyama, Isamu Kamimaki, Nobuaki Shikoro, and Ronald G. Barr. 2012. Effectiveness of educational materials designed to change knowledge and behavior about crying and shaken baby syndrome: A replication of a randomized controlled trial in Japan. *Child Abuse and Neglect* 36 (9): 613–20.

Gordon, Robert 1983. An operational classification of disease prevention. *Public Health Reports* 98:107–9.

Gustavsson, Nora, and Ann E. MacEachron. 2010. Poverty and child welfare, 101 years later. *Social Work* 55 (3): 279–80.

Haskins, Ron. 2021. Child welfare financing: What do we fund, how, and what could be improved? *The ANNALS of the American Academy of Political and Social Science* (this volume).

Helfer, Ray E. 1987. The perinatal period, a window of opportunity for enhancing parent-infant communication: An approach to prevention. *Child Abuse and Neglect* 2:565–79.

Herrenkohl, Todd I., M. Kim, and J. Anderson. 2018. Child maltreatment in the context of poverty and other forms of adversity. In *The APSAC handbook on child maltreatment*, 4th edition, eds. J. Bart Klicka and Jon R. Conte, 34–46. Thousand Oaks, CA: Sage Publications.

Herrenkohl, Todd I., Rebecca T. Leeb, and Daryl Higgins. 2016. The public health model of child maltreatment prevention. *Trauma Violence and Abuse* 17 (4): 363–65.

Hill, Robert B. 2004. Institutional racism in child welfare. *Race and Society* 7 (1): 17–33.

Institute of Medicine and National Research Council. 1998. *Violence in families: Assessing prevention and treatment programs*. Washington, DC: The National Academies Press.

Kairys, Steven 2020. Child abuse and neglect: The role of the primary care pediatrician. *Pediatric Clinics of North America* 67:325–39.

Kelleher, Kelly, Jason Reece, and Megan Sandel. 2018. The healthy neighborhood, healthy families initiative. *Pediatrics* 142 (3): e20180261.

Kelly, Patrick, Kati Wilson, Aqeela Mowjood, Joshua Friedman, and Peter Reed. 2016. Trialing a shaken baby syndrome prevention programme in the Auckland District Health Board. *New Zealand Medical Journal* 129 (1430): 39–50.

Kimbrough-Melton, Robin J., and Gary B. Melton. 2015. "Someone will notice, and someone will care": How to build strong communities for children. *Child Abuse and Neglect* 41:67–78.

Klevens, Joanne, Feijun Luo, Likang Xu, Cora Peterson, and Natasha E. Latzman. 2016. Paid family leave's effect on hospital admissions for pediatric abusive head trauma. *Injury Prevention* 22 (6): 442–45.

Klevens, Joanne, Brian Schmidt, Feijun Luo, Likang Xu, Katie A. Ports, and Rosalyn D. Lee. 2017. Effect of the earned income tax credit on hospital admissions for pediatric abusive head trauma. *Public Health Reports* 132 (4): 505–11.

Klicka, J. Bart, Shawna Lee, and Joyce Y. Lee. 2018. Prevention of child maltreatment. In *The APSAC handbook on child maltreatment*, 4th edition, eds. J. Bart Klicka and Jon R. Conte, 235–51. Thousand Oaks, CA: Sage Publications.

Krugman, Richard D. 1995. Future directions in preventing child abuse. *Child Abuse and Neglect* 19 (3): 273–79.

Leventhal, John M., Andrea G. Asnes, and Kirsten Bechtel. 2017. Prevention of pediatric abusive head trauma: Time to rethink interventions and reframe messages. *JAMA Pediatrics* 171 (3): 218–20.

Levey, Elizabeth J., Bizu Gelaye, Paul Bain, Marta B. Rondon, Christina P. C. Borba, David C. Henderson, and Michelle A. Williams. 2017. A systematic review of randomized controlled trials of interventions designed to decrease child abuse in high-risk families. *Child Abuse and Neglect* 65:48–57.

Lopes, Nahara Rodriguez Laterza and Lúcia Cavalcanti de Albuquerque Williams. 2016. Pediatric abusive head trauma prevention initiatives: A literature review. *Trauma, Violence, & Abuse* 19 (5): 555–66.

McDonell, James R., Asher Ben-Arieh, and Gary B. Melton. 2015. Strong communities for children: Results of a multi-year community-based initiative to protect children from harm. *Child Abuse and Neglect* 41:79–96.

McGowan, Brenda G., and Edith M. Walsh. 2000. Policy challenges for child welfare in the new century. *Child Welfare* 79 (1): 11–27.

McLeigh, Jill D., Paulette Grate, Doris Cole, and Gary B. Melton. 2020. One person can make a differ-ence: Stories of Strong Communities and their outreach workers. *International Journal on Child Maltreatment: Research, Policy, and Practice* 3:177–96.

Medical Home Initiatives for Children With Special Needs Project Advisory Committee. 2002. The Medical Home. *Pediatrics* 110 (1): 184–6.

Melton, Gary, and Jill D. McLeigh. 2020. The nature, logic, and significance of Strong Communities for Children. *International Journal on Child Maltreatment: Research, Policy and Practice* 3:125–61.

Merritt, Darcey. 2021. How do families experience and interact with CPS? *The ANNALS of the American Academy of Political and Social Science* (this volume).

Merritt, Darcey, Kathryn Maguire-Jack, and Tori Negash. 2018. Effective program models for the preven-tion of child maltreatment. In *The APSAC handbook on child maltreatment*, 4th edition, eds. J. Bart Klicka and Jon R. Conte, 252–71. Thousand Oaks, CA: Sage Publications.

Molnar, Beth E., Robert M. Goerge, Paola Gilsanz, Andrea Hill, Subu V. Subramanian, John K. Holton, Dustin T. Duncan, Elizabeth D. Beatriz, and William R. Beardslee. 2016. Neighborhood-level social processes and substantiated cases of child maltreatment. *Child Abuse and Neglect* 51:41–53.

Muñoz, Abigail C., Juan Alan Román Olmos, and Noé González García. 2018. Abusive head trauma and the strategies for its prevention. In *Child abuse: Harm and solutions*, eds. Arthuro Lredo Abdalá, Hugo Juárez-Olguín, and Abigail C. Muñoz, 27–46. New York, NY: Nova Science Publishers.

National Research Council. 1993. *Understanding child abuse and neglect*. Washington, DC: National Academy of Sciences Press.

Orpana, Heather M., and Louise Lemyre. 2004. Explaining the social gradient in health in Canada: Using the National Population Health Survey to examine the role of stressors. *International Journal of Behavioral Medicine* 11 (3): 143–51.

Palusci, Vincent J. 2017. Child protection and the development of child abuse pediatrics in New York City. *Journal of Forensic and Legal Medicine* 52:159–67.

Palusci, Vincent J., Rosalynn Bliss, and Pat Crum. 2007. Outcomes after groups for children exposed to violence with behavior problems. *Trauma and Loss: Research and Interventions* 7 (1): 27–38.

Palusci, Vincent J., Pat Crum, Rosalynn Bliss, and Stephen J. Bavolek. 2008. Changes in parenting atti-tudes and knowledge among inmates and other at-risk populations after a family nurturing program. *Children and Youth Services Review* 30 (1): 79–89.

Palusci, Vincent J., Ralph A. Hicks, and Frank E. Vandervort. 2001. "You are hereby commanded to appear": Pediatrician subpoena and court appearance in child maltreatment. *Pediatrics* 107 (6): 1427–30.

Palusci, Vincent J., and Jessica Perfetto. 2018. An overview of published medical research about child abuse and neglect during 2006–2015. *APSAC Advisor* 31 (1): 12–23.

Palusci, Vincent J., and Frank E. Vandervort. 2014. Universal reporting laws and child maltreatment report rates. *Children and Youth Services Review* 38:20–28.

Palusci, Vincent J., Wilma Zeemering, Rosalynn Bliss, Amy Combs, and Michael A. Stoiko. 2006. Preventing abusive head trauma using a directed parent education program. Paper presented at the Sixth North American Conference on Shaken Baby Syndrome, at the Pediatric Academic Societies Meeting, Atlanta, GA.

Powell, John, Stephen Menendian, and Wendy Ake. 2019. *Targeted universalism: Policy & practice*. Berkeley, CA: Haas Institute for a Fair and Inclusive Society, University of California, Berkeley.

Raissian, Kerri M., and Lindsey Rose Bullinger. 2017. Money matters: Does the minimum wage affect child maltreatment rates? *Children and Youth Services Review* 72 (C): 60–70.

Reese, Laura S., Erin O. Heiden, Kimberly Q. Kim, and Jingzhen Yang. 2014. Evaluation of Period of PURPLE Crying, an abusive head trauma prevention program. *Journal of Obstetric, Gynecologic & Neonatal Nursing* 43 (6): 752–61.

Ridings, Leigh E., Lana O. Beasley, and Jane F. Silovsky. 2016. Consideration of risk and protective factors for families at risk for child maltreatment: An intervention approach. *Journal of Family Violence* 32:179–88.

Roygardner, Debangshu, Kelli N. Hughes, and Vincent J. Palusci. Forthcoming. A structured review of the literature on abusive head trauma prevention. *Child Abuse Review*.

Roygardner, Debangshu, Vincent J. Palusci, and Kelli N. Hughes. 2019. Advancing prevention zones: Implementing community-based strategies to prevent child maltreatment and promote healthy families. *International Journal on Child Maltreatment* 3:81–91. Available from https://doi.org/10.1007/s42448-019-00039-0.

Runyan, Christine N. 2018. Assessing social determinants of health in primary care: Liability or opportunity? *Families, Systems, & Health* 36 (4): 550–52.

Showers, Jacy 2001. Preventing shaken baby syndrome. In *Shaken baby syndrome: A multidisciplinary approach*, eds. S. Lazoritz and V. J. Palusci, 349–65. London: Hayworth Press.

Slack, Kristen, Bong Joo Lee, and Lawrence Berger. 2007. Do welfare sanctions increase child protection system involvement? A cautious answer. *Social Service Review* 81 (2): 207–28.

Smedley, Audrey, and Brian D. Smedley. 2005. Race as biology is fiction, racism as a social problem is real: Anthropological and historical perspectives on the social construction of race. *American Journal of Psychology* 60 (1): 16–26.

Sprague-Jones, Jessica, Jacqueline Counts, Mallory Rousseau, and Casandra Firman. 2019. The Development of the Protective Factors Survey, 2nd edition: A self-report measure of protective factors against child maltreatment. *Child Abuse & Neglect* 89:122–34.

Stolz, Heidi E., Denise J. Brandon, Heather S. Wallace, and Emily A. Tucker. 2017. Preventing shaken baby syndrome: Evaluation of a multiple-setting program. *Journal of Family Issues* 38 (16): 2346–67.

Testa, Mark F., and David Kelly. 2021. The evolution of federal child welfare policy through the Family First Prevention Services Act of 2018: Opportunities, barriers, and unintended consequences. *The ANNALS of the American Academy of Political and Social Science* (this volume).

Thompson, Ross A. 2015. Social support and child protection: Lessons learned and learning. *Child Abuse and Neglect* 41:19–29.

Tlapek, Sarah Meyers, Wendy Auslander, Tonya Edmond, Donald Gerke, Rachel Voth Schrag, and Jennifer Mary Threlfall. 2017. The moderating role of resiliency on the negative effects of childhood abuse for adolescent girls involved in child welfare. *Children and Youth Services Review* 73:437–44.

U.S. Advisory Board on Child Abuse and Neglect. 1991. *Creating caring communities: Blueprint for an effective federal policy on child abuse and neglect*. Washington, DC: Department of Health and Human Services.

U.S. Advisory Board on Child Abuse and Neglect. 1993. *Neighbors helping neighbors: A new national strategy for the protection of children*. Fourth report. Washington, DC: U.S. Department of Health and Human Services.

U.S. Children's Bureau. 2019. *Strong and thriving families: 2019 prevention resource guide*. Washington, DC: Government Printing Office.

U.S. Commission to Eliminate Child Maltreatment Fatalities. 2016. *Within our reach: A national strategy to eliminate child abuse and neglect fatalities*. Washington, DC: U.S. Government Printing Office.

van Dijken, Maartje W., Geert-Jan J. M. Stams, and Micha de Winter. 2016. Can community-based interventions prevent child maltreatment? *Children and Youth Services Review* 61:149–58.

The Social Welfare Policy Landscape and Child Protective Services: Opportunities for and Barriers to Creating Systems Synergy

By
MEGAN FEELY,
KERRI M. RAISSIAN,
WILLIAM SCHNEIDER,
and
LINDSEY ROSE
BULLINGER

Contemporary child welfare policies in the United States are well-suited for prevention of child abuse but fail to account for the relationship between family financial hardship and neglect, that is, the lack of safe and consistent care. We argue that rates of child neglect have been stagnant because of two failures: (1) lack of recognition of financial hardship as a causal mechanism of neglect and (2) federal policy that purposefully omits alleviation of financial hardship as a solution to the occurrence of neglect. Because U.S. antipoverty programs operate independently of one another, our siloed policy structure misses opportunities for the alleviation of child maltreatment and, worse, creates negative and unintended consequences in child welfare. We present a model for change: systems synergy for the promotion of safe and consistent care that makes reduction of child maltreatment the responsibility of every social service program in the United States.

Keywords: systems synergy; financial hardship; neglect; outcomes; safe and consistent care

At a conference in 2019, the keynote speaker shared a story from his early days as a Child Protective Services (CPS) case worker. His experiences are captured below and demonstrate the need for a new model; what we call systems synergy. This is what he shared:

> In the mid-1990s, when I was a young caseworker, I responded to the home of a young family. There I saw dire neglect. A family of five was living in dirty and unsafe conditions. As was recommended by Child Protective Services

Megan Feely is an assistant professor at the University of Connecticut School of Social Work. Her research focuses on child welfare systems and primary and secondary prevention of child maltreatment.

Kerri M. Raissian is an associate professor of public policy at the University of Connecticut. Her research focuses on child and family policy with an emphasis on understanding how policies affect fertility, family formation, and family violence.

Correspondence: kerri.raissian@uconn.edu

DOI: 10.1177/0002716220973566

(CPS), I initiated the process to remove the children from the home. The children were at school, and so I went to school and explained to one of the daughters, Brittany, that she would need to come with me to stay in a new place that was clean and safe.

Brittany did not want to go. She wanted her mother. She was scared of the unknown—even if it was clean and safe. I began to doubt myself: maybe I should have brought her mother along to explain . . . maybe Brittany would be less scared? But parent involvement was not part of CPS "best practice," and so I did not think of this concession until it was too late.

Then I learned the family's home was rented. And a new doubt came to my mind: should I have instead held the landlord responsible for the living conditions? Could I have been an advocate instead of an enforcer?

Finally, I learned of the father's substance abuse illness and his trouble keeping a steady job. I initiated substance abuse treatment, but I was at a loss when it came to employment options for the father. I had followed agency protocols. My work was done, but yet, I've always felt like the system let Brittany and her family down.

The last 30 years have witnessed stark declines in child physical and sexual abuse rates. In contrast, child neglect, which composes 75 percent of child maltreatment reports, has remained steady and high (Finkelhor, Saito, and Jones 2016; U.S. Department of Health and Human Services 2020). Scholars, practitioners, and policy-makers face a conundrum: why are abuse rates declining while neglect rates remain seemingly intractable and high? Although they sometimes overlap, child neglect and child abuse are distinct from one another. Child neglect is an act of omission, or failure to act, that results in imminent harm. In contrast, child abuse is an act of commission—something that is done—that results in real or imminent harm to a child.

Making progress in the child welfare system first requires understanding the origins of current policies and practices. Our current response, which is well-suited for abuse prevention, fails to account for the relationship between financial hardship and neglect. This makes the system unresponsive to the underlying needs of neglect. Since any discussion of child maltreatment in the United States is inherently linked to the Child Abuse Prevention and Treatment Act of 1974 (CAPTA), and because CAPTA serves a number of functions that are important for how the problems of child abuse and neglect are addressed, we review this legislation's history and its role in prevention, and we present a

William Schneider is an assistant professor of social work at the University of Illinois at Urbana-Champaign. His research focuses on the role of social policy, inequality, poverty, and family structure in the risk for child maltreatment and the promotion of child well-being.

Lindsey Rose Bullinger is an assistant professor of public policy at Georgia Tech. Her research examines the role of public policies in child and family health and well-being.

NOTE: All authors contributed equally to this manuscript. The authors are grateful to the organizers of this volume, especially Lonnie Berger and Kristi Shook Slack. We are also grateful to the participants of the 2020 AAPSS *ANNALS* conference. A special thanks to Reggie Bicha for sharing his professional knowledge and experience with us. We thank Will Butler and Hannah Nguyen for careful research assistance. Finally, we thank the Doris Duke Fellowship for the Promotion of Child Well-Being for connecting us to each other, this topic, and inspiring us to form the KIDS research team. Most importantly, we thank the many professionals and scholars dedicated to ending child abuse and neglect.

critique of CAPTA's design. We then explore the issue of child neglect, present a theory of how financial hardship can cause neglect, and discuss what is needed to prevent neglect.

We submit that the immobility of neglect rates has two root causes: (1) our collective failure to view financial hardship as a causal mechanism in neglect's perpetration and (2) our crafting of federal policy to purposefully omit the alleviation of financial hardship as a solution to the occurrence of neglect.

We then present our model for change: systems synergy. The United States has a number of financial hardship alleviation programs and policies, but in their current form no person can fully leverage their effectiveness. These programs operate independently, and this siloed structure has allowed for missed opportunities to significantly reduce financial hardship (and thereby reduce neglect) among low-income families. Furthermore, the siloed approach has also been harmful because it has helped to create negative and unintended consequences, especially as it relates to child welfare. Our model is motivated by Brittany's (a pseudonym) story, and her then-caseworker's reflection on how powerful a synergistic system could be for children, their families, communities, and the caseworkers who serve them.

A synergistic system would make reducing child maltreatment the responsibility of every social service program in the United States. In the current framework, this responsibility falls solely to CPS, but CPS is a response agency, not a preventive agency. Moreover, what is needed to prevent most forms of neglect is alleviation of financial hardship, and that will always be outside of CPS's scope. However, financial hardship alleviation is the goal of myriad social and antipoverty programs. Requiring programs external to CPS to consider child welfare in their program outcomes and decisions will ensure our policies and programs are promoting families' needs. Families will be better served, and hopefully diverted from CPS altogether; but when a family does come before CPS, many social safety net services will already be in place, making the job of CPS realistic.

As we present the necessary changes for implementing this synergistic strategy, we show that it is not only achievable but also the most pragmatic response available. It builds on systems that are currently in place, is efficiency enhancing, and, most importantly, provides a path forward for reducing child neglect in the United States.

Child Welfare in the United States

For much of our history, the United States has collectively held the belief that parents' treatment of children is a private, family matter. No federal legislation regarding child maltreatment was enacted until 1935 when the Social Security Act provided grants to states to create child welfare agencies, and no federal definition of maltreatment was adopted until the passage of CAPTA in 1974.

In 1962, Kempe and colleagues published a groundbreaking report describing the extent and consequences of what they termed "battered-child syndrome." This work differed significantly from prior approaches by placing a focus on the medical determination of maltreatment and its psychopathological origins. In addition, the authors highlighted that maltreatment was not restricted to low-income families, but that it also occurred among "people with good education and stable financial and social backgrounds [and that] . . . it would appear that in these cases, too, there is a defect in character structure which allows aggressive impulses to be expressed freely" (p. 145).

Child abuse versus child neglect

Common across both the medical and sociological child maltreatment literatures is a conflation—or overlooking—of the distinction between child abuse and child neglect (Dubowitz 1999). One strain of research argues that both child abuse and child neglect are the result of poor parenting, which can be addressed by interventions designed to improve parenting skills (Waldfogel 2010). A second line of research contends that both are caused by psychopathology and can be addressed through mental health services (Wolfe 1999). More complex theories rely on social stress explanations (Elder 1974; Garbarino 1976), which examine the interaction between individuals and their contexts (Cicchetti and Rizley 1981), or ecological models, which account for the multiple nested spheres in which families live (Belsky 1980). Although social-ecological models point to the need for interventions that are external to the family, child welfare interventions have continued to focus on family behaviors rather than family circumstances.

Poverty or low socioeconomic status is a risk factor for child neglect (Berger 2004; Garbarino 1982). A growing literature has sought to identify the causal effect of poverty on child neglect. Researchers have taken up a number of innovative methods—leveraging plausibly exogenous variation in neighborhoods, macro-policy, and business cycles—to demonstrate that poverty may be causally linked to child neglect (Berger et al. 2017; Raissian and Bullinger 2017; Paxson and Waldfogel 2003; Klevens et al. 2015; Lindo, Schaller, and Hansen 2018; Raissian 2015; Schenck-Fontaine, Gassman-Pines, and Hill 2017).

If the causes of neglect and abuse differ, then the effective treatment or prevention of neglect may be fundamentally different than for abuse. Neglect is an act of *omission*, or the failure to provide for a child's basic needs and safety, and is often unintentional.[1] This type of maltreatment contrasts with abuse, which is an act of *commission*. Physical and sexual abuse are entirely a result of parental or caretaker behaviors that (usually) occur intermittently. The inverse of abuse is to not engage in abusive acts, often replacing this behavior with more positive behavior and/or removal of the perpetrator from the setting. In cases of abuse, it is appropriate to provide the family with psychosocial interventions. However, the inverse of neglect is more complex; it is to provide safe, consistent supervision and constantly provide for children's basic needs (hereafter SCC for safe and consistent care).

While financial hardship and neglect do not share a deterministic relationship, empirical evidence points to a probabilistic causal relationship—meaning as financial hardship increases, the likelihood of neglect occurring increases; and the increase appears to be explained by financial hardship, itself, rather than other, related factors. Moreover, financial hardship remains one of the few preventative factors that is unaddressed in the current policy context. Rates of child neglect have remained steadily high, perhaps because neglect is fundamentally different than abuse—stemming primarily from poverty rather than parenting behaviors—and is resistant to prevention efforts focused on parenting modifications (Bullinger et al. 2019). There are numerous parenting or parent behavioral training programs that are offered to and sometimes mandated for families at risk of maltreatment or CPS-involved families; however, thus far, the evidence that parent behavioral training programs reduce neglect is slim. An exception is SafeCare, which undertakes parent education in participants' homes and has a particular focus on home safety, and which has shown significant reductions in neglect (Chaffin et al. 2012). Preventing neglect is likely the result of a complex combination of circumstances, environment, and parent capacity that allows a parent or family to *provide SCC all of the time*. Preventing neglect involves preventing or reducing family financial hardship, and systems that address this underlying mechanism of neglect are required to prevent neglect.

CAPTA: Its focus and history

The articles by Testa and Kelly (this volume) and Haskins (this volume) provide a comprehensive history of child welfare policy in the United States. To complement, we focus on important policy developments that lead to the siloed nature of our current child welfare system. By the 1970s, policy-makers and the public recognized that child maltreatment was a serious and widespread problem, and this growing recognition initiated the creation of CAPTA. However, as Barbara Nelson (1984) wrote in her history of CAPTA, Democrats feared that President Nixon might veto CAPTA, as he had the Comprehensive Child Development Act, if it were viewed as being too closely connected to poverty. Senator Mondale (Democrat from Minnesota, sponsor of the legislation, and later President Carter's vice president), for example, made great efforts to make clear that maltreatment could happen to anyone, regardless of social class. In testimony by David Gil, a professor at Brandeis University and a pioneer in child maltreatment research, Senator Mondale pressed to frame the problem broadly:

> Mr. Gil: . . . As I have said on another occasion, the factors that lead to abuse among the well-to-do are the same that also lead to abuse among the poor. The poor have in addition many more factors.
> Sen. Mondale: I know you are going to get to that. But this is not a poverty problem; it is a national problem.
> Mr. Gil: That is correct.

Notably, the act ambitiously encapsulated two very different forms of maltreatment—abuse and neglect—without acknowledging or planning for different causal mechanisms. And to create this broad reach, the act had to decouple poverty from child maltreatment. The result was the creation of a child welfare system that was parallel to, but siloed from, existing social welfare programs; one that was, by design, focused solely on the psychopathological antecedents of maltreatment. The effect was a framework that was very good at responding to abuse but that did not meet the needs of children suffering from neglect. As Nelson writes in her history (1984), John T. Allen, the chairman of the American Academy of Pediatrics' Subcommittee on Child Abuse, noted the following in his testimony:

> Dr. Allen: What we are really talking about, whether we want to admit it or not, is . . . the physically abused child.
> Senator Mondale: I am glad you made that point. Unless you do that, you get into the question of sort of basic social health, which is beyond the reach of legislation that we can possibly do.

The framers of CAPTA were faced with challenges—many stemming from the political economy of the time—and they made the necessary trade-offs to pass the legislation. The bill made no effort to separate prevention of child neglect, which was viewed as being too closely linked to poverty, and it paved a road toward deep linkages with the mental health services fields. Because CAPTA funding was tied to the psychopathological origins of child maltreatment, funds flowed toward these services. The National Academies reports that a majority of interventions funded through CAPTA focus on changing parents and the home environment, improving cognitive-behavioral skills, or altering the psychodynamic interplay in relationships and family systems (National Research Council 1993).

What has this legislative structure meant for the prevention of child maltreatment in the ensuing 45 years? The child welfare system has been successful at reducing the forms of child maltreatment that it set out to reduce, namely abuse. That financial hardship was separated from the act is particularly problematic because it leaves CPS with no mechanisms to respond to a core cause of neglect. In this sense, siloed systems effectively capture families in a CPS system that is not designed to respond to their needs.

Understanding the Underlying Causes of Neglect and the Potential of Systems Synergy

The vignette at the beginning of this article summarizes how the misdiagnosis of the underlying driver of neglect has led to inappropriate and ineffective treatment of neglect. The sole assignment of neglect to CPS perpetuates the misidentification of the underlying problem. While a complete understanding of all potential causes and relevant mechanisms leading to neglect would be beneficial, children and families cannot, and should not have to, wait for such a discovery before policy solutions are offered.

Research has demonstrated that poverty plays an important role in the etiology of child maltreatment. In particular, neglect occurs far more frequently in resource-poor families and communities (Bullinger et al. 2019; Slack et al. 2003). At the individual level, research has found that poverty and low income are associated with increased risk for child neglect (Berger 2004) and child maltreatment overall (Pelton 1994, 2015; Sedlak et al. 2010). Similarly, extensive evidence has linked community-level indicators of poverty to increased risk for child maltreatment (Coulton et al. 1995; Drake and Pandey 1996). This work indicates that social disorganization, resource availability, and concentrated poverty all contribute to child abuse and neglect. Finally, a growing body of research has sought to leverage variation in policies—such as the Earned Income Tax Credit (Berger et al. 2017), the minimum wage (Raissian and Bullinger 2017), and child support enforcement (Cancian, Yang, and Slack 2013)—to examine the impact of economic hardship on child maltreatment.

This research suggests that macrosystem policies have a role in causing and preventing maltreatment. Recent attention has tried to refocus maltreatment prevention efforts on this broader context (Bullinger et al. 2019). This growing literature provides compelling evidence that poverty is causally linked to child maltreatment. If we accept that poverty, at least in some way, is a causal factor in the perpetration of neglect, we can begin to reduce neglect (and its consequences) long before the exact mechanisms are understood.

We do not know exactly how financial resources serve as a protective factor among families, but understanding the mechanism is not required to begin the necessary policy work. Moreover, public health history is replete with examples of scientists knowing through scientific observation that A causes B, but not knowing precisely why such a relationship exists. A classic example is John Snow's investigation of the cholera outbreak in Soho, London, in 1854. Through observation he learned that people drinking water from the Broad Street pump had higher cholera infection rates, but he did not know what about the water was dangerous. Nevertheless, Snow convinced officials to discontinue water supply from the Broad Street pump, and after that was done, the cholera outbreak stopped (Hempel 2007). Snow only knew that ingestion was clearly leading to illness and that it must be stopped. In the same way, we know financial hardship creates the conditions for neglect, and as a society, we are obligated to respond.

In examining the potentially relevant factors in the macrosystem, the critical role of systems, policies, and programs outside of CPS becomes clearer. Housing policy, food policy, employment opportunities, and transportation all factor into the macrosystem. According to ecological theory (Belsky 1980), a more robustly supportive macrosystem, which comes about through intentional public policy decisions, would create a different context for communities, families, and individuals in their efforts to provide and achieve SCC.

Moving from neglect to SCC

Providing SCC is highly dependent on the environments, contexts, and resources under which caretakers operate. This context of care varies widely and, as Belsky's (1980) model implies, is largely shaped by the resources available to a family unit. Financial hardship—which might include insufficient income or poverty, transportation limitations making employment and social service engagement challenging, and unsafe and/or unstable housing—is key and, often, an external component in the family's ability to provide SCC for children. As these resources are external to the family unit, they have not been traditionally taken into account in interventions occurring under the CAPTA model.

We propose expanding the definition and focus of primary prevention, especially as it relates to neglect. Traditional primary maltreatment prevention has focused on expanding the accessibility of targeted programs more closely related to parenting (including promoting child health and development); see Jones Harden et al. (this volume) for a full discussion. But these expansions will only be effective if (1) they address the actual cause of the neglect, and (2) programs are able to identify and engage with the "right" families. With respect to the first, expansion of traditional primary prevention has been an effective strategy for abuse reduction, but currently there are not effective interventions for neglect that can simply be expanded (Macmillan et al. 2009).

The second prerequisite is identifying and engaging the at-risk families. As a result of the state of the research and the complex nature of providing SCC, it has been difficult, even with recent advances, to accurately identify who is at risk of neglect. Efforts to correctly identify high-risk families fail to identify many families who will be reported for maltreatment (Putnam-Hornnstein and Needell 2011; Goldhaber-Fiebert and Prince 2019). These challenges suggest that a broad (or more universal) approach that encompasses all families that experience significant financial hardship is more likely to substantially reduce neglect than a targeted approach that focuses on only the highest-risk families. Adopting a broad-based approach will require a concerted and coordinated effort across public sector service systems. Policy-makers and program leaders will need to embrace their role in developing systems synergy to promote SCC.

An emerging body of research suggests that neglect rates are responsive to macro-level conditions. We draw on this evidence to propose an integrated policy framework to support families and protect children. If neglect, or even some forms of neglect, is, at least in part, caused by poverty, then poverty alleviation programs have a role to play in helping families to provide SCC, that is, to prevent neglect. In this vision, "neglect prevention" would no longer be the sole responsibility of CPS, but rather it would also be the responsibility of agencies such as the U.S. Departments of Housing and Urban Development, Health and Human Services, Agriculture, and so on. This approach would leverage the existing programs and the workforce of public agencies to increase families' access to the social services for which they are eligible. Refocusing social services will be challenging, but it would create a social landscape that allows families to safely care for their children.

Why other social policies may be counterproductive

Currently, in the United States, social services are often delivered through agencies that are typically charged with changing a distinct set of outcomes. Moreover, agencies may be bound by a jurisdiction or need to act within certain policy parameters. These constraints have not only created siloed policies; they have made siloed service delivery an entrenched feature of social policies. Programs and services may have ambitious goals, but the way in which they achieve them is limited. For example, the child welfare system focuses on the prevention and, especially, treatment of child abuse and neglect, but CPS can only intervene in the family unit—and not in the family's broader context—to address maltreatment. Temporary Assistance for Needy Families (TANF) seeks to promote economic self-sufficiency, but its main policy lever is to move clients off caseloads and into employment. The goal of the Supplemental Nutrition Assistant Program (formerly Food Stamps) is to reduce hunger, and it does so by offering food subsidies. Medicaid seeks to improve health and, while providing health insurance allows access to medical treatment, its focus is on treating illness.

While each of these programs has laudable goals, when pursued in isolation these programs overlook families' multifaceted and complex realities and may not fully promote the well-being of children or the family unit. This may also reduce the efficacy of their societal impact. When developed and executed in isolation, policies may achieve their core function and may indeed improve outcomes in a particular domain, but due to tunnel vision, they may inadvertently create greater complexity or problems in other domains.

Narrowly focused policies often force families into "no-win" situations. For example, when the Personal Responsibility and Work Opportunities Reconciliation Act (PRWORA) first authorized TANF, a major legislative goal was to move program participants—predominantly low-income single mothers—from welfare to work. However, what was not considered was what families need when a parent, especially a single parent, enters the labor force. Failure to account for the needs of children meant that the policy overlooked potential effects on child maltreatment and foster care entrance, and TANF program workers were not held accountable for negative outcomes outside of the federally stated self-sufficiency measures. Indeed, one of the negative consequences of TANF was increased demands on the child welfare system in the form of more CPS caseloads and children entering foster care and staying longer (Paxson and Waldfogel 2003; Slack et al. 2003; Wells and Guo 2006).

There are other examples of a siloed approach leading to unintended consequences. Employment programs that focus exclusively on job training and employment without considering issues related to transportation or child care are likely to help one problem (employment), but also create another (child care). The Moving to Opportunity (MTO) experiment is another example. Although this program offered families housing vouchers to move to better neighborhoods, many families did not take the opportunity because moving would mean losing their social support system.

Similarly, stated goals of social policies vis-à-vis child well-being outcomes and programmatic decisions do not always align. For example, although the child support system often claims to be focused on providing economic support for children, there are several program features that focus the program on cost recovery, rather than aiding families (Cancian, Yang, and Slack 2013). Mothers on TANF and Medicaid must cooperate with child support enforcement to receive benefits, regardless of whether they believe it to be in their best interests. They must also assign their rights to collected child support to the state, meaning that child support payments go to TANF coffers rather than families. Indeed, evidence has shown that custodial families' receipt of all the child support they are owed, rather than states keeping a portion to offset TANF expenses, reduces child maltreatment (Cancian, Yang, and Slack 2013). The child support enforcement program is just one, among many, social policy examples of siloed policies.

In contrast, Head Start takes a "whole family" approach. Although the program's primary goal is providing quality early care and education, it is also deeply concerned with social-emotional development and parental well-being. As a result, parents with children in Head Start have the ability to enroll in GED classes and receive employment services and parenting classes. In addition, Head Start recognizes the importance of meeting families' financial, food, and housing related needs for children to thrive, and it provides key linkages to other social welfare programs as a result. While Head Start services do not have perfect take-up rates, nor capacity to serve all eligible families, the program's engagement with factors contributing to a family's financial hardship provide an example of synergistic, or nonsiloed, program offerings.

We advance a model that recognizes the relationship between financial hardship and neglect and enlists antipoverty policies and programs as part of the solution. As it stands now, each program defines its own goals and creates a government at odds with itself, certainly with its children and families. This internal strife could be greatly reduced if systems worked synergistically with CPS, rather than the current practice of child welfare ambivalence.

Systems Synergy: How a New Approach to Policies Could Support Systems Collaboration

What does a synergistic model look like? We argue for a child-centered approach like that illustrated in Figure 1. By requiring child outcomes to be considered in all domains of service provision, families and children are better served; this model ensures that children's full range of needs are more likely to be addressed. The model also requires agencies to anticipate the impacts of their service provision, to understand its consequences, both intended and unintended, and holds agencies accountable for their core mission outcomes alongside promoting SCC. There are two key components of this approach. The first is a shift in policy focus and development where children's holistic needs are considered as the primary concerns of policies; a related, but slightly different, issue is that the unintended consequences for children would become a central concern. The end result is that if policies, and consequently agencies and programs implementing these policies, are accountable for unintended consequences for children, they will have an incentive to increase families' access to and uptake of other social programs, which would increase family resource and stability, allowing more children to experience SCC and thus reduce neglect.[2]

Table 1 demonstrates the targeted focus of several federal programs and their potential effects on families' resources. By enhancing one of these domains, these programs may alleviate child maltreatment. However, these programs may also detract from other aspects of families' lives, potentially threatening children's well-being in other ways.

Federal Antipoverty Programs or Policies That Could Better Affect SCC

Table 1 illuminates several things. The first is that a range of social programs contributes to SCC. Second, programs typically affect family resources in one of two ways: by changing the parents' "money" or by changing the "time" a parent has available. Money broadly refers to economic resources, such as food stamps, housing subsidies, and childcare subsidies. If a program allows parents more leisure time, parent–child interactions may increase. Alternatively, programs like Head Start or public schools, may reduce parental childcare time commitments. This would give parents more time for employment or a respite from providing care. Time and money seem to be the two core resources a family needs at the micro-level. Programs that increase both time and money are optimal; there are no trade-offs for families to make when accepting this assistance. However, programs that increase one resource (money, for example), while decreasing the other (time, for example) may lead to unintended and negative consequences for families and children. These programs must recognize their potential for and seek to mitigate harm. This kind of internal program reflection with an outward look to SCC is both novel and necessary.

Table 1 also shows total federal spending, program's classification as entitlement or capped, and annual caseloads of these programs. It is clear that millions of people, of which the majority are likely families with children, receive billions of dollars in benefits each year through services and programs designed to relieve and prevent financial hardship. This is a testament to our national desire to alleviate suffering. At the same time, by implementing each program in a siloed fashion, opportunities to leverage dollars more effectively are lost. These federal dollars, and the extensive state and local dollars that accompany them, could be used to achieve their primary legislative function *and*—in an environment of systems synergy—be used to more thoughtfully support SCC, which is already central to their intended purpose.

A potentially important feature of systems synergy is universality. An example of one service sector more fully integrating the delivery of other services into

TABLE 1
Federal Antipoverty Programs or Policies That Could Better Affect SCC

Federal Policy or Program	Program's Targeted Outcome	Average Predicted Effect on Families' Resources		Potential for Unintended Consequences	Total Federal Spending	Entitlement vs. Capped	# of People Assisted
		Money	Time				
Cash assistance							
Temporary Assistance for Needy Families (TANF)	Self-sufficiency	↔	→	X	$16.5B (2019)	Capped	1.2 million families (2018)
Earned Income Tax Credit (EITC)	Employment	↑	—		$63B (2019)	Entitlement	22.1 million (2018)
Child Tax Credit (CTC)	Income support for parents	↑	—		$49B (2017)	Entitlement	16.3 million (2018)
Unemployment Insurance (UI)	Short-term economic relief	↑	←		$31.29B (2019-2020)	Entitlement	1,766,000 (2019)
Social Security Disability Insurance (SSDI)	Income support for disabled	↑	←		$144B (2018)	Entitlement	9.9 million (2018)
Medical assistance							
Medicaid/Children's Health Insurance Program (CHIP)	Affordable healthcare	↑	—		$15.6B (2016)	Entitlement	9.6 million (2018)
Health Center Program (HCP)	Healthcare access	↑	—		$10.154B	Capped	25 million (2019)
Food support							
Supplemental Nutrition Assistance Program (SNAP)	Hunger and malnutrition	↑	—		$68B (2018)	Entitlement	40 million (2018)
National School Lunch Program (NSLP)	Health and nutrition	↑	←		$13.8B (2018)	Entitlement	29.7 million (2019)
Women, Infants, and Children (WIC)	Food and nutrition education	↑	—		$5.3B (2018)	Capped	6.9 million (2018)

(continued)

TABLE 1 (CONTINUED)

Federal Policy or Program	Program's Targeted Outcome	Average Predicted Effect on Families' Resources	Potential for Unintended Consequences	Total Federal Spending	Entitlement vs. Capped	# of People Assisted
Housing programs						
Housing Choice Voucher Program	Safe and affordable housing	↑	—	$23.9B (2020)	Capped	5 million (2017)
Low-Income Housing Tax Credit (LIHTC)	Development of affordable housing	↑	—	$9B (2019)	Capped	2.97 million units (2018)
Energy and utilities assistance						
Low-Income Home Energy Assistance Program (LIHEAP)	Energy burden	↑		$3.69B (2019)	Capped	7.7 million families (2016)
Education programs						
Head Start	Emotional, social, health & psychological needs	↑		$9.127 billion (2018)	Capped	873,019 children (2019)
Public Education	Education	↑		$79 billion (2014)	Entitlement	56.6 million (2019)
Family support						
Child Support Enforcement (CSE)	Reduced public expenditures; stronger families	↔	X	$5.9B (2018)	Entitlement	14.7 million (2018)
Family Leave (Unpaid)	Work and family balance	↓		NA	Entitlement	20 million (2017)

NOTE: The numbers in this table were culled from the following sources: Administration for Children and Families, Center for American Progress, Center on Budget and Policy Priorities, Congressional Research Service, Health Resources and Services Administration, Medicaid and CHIP Payment Access Commission, National Center for Education Statistics, National Low Income Housing Coalition, Tax Policy Center, United States Department of Agriculture Economic Research Service, and Urban Institute.

FIGURE 1
All Programs Seek to Achieve Safe and Consistent Care (SCC) of Children

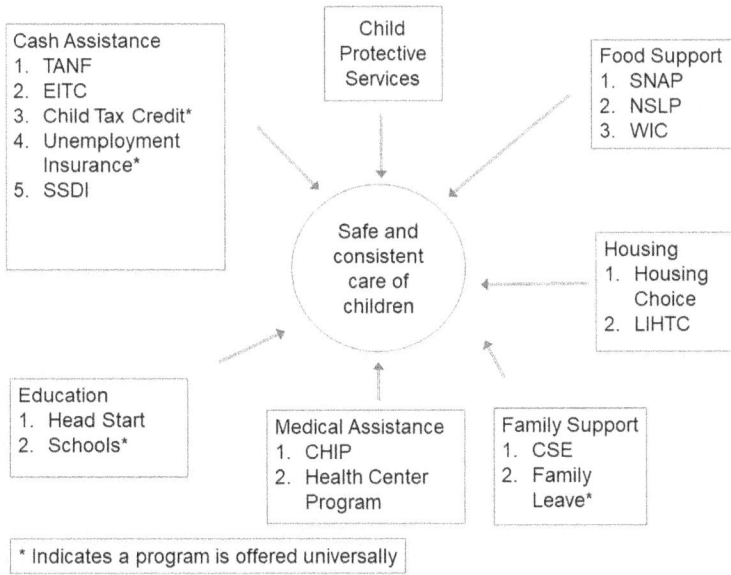

Cash Assistance
1. TANF
2. EITC
3. Child Tax Credit*
4. Unemployment Insurance*
5. SSDI

Child Protective Services

Food Support
1. SNAP
2. NSLP
3. WIC

Safe and consistent care of children

Housing
1. Housing Choice
2. LIHTC

Education
1. Head Start
2. Schools*

Medical Assistance
1. CHIP
2. Health Center Program

Family Support
1. CSE
2. Family Leave*

* Indicates a program is offered universally

their programming is universal free meals in schools. Childhood hunger inhibits development and learning. Although nutrition is beyond the traditional scope of educational services, schools are realizing the power of providing meals to all children—not just children from low-income households—and it is paying off. For example, many New York City public schools have implemented a universal free meals program to their students in the past decade. Research has found this program to improve academic test scores in both English language arts and mathematics (Schwartz and Rothbart 2019). Importantly, these improvements were present for children from both high- and low-income households, demonstrating the power of universal eligibility.

Our model's core tenant is that services from Table 1 work together to achieve SCC; this is visually depicted in Figure 1. Lack of SCC caused by financial hardship is too big for CPS to tackle alone, and caseworkers do not have the necessary resources to do so. However, financial hardship cannot be ignored. If we combine the efforts of our federal antipoverty programs,[3] alleviating financial hardship becomes achievable. Importantly, although the U.S. safety net has shifted its orientation in the past two decades toward working families, our model is not just about income supports. Instead it highlights the roles of time and resources, including access to childcare, transportation, housing, and food, among others. These factors can certainly be enhanced with more money, but do not necessarily require it from safety net programs. Instead of increasing the administrative burden for each of these programs, we are simply arguing that there is room for more take up among those who are eligible. Many people will not know if they are eligible unless they are told.

What would service integration that prevents unintended consequences look like? Imagine if the PRWORA had expanded its outcomes to include moving recipients (or single mothers) off of welfare *in a way that promotes SCC for children*. Caseworkers might have been tasked with helping mothers obtain childcare assistance and after school care, or strategizing about how to ensure critical medical appointments were not missed due to the mother's new employment hours, for example. This type of systems synergy is not just about alleviating current financial hardships among families but about improving long-term child outcomes. Recent research shows that children experiencing both poverty and neglect are at higher risk of adverse outcomes than children experiencing poverty alone (Font and Maguire-Jack 2020). In other words, focusing on the needs of the whole family and recognizing how changing one facet of family life may affect another is important, especially because, historically, this point has not been emphasized.

The role of CPS in systems synergy

Successful systems synergy will mean that over time, cases of neglect that come to the attention of CPS will likely be ones that have connections to psychopathology, substance use disorders, or significant parenting-related problems. However, systems synergy will aid these families as well. Under the current approach, many families are unable to benefit from traditional CPS programs because material hardship has made their lives too unstable to fully participate in services (Lewis et al. 2020). Support in the form of time and money will clearly aid families receiving traditional CPS interventions related to mental health or parenting skills.

Nevertheless, some families will likely make primary contact with CPS for financial hardship–related neglect. Here, systems synergy may provide a form of an economic differential response, allowing CPS workers to link families to services that will address the actual core problems they face rather than providing them mismatched services through the child welfare system. In many ways, this is a form of enhanced differential or alternative response (see Berger and Slack, this volume, for a discussion of differential/alternative response programs). Differential response typically focuses on CPS partnerships with nonprofit agencies to provide services to families who are at low risk, rather than involving them in the formal CPS system or creating a new system (Lindsey 1994; Waldfogel 1998). Our proposal extends the existing service framework by creating synergies with social welfare agencies. Unlike a differential response, our proposal allows families to have increased access to services for basic needs without contact with CPS. Notably, the reauthorization of CAPTA in 2010 includes a broad definition of differential response, making such implementation accomplishable.

Brittany's alternative ending

To examine how this new system might affect children and families, let us first imagine how the opening vignette might have been different with system-level synergies. There were several opportunities for intervention, outside of CPS, that, because they were outside of traditional practice, left the CPS response disruptive to Brittany and her family.

First, Brittany resided in a community that was plagued by poverty and responsible for a high number of referrals. Social service agencies, which exist outside of CPS, should have been offering a range of community supports, advocacy, and family supports, and enhanced public assistance that could have benefited the neighborhood and Brittany's family.

The family rented their dwelling. Why were property codes not better enforced? If some of the home's squalor came from structural deficits, then the local government should have stepped in to enforce standards, striving for the outcome that all children in their jurisdiction live in safe housing.

While Brittany's story predates TANF welfare reform, lessons are still applicable. Opportunities for job training, both for the mother and father, as well as substance use interventions, were missed. At the time, only incarcerated or severely addicted persons were offered substance use treatment through Medicaid, but Brittany's father needed this service. Help to integrate childcare into the family's needs were also missed. Could more robust and free afterschool activities have relieved Brittany's family of stress (an opportunity to increase financial and time resources for the family)? What else could have been done if more government agencies were considering Brittany and her family's well-being as a required outcome of their service provision?

If these interventions had happened, the caseworker, if still needed, would have had a better foundation on which to begin his work. Instead, he was tasked with intervening in a family with no supports and little hope of achieving kin care. In a more stable setting and with different institutional practices, temporary housing could have been offered to the family to maintain the family unit—likely a much more cost-effective alternative compared to removing the child. In an emergency situation, CPS cannot be expected to work miracles. Had the education, housing, medical, code enforcement, CPS, or any combination of systems been working together, Brittany might have never been removed.

A synergistic system offers CPS two things: (1) a set of supports to reduce the likelihood that they are ever called, making them the last rather than first responder; and (2) when CPS is called, caseworkers will have a stronger foundation on which to add, not start, family-centered services.

COVID-19 response: A partial systems synergy for children

Between February and March 2020, states and the federal government were forced to enact emergency public health measures to prevent the spread of the novel coronavirus (COVID-19). The scale and swift implementation of safety measures, which included strict social distancing, universal and prolonged school cancellations, and mass industry and business closures, were unprecedented. These sudden shifts combined financial hardship and isolation, likely placing children and families in dangerous situations.

The COVID-19 response has provided both examples of and missed opportunities for systems synergies that would promote child and family well-being.

Examples of systems synergy include Congress's federal stimulus package, which included a $500 per child credit. When schools implemented distance learning, decision-makers considered what critical services children needed. Food delivery systems and electronic learning devices for low-income children were coordinated. In both of these examples, child and family well-being were considered as outcomes and goals. This is the policy mindset shift we are advocating for, and the COVID-19 response demonstrates that such considerations can be made in our current policy landscape.

Of course, the COVID-19 response has not been perfect; we do not dispute that children may be at higher risk of maltreatment, with fewer opportunities for it to be identified, and parents have experienced extraordinary strain in the absence of their usual supports for child care. However, if child and family well-being were a central focus or consideration in the policy response to this crisis, certain problems might have been mitigated. For example, should the magnitude of unemployment insurance benefits differ based on family size? Can social safety net intake or guidelines be modified to ease administrative burdens during this time? How can childcare be provided for essential workers, so that children are not placed in precarious situations while their parents perform necessary services and earn a paycheck? Our proposal is straightforward: whenever decision-makers craft, renew, or modify a policy or procedure, they should ask, "How does this benefit or harm children and families?" and then reconsider the policy accordingly.

Achieving Systems Synergy: How Do We Get There?

Make maltreatment visible in policy development and analysis

This piece is the most critical because it will drive action and innovation in the other areas. All social service agencies and programs contribute to the promotion of SCC. This process should be visible. Incorporating accountability for SCC into programs would increase the sense of shared responsibility and make it easier to assess the impact of more distal policies on maltreatment. The impact on SCC should then be assessed as part of the standard assessment of the cost and impact of all policies. An adverse impact on children should be considered a cost of the program. Conversely, programs that reduce maltreatment should be correspondingly credited with that positive externality. For example, just as many proposed policies are assessed for their potential impacts on the environment or employment rates, the protection of children should be a required outcome, as well. Perhaps the reason that positive and negative externalities of policies on children have not be accounted for is that the outcomes are distal and potentially difficult to assess. While true, this challenge has been addressed in other contexts. The environmental sustainability movement provides an example. By emphasizing the effect that individuals' decisions have on climate change, this movement has effectively brought a distal outcome to the forefront for many. However, the ultimate goal of the environmental movement is—as it should be for child welfare advocates—to create policy that affects not only individuals but systems writ large. We view this as in incremental improvement to programs and expect the return on this change to be quite large.

Information and advocacy

The literature on the effects of macro-level factors on child maltreatment is in its infancy. Part of the reason for the scant evidence base is the lack of data integration. The ability to link data across agencies will vastly increase our understanding of the effects of antipoverty programs on child neglect, identify the maltreatment-related efficacy of programs outside of CPS, help to understand the role of rationed services (such as housing), and allow for easier collaboration across agencies. In particular, linked data will help researchers to better understand the issue, identify possible solutions, and track the efficacy of program approaches.

Linked data would allow administrators to track the impact of policy changes in a given agency on children and families. For example, does a change in housing policy increase family homelessness, or neglect reports, or adverse educational outcomes for children as a result of a disrupted school year? It would also allow for more granular analyses of the effects of service limits and rationing on individual families.

Predictive modeling with linked data, which in child welfare has thus far been focused on assessment of risk at the point of contact with CPS (see Drake and colleagues, this volume), could also be applied more broadly to understand why certain factors are associated with maltreatment risk, and the differences across families with similar risk profiles that are and are not reported for neglect. This data enhancement could inform programming possibilities or alternative early intervention approaches. For example, frequent address changes of a high-risk family could suggest a need for stable housing. The elevated risk of a family member going to jail or prison might indicate a loss of income for a family and the need for additional financial support. At the service level, integrated data might also be useful in identifying eligibility for other income-support programs in which families are not currently enrolled. A small number of states and state-university partnerships have begun to take up this task. For example, programs in Rhode Island, Michigan, and Georgia have created integrated data systems to evaluate the effectiveness of particular policies, redirect resources to areas of need, and increase participation in programs and services.

There is substantial evidence that financial hardship has a negative effect on families' ability to provide SCC, but this research must be better disseminated and translated to policy-makers, decision-makers, and program providers. To do so, CPS can first advocate at all levels for other social service and welfare programs, and these other programs must highlight their impacts on supporting SCC. Second, researchers and public agencies should enhance their collaboration efforts to get the word out about data-driven findings.

Incentives for innovation and accountability

We acknowledge that systems synergy may not be an easy task across all policy domains. One way to facilitate the process is to provide incentives for adopting this model. An incentive system awarding federal funds to states that develop successful cross-system efforts to reduce child neglect would encourage innovation. States could be laboratories potentially producing different models for effective collaboration. Tested and effective strategies could be incentivized for lagging or later-adopting states.

President Obama's "race to the top" provides a roadmap for such a process. Race to the top provided nearly $4 billion in funding to states in an effort to spur innovation in education policy. In particular, it focused on developing data systems and rigorous interventions. A race to the top in child maltreatment prevention might encourage states to integrate data systems, develop innovations for merging siloed social welfare policies, and prioritize child neglect prevention as a primary outcome across government agencies.

Limitations

Our proposal does not come without necessary trade-offs and possible drawbacks. We do not know the costs of creating systems synergy. The process will necessarily involve training not only for CPS workers, but also for a host of administrators and providers across social welfare agencies. Similarly, it may be that other social welfare programs are insufficiently funded, have lower benefit levels than needed, or are not universally available. In this case, it may be that even systems synergy cannot provide the resources necessary for families to provide SCC. However, it may also be that the process increases take-up of these programs and that, when combined, they have complementary effects that magnify their power to reduce neglect. Although there are potential obstacles, we should draw on the record of the public health interventions described here and take action, even if the outcome is uncertain.

We have yet to test the scope of the solutions proposed here. One study has provided a glimpse into this idea. Project GAIN (Getting Access to Income Now) provided families with closed CPS cases support in obtaining access to programs such as TANF, housing, and transportation benefits (Slack et al., forthcoming). Results from this research, however, have shown that the program did not significantly reduce reports of child maltreatment. One potential explanation for GAIN's lack of success is that the support remained below the threshold of an adequate amount and duration of support. In other words, the program offered pennies when families needed dollars. Additionally, this intervention differs from our recommendation insofar as it does not link child welfare and social welfare agencies to a common goal or better integrate these siloed systems—rather families were referred to economic support workers after already having been reported to CPS. We propose that synergy in this manner will prioritize prevention of child neglect and provide added benefits.

Similar to Project GAIN in the context of families and economic stability, there may be a threshold effect. In other words, there is a minimum level of resources that will prevent the family from tipping into crisis and allow them to adequately provide SCC. Services and programs that provide a small amount of relief—either in finances, time, or stress—may not provide for incremental improvements. Even with systems synergy, these programs may be insufficient to get a family over the threshold of economic stability that allows them to provide SCC, which could limit the efficacy of this model.

CPS provides services to families that are in dire situations. Other programs do not always serve this role. To the extent that resources would get diverted from CPS to adopt this model, families in the most severe situations could be undertreated. Furthermore, there could be substantial trade-offs, since, at least at the state level, most budgets need to be balanced. Nonetheless, neglect rates have remained steady for decades; a new direction might be the innovative change that is needed.

Notes

1. In this work, we focus on supervisory and physical neglect. Berger and Slack (this volume) provide an in-depth discussion of the types of child neglect.

2. In many ways, a child allowance would likely be the most efficient strategy to reduce neglect. For example, simulations produced by the National Academy of Sciences (NAS) show that a child tax credit of $3,000 per child per year would reduce deep child poverty by 50 percent. Since research has shown that much smaller income boosts (e.g., $100–$1,500 per year) help to reduce maltreatment, $3,000 could go much further for families. Nonetheless, the feasibility of a child allowance of this magnitude in contemporary times seems unlikely.

3. While we focus on federal services, this model should also be applied at state and local levels. Many federal policies are implemented at the state level; this extension is natural and necessary.

References

Belsky, Jay. 1980. Child maltreatment: An ecological integration. *American Psychologist* 35 (4): 320–35.

Berger, Lawrence M. 2004. Income, family structure, and child maltreatment risk. *Children and Youth Services Review* 26 (8): 725–48.

Berger, Lawrence M., Sarah A. Font, Kristen S. Slack, and Jane Waldfogel. 2017. Income and child maltreatment in unmarried families: Evidence from the Earned Income Tax Credit. *Review of Economics of the Household* 15 (4): 1345–72.

Berger, Lawrence M., and Kristen S. Slack. 2020. The contemporary U.S. child welfare system(s): Overview and key challenges. *The ANNALS of the American Academy of Political and Social Science* (this volume).

Bullinger, Lindsey Rose, Megan Feely, Kerri M. Raissian, and William Schneider. 2019. Heed neglect, disrupt child maltreatment: A call to action for researchers. *International Journal on Child Maltreatment: Research, Policy and Practice*. https://doi.org/10.1007/s42448-019-00026-5.

Cancian, Maria, Mi-Youn Yang, and Kristen Shook Slack. 2013. The effect of additional child support income on the risk of child maltreatment. *Social Service Review* 87 (3): 417–37.

Chaffin, M., D. Hecht, D. Bard, J. F. Silovsky, and W. H. Beasely. 2012. A statewide trial of the SafeCare home-based services model with parents in Child Protective Services. *Pediatrics* 129 (3): 509–15.

Cicchetti, Dante, and Ross Rizley. 1981. Developmental perspectives on the etiology, intergenerational transmission, and sequelae of child maltreatment. *New Directions for Child and Adolescent Development* 1981 (11): 31–55.

Coulton, C. J., J. E. Korbin, M. Su, and J. Chow. 1995. Community level factors and child maltreatment rates. *Child Development* 66 (5): 1262–76.

Drake, B., and S. Pandey. 1996. Understanding the relationship between neighborhood poverty and specific types of child maltreatment. *Child Abuse & Neglect* 20 (11): 1003–18.

Drake, Brett, Melissa Jonson-Reid, Maria Gandarilla Ocampo, Maria Morrison, and Daji Dvalishvil. 2020. A practical framework for considering the use of predictive risk modeling in child welfare. *The ANNALS of the American Academy of Political and Social Science* (this volume).

Dubowitz, Howard. 1999. *Neglected children: Research, practice, and policy.* Thousand Oaks, CA: Sage Publications.

Elder, Glen H., Jr. 1974. *Children of the Great Depression: Social change in life experience.* 1st ed. Chicago, IL: University of Chicago Press.

Finkelhor, D., K. Saito, and L. Jones. 2016. *Updated trends in child maltreatment, 2014.* Durham, NH: Crimes against Children Research Center.

Font, Sarah A., and Kathryn Maguire-Jack. 2020. It's not "just poverty": Educational, social, and economic functioning among young adults exposed to childhood neglect, abuse, and poverty. *Child Abuse & Neglect* 101 (January). https://doi.org/10.1016/j.chiabu.2020.104356.

Garbarino, James. 1976. A preliminary study of some ecological correlates of child abuse: The impact of socioeconomic stress on mothers. *Child Development* 47 (1): 178–85.

Garbarino, James. 1982. *Children and families in the social environment.* New York, NY: Aldine Publishing Company.

Goldhaber-Fiebert, J. D., and L. Prince. 2019. *Impact evaluation of a predictive risk modeling tool for Allegheny county's child welfare office.* Allegheny, PA: Allegheny County Analytics.

Haskins, Ron. 2020. Child welfare financing: What do we fund, how, and what could be improved? *The ANNALS of the American Academy of Political and Social Science* (this volume).

Hempel, Sandra. 2007. *The strange case of the Broad Street Pump.* Los Angeles, CA: University of California Press.

Jones Harden, Brenda, Cassandra Simons, Michelle Johnson-Motoyama, and Richard Barth. 2020. The child maltreatment prevention landscape: We are we now and where should we go? *The ANNALS of the American Academy of Political and Social Science* (this volume).

Kempe, C. H., F. N. Silverman, B. F. Steele, W. Droegemueller, and H. K. Silver. 1962. The battered-child syndrome. *JAMA* 181 (July): 17–24.

Klevens, Joanne, Sarah Beth L. Barnett, Curtis Florence, and DeWayne Moore. 2015. Exploring policies for the reduction of child physical abuse and neglect. *Child Abuse & Neglect* 40 (February): 1–11.

Lewis, Ericka M., Cole Hooley, Megan Feely, Paul Lanier, Suzanne J. Korff, and Patricia L. Kohl. 2020. Engaging child welfare–Involved families in evidence-based interventions to address child disruptive behavior disorders. *Journal of Emotional and Behavioral Disorders* 28 (1): 43–51.

Lindo, Jason M., Jessamyn C. Schaller, and Benjamin Hansen. 2018. Caution! Men not at work: Gender-specific labor market conditions and child maltreatment. *Journal of Public Economics.* https://doi.org/10.1016/j.jpubeco.2018.04.007.

Lindsey, D. 1994. *The welfare of children.* New York, NY: Oxford University Press.

Macmillan, Harriet L., C. Nadine Wathen, Jane Barlow, David M. Fergusson, John M. Leventhal, and Heather N. Taussig. 2009. Interventions to prevent child maltreatment and associated impairment. *The Lancet* 373 (9659): 250–66.

National Research Council. 1993. *Understanding child abuse and neglect.* Washington, DC: National Research Council.

Nelson, B. J. 1984. *Making an issue of child abuse.* Chicago, IL: University of Chicago Press.

Paxson, Christina, and Jane Waldfogel. 2003. Welfare reforms, family resources, and child maltreatment. *Journal of Policy Analysis and Management* 22 (1): 85–113.

Pelton, Leroy H. 1994. The role of material factors in child abuse and neglect. In *Protecting children from abuse and neglect: Foundations for a new strategy,* 131–81. New York, NY: Guilford Press.

Pelton, Leroy H. 2015. The continuing role of material factors in child maltreatment and placement. *Child Abuse & Neglect* 41 (March): 30–39.

Putnam-Hornstein, E., and B. Needell. 2011. Predictors of child protective service contact between birth and age five: An examination of California's 2002 birth cohort. *Children and Youth Services Review* 33 (8): 1337–44.

Raissian, Kerri M. 2015. Does unemployment affect child abuse rates? Evidence from New York State. *Child Abuse & Neglect* 48 (October): 1–12.

Raissian, Kerri M., and Lindsey Rose Bullinger. 2017. Money matters: Does the minimum wage affect child maltreatment rates? *Children and Youth Services Review* 72: 60–70.

Schenck-Fontaine, Anika, Anna Gassman-Pines, and Zoelene Hill. 2017. Use of informal safety nets during the Supplemental Nutrition Assistance Program benefit cycle: How poor families cope with within-month economic instability. *Social Service Review* 91 (3): 456–87.

Schwartz, A. E., and M. W. Rothbart. 2019. Let them eat lunch: The impact of universal free meals on student performance. *Journal of Policy Analysis and Management* 39 (2): 376–410.

Sedlak, Andrea J., Jane Mettenburg, Monica Basena, Ian Petta, Karla McPherson, Angela Greene, and Li Spencer Li. 2010. *Fourth National Incidence Study of Child Abuse and Neglect (NIS–4): Report to Congress.* Washington, DC: U.S. Department of Health and Human Services, Administration for Children and Families.

Slack, Kristen Shook, Lawrence M. Berger, J. M. Collins, A. Reilly, and E. K. Monahan. Forthcoming. Preventing child protective services intervention with economic support: Results from a randomized control trial.

Slack, Kristen Shook, Jane L. Holl, Bong Joo Lee, Marla McDaniel, Lisa Altenbernd, and Amy Bush Stevens. 2003. Child protective intervention in the context of welfare reform: The effects of work and welfare on maltreatment reports. *Journal of Policy Analysis and Management* 22 (4): 517–36.

Testa, Mark F., and David Kelly. 2020. The evolution of federal child welfare policy through the Family First Prevention Services Act of 2018. *The ANNALS of the American Academy of Political and Social Science* (this volume).

U.S. Department of Health and Human Services, Administration for Children and Families, Administration on Children, Youth and Families, Children's Bureau. 2020. Child maltreatment 2018. Available from https://www.acf.hhs.gov/cb/research-data-technology/statistics-research/child-maltreatment.

Waldfogel, Jane. 1998. Rethinking the paradigm for child protection. *The Future of Children* 8 (1): 104–19.

Waldfogel, Jane. 2010. *What children need.* Cambridge, MA: Harvard University Press.

Wells, Kathleen, and Shenyang Guo. 2006. Welfare reform and child welfare outcomes: A multiple-cohort study. *Children and Youth Services Review* 28 (8): 941–60.

Wolfe, David A. 1999. *Child abuse: Implications for children development and psychopathology.* 2nd ed. Thousand Oaks, CA: Sage Publications.

A Practical Framework for Considering the Use of Predictive Risk Modeling in Child Welfare

By
BRETT DRAKE,
MELISSA JONSON-REID,
MARÍA GANDARILLA
OCAMPO,
MARIA MORRISON,
and
DAREJAN (DAJI)
DVALISHVILI

Predictive risk modeling (PRM) is a new approach to data analysis that can be used to help identify risks of abuse and maltreatment among children. Several child welfare agencies have considered, piloted, or implemented PRM for this purpose. We discuss and analyze the application of PRM to child protection programs, elaborating on the various misgivings that arise from the application of predictive modeling to human behavior, and we present a framework to guide the application of PRM in child welfare systems. Our framework considers three core questions: (1) Is PRM more accurate than current practice? (2) Is PRM ethically equivalent or superior to current practice? and (3) Are necessary evaluative and implementation procedures established prior to, during, and following introduction of the PRM?

Keywords: risk assessment; child protective services; predictive risk modeling; child welfare policy

The past four decades have witnessed the dawn of the information age, and with its arrival has come an array of data tools useful to researchers. Advances in computer storage have allowed a vast amount of data to be held essentially for free and processed with breathtaking speed. Advances in a broad array of analytic approaches (e.g., propensity score matching, various regression techniques, machine learning

Brett Drake is a professor at the Brown School at Washington University in St. Louis. His research interests include applying big data to understanding child maltreatment, particularly "front-end" services and issues of class and race. He has coauthored an ethical review of potential predictive risk modeling uses in California.

Melissa Jonson-Reid is the Ralph and Muriel Pumphrey Professor of Social Work Research and director of the PhD program in social work at the Brown School at Washington University in St. Louis. Her research emphasizes improving outcomes for children in public child welfare using a systems perspective.

Correspondence: brettd@wustl.edu

DOI: 10.1177/0002716220978200

applications) have allowed data to be used to more accurately answer a range of critical practice and policy questions.

Complex algorithms simply *could not be executed* on large datasets in a reasonable timeframe on generally available computer platforms 30 years ago. Some authors of this article recall spending tens of thousands of dollars to procure storage for datasets that took months of processing time to analyze. Far larger datasets are now transferred routinely across the internet in seconds or minutes, and far more complex analyses are routinely conducted in minutes or, at worst, hours. Put simply, sophisticated analytic methods that use big datasets, like predictive risk modeling (PRM), are newly available for application in fields like child welfare. All new technologies come with risk, however. It is important to fully understand both the potential benefits and the potential risks that adoption of PRM might bring. The obvious question arises: Should we embrace such technologies?

Our Approach to Evaluating Predictive Risk Models in Child Welfare

There is a natural and quite healthy human tendency to be wary of the new. Premature adoption of new technologies or practices can have catastrophic results. One clear example can be found in the heroic actions of Dr. Frances Oldham Kelsey in forestalling the adoption of Thalidomide in the United States. Her caution, based on what she found to be inadequate prior trials, along with other concerns, spared our country the devastating level of impact experienced by various European countries (Rice 2019). Of course, there have also been historical instances where effective new treatments or interventions have been unnecessarily delayed. There is a balance that must be found.

This article is concerned with the application of one particular new analytic tool—PRM—to child welfare programming and policy. PRM is a kind of analysis that uses existing data and machine learning to predict the likelihood of outcomes among people. The prediction of human behavior is both innately complex and has ethical implications. In our view, there are three core conceptual questions that must be answered to evaluate the use case for PRM: (1) Compared to currently available tools and current practice, can PRM approaches more accurately

María Gandarilla Ocampo is a social work doctoral student at Washington University in St. Louis. Her research interests include child maltreatment, child protection systems, and the impact of mandated reporting policies on families and child welfare system outcomes.

Maria Morrison is a social work doctoral student at Washington University in St Louis. She has worked for over a decade for the Equal Justice Initiative. Her research focuses on cumulative traumatic stress among incarcerated and formerly incarcerated men in the context of current and historical racial injustice.

Darejan (Daji) Dvalishvili is completing her PhD in social work from the Brown School at Washington University in St. Louis. She has been working with UNICEF and other international and local nonprofit organizations focusing on child welfare. Her research interests are child maltreatment, gender-based violence, poverty, and economic strengthening interventions.

predict outcomes of interest to child welfare policy and practice, both overall and for subpopulations (e.g., racial/ethnic groups, class, age, geography/setting)? (2) Compared to existing options, is PRM ethically inferior, equivalent, or superior? and (3) Are the key factors related to a successful implementation of a PRM in place? Surrounding these are a range of other subsidiary or related practical questions, particularly related to implementation, such as how appropriate use of a PRM is dependent on factors such as workforce training, agency policies, and ongoing empirical monitoring. Our framework for evaluating PRMs builds upon the "validity/equity/reliability/usefulness" model (Coohey et al. 2013; Hughes 2018; Russell 2015), with which it broadly aligns. Their validity and equity components correspond to concerns with accuracy both in general and for subgroups, while their reliability and usefulness components refer to implementation issues. Our focus builds on these factors by adding a focus on ethical issues.

We argue that these questions cannot be addressed in a general or abstract sense but can only be answered with reference to individual use cases. We define a use case as that situation, purpose, and actual use to which the PRM is applied. Absent a clearly operationalized use case, we cannot make judgments about the utility of any tool. A related point that we would like to stress is that a PRM is a tool and must be evaluated as such. For example, you could confidently say, "A hammer is better than a wrench at driving a three-inch nail through a half inch plank of oak"; but it is nonsensical to say, "A hammer is a better tool than a wrench." Moreover, some issues relating to reliability and validity will be site-specific. For example, larger jurisdictions have a distinct advantage in obtaining sufficiently large training samples. In addition, predictors that are very rare in smaller jurisdictions may not be stable enough to use.

As the title of this article implies, we come at our subject with a clear practical and empirical bias—we favor arguments that are subject to empirical validation over arguments that are purely theoretical or untestable. For example, while we certainly consider what theoretically might occur when PRM is employed, we believe that policy decisions should be based on what can be shown empirically to actually occur when PRM is employed in particular use cases. Implicit in these arguments is the assumption that the ethical and predictive value of any tool is always relative to other available alternatives. PRM cannot be "ethically sound" or "ethically troubling" in any particular use case except compared to other best available practices.

Finally, we acknowledge the difficulty of decision-making in the child protective services (CPS) context. Child welfare hotline screening is important but is often based on scant information. Inclusion or exclusion of particular data elements can have profound, and often counterintuitive, consequences. For example, "ban the box" policies were an attempt to increase the hiring of minority males by forbidding decision-makers (employers) from asking about criminal history. These policies actually reduced hiring of minority males (Doleac and Hansen 2020; Agan and Starr 2016). For us, this highlights the potential chasm between theory or intent and measurable empirical outcome. Throughout this article, we emphasize the need for empirical testing, and we feel this need is especially strong in low-information contexts where unpredictable events may likely occur.

What Are Predictive Analytics, Machine Learning, and Predictive Risk Modeling?

Predictive analytics is a broad term referencing the use of preexisting data to develop models to predict a future outcome. *Machine learning* refers to those approaches in which computers learn (in part) on their own. Machines can do this through exposure to existing datasets, which can be used to "train" the computer to create an algorithm that predicts the desired outcome as well as possible. This can only be done when both the predictive variables and the outcome variable are available. In simple terms, if you know a number of things about a situation (e.g., the information contained in an initial child welfare referral), and you also know about a later outcome (e.g., having a subsequent rereport or not) for those same cases, you can use a machine learning approach to try to create a predictive model. PRM falls under both the domain of predictive analytics and machine learning. It is a broad term for a set of tools that identify which variables can best predict the outcome that the model is trained on and create a predictive model that results in a risk score for each case. This risk score can be scaled as desired (e.g., 1–100 or 1–20). Some common PRM methods include regression and random forest models, which have the same purpose but have different internal processes. PRM has been considered for use in many child welfare systems, and for a variety of different purposes. It has also been formally employed as standard practice to aid risk assessment in some places, such as Allegheny County, Pennsylvania.

What risk assessments are used currently?

Actuarial risk assessment tools dominate current common practice in risk and safety assessment in child welfare. The history of these tools' adoption can be traced back 50 years. At that time, child welfare decisions were commonly made using unaided worker judgment, often with a supervisor clearing the decision. Those in child welfare quickly realized that there should be a formal way of determining risk that could support worker decision-making (Pecora, Chahine, and Graham 2013). The system consulted experts and developed "consensus-based" instruments that were theoretically predictive of maltreatment. These instruments, in turn, gave way to "actuarial" instruments, which were quite different in derivation. While consensus-based tools included items *believed* to be predictive of maltreatment, actuarial tools, as the name implies, included items *empirically demonstrated* to be predictive of maltreatment. Over the past 20 years, research has found that the use of actuarial tools outperforms both the use of consensus-based tools and unaided worker judgment (Grove and Meehl 1996; D'Andrade, Austin, and Benton 2008; Baird and Wagner 2000). Most empirical research in this area uses system outcomes, such as rereferral as outcome measures. Risk assessment tools, including PRM, can be implemented in many ways. When an individual or family receives a very high-risk score, child welfare generally takes a given course of action (e.g., a referral is accepted), but overrides in the system also exist. For example, a decision not to intervene when a very high-risk score is generated might require supervisory approval. The agency's risk assessment protocols go far beyond selecting an appropriate tool. Policies and worker training must be designed to optimize the utility of the selected instrument. Workers must be aware of the specific role that risk assessments are intended to play, and the centrality of their own clinical judgment.

One cannot address the advisability of adopting PRM without an understanding of what technology the PRM seeks to supplant. According to Coohey and colleagues (2013, 151), "Actuarial risk assessment is a statistical procedure for estimating the probability that a critical event, such as child maltreatment, will occur in the future." More specifically, these tools assign probability weights to risk factors statistically known to be associated with child maltreatment to determine the risk level, based on predetermined cut points, of maltreatment reoccurring. These validated tools assign a level of risk to a family, and the tools are used to complement child protective services workers' clinical judgement throughout critical decision-making points. There are several types of actuarial risk assessments that the child welfare system uses, each with varying levels of support and validation.

One of the most commonly used actuarial systems is structured decision making (SDM). Initiated in 1998, the goal of SDM is to assist CPS workers in making consistent and valid assessments regarding child risk and safety throughout various critical points in the child welfare process including initial screening (National Council on Crime and Delinquency [NCCD] 2019). These critical points include the initiation (screening in or out) and disposition of an investigation, case planning, ongoing case evaluation, reunification, and case closure (NCCD 2019). In one study, 27 percent of families identified as having high or very high risk of recurrence had a rereport within six months (Children's Research Center 2008). Families identified as having low or moderate risk had less than 6 percent rereport rates.

How is PRM different?

PRM models are capable of considering a much broader array of variables than risk assessment instruments used in the field, including those that may be available from data sources other than the individual reporting the concern about a child, or that which is observed by an investigative caseworker. The use of predictive analytics in child welfare may address some of the challenges and limitations of actuarial risk assessment tools (Cuccaro-Alamin et al. 2017). Generally, the application of PRM to CPS has shown promising results when CPS has identified an appropriate use case. A common measurement of predictive accuracy for PRM is the receiver operating characteristic (ROC) curve. This curve plots the sensitivity (true positive rate) and specificity (false positive rate) for each risk score vis-à-vis a specified subsequent outcome (Coohey et al. 2013). The area under the curve (AUC) indicates the probability that the classification model will assign a higher probability of an outcome to families that truly have higher risk for that outcome. AUC values range from 0 to 1, with AUC values of .70 or higher being desirable. Several studies have evaluated how well these models perform. For example, in one early study by Vaithianathan and colleagues (2013), the prediction of maltreatment risk by PRM model had an AUC of .76.

Illustrative Case Studies

Fields outside of child welfare have historically used predictive analytics (Church and Fairchild 2017). These include, among others, health (Duncan 2011) and criminal justice (Hannah-Moffat 2019). To provide some concrete orientation to the issues addressed in this article, we present two very brief case studies of the use of PRM in a child welfare context. These divergent cases illustrate how important the appropriate "use case," as well as development, testing, and implementation contexts are.

The Illinois experience with Eckerd's Rapid Safety Feedback Program

We chose the first case study because it both appears to be an example of a predictive analytic approach that failed to perform and directly illustrates many of the key questions and issues we raise in this article. Although Illinois' deployment of Eckerd's Rapid Safety Feedback Program (ERSF) is commonly discussed in both academic and nonacademic sources, we, like Gillingham (2019), believe that all available sources on this matter trace back to a single newspaper article in the *Chicago Tribune* (Jackson and Marx 2017). The *Tribune* article asserts that George Sheldon, then-director of the Illinois Department of Children and Family Services (DCFS), set up and used an internal grant mechanism, rather than an open bidding mechanism, to hire Eckerd, and that the grant was given to prior associates of Sheldon. Sheldon hired Eckerd to implement the ERSF, which used existing data from Illinois DCFS to predict if children reported to the DCFS hotline would be "killed or severely injured" (Jackson and Marx 2017).

As it turned out, the ERSF predictions were catastrophically flawed, with more than four thousand children being flagged as having a 90 percent probability of death or injury and almost four hundred children being classified as having a 100 percent chance of serious injury or death. Setting aside the obvious fact that predicting anything at such high levels of certainty is remarkable, the raw predicted numbers were obviously far too high. For example, during 2015, Illinois reported seventy-seven child fatalities (U.S. Department of Health and Human Services [DHHS] 2017), a rate not inconsistent with national averages. In addition to this very high range of false positives, the system had a large number of false negatives, failing to accurately predict maltreatment-related fatalities that did, in fact, occur. The *Tribune* describes how the program that the DCFS director discontinued and quotes the current director of DCFS, Beverly Walker, who said, "We are not doing the predictive analytics because it didn't seem to be predicting much."

This case study is remarkable in that, to the degree the *Tribune*'s reporting is accurate, this use of predictive analytics violated most or all of the key principles necessary for a practical and ethical use of such a method. In particular, it appears that DCFS did not adequately pretest the program, else it is difficult to understand how so many children could have been classified at such a high level of risk. The algorithm was apparently proprietary and therefore not transparent, so the application of predictive analytics in this use case is intrinsically suspect. Further, the use case itself is highly suspect, as there are no known analytic methods of any kind that can effectively tackle the "haystack problem" (see our discussion of the critiques of PRM).

Allegheny County's Family Screening Tool

Perhaps the most thoroughly evaluated PRM in use in child welfare is Allegheny County's Allegheny Family Screening Tool (AFST). Hotline workers use the AFST to help them decide if a case should be screened in or screened out, a decision-making point where there is often limited information with a very brief window of time to make a decision. The AFST is a PRM that uses a large number of data elements derived from the internal CPS data as well as from other state systems, including jail records, juvenile probation records, behavioral health records, and birth records. The AFST uses data relating to both children and adults in a family. An early version of the AFST used public benefit records, but the current version does not use these data (Vaithianathan et al. 2019). Variable inclusion decisions are often both empirical and political, with many localities making decisions to exclude "hot button" variables, such as the race of the family, particularly when they do not markedly improve instrument accuracy. The AFST generates a score between 1 and 20.

Several elements of the AFST development and adoption process are noteworthy. First, the actors involved made concerted and continuing efforts to be transparent and consciously attend to ethical concerns, both in the form of direct outreach and through a large array of publications, even including a periodically updated online Frequently Asked Questions (Allegheny County DHS 2019a, 2019b). This tool was developed over several years and involved an open solicitation of proposals, community outreach, and feedback, a long series of publications describing the nature and use of the instrument (e.g., Vaithianathan et al. 2019), a process evaluation (Hornby Zeller Associates 2018), and a review of the ethical considerations attendant to the use of the instrument (Dare and Gambrill 2017). The discussion over the advisability of the instrument flowed into the public square, with commentary both supportive of and opposed to being easily accessible in various high-profile publications, such as the *New York Times* and *Wired* (e.g., Hurley 2019; Miller 2018; Giammarise 2019; Eubanks 2018). It is also notable that workers were not chained to the recommendations of the AFST—their decisions could vary from what the machine suggested (Vaithianathan et al. 2019).

Second, established scientists with a prior history of developing predictive risk models in child welfare developed the AFST. Early publications that described the AFST detailed the methods and algorithms used and included demonstrations of the predictive utility of the tool compared to prior known screener accuracy and also, importantly, against non-CPS outcomes (see "feedback loop" discussion). The AFST was thoroughly pretested by internal and external team members (Vaithianathan et al. 2019) to determine the degree to which the risk score predicted unwanted outcomes (e.g., rereport) both in general and for particular population subgroups. The developers conducted the analyses before DHS deployed the AFST. They were able to model what a predictive model would have determined about historical cases and assess those risk determinations through checking historical outcomes and comparing them to what decisions were actually made, historically. This pretesting or "virtual test drive" of a system is one of the key advantages of predictive analytics—you can use history to validate different algorithms.

Testing what an instrument recommends against prior action is not, however, the same as human beings testing the instrument. To do this, DHS commissioned an independent quasi-experimental (pre/post) review (Goldhaber-Fiebert and Prince 2019). The review found that use of the AFST modestly improved sensitivity (reduced false positives), had a very small degradation in specificity (slightly increased false negatives), did not result in higher workload (the number of screen-ins did not go up), reduced racial disparities, and improved consistency among hotline staff. Both the independent evaluators and Allegheny County found the implementation of the AFST to improve practice, and the county is moving forward with the algorithm and is attempting to further improve both the algorithm and how it uses it.

Highlighting the issues of sensitivity (capturing true positives) and specificity (capturing true negatives) is useful. We argue that the human cost of low specificity (failing to see a low-risk situation correctly) increases with deeper CPS involvement. Wrongly terminating parental rights is worse than wrongly removing a child, which is worse than wrongly substantiating a case, which is worse than unnecessarily screening a case in. On the other hand, the cost of low specificity (failing to see real risk) can be lethal to a child at any point in the process. This is why decision thresholds are lowest at the screen-in level and become more restrictive as CPS involvement continues. Ideally, information, which accrues during engagement with CPS, enhances specificity. Procedures that set thresholds for all risk assessment tools should take this into account.

The Public and Academic Discourse: Time to Embrace Change or Hit the Panic Button?

The public and academic discussions around PRM are contentious. Fortunately, the terms of the debate are fairly well established, with key concerns being divisible into general categories, including issues of accuracy, ethics, and implementation. We outline major arguments both for and against PRM and consider them alongside empirical data and ethical principles.

In our view, almost any discussion about child maltreatment practice or policy can benefit from paradigmatic clarity about the role of CPS. CPS could be framed as akin to a criminal justice or emergency medical system, responding to events after they occur and providing services to ensure immediate safety. This has been colorfully and distressingly illustrated with the "ambulance at the bottom of the cliff" metaphor (Keddell 2019). An alternate paradigm is that CPS is intended to *also* have a preventative role through provision of services—a public health model. How CPS is viewed fundamentally impacts the choice of how we evaluate success (operationalizing outcome metrics). Under the first paradigm, immediate outcomes make sense; but under the second paradigm, longer-term outcomes such as rereporting and foster care subsequent to future reporting also make sense. Reviewing the mission statements of most state CPS programs suggests that the second paradigm more accurately captures the intent of most states, and it is one we support. It is heartening to note that the outcome variables chosen in many evaluations of PRM (e.g., Allegheny County) include longer-term measures consistent with the evaluation of a preventative role of CPS. In this section, therefore, we conceptualize CPS as having both an emergency response and a preventative role.

Arguments for how PRM may support ethical, effective practice and social justice

Proponents of PRM claim that the modeling offers an accurate way to assess risk and that accurate risk assessment is ethically valuable. While PRM could be used for other child welfare functions besides risk assessment, including targeting service delivery and evaluating internal agency processes (Hughes 2018) or even case-finding (Putnam-Hornstein and Vaithianathan 2018), the heart of the current debate is focused on the use of PRM at the hotline screening level. Accuracy is the *sine qua non* of risk assessment—without accuracy, assessment serves no purpose. The core assertion that proponents of PRM must make is, therefore, that accuracy is improved.

The instrument itself must be more accurate. That is, the risk assessment scores that the PRM generates must be more accurate than the risk assessment scores that the tools currently in use generate. In addition, this accuracy must extend to subgroups of the population. These two requirements conform to the "accuracy" and "equity" elements of the accuracy/equity/utility/reliability model. Concerns about accuracy within subpopulations stem largely from long-standing concerns among scientists (e.g., Dettlaff and Rycraft 2008) as well as nonscientists (e.g., Wexler 2017) that public systems may discriminate against families by class or ethnic/racial characteristics. Any system that, for example, markedly increases the rate of false positives among screened-in African Americans would be ethically unacceptable. It is important to note that this concern is not unique to screening but has been expounded across all decision points in the child welfare system, from screening to service delivery to substantiation to foster care entry.

Which brings us to ethics. Accuracy is every bit as much an ethical as a techni-cal issue. There is a positive ethical value in using better tools, particularly when the use of these tools impacts people's lives. In the same way that it is obviously ethically preferable for a surgeon to use a sharp scalpel or a radiologist to use the most detailed available image, it is ethically preferable for child welfare systems to employ a more accurate risk assessment tool. More accurate risk assessment can have benefits accompanying increased sensitivity, such as improving the agency's likelihood of responding to high-risk situations, as well as benefits atten-dant to increased specificity, such as reducing concerns regarding possible trauma and stigma resulting from unnecessary contact.

New Zealand, Allegheny County, and California (Dare 2013; Dare and Gambrill 2017; Drake and Jonson-Reid 2018) commissioned separate ethical analyses in contemplating of the use of PRM in child welfare. All three reports found that, in sum, the ethical advantages of employing PRM exceeded the ethi-cal problems raised, and that there could, in fact, be ethical issues in *not* adopting the most accurate tool available.

Other advantages of using PRM to augment human decision-making include speed and breadth of data that can be reviewed. PRM can be automatically and instantly generated at the level of a hotline call, partly using information residing in the system before the call is even made. In terms of breadth of available data, a PRM will consider any information from any case or other data element that you want. It is subject to some of the same limitations as human review (e.g., reliance on incomplete or missing data) but is not subject to others (e.g., failing to notice a data element or not being able to take the time to adequately review a file).

An additional advantage of PRM over actuarial tools is that it can be consist-ently generated. Actuarial instruments, even those following a SDM approach, must take input from human beings, who are fallible and can be inconsistent in their behaviors. This is one reason why so much of the literature on the use of actuarial instruments focuses on adequate training of the people who will admin-ister them (Cuccaro-Alamin, Vaithianathan, and Putnam-Hornstein 2017). PRM is also vulnerable to wrong data inputs, but to the degree that it draws on scores of fields, rather than a few, the impact of a single incorrect data element is minimized.

Arguments for how PRM may threaten ethical, effective practice and impede social justice

Concerns regarding the use of PRM in a child welfare context also fit into the "accuracy/ethics/implementation" structure. Various concerns exist regarding system accuracy, including the familiar and potent "GIGO" concern (Glaberson 2019). "GIGO" is an old computer science term meaning "garbage in, garbage out." Given that PRM relies on preexisting data in computerized systems, critics have raised concerns that any predictions based on such data will be inherently inaccurate. "Bias in, bias out" (BIBO) is an associated problem, one that the criminal justice PRM literature frequently discusses (Howcroft and Rubery 2019). It is also present in the use of PRM in child welfare (Glaberson 2019). From a technical perspective, we might conceptualize GIGO as encompassing both random and systematic error. BIBO asserts that biased data cause systematic error. In particular, data biased against class or, more commonly, racial minorities will cause more false positives (lower specificity) among those populations. For example, if Black adults are disproportionately likely to be arrested simply because of their race, and if arrest is an element in a predictive model of maltreatment risk, then that model could advance this systematic bias into its risk score.

Glaberson (2019) is representative of those who are concerned that PRM may not recognize and account for historical changes—the so-called Zombie Prediction problem. Yet another issue can be found in potential "feedback loops" (Keddell 2019). Feedback loops may occur when within-system indicators of risk, particularly previously accepted CPS reports, are used as an element in a predictive model. In such cases, people may be screened in partly because they were screened in before, theoretically causing a self-perpetuating loop in the system.

Accountability is another frequent issue. For example, a high-risk score for a given individual in random forest models will depend on the outcomes of a vast number of randomly generated decision trees. The way in which they come together to yield a given score in any given case is certainly mathematically knowable but cannot be easily explained to a person, as it involves a massive number of pathways. Accountability problems are multiplied when the public has no ability to examine the algorithms that the model used. For this reason, proprietary algorithms are particularly ethically troubling (Church and Fairchild 2017).

Finally, some have concerns that computer algorithms in child welfare may tend to degrade or dehumanize the quality of clinical social work (Gillingham and Graham 2016). This is not an attack on PRM per se but, instead, a set of concerns about the de-professionalization of workers as they are theoretically reduced to feeding information into and taking orders from machines. We are warned of a "modern times"–like dystopia where workers are mere cogs in machines (Gillingham 2016). Such a concern is present whenever new empirical technologies or approaches become available, such as in discussions of the utility of evidence in practice (e.g., Guyatt et al. 1992). Oak (2016) raises the science fiction film *Minority Report* as an exemplar of how predictive methods can lead otherwise reasonable people to engage in unjust practices through an uncritical application of risk assessments.

While some scholars have energetically forwarded practical and technical arguments against PRM, we can find the primary objections to PRM in the realm of ethics. Concerns exist about the loss of privacy, specifically the failure to obtain consent for the use of personal data. In addition, there are concerns that a PRM with low specificity could be stigmatizing. In this case, stigma is defined as a personal or social disgrace associated with an unnecessary (false positive) child welfare screen-in or subsequent determination.

Many of the issues regarding the use of predictive analytics in child welfare are not new and have been subject to substantial consideration in other disciplines.

For example, in the criminal justice literature, PRM has been used in endeavors such as "predictive policing" (Meijer and Wessels 2019) and in sentencing (Robinson 2017). Many of the same key issues are encountered—the centrality of the use case, the ethical necessity of transparency, concerns over the quality and applicability of the data that the model uses, and the need to prove increased accuracy, both overall and especially for vulnerable subgroups. Many of the key recommendations are also the same—improve data quality, use careful and public analysis of models and outcomes, and avoid the proprietary firms that refuse to make their algorithms public.

Unmuddying the Waters: Evaluating Arguments for and against PRMs in Screening

In writing this article, we were struck by how common it is for there to be a very high level of overlap between those issues that detractors of PRM highlight and those issues that proponents of PRM cite as being necessary to overcome prior to the successful implementation of the technology. In other words, both sides agree on the core issues but disagree on if they can be addressed successfully. We argue that this is an issue that is amenable to the application of evidence *with regard to particular use cases*.

Many criticisms of PRM are not really specific to PRM

Many of the criticisms of PRM are criticisms of risk assessment in general and not criticisms of PRM in particular. As such, they are not reasonable grounds to oppose the introduction of PRM, unless the advocates of such arguments are willing to apply similar criticisms to all risk assessment tools. These concerns are not trivial or unimportant. Many are central and critical. However, they do not constitute arguments against the use of PRMs per se, which is the focus of this article. The following passage from Church and Fairchild (2017, 73) is illustrative:

> Child welfare's embrace of predictive analytics has brought three challenges to surface. First, there is very little known about how or why a tool is making a prediction or recommendation. In other words, we have very little algorithmic detail on any of the tools. Second, these algorithms focus on predicting rare events, such as identifying high risk cases early in a case, typically at or shortly after intake. Finally, each algorithm's output is a single numerical risk score, which no doubt oversimplifies most matters.

None of these issues is specific to PRM. The second issue that the passage describes—the difficulty of predicting rare events (i.e., needle in the haystack problem)—is undoubtedly one of the most serious challenges in social science (Lanier et al. 2020), but it exists irrespective of the method used to make the prediction. This is a characteristic of the use case (e.g., trying to predict fatalities vs. trying to predict rereport) not the method. Similarly, why oppose PRM on the basis that it generates a single risk score when many currently used risk assessment tools share this characteristic?

In addressing the first issue in the quotation, we could easily argue that we do not know how or why an actuarial risk assessment tool is making a certain recommendation. We can certainly explain, "Well, it is because we checked this box," but that is not the same as understanding *how or why* that item is predictive. Actuarial items are definitionally selected because of correlations with a given outcome, not because we theoretically understand how or why they are related. Deriving questions from how and why was, in fact, the first formal approach that risk assessment used, and those consensus-based tools did not work well. For example, single-parent status, maternal age at birth, and poverty are all highly predictive of maltreatment as individual items. We do not know, however, how or why these items are predictive. Why is single-parent status predictive of maltreatment? Is it due to greater stress burden? Is it due to frequently accompanying poverty? Is single-parent status, itself, particularly at a young age, a proxy for other underlying personal, family, or community issues? We have yet to generate a strong body of explanatory knowledge about the mechanisms for the association between various risk and protective factors and maltreatment risk. This is a fundamental problem for the development of interventions, but it is less of a problem if the aim of the tool is merely to accurately identify families most in need of further assessment.

The GIGO and BIBO problems also largely fall into this category. To the degree that current risk assessment tools or workers focus on similar data points that are subject to either random or systematic error, they share these issues with PRM applications. For example, there is little difference between a worker entering potentially erroneous information about a child's age into a risk assessment tool and a PRM automatically extracting the same erroneous information and using it.

This same issue applies to the feedback loop problem. Prior child welfare reports are commonly among the most predictive elements in current risk assessment tools. In this way, current tools have the capacity to promulgate this issue, although an argument can be made that the breadth of variables that PRM uses allows for more possibilities for feedback loops to manifest. On the other hand, a risk assessment tool largely driven by prior reports is of little use for assessing risk for families at the time of their first CPS contact. A PRM with access to a broader range of preexisting risk factors may help to overcome this problem. Despite this, we think the feedback loop problem is concerning, and we discuss it further here.

The zombie problem—that of instruments losing predictive utility due to changing conditions in the world (the classic threat to validity usually termed "history")—is clearly worse for standardized risk assessment tools than for PRM. While local PRM can and should be tuned on an ongoing basis, standardized risk assessment tools are updated far less frequently.

Remaining criticisms of PRM and means to address them

The nonspecific criticisms of PRM may well be valid in whole or in part depending on the context and certainly demand ongoing attention as PRM is implemented. They do not, however, constitute reasons for electing to stay with current procedures over PRM. Many specific concerns surrounding the implementation of PRM remain, however, which we discuss next, along with an account of how these issues have been addressed by those advocating for or adopting PRM.

Accuracy and implementation remain central issues. PRM must be evaluated rigorously and continuously for accuracy, including sensitivity and specificity, both in general and with subgroups (e.g., Goldhaber-Fiebert and Prince 2019). We strongly oppose any initial or ongoing use of PRM (or any other risk assessment) that does not do this. We further divide the ability to evaluate accuracy into at least two stages.

Prior to implementation, a PRM should be trained and evaluated on historical data, a kind of "virtual test drive." For example, the AFST was evaluated by external experts prior to implementation (Vaithianathan et al. 2019) to determine if the risk assessment scores generated using historical predictors and outcomes were more accurate than categorizations generated by actual practice. This analysis was extended to specific subgroups and also extended to non–child welfare system outcomes (e.g., hospital-recorded injury). Verification that the predictive model was not biased against subgroups (e.g., did not increase false positives) was necessary to satisfy the requirement for the ethical standard related to it being an equitable instrument. Verification against non–child welfare outcomes is a useful shield against the possibility of feedback loops. This is because, while feedback loops are theoretically capable of influencing outcomes within the child welfare system (e.g., future screening in or substantiation or placement), it is harder to argue that they might influence outcomes beyond the child welfare system, such as hospital-recorded injury, hospital-recorded abusive injury, or suicide, all of which the AFST score predicted (Vaithianathan et al. 2019). Using these two approaches—rigorous subgroup analysis and use of external outcome measures—can effectively address key ethical concerns about bias and feedback loops.

Following implementation, it is necessary for the implementing agency to evaluate system outcomes while the PRM is in use. This is very different from the preimplementation test drive. While the goal of preimplementation modeling is to see if the generated risk score is predictive of a given outcome (e.g., rereport), the purpose of postimplementation testing is to see if system accuracy improves once the PRM is actually in use. In this way, the second test verifies both instrument accuracy and the implementation of that instrument. Randomized controlled trials in such evaluations are ideal to minimize the chances of spurious causality (e.g., historical or unrelated program effects), but the near necessity of implementing such system changes universally will often necessitate quasi-experimental designs, such as the AFST used.

Moreover, even when a model seems to "work," it may not work for everyone. For instance, a diagnostic test/model that has been validated in a high-prevalence group will have different predictive values when applied to groups with a lower prevalence. Thus, evaluation should be ongoing and should address overall accuracy and subgroup accuracy, and should use internal and external outcomes as measures. One unresolved weakness of this approach is that, as time goes on, it will be less and less possible to compare current PRM benchmarks to an increasingly distant pre-PRM condition. This is, again, not specific to PRM but is true of any similar evaluation of an assessment tool.

Beyond outcome evaluation per se, the implementation of any new tool, practice, or policy must be carefully planned, monitored, and evaluated. Again, this is not unique to PRM. Training is a key ethical and practical consideration for the implementation of any tool. Again, the issues we raised could apply equally well to any risk assessment tool and are not specific to PRM. Drake and Jonson-Reid (2018), drawing on Dare and Gambrill (2017), identified the following key areas for training. First, workers must understand the intended use of the tool and how it fits into their work and overall agency procedures. Perhaps most critically, workers must clearly understand that any risk assessment tool (including a PRM) is just that—a *tool* to assist human decision-making, not to replace it. With any risk assessment tool, it is likely that agencies will establish guidelines, and workers must be trained in these. For example, such guidelines might require that any hotline risk score over a specific (very high) threshold requires an investigative response unless supervisory override is given.

Ethical concerns. Key ethical concerns (beyond those we have already discussed) include concerns with loss of privacy, lack of consent for utilizing personal data, the use of data for reasons other than for which they were obtained, and increased stigma. Addressing the last first, we find that this concern is completely subsumed under the accuracy criterion. In the case of the use of PRM for hotline screening, stigma is only a concern in false positive cases, that is, unnecessary investigations. The question of ethical harm from increased stigma, therefore, is the same as the question of accuracy, particularly specificity (assuming the overall screen-in rate does not rise). To the degree that a PRM enhances specificity, it reduces ethical concerns regarding stigma. The child welfare system should not employ a PRM that degrades specificity in the first place.

We now turn to issues of privacy, lack of consent, and use of data for reasons other than for originally collected. It is critical that each separate use case be analyzed individually. To take the simplest possible case, a PRM that the State of California considered as a screening tool (Drake and Jonson-Reid 2018) used only data that the child welfare agency already held and currently used. In a case such as this, there is no expansion of privacy concerns, and the concerns are moot. To expand on this, we argue that, in cases where the child welfare agency has already been granted access to data sources, the use of those data sources poses no new ethical concerns. In a different use case, and if pressed, one could frame a question such as, "Is it ethical to use data you are already using but more comprehensively?" Is it ethical to use records that could have been accessed prior to the PRM but often were not (e.g., arrest data that formerly required time to obtain)? In such a case, one might justify the expanded use of a dataset they already have permission to use, but this is something of a fine distinction given that they already had access.

Concerns regarding consent, loss of privacy, and use of data for purposes other than originally collected are similar and can be dealt with concurrently rather than sequentially. We argue that, again, the use of a PRM is no different from the use of any other method. Consent is most prominent in terms of individual decisions (such as consenting to medical care) and in consenting to be a research subject. Under the Common Rule, which governs human subjects policy in the United States (DHHS 2020), within-agency evaluations are exempted from the requirement to obtain informed consent. For example, if a hospital reviews its own patient records in a study meant to optimize its own triage procedures, that review is not subject to oversight. In such a case, the data are being used for a purpose other than that for which they were collected. For these reasons, we believe that agencies using their own data are largely exempt from these concerns, as long as they use them for the same general purposes (e.g., case decisions) and with the same degree of confidentiality. This situation can easily expand, however. In the case of the AFST, data were used outside the child welfare system. In such cases, ethical access to those data must be justified by the same means that using such data for any other agency purpose should be justified. Again, a PRM's use of such data is not unique or different or a new frontier in any way. Traditional justifications, safeguards, and oversight should be employed by the implementing agency, ideally in conjunction with stakeholders and outside experts, as they would in any other case.

We also stress an overarching principle that we believe applies to all aspects of any public policy: transparency. In our view, maximizing transparency is key both for ethical reasons and for improving the system in question. Several steps can be taken to support transparency. In our view, all algorithms used must be public. Proprietary agencies that refuse to share their models should never be used. Not only is there a high ethical cost in lost transparency (Church and Fairchild 2017), but secret algorithms cannot be part of the process of knowledge building, which is a bedrock principle of science. In this way, proprietary algorithms are damaging both to the entity contracting for their use and to the advancement of science and the field in general.

Transparency is not a passive concept. In our view, employing any tool requires community engagement in the form of active outreach to stakeholders. This is especially true in the case of big data, which is new and is understandably frightening to many. This should not be a "We're doing this to check off a box" enterprise, but a sincere attempt to engage stakeholders in design and evaluation from the earliest stages and on a continuing basis.

Transparency is also fostered by documentation of all stages of the consideration, specification, ethical justification, pretesting, process, and implementation analyses. As an example, Allegheny County has produced comprehensive documents covering all these issues, which are available on a public website. Such efforts are, in our view, not only possible but necessary. While there are fears that a screening PRM could become "a silver bullet inside a black box buried deep in a haystack" (Church and Fairchild 2017, 17), this certainly need not be the case.

Concerns regarding de-professionalization as a result of automation date back at least a century and are not new to the use of PRM. We fully agree that

FIGURE 1
A Framework for Implementing, Evaluating, and Assessing a PRM-Based Hotline
Screening Process

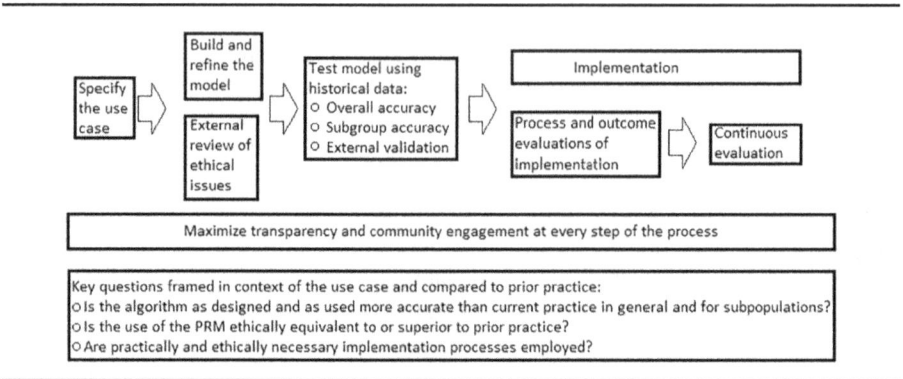

caseworkers are professionals and must not be transformed into mindless screen readers and button pushers. Workers must be trained in the use of any new tool and this concern is vibrant in the literature on actuarial risk assessment tools. A risk score that an SDM generates and a risk score that a PRM generates are similar. All ethical reviews of PRM that we are aware of place a fundamental emphasis on the necessity to train workers that PRM is a fallible tool, and not a celestial mandate.

Specifying a Proposed Framework for Implementing and Evaluating PRM in Child Welfare

We suggest a framework for adopting PRM and evaluating its utility in a child welfare context (see Figure 1). While it may seem strange to conflate implementation and assessment, understanding PRM in a child welfare context must simultaneously consider how the program is conceptualized, evaluated, and executed. Many of the elements in this model are not attributable to the authors, as the key elements and process are closely parallel to those that entities (e.g., Allegheny County) have adopted in designing, implementing, and evaluating their models. We do not specify the minutiae of each phase of the model, as we have already discussed our views on the mechanisms for ensuring transparency, equity, and ethical acceptability. Rather, this section is primarily to bring the previous parts of this article together in a simple visual format. The proposed model is not the only viable approach, but it is consistent with and illustrative of the points we have raised.

The model in Figure 1 emphasizes the centrality of the use case. No program can be contemplated or assessed without a clear, operationalized description of what it is to be used for. Implementing agencies should build and refine their PRM in parallel with an (ideally) external review of the ethical issues attendant to the use case. They should then do preliminary model testing prior to actual implementation. Community engagement and establishing transparency should begin as the use case is being specified. Historical data can then be used to evaluate and refine the accuracy of the PRM, with promising models being advanced to implementation, again with ongoing evaluation. The lower box is included in the model as a reminder that the three dimensions of accuracy, ethical acceptability, and implementation are ongoing considerations for all stages of the process. There is never a point at which concerns about accuracy, ethics, or implementation are "put to bed"—they remain concerns from initial conceptualization through ongoing evaluation.

Conclusion

We see no insurmountable obstacles to the use of PRM in child welfare practice. We also do not wish to minimize the difficulty or necessity of assuring accuracy, ethical acceptability, and proper implementation. The advisability of adopting PRM as a tool is dependent on the specified use case and the demonstrated empirical performance of the tool, particularly its accuracy. Overall accuracy must be higher than current practice. The model must not systematically disadvantage subgroups. The model should be tested against external outcomes to assess the threat of feedback loops. Ethical concerns are central. While most ethical concerns regarding PRM will be similar to ethical concerns about existing models, implementing agencies must review and implement specific steps to address potential issues such as overreliance on the instrument. Community engagement and transparency are absolutely essential. Implementation of any PRM system must depend on demonstrated superiority to current practice and must address ethical and practical concerns. Processes and tools exist currently to allow for the safe and effective use of this technology, at least for the screening use case. As with all tools that powerfully impact people's lives, ongoing evaluation, adjustment, and improvement of the tool are absolutely necessary.

References

Agan, Amanda Y., and Sonya B. Starr. 2016. Ban the box, criminal records, and statistical discrimination: A field experiment. University of Michigan Law and Economics Research Paper No. 16-012. Ann Arbor, MI: University of Michigan.

Allegheny County DHS. 2019a. Frequently asked questions. Available from https://www.alleghenycounty analytics.us/wp-content/uploads/2019/05/FAQs-from-16-ACDHS-26_PredictiveRisk_Package_050119_FINAL-8.pdf.

Allegheny County DHS. 2019b. Impact evaluation summary of the Allegheny Family Screening Tool. Available from https://www.alleghenycountyanalytics.us/wp-content/uploads/2019/05/Impact-Evaluation-Summary-from-16-ACDHS-26_PredictiveRisk_Package_050119_FINAL-5.pdf.

Baird, Christopher, and Dennis Wagner. 2000. The relative validity of actuarial-and consensus-based risk assessment systems. *Children and Youth Services Review* 22 (11–12): 839–71.

Children's Research Center. 2008. *The structured decision making model: An evidence-based approach to human services*. Madison, WI: National Council on Crime and Delinquency.

Church, Christopher E., and Amanda J. Fairchild. 2017. In search of a silver bullet: Child welfare's embrace of predictive analytics. *Juvenile and Family Court Journal* 68 (1): 67–81.

Coohey, Carol, Kristen Johnson, Lynette Renner, and Scott Easton. 2013. Actuarial risk assessment in child protective services: Construction methodology and performance criteria. *Children and Youth Services Review* 35 (1): 151–61.

Cuccaro-Alamin, Stephanie, Regan Foust, Rhema Vaithianathan, and Emily Putnam-Hornstein. 2017. Risk assessment and decision making in child protective services: Predictive risk modeling in context. *Children and Youth Services Review* 79:291–98.

D'Andrade, Amy, Michael J. Austin, and Amy Benton. 2008. Risk and safety assessments in child welfare: Instrument comparisons. *Journal of Evidence Based Social Work* 5 (1–2): 31–56.

Dare, Tim. 2013. Predictive risk modelling and child maltreatment, an ethical review. Available from https://www.msd.govt.nz/documents/about-msd-and-our-work/publications-resources/research/predictive-modelling/00-predicitve-risk-modelling-and-child-maltreatment-an-ethical-review.pdf.

Dare, Tim, and Eileen Gambrill. 2017. Ethical analysis: Predictive risk models at call screening for Allegheny County. Available from https://www.alleghenycountyanalytics.us/wp-content/uploads/2019/05/Ethical-Analysis-16-ACDHS-26_PredictiveRisk_Package_050119_FINAL-2.pdf.

Dettlaff, Alan J., and Joan R. Rycraft. 2008. Deconstructing disproportionality: Views from multiple community stakeholders. *Child Welfare* 87 (2): 37–58.

Doleac, J. L., and B. Hansen. 2020. The unintended consequences of "ban the box": Statistical discrimination and employment outcomes when criminal histories are hidden. *Journal of Labor Economics* 38 (2): 321–74.

Drake, Brett, and Melissa Jonson-Reid. 2018. Administrative data and predictive risk modeling in public child welfare: Ethical issues relating to California. Available from https://www.datanetwork.org/wp-content/uploads/ethical-review-of-predictive-risk-modeling.pdf.

Duncan, Ian. G. 2011. *Healthcare risk adjustment and predictive modeling*. Greenland, NH: Actex Publications.

Eubanks, Virginia. 15 January 2018. A child prediction model fails poor families. *Wired*. Available from https://www.wired.com.

Giammarise, Kate. 6 May 2019. Can an algorithm keep kids safe? So far, Allegheny County's screening tool is improving accuracy. *Pittsburgh Post-Gazette*.

Gillingham, Philip. 2016. Predictive risk modelling to prevent child maltreatment and other adverse outcomes for service users: Inside the "black box" of machine learning. *British Journal of Social Work* 46 (4): 1044–58.

Gillingham, Phillip. 2019. Can predictive algorithms assist decision-making in social work with children and families? *Child Abuse Review* 28 (2): 114–26.

Gillingham, Phillip, and Timothy Graham. 2016. Designing electronic information systems for the future: Social workers and the challenge of new public management. *Critical Social Policy* 36 (2): 187–204.

Glaberson, Stephanie. 2019. Coding over the cracks: Predictive analytics and child protection. *Fordham Urban Law Journal* 46 (2): 307–63.

Goldhaber-Fiebert, Jeremy, and Lea Prince. 2019. Impact evaluation of a predictive risk modeling tool for Allegheny county's child welfare office. Available from https://www.alleghenycountyanalytics.us/wp-content/uploads/2019/05/Impact-Evaluation-from-16-ACDHS-26_PredictiveRisk_Package_050119_FINAL-6.pdf.

Grove, William M., and Paul E. Meehl. 1996. Comparative efficiency of informal (subjective, impressionistic) and formal (mechanical, algorithmic) prediction procedures: The clinical-statistical controversy. *Psychology, Public Policy, and Law* 2 (2): 293–323.

Guyatt, Gordon, John Cairns, David Churchill, Deborah Cook, Brian Haynes, Jack Hirsh, Jan Irvine, Mark Levine, Mitchell Levine, and Jim Nishikawa, et al. 1992. Evidence-based medicine: A new approach to teaching the practice of medicine. *JAMA* 268 (17): 2420–25.

Hannah-Moffat, Kelly. 2019. Algorithmic risk governance: Big data analytics, race and information activism in criminal justice debates. *Theoretical Criminology* 23 (4): 453–70.

Hornby Zeller Associates. 2018. Allegheny County Predictive Risk Modeling Tool implementation: Process evaluation. Available from https://www.alleghenycounty.us.

Howcroft, Deborah, and Jill Rubery. 2019. "Bias in, bias out": Gender equality and the future of work debate. *Labour & Industry: A Journal of the Social and Economic Relations of Work* 29 (2): 213–27.

Hughes, Karissa. 2018. Research summary: Innovative technologies in child welfare services. Available from https://theacademy.sdsu.edu/wp-content/uploads/2018/05/innovative-technology-in-cw-may-2018.pdf.

Hurley, Dan. January 2019. Can an algorithm tell when kids are in danger? *New York Times Magazine*.

Jackson, David, and Gary Marx. 6 December 2017. Data mining program designed to predict child abuse proves unreliable, DCFS says. *Chicago Tribune*.

Keddell, Emily. 2019. Algorithmic justice in child protection: Statistical fairness, social justice and the implications for practice. *Social Sciences* 8 (10): 281.

Lanier, Paul, Maria Rodriguez, Sara Verbiest, Katherine Bryant, Ting Guan, and Adam Zolotor. 2020. Preventing infant maltreatment with predictive analytics: Applying ethical principles to evidence-based child welfare policy. *Journal of Family Violence* 35 (1): 1–13.

Meijer, Albert, and Martijin Wessels. 2019. Predictive policing: Review of benefits and drawbacks. *International Journal of Public Administration* 42 (12): 1031–39.

Miller, Alex. 26 July 2018. Want less biased decisions? Use algorithms. *Harvard Business Review*.

National Council on Crime and Delinquency. 2019. The SDM model in child protection. Available from https://www.nccdglobal.org/assessment/sdm-structured-decision-making-systems/child-welfare.

Oak, Eileen. 2016. A minority report for social work? The Predictive Risk Model (PRM) and the Tuituia Assessment Framework in addressing the needs of New Zealand's vulnerable children. *British Journal of Social Work* 46 (5): 1208–23.

Pecora, Peter, Zeinab Chahine, and Christopher Graham. 2013. Safety and risk assessment frameworks: Overview and implications for child maltreatment fatalities. *Child Welfare* 92 (2): 143–60.

Putnam-Hornstein, Emily, and Rhema Vaithianathan. 2018. Injury and mortality among children identified as at high risk of maltreatment. *Pediatrics* 141 (2). doi:https://doi.org/10.1542/peds.2017-2882.

Rice, Kaylee J. 2019. The thalidomide tragedy and the United States. *Tenor of Our Times* 8 (1): 10.

Robinson, David G. 2017. The challenges of prediction: Lessons from criminal justice. *ISJLP* 14 (2): 151–86.

Russell, Jesse. 2015. Predictive analytics and child protection: Constraints and opportunities. *Child Abuse & Neglect* 46:82–89.

U.S. Department of Health and Human Services. 2017. Child maltreatment 2015. Available from http://www.acf.hhs.gov/programs/cb/research-data-technology/statistics-research/child-maltreatment.

U.S. Department of Health and Human Services. 2020. Federal policy for the protection of human subjects ("Common Rule"). Available from https://www.hhs.gov/ohrp/regulations-and-policy/regulations/common-rule/index.html.

Vaithianathan, Rhema, Emily Kulick, Emily Putnam-Hornstein, and Diana Prado. 2019. Allegheny Family Screening Tool, methodology, version 2. Available from https://www.alleghenycountyanalytics.us/wp-content/uploads/2019/05/Methodology-V2-from-16-ACDHS-26_PredictiveRisk_Package_050119_FINAL-7.pdf.

Vaithianathan, Rhema, Tim Maloney, Emily Putnam-Hornstein, and Nan Jiang. 2013. Children in the public benefit system at risk of maltreatment: Identification via predictive modeling. *American Journal of Preventive Medicine* 45 (3): 354–59.

Wexler, Richard. 25 April 2017. From denial to desperation: Misinterpretations on child welfare and race. *The Chronicle of Social Change*.

Who Is and Is Not Served by Child Protective Services Systems? Implications for a Prevention Infrastructure to Reduce Child Maltreatment

By
KRISTEN S. SLACK
and
LAWRENCE M. BERGER

The majority of alleged abuse or neglect reports to the U.S. child welfare system are either screened out prior to an investigation (i.e., at the "hotline" stage) or investigated only to be closed with no finding of immediate child safety concerns. Yet while many of these children and families are at risk of subsequent incidents of child maltreatment or child welfare system involvement, they are not systematically offered services or benefits intended to reduce this risk at the point that child protective services (CPS) ends its involvement. This article provides an overview of the "front end" of the child welfare system, commonly referred to as CPS, highlighting which families are served and which are not. We then argue for a systematic and coordinated child maltreatment prevention infrastructure that incorporates elements of "community response" programs that several U.S. states have implemented in recent years. Such programs are focused on families that have been reported to, and sometimes investigated by, CPS, but no ongoing CPS case is opened. We further argue that such programs need to pay particular attention to economic issues that these families face.

Keywords: child abuse and neglect prevention; child maltreatment prevention; child protective services; child welfare system; community response

Although the federal government created the Children's Bureau in 1912, with the mission to study and report on a wide range of matters affecting the welfare of children, child protective services (CPS) in the United States were not formally codified by the federal government until 1962. In that year, Congress passed amendments to the Social Security Act

Kristen S. Slack is a professor at the University of Wisconsin–Madison School of Social Work. Her research focuses on understanding the role of poverty and economic hardship in the etiology of child maltreatment, caseload dynamics of child welfare systems in relation to other public benefit systems, and community-based programs designed to prevent child maltreatment.

Correspondence: ksslack@wisc.edu

DOI: 10.1177/0002716220980691

that required states to establish statewide child welfare systems by 1975. Prior to the passage of these amendments, child protection activities were a function of nongovernmental entities, often called "Societies for the Prevention of Cruelty to Children" (SPCCs), which were not uniformly available within or across states (Myers 2004). The Title IV-E amendments to the Social Security Act established a dedicated funding stream to states to partially support (along with state-matching funding) the care and service needs of children who meet federal eligibility requirements and are placed in out-of-home care (e.g., foster care, institutional care) for reasons of abuse or neglect, and later for adoption and kinship guardianship assistance.

Several other major laws influencing child protection practice have passed since the early 1960s, but our approach to child protection in the United States is now at an inflection point. After steadily declining from 2002 to 2012, foster care caseloads have increased substantially since 2012 and are now at their highest level in more than two decades (Child Trends Databank 2019; Radel et al. 2018; U.S. Department of Health and Human Services 2019). Moreover, they may become more pronounced in the midst and aftermath of the COVID-19 pandemic to the extent that the pandemic creates or exacerbates economic stress within families, a known risk factor for child maltreatment (Slack, Berger, and Noyes 2017). This uptick may occur despite that child maltreatment reports decreased substantially during periods of school closures and state and local lockdowns due to a corresponding decline in children's face-to-face interactions with mandated reporters in schools, childcare centers, and other child-serving systems (Stewart 2020; Welch and Haskins 2020). In addition, new evidence and new opportunity afforded by policy combine to warrant a rethinking of the approach to child protection in the United States, including research illustrating the striking cumulative incidence of childhood CPS system involvement (Kim et al. 2017; Wildeman et al. 2014), the exorbitant economic costs of child maltreatment (Peterson, Florence, and Klevens 2018), persistent disproportionality in CPS involvement by race and ethnicity (Dettlaff et al. 2011; Drake et al. 2011; Johnson-Motoyama et al. 2015; Wildeman et al. 2014), and the recent passage of the Family First Prevention Services Act of 2018 (P.L. 115-123) to expand the scope of child welfare systems further into the prevention realm.

In this article, we focus on the "front-end" of the U.S. child welfare systems, which comprises CPS functions, where reports of abuse and neglect are screened, and decisions are made to investigate and initiate services to address situations of child maltreatment. We review who is currently served by CPS and how effective these systems are in identifying maltreatment, and we attend to an important overlooked population of families at risk for child maltreatment—those reported to CPS, but that, upon further screening and investigation, are not ultimately served by that system. We then propose a prevention infrastructure that attends

Lawrence M. Berger is Vilas Distinguished Achievement Professor of Social Work and former director of the Institute for Research on Poverty at the University of Wisconsin–Madison. His research focuses on the ways in which economic resources, sociodemographic characteristics, and public policies affect parental behaviors and child and family well-being.

to this population, and we highlight the multiple systems external to CPS positioned to influence rates of child maltreatment.

Whom Do CPS Systems Serve and Not Serve?

Currently, CPS systems in the United States have four primary functions: (1) vetting referrals of alleged abuse and neglect incidents that an array of professionals and the general public report, (2) further assessing or investigating the referrals that appear to meet state statutory definitions of child maltreatment, (3) providing in-home services to families as well as services to families whose children are removed for safety concerns and placed in out-of-home care, and (4) closing cases of abuse or neglect through service plan completions or establishment of permanent placements for children who cannot remain or be reunified with their families of origin (Institute of Medicine and National Research Council [IOM and NRC] 2014).

The passage of the Adoption and Safe Families Act of 1997 established federal regulations for "Child and Family Service Reviews," which carried the mandate of ensuring the safety, permanency, and well-being of children once they are involved in CPS. Notably, none of these functions and mandates supports the *prevention* of child abuse and neglect—rather, CPS systems are explicitly charged only with *responding* to allegations of child maltreatment and attending to the service needs of children and families once they are involved with CPS. With the recent passage of the Family First Prevention Services Act of 2018, states may now use Title IV-E (as well as Title IV-B[1]) funding for the purpose of preventing out-of-home placements of children. Testa and Kelly (this volume) offer an overview of this new law and its implications for child welfare systems; Haskins (this volume) offers an overview of child welfare funding.

Over the last 25 years, many states have established "alternative response" (AR) (also called "differential response") pathways within their CPS systems. States established AR pathways primarily in reaction to traditional CPS system practices that tended to treat families similarly despite variation in the level and nature of presenting risk and protective factors. Families with fewer and less serious risks or child safety concerns could be placed on an AR path characterized by greater collaboration between CPS and the family, and an "assessment" rather than an "investigation" approach to developing a service plan (Maguire-Jack, Slack, and Berger 2014). Under an AR model, families reported for less severe situations of maltreatment or maltreatment risk are offered voluntary services by CPS. The focus of the CPS caseworker's initial contacts with a family is on collaborative needs assessment and developing a service plan to maintain child safety in the home and reduce the likelihood of maltreatment risk escalating. Under a traditional CPS model, an investigative approach is taken to determine whether maltreatment allegations should be substantiated and whether to open an ongoing case, remove a child from the home, and require services that are typically court-ordered and thus mandatory. The distinction between the two

FIGURE 1
Family Pathways in Child Protective Services (CPS) Systems

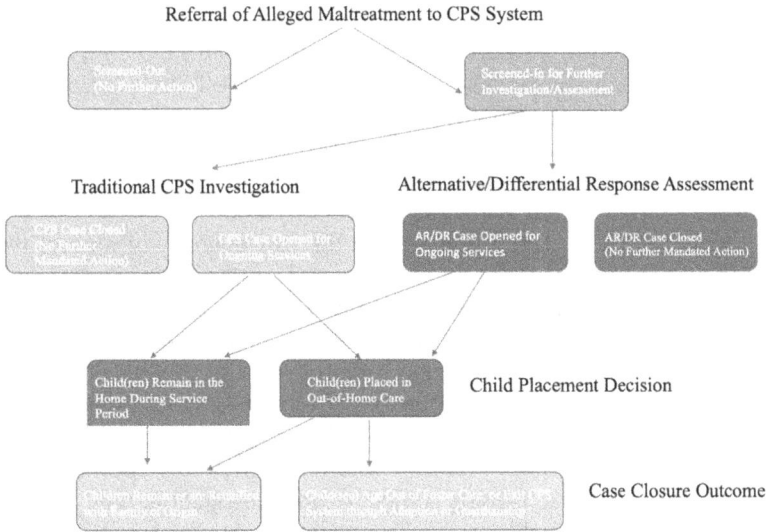

models or tracks is partly a function of how a caseworker approaches and engages with a family and partly a function of the stakes being much higher for a family under the traditional CPS model. We should note, however, that even families referred to an AR track are at risk of having a child removed from the home if caseworkers determine that the situation becomes unsafe for a child. Thus, despite the more collaborative model of AR, AR services are not entirely voluntary, given that families are most likely keenly aware of the potential for more intrusive levels of CPS involvement. Figure 1 provides an overview of the various decision points that capture the primary CPS functions, beginning with a report of child maltreatment to CPS, followed by a screening decision, an investigation or assessment decision, a child removal decision, and a case closure outcome.

The most recent data from the U.S. Department of Health and Human Services (2020) indicate that, in 2018, CPS systems received 4.3 million referrals (reports) of suspected child abuse or neglect involving 7.8 million children (5.9 percent of all U.S. children). Approximately 56.0 percent of these referrals were screened in for a CPS response (either AR or a traditional investigation), while 44.0 percent were screened out at the referral stage, meaning that CPS did not pursue these cases further. In all, 4.8 percent of U.S. children were the subject of a CPS investigation for alleged maltreatment. Of these, CPS determined 16.8 percent to be a child maltreatment victim (received a case disposition that the maltreatment allegations were substantiated or indicated),[2] 14.0 percent received AR (such that they were not subject to the substantiation decision process), and 56.3 percent received a case disposition that the maltreatment allegations were unsubstantiated. As such, 9.2 per 1,000, or nearly 1.0 percent of U.S. children, were deemed to be maltreatment victims, with 84.5 percent of victims experiencing a single type of (substantiated) abuse or neglect[3] and 15.5 percent experiencing multiple types.[4] The vast majority of perpetrators were children's parents (77.5 percent). Among those children who were investigated, 60.7 percent of children deemed victims and 29.0 percent deemed nonvictims (e.g., siblings of victims) received some postinvestigation services; these figures include the 22.9 percent of victims and 1.9 percent of nonvictims who were removed from their homes. Federal data do not provide information on the rate of cases opened for ongoing CPS services, so these percentages may not fully capture all families with continued CPS involvement following an investigation.

Taken together, these data highlight that the vast majority of reports result in no ongoing CPS intervention for the children and families who are their subjects. Specifically, the data indicate that (1) 44.0 percent of reports do not receive an investigation; (2) among the 56.0 percent of reports that are investigated, only 16.8 percent result in a maltreatment substantiation; and (3) only 60.7 percent of children deemed victims and 29.0 percent of those deemed nonvictims receive services. This suggests that only about 19.3 percent of reports result in ongoing (postinitial CPS response) services, whereas fully 80.7 percent do not. Furthermore, among those reports subject to an investigation, only 34.3 percent receive ongoing services, whereas 65.7 percent do not. Yet families referred to CPS only to have their case screened out or to have an investigation that does not result in a substantiation that abuse or neglect occurred—as measured by current legal thresholds—subsequently become reinvolved with CPS at high rates (Drake et al. 2003; Hindley, Ramchandanli, and Jones 2006; Jedwab, Harrington, and Dubowitz 2017). For example, recent evidence from Wisconsin indicates that between 2004 and 2016, 26.5 percent of families that experienced a report that was initially screened in (investigated) but received an unsubstantiated case disposition were rereported to CPS, and 22.1 percent had a subsequent screened-in report and 4.4 percent a subsequent substantiated report, within 12 months of the initial report.[5] Despite concerning rates of subsequent (and escalating) CPS involvement, however, preventive interventions are not systematically offered to this group of families, some portion of whom may never be in need of CPS intervention, some who may have had their CPS cases incorrectly closed at the screening or investigation stage, and some of whom may have persistent or increasing needs related to child safety that only become evident over time.

There is widespread variation across states in terms of mandatory-reporting laws, child abuse and neglect definitions and associated levels of evidence required for substantiation, and CPS system structures and features, as well as referral, investigation, substantiation, and postresponse service receipt (including out-of-home placement) rates. A discussion of variation in mandated-reporting laws and maltreatment definitions and levels of evidence required for substantiation is provided by Berger and Slack (this volume) and Font and Maguire-Jack (this volume). Key dimensions of state CPS system structures and features include the extent to which a system is state or county administered and whether a state (or county) has implemented AR. In all, forty states (including Washington, D.C., and Puerto Rico as states for this purpose) operate state-administered systems. Ten states operate county-administered but state-supervised systems (California, Colorado, Minnesota, New York, North Carolina, North Dakota, Ohio, Pennsylvania, Virginia, and Wyoming), and two states (Nevada and Wisconsin) operate hybrid systems in which some CPS functions are administered at the state level and others at the county level (Child Welfare Information Gateway, 2018). Centralized and decentralized CPS systems may produce different patterns across the systems' decision points, leading to more or less consistent practice depending on the model. Currently, twenty-three states report AR data to the federal government, though additional states may engage in AR at the county or, to some extent, state level. Moreover, AR program designs vary across states.

There is also widespread variation across states in CPS reports (with rates ranging from 1.6 percent of children in Hawaii to 16.8 percent of children in Vermont), investigation (1.3 percent of children in Hawaii to 14.4 percent of children in West Virginia), substantiation (0.18 percent of children in Pennsylvania to 2.4 percent of children in Kentucky), and postresponse service receipt (18.7 percent of child maltreatment victims in Illinois to 100 percent of victims in Iowa and Tennessee; out-of-home placement rates among victims range from 5.2 percent in Kentucky to 48.8 percent in Hawaii) rates.[6] In addition, there is considerable county-level variation in these rates, as well, typically reflecting differences in both CPS practices and underlying sociodemographic characteristics of the population, as well as in the economic and sociopolitical contexts. Such variation may have substantial implications for the likelihood that children and families receive CPS services, which children and families receive services, and what types of services they receive. They may also reflect or affect CPS's capacity to respond to and serve the population at risk in a specific locale.

How Well Does the CPS System Work in Identifying Child Maltreatment?

Given the profound implications of child maltreatment for children's concurrent well-being and their ongoing well-being over the life course, as well as the extraordinarily intrusive and intensive nature of governmental intervention in response to child safety concerns, the stakes are high for CPS systems to simultaneously achieve high levels of sensitivity (the ability to correctly identify and serve families experiencing maltreatment) and high levels of specificity (the ability to correctly exclude families not experiencing maltreatment from CPS intervention).[7] Higher rates of sensitivity almost certainly lead to the *overinclusion* of families, whereas higher rates of specificity may lead to the *underinclusion* of families, two issues that have plagued CPS systems for decades (Waldfogel 1998). To date, the United States has conducted four National Incidence Studies (NIS) to estimate rates of child maltreatment in the general population, regardless of CPS involvement. Results from the most recent study, NIS-4, conducted in 2006, suggest an incidence rate of 17 per 1,000 children using a conservative standard, and 40 per 1,000 children using a more inclusive standard (Sedlak et al. 2010). That the NIS estimates of child maltreatment known to "community sentinels" well exceed rates of CPS involvement indicates that many children who may be victims of abuse or neglect are not known to CPS. Dettlaff and Boyd (this volume) provide insight about disparities in CPS involvement across racial and ethnic groups, stemming from historical, structural, and environmental challenges associated with racially biased practices, policies, and resource allocation contexts. New laws, the economy, changes to the social safety net, media coverage of egregious incidents of child maltreatment, and issues related to CPS system capacity can also affect patterns of overinclusion and underinclusion, as well as public health crises like the COVID-19 pandemic, currently depressing CPS reports around the country (Welch and Haskins 2020). In sum, there are a wide range of reasons that families may be overincluded or underincluded in CPS systems, some of which can be changed or influenced by these systems, and some of which cannot.

While not all families in need of intervention are reported to CPS systems, families at risk for child maltreatment may be served outside of the CPS system through participation in voluntary, community-based services, some of which are specifically designed to prevent child abuse and neglect. Jones Harden and colleagues (this volume) provide a broad overview of such prevention services, many of which have demonstrated effectiveness. One of the key challenges in the child maltreatment prevention field is getting families to participate and engage in prevention services when they are not asking for or seeking support. This may be particularly problematic in the child maltreatment prevention arena, where issues of child safety are paramount. Families who elect to participate in voluntary services may not be the families most in need of an intervention to prevent child maltreatment. This selection problem has not been adequately studied, leaving open the question of whether some evidence-based voluntary prevention services are effective for families with higher levels of need. The existing research on predictors of participation and engagement tends to focus on samples that have had some form of contact with program staff, rather than the universe of eligible participants regardless of whether program contact is made, or "enrollment" is measured as the percentage of available spots that participants fill (Maternal, Infant, and Early Childhood Home Visiting Technical Assistance Coordinating Center [MIECHV TACC] 2015). This hinders our ability to learn how to engage high-risk populations, where the very reasons behind the need for prevention services may prevent families from seeking them out on their own. It also motivates the need for intent-to-treat evaluation designs, where eligible participants are randomly assigned to a treatment or control condition and information is collected about them prior to offering the treatment group intervention services. Such designs afford the ability to better understand which participants are most likely to engage in treatment services, and whether engagement and persistence in services is tied to different types and degrees of need.

Turning back to the CPS system, another consideration for system performance—one that internal system factors can arguably influence—is how often families reported to, but ultimately *unserved* by CPS, are rereported to

CPS at some future point. If the system correctly ends involvement with families whose risk for maltreatment is low or nonexistent, then CPS recurrence among such families should be relatively low. However, several studies have demonstrated concerning rates of short-term CPS recurrence among families whose initial reports were unsubstantiated (Drake et al. 2003; Hindley, Ramchandani, and Jones 2006; Jedwab, Harrington, and Dubowitz 2017), suggesting that the system may be ending involvement with families who are actually in need of intervention to prevent child maltreatment—even if legally defined maltreatment has not yet occurred. These potential scenarios are further complicated by the fact that many families come to the attention of CPS for reasons related to poverty and material hardship (Slack et al. 2011), begging the question of whether their needs are best served by the CPS system. For the remainder of the article, we focus on the group of families for whom CPS involvement ends at the point of initial screening or investigation of a report of maltreatment. Little attention has, to date, been paid to this population at the point that CPS ends its involvement, even though this moment of contact creates an opportunity to assist families that may need and want assistance external to the child welfare system, and for whom such assistance may reduce future involvement with that system.

Families with Maltreatment Reports That Do Not Result in Ongoing CPS Involvement: An Underserved Population in Need of Services

As we described, approximately 80 percent of abuse and neglect reports do not result in ongoing intervention by CPS systems (U.S. Department of Health and Human Services 2020). Yet research suggests that a sizable percentage of families with this result are rereported to the system within a relatively short time frame. As such, families that come to the attention of CPS but are not provided ongoing services by that system constitute a population that may benefit from interventions to prevent the recurrence or escalation of risk factors for child maltreatment. Furthermore, families in this population may not be self-selecting into voluntary prevention programs in their community, rendering them underserved and, in most states, overlooked altogether.

Few existing services available to families at risk for or experiencing child maltreatment systematically attempt to engage or tailor services to meet the needs of families immediately following a CPS contact, when that contact does not result in ongoing CPS services. This is not to say that families who are reported to CPS are uninvolved in other service systems. In Wisconsin, for example, more than three-quarters of families whose cases are screened in for further investigation received Supplemental Nutrition Assistance Program (SNAP) benefits, and approximately 71 percent had BadgerCare (Wisconsin's combined Medicaid and State Children's Health Insurance program) coverage in the year prior to their CPS report.[8] However, such means-tested benefits may only partially address a family's needs in terms of types or extent, or both. Furthermore, benefits tied to a family's income and subject to regular redetermination requirements may fluctuate, creating economic stress and other hardships for a family (Ettinger de Cuba et al. 2019; Lee, Slack, and Lewis 2004). And families who are eligible for certain benefits may not take them up, sometimes by choice and other times because administrative burdens and hurdles prevent completion of the application process (Herd and Moynihan 2019; Wu and Eamon 2010). Moreover, these programs and benefits, which are intended to help families maintain stability, are not systematically enacted as part of a maltreatment prevention strategy.

In 2006, Wisconsin was one of the first states to design and implement a program, called community response (CR), which explicitly seeks to voluntarily engage families at the point that CPS decides not to open an ongoing case.[9] It is important to note that CR is not synonymous with AR programs that have proliferated in CPS systems around the country in recent decades. AR approaches are typically delivered within the context of CPS systems, whereas community-based prevention agencies that have no oversight by CPS provide CR services. Thus, CR participation is truly voluntary. CR fills a gap in the child maltreatment prevention continuum by serving families who "touch" the CPS system, but who are not further served by that system because their circumstances do not currently meet statutory definitions of maltreatment. This group may be offered ad hoc referrals to community services at the point of diversion from CPS, but typically they receive little to no further assistance at this juncture. The motivating rationale for contemporary CR programs is not a new story in the U.S. history of child welfare. As Testa and Kelly (this volume) describe, amendments to the Social Security Act in the mid-twentieth century laid a foundation for social services to promote stability for families receiving income support as an explicit means for keeping families intact. While these services were not offered at the same system point as CR programs, they targeted a largely similar population—disadvantaged families whose economic stressors could easily be conflated with "child neglect."

CR programs aim to promote stable home environments for families experiencing stressors, prevent child maltreatment, and reduce rereferrals to CPS. CR interventions are meant to be short term (i.e., 12–16 weeks) and typically include at least one home visit from the CR worker; an assessment of family strengths, needs, and stressors; collaborative goal-setting between the primary caregiver(s) and the CR worker; and flexible funds for addressing critical immediate financial stressors. In many ways, CR programs mirror the premise and nature of kinship navigator programs that are eligible for federal funding through the Family First Prevention Services Act of 2018, discussed in Testa and Kelly (this volume), with the critical difference that CR programs are intended to keep children with their families of origin, rather than focusing on supporting kinship arrangements that emerge in response to the breakdown of a child's birth or adoptive home, a point to which we return.

Using information from family assessments, staff work with the primary caregiver(s) to collaboratively set and prioritize goals to address select economic and/or psychosocial needs and assist with connecting the family to formal and informal resources (e.g., in-kind and cash benefits, parenting supports, mental health treatment, and child health and development services). Through the

FIGURE 2
Community Response Case Flow

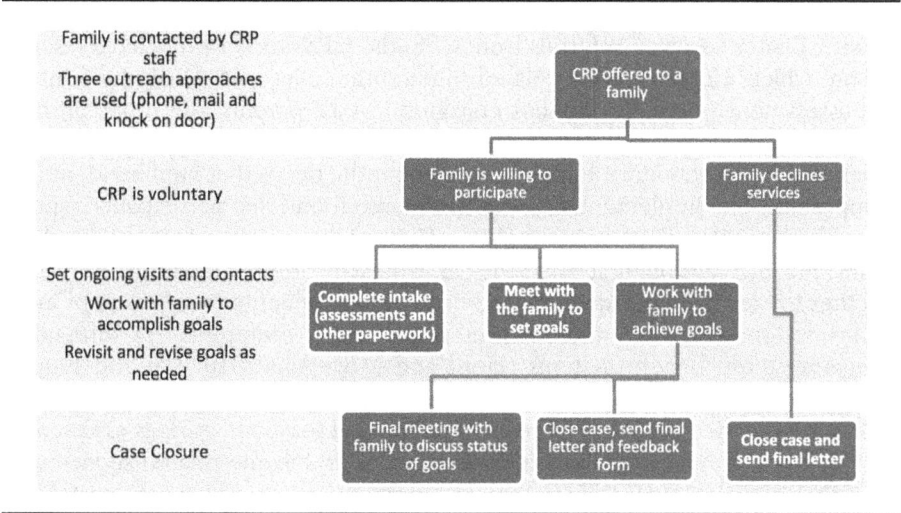

course of the intervention, the worker has at least biweekly contact with the participating family. Contacts include phone calls and in-home visits or face-to-face visits in a location convenient for the primary caregiver. Figure 2 illustrates the case flow of the intervention.

While the goal of expanding the child maltreatment prevention continuum by adding the CR component is laudable, whether CR was a feasible service model that families would want to access voluntarily, particularly on the heels of a CPS contact, was unknown. The initial six CR sites in Wisconsin participated in an implementation evaluation that allowed the Wisconsin Child Abuse and Prevention Board, Wisconsin Department of Children and Families, and site teams to learn whether and the extent to which families would participate in CR, the types of needs these families expressed, and their progress once enrolled in the program. The evaluation also allowed sites time to work through the initial stages of coordinating referrals from county CPS agencies. Given the novelty of working on a larger scale with families diverted from CPS, primary foci of the implementation evaluation were issues and concerns related to information-sharing, child safety, and how best to conduct outreach with the intended service population.

From the implementation evaluation, several key findings emerged (Maguire-Jack, Slack, and Berger 2014). First, the program acceptance rate by families ranged from 28 percent to 83 percent across sites, with an overall acceptance rate of about half. This exceeded the expectations of many of the program stakeholders. Second, sites that focused on families whose CPS involvement ended at the investigation stage tended to have higher participation rates than sites focusing on families that were screened out at the report stage. This made sense, given that families screened out at the report stage often had less accurate contact information. They also typically had no knowledge that they were the subject of a CPS report alleging child maltreatment, and many declined services out of concern that involvement in CR would lead to more unwanted surveillance. When CR sites received referrals from CPS, the CPS worker provided a referral reason, which was most often related to parenting concerns. During the intake and assessment phase for families engaging in CR, parents and other primary caregivers most often defined their primary needs as economic and material. Given that CR is voluntary, having insight about the needs that families identified is important. The implementation evaluation also found that participants' reports of public benefit receipt were modest at CR intake, despite very low levels of family income; although it was unclear from the implementation evaluation whether the lower-than-expected take-up of public benefits was a result of ineligibility for reasons other than income level, family preference, or difficulties navigating these benefit systems (Herd and Moynihan 2019; Wu and Eamon 2010). On the whole, 70 percent of participants made significant progress toward at least one service goal, and 57 percent attained at least one goal, as assessed by the CR worker. Notably, family identification of an income-related service goal was highly predictive of goal attainment (although this could have, in part, been a function of income-related service goals being more easily attained than other types of service goals).

In 2017, the Wisconsin Child Abuse and Neglect Prevention Board collected data on seven CR sites to assess program participation and engagement. In this group of CR programs, the average service take-up rate was lower than it was for the earlier group of programs (fielded in the late 2000s), ranging across sites from only 5 percent to nearly 30 percent, with an average acceptance rate of 12 percent.[10] Roughly one-third (31 percent) of CR participants had a service goal related to housing, followed by goals related to accessing resources (28 percent), parenting needs (25 percent), employment (24 percent), and mental health (22 percent). Goals related to economic needs (transportation, accessing means-tested benefits, utilities, basic needs, employment, housing, and other financial needs) were collectively identified by 53 percent of CR participants. Using an intent-to-treat randomized control trial design, we are currently conducting a program impact evaluation to determine if the CR program led to reductions in future CPS involvement.

Following Wisconsin's CR initiative, which the state launched in 2006, other states have developed and adapted CR models and engaged in evaluation activities. In Colorado's CR program, the take-up rate for services was 23 percent, and like in Wisconsin, income-related needs were most prevalent among participants (Colorado Office of Early Childhood 2019). Pre-post tests showed significant improvement in protective factors and a decrease in prevention needs, and a comparison of CR participants to a matched control group showed less maltreatment and fewer out-of-home placements of children in the CR group. Nebraska's CR program also found income-related needs to be most prevalent, and retrospective pre-post tests showed improvements in four out of five domains (Jackson, Tourek, and Skoglund 2019).[11]

Marathon County, Wisconsin, a small rural region of the state, also evaluated CR. The take-up rate for CR services was approximately 50 percent, and a comparison of families whom the program served and eligible families whom the program did not serve due to program capacity limitations (i.e., a waitlist group) showed lower rates of subsequent CPS involvement, including CPS contacts that resulted in the out-of-home placement of children, for those who received CR services (Maguire-Jack and Bowers 2014).

Milwaukee County implemented a version of Wisconsin's CR model, Project GAIN (Getting Access to Income Now), which focused exclusively on assisting families with economic needs (it did not address psychosocial needs). An intent-to-treat randomized control trial evaluated Project GAIN, and the treatment group participation rate for the later cohort of families was 22 percent.[12] Results showed statistically insignificant effects, on the whole. However, although still not statistically significant, effect sizes tended to favor the treatment group for later cohorts (i.e., those selected into the sample after the first two years of the evaluation) and especially for economically disadvantaged families (Slack et al. 2020). Specifically, for the most disadvantaged income subgroups, effect sizes tied to reductions in CPS recurrence ranged from 10 to 24 percent, suggesting that subgroup analyses may have simply lacked sufficient statistical power to attain statistical significance. For higher-income families, statistically insignificant effects were in the opposite direction, however, such that those with higher incomes who were in the treatment group were *more likely* to have CPS reinvolvement than those with similar income levels in the control group. In sum, the CR model is not a panacea for child maltreatment prevention, and it may not be equally effective for all families who are reported to CPS. Nonetheless, it does show promise with some families. Ongoing research is needed to understand the complexities of this intervention vis-à-vis the needs and circumstances of particular families.

Taken together, the various CR initiatives under way in the United States suggest that (1) some families whose CPS involvement ends at the maltreatment report screening or investigation stage are willing to participate in voluntary services to help meet their needs; (2) the needs that families identify are largely economic in nature; and (3) participation in CR services may reduce the likelihood of future CPS involvement, at least in the short term and for families experiencing high levels of economic hardship. The fact that the CR model operates externally to CPS and involves case management to help families access a variety of community-based services and resources, as well as means-tested benefits and supports related to employment and housing, situates CR in a larger context. That is, as Feely and colleagues (this volume) discuss, other systems that serve children and families are inextricably tied to efforts to reduce child maltreatment—systems that are designed to serve high-risk populations (e.g., criminal justice, mental health, economic support systems), as well as more universal systems and resources, such as schools, health care systems, and childcare. Feely and colleagues, therefore, argue that systems should recognize their role in child maltreatment prevention, something that is currently hindered by the siloed nature of the social welfare landscape in the United States.

FIGURE 3
Components of a Child Maltreatment Prevention Infrastructure

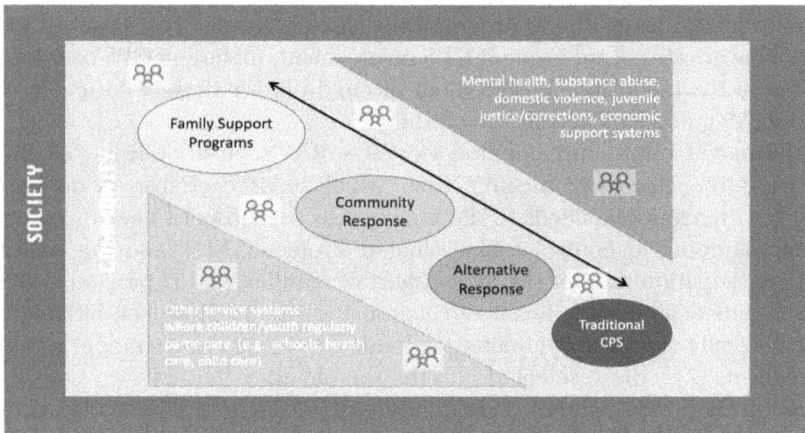

But in the absence of a formalized system of services, benefits, and resources that authentically work together to reduce child abuse and neglect, is it possible to think about creating a child maltreatment prevention infrastructure? Our various social welfare, education, and health systems, among others, are heavily siloed, and individuals and families are faced with a maze of different eligibility and application procedures, rules, and regulations that can be difficult to navigate (Herd and Moynihan 2019; Slack et al. 2014; Wu and Eamon 2010), and about which families often lack information (Anderson 2002; Lee, Slack, and Lewis 2004). CR offers promise as a tool for helping families at risk for deeper-end involvement with CPS to access these systems as their needs and situations change. Such an approach is similar to the kinship navigator programs that the Family First legislation has authorized, and for which federal funding is available. Given that kinship navigator programs have garnered support in federal law despite not having a solid evidence base of their effectiveness, it can be argued that CR programs, which do show some evidence of effectiveness, may be better positioned to serve families at risk of deeper involvement with child welfare systems, including the placement of children into foster care (including kinship foster care), and to closely monitor these programs through rigorous evaluation.

Figure 3 offers an illustration of the various organizational and system components of a proposed prevention infrastructure. In the upper left corner of the figure, family support programs are community-based, voluntary programs that serve individuals or families universally (e.g., all resident families in a community), or selectively (e.g., families referred from other service providers due to the presence of risk factors for child maltreatment), regardless of past or current child welfare system involvement. In the lower right corner of the figure, traditional CPS systems intervene with children, parents, and families following a report of abuse or neglect that necessitates (as determined by an investigation and findings that align with the statutory scope of CPS) ongoing CPS involvement. AR programs serve families deemed to have low to moderate levels of risk following a maltreatment report, most commonly as an arm of CPS. CR programs are intended for families reported to CPS, but whose cases CPS closes at the point of a maltreatment report screening or investigation. Although CR programs are typically intended only for families reported to and diverted from CPS, they could potentially serve families who self-refer, as some CR programs in Wisconsin later chose to do. Families may move along this continuum at various points, according to their constellation of risk and protective factors and the service capacity of each component of the continuum.

Figure 3 also depicts service systems in which families may be dually involved, or which they may potentially access. These include involuntary systems such as corrections, systems designed to address other types of risk factors (e.g., mental health, economic support), as well as more universal or normative systems and programs, such as education, health care, and childcare. Throughout and across the formal components depicted in the figure are informal networks of kin, neighbors, and community members who interact with families on a regular basis, serving as sources of support (or impediments) to family functioning. Finally, this infrastructure must be attuned and responsive to community and societal influences that affect child maltreatment trends and outcomes, including changes in policies, economic shifts, and changes in community demographic composition.

All of these programs, systems, and networks may function independently or interactively in ways that can be supportive, but they may also operate in ways that can serve as barriers to child and family well-being (see Feely et al., this volume; Merritt, this volume). And when they operate in a siloed fashion, even if channels of information sharing and communication are established among them, child maltreatment prevention results are not necessarily achieved. A report from IOM and NRC (2014) articulates several elements deemed essential to building an "integrated system of care," which can be grouped according to their focus on planning and collaboration activities (i.e., foundational infrastructure); operations and workforce development (implementation infrastructure); and fiscal capacity, community and political support, communications, and evaluation (sustaining infrastructure). The report highlights, in particular, the roles of organizational culture in program delivery and characteristics and contexts of interagency networks that are believed to engender and sustain interagency collaboration. In short, there are numerous and complex factors that need consideration in efforts to effectively design and leverage components of a prevention infrastructure. However, nearly 40 percent of U.S. children experience a CPS investigation at some point in their childhoods (Kim et al. 2017)—an astonishing statistic that warrants a commensurate policy response. It is nothing short of imperative that we establish a sustainable and well-resourced prevention infrastructure that can create meaningful reductions in child maltreatment.

One potential conclusion from our focus on CPS-diverted families and their high risk for reinvolvement with the CPS system is that the system should broaden its capacity to serve such families—that is, that more of these diverted families should actually be screened in for ongoing CPS services. We do not endorse this view for several reasons. First, CPS involvement tends to be unwelcomed by families, highly stigmatized, intrusive, antagonistic, and traumatic for families (see Dettlaff and Boyd, this volume; Merritt, this volume).

Second, decades of research on the etiology of child maltreatment have demonstrated that poverty and various measures of economic hardship are repeatedly correlated with indicators of child maltreatment and CPS involvement (Gelles 1992; Gil 1970; Giovannoni and Billingsley 1970; IOM and NRC 2014; Pelton 1978, 1981, 1994, 2015, 2016; Wolock and Horowitz 1979). Large-scale cross-sectional studies, such as the National Incidence Studies and the National Family Violence Surveys, have demonstrated an inverse association between income and maltreatment (Sedlak and Broadhurst 1996; Sedlak et al. 2010; Berger 2004; Gelles 1992). Research has also shown that various indicators of maltreatment correlate with community- or state-level poverty rates (Coulton et al. 2007, 1995; Drake and Pandey 1996; Maguire-Jack 2014), income inequality (Eckenrode et al. 2014), and welfare receipt rates and benefit levels (Paxson and Waldfogel 2002; Slack et al. 2003). Furthermore, within low-income populations or populations at elevated risk of child maltreatment, research has shown that economic hardship (e.g., welfare sanctions, utility shut-offs, unemployment, housing moves, self-reported material hardship) increases the risk of CPS involvement (McDaniel and Slack 2005; Courtney et al. 2005; Slack, Lee, and Berger 2007; Slack et al. 2004, 2011). And a growing body of national and international research suggests that this relationship is causal (Berger et al. 2017; Cancian, Yang, and Slack 2013; Lindo, Schaller, and Hansen 2013; Raissian and Bullinger 2017; Schneider, Waldfogel, and Brooks-Gunn 2017; Wildeman and Fallesen 2017).

Third, studies that exploit exogenous changes to the economic safety net in the United States suggest that maltreatment rates and risks are sensitive to the accessibility and generosity of social welfare benefits (Berger et al. 2017; Cancian, Yang, and Slack 2013; Raissian and Bullinger 2017). Finally, the United States has a residual welfare state, which is characterized by siloed systems with policies and rules that can be complex to navigate and even conflictual in their requirements, and an increasing reliance on policy levers and administrative practices that restrict access to the safety net (Herd and Moynihan 2019; Fox and Feng 2019). These factors, coupled with the knowledge that families diverted from CPS identify economic stressors as their primary concern, points us in the direction of taking a closer look at how various social welfare benefit programs and systems might more adequately address the basic needs of families struggling on the economic margins. We concur with Feely et al. (this volume) that a more synergistic system is needed that considers the provision of basic needs a necessary component for the "safe and consistent care" of children and see their mission as one aligned with child maltreatment prevention. And like Roygardner, Hughes, and Pulasci (this volume), we believe that secondary prevention efforts, such as CR, in the context of larger scale efforts to prevent child maltreatment, are a critical component of a prevention infrastructure.

Leroy Pelton was one of the earliest scholars to draw attention to the role of poverty in the child welfare system and as a risk for one's involvement in it (Pelton 1978, 1981, 1994, 2015, 2016). He was particularly concerned about what he viewed as a tendency for the child welfare system to conflate poverty with child neglect and to place the onus of responsibility for perceived neglect on the parent, rather than on the systems and contexts in which a family is situated. One policy recommendation from Pelton deserves particular attention: he recommended that a "social dividend, an annual common cash benefit would be allocated to every member of the community, adjusted only for household size, and would replace current public assistance and entitlement cash distribution programs, as well as tax-break programs" (Pelton 2015, 36; see also Pelton 2005). This recommendation is similar to contemporary calls for a universal basic income (UBI) (Hughes 2020), an idea first seriously considered in the United States by President Nixon, in the form of a guaranteed minimum income, proposed as part of his Family Assistance Plan (Quadagno 1990). Although Nixon's proposal was ultimately defeated, it has renewed relevance today. Given the complexities of and costly system oversight required for the myriad means-tested benefits that compose the U.S. economic safety net, coupled with the growing evidence that safety net transfers have the potential to prevent child maltreatment, a UBI has the potential to create a minimal standard of economic stability for families and reduce the need for deeper-end systems involvement. Indeed, the National Academies of Sciences, Engineering, and Medicine's (2019) recent report *A Roadmap to Reducing Child Poverty*, estimates that providing a modest monthly universal child allowance could lead to a dramatic reduction in poverty for families with children.

In sum, we make three policy recommendations stemming from our review of whom the CPS system serves and does not serve, and the implications for child maltreatment prevention. First, systems that serve children and families external to the child welfare system should develop—through workforce training, policies, and practice shifts—a greater understanding of their role in child maltreatment prevention, and their capacity to reduce demands on deep-end systems like child welfare. Second, programs such as CR should be eligible for Family First funding, given their similarity to kinship navigator programs (already eligible under this legislation), their emerging evidence base, and their ability to reach an *identified* population known to be at high risk for future CPS involvement. We also urge that such programs be subject to rigorous evaluation. Third, given the staggering rates of childhood CPS involvement in the United States, the robust evidence that economic stress and instability contribute to this involvement, and the inherent complexity of this country's siloed economic safety net, we argue that a universal child allowance would contribute to a meaningful reduction in the need for CPS intervention. We recognize that our final recommendation may face more of an uphill battle than the previous two and, if it were to be enacted, may reduce (but not eliminate) the need for the first two proposals. However, we believe that with this policy solution, we would likely see immediate impact on child maltreatment rates that would generate longer-term savings to society.

Conclusion

In this article, we have provided an overview of the "front end" of the child welfare system, commonly referred to as child protective services or CPS, and its performance with respect to identifying families in which child maltreatment has occurred or is at risk of occurring. This review is offered at a moment when child protection practices in the United States are shifting to encompass more prevention-oriented services, which necessitates a critical look at the infrastructure currently in place for preventing child abuse and neglect. We present components of a prevention system that should be considered in efforts to better coordinate and deliver proactive services to families at risk of child maltreatment and CPS involvement, with particular attention to a previously overlooked population—families reported to but diverted from CPS.

This population is the largest group to encounter CPS, yet historically the system has done little to engage and offer them services to prevent maltreatment recurrence and rereports to CPS. We argue that the diversion of families reported to CPS should not necessarily be considered a failure of CPS systems but, rather, a reflection of the insufficient social safety net for disadvantaged families in the United States. Meaningful and significant reductions in child maltreatment in the United States will not likely be accomplished without attending to safety net programs and systems to ensure that they are facilitating (and not hindering) access by eligible families, providing reasonable levels of support, and working together to coordinate service delivery. More robust antipoverty policies and programs are not the panacea for child maltreatment; nor will they diminish maltreatment risk for every child. However, given the extensive evidence demonstrating a strong relationship between economic disadvantage and child maltreatment, including evidence that this relationship is causal, concerted efforts to address poverty are a worthwhile investment from a prevention perspective.

Notes

1. Title IV-B of the Social Security Act was established in 1967 and provides some funding to states, tribes, and territories for child maltreatment prevention and child welfare services.

2. States use different terms to reflect an allegation that is found to have merit, including "substantiated," "indicated," and "founded." We use the term "substantiated" to capture all of these statuses.

3. Of these, 60.8 percent of victims experienced only neglect, 10.7 percent experienced only physical abuse, and 7.0 percent experienced only sexual abuse (U.S. Department of Health and Human Services 2020).

4. There were 1,738 maltreatment-related child fatalities in 2018, a rate of 2.39 per 100,000 U.S. children, representing 0.000004 percent of all U.S. children (U.S. Department of Health and Human Services 2020).

5. Authors' calculations, available on request.

6. Postresponse service receipt rates for nonvictims range from 2.0 percent in Maine to 100 percent in Iowa; out-of-home placement rates among nonvictims range from 0.1 percent in Oklahoma and Utah to 6.7 percent in Wisconsin (U.S. Department of Health and Human Services, 2020).

7. There are additional concerns related to whether the nature or even the fact of CPS involvement benefits, harms, or has no effect on the welfare of children; however, this article focuses on the decision to serve or not serve families at the system's front end, and not on how well the system works once families become more deeply involved.

8. Authors' calculations, available on request.

9. The programs operated at a county or regional level, primarily supported (until 2019) by the Wisconsin Child Abuse and Neglect Prevention Board (formerly Wisconsin Children's Trust Fund). Although not a statewide initiative, approximately twenty-four counties (out of seventy-two) have implemented CR at some point since 2006.

10. The lower take-up rate in 2017 was due to the referral population consisting of all cases closed after a report or investigation; whereas, in the earlier pilot program, some sites had additional eligibility criteria that may have made families easier to locate and engage.

11. The take-up rate in Nebraska's CR program was not reported.

12. Participation rates reached over 60 percent in the final year of the intervention, but there were some key differences in recruitment in this final year, tied to requiring completion of an in-person survey prior to randomization.

References

Anderson, Steven G. 2002. Ensuring the stability of welfare-to-work exits: The importance of recipient knowledge about work incentives. *Social Work* 47:162–70.

Berger, Lawrence M. 2004. Income, family structure, and child maltreatment risk. *Children and Youth Services Review* 26 (8): 725–48.

Berger, Lawrence M., Sarah A. Font, Kristen S. Slack, and Jane Waldfogel. 2017. Income and child maltreatment in unmarried families: Evidence from the Earned Income Tax Credit. *Review of Economics of the Household* 15 (4): 1345–72.

Berger, Lawrence M., and Kristen S. Slack. 2021. The contemporary U.S. child welfare system(s): Overview and key challenges. *The ANNALS of the American Academy of Political and Social Science* (this volume).

Cancian, Maria, Mi-Youn Yang, and Kristen S. Slack. 2013. The effect of additional child support income on the risk of child maltreatment. *Social Service Review* 87 (3): 417–37.

Child Welfare Information Gateway. 2018. *State vs. County Administration of Child Welfare Services.* Washington, DC: U.S. Department of Health and Human Services, Children's Bureau.

Child Trends Databank. 2019. *Foster care.* Available from https://www.childtrends.org/?indicators=foster-care.

Colorado Office of Early Childhood. 2019. Colorado Community Response Evaluation Findings: 2014–2018. Evaluation Brief. Denver, CO: Colorado Office of Early Childhood.

Coulton, Claudia, David Crampton, Molly Irwin, James Spilsbury, and Jill Korbin. 2007. How neighborhoods influence child maltreatment: A review of the literature and alternative pathways. *Child Abuse and Neglect* 31 (11–12): 1117–42.

Coulton, Claudia, Jill Korbin, Marilyn Su, and Julian Chow. 1995. Community level factors and child maltreatment rates. *Child Development* 66 (5): 1262–76.

Courtney, Mark E., Amy Dworsky, Irving Piliavin, and Andrew Zinn. 2005. Involvement of TANF applicant families with child welfare services. *Social Service Review* 79 (1): 119–57.

Dettlaff, Alan J., and Reiko Boyd. 2021. Racial disproportionality and disparities in the child welfare system: Why do they exist, and what can be done to address them? *The ANNALS of the American Academy of Political and Social Science* (this volume).

Dettlaff, Alan J., Stephanie L. Rivaux, Donald J. Baumann, John D. Fluke, Joan R. Rycraft, and Joyce James. 2011. Disentangling substantiation: The influence of race, income, and risk on the substantiation decision in child welfare. *Children and Youth Services Review* 33:1630–37.

Drake, Brett, Jennifer M. Jolley, Paul Lanier, John Fluke, Richard P. Barth, and Melissa Jonson-Reid. 2011. Racial bias in child protection? A comparison of competing explanations using national data. *Pediatrics* 127 (3): 1–8.

Drake, Brett, Melissa Jonson-Reid, Ineke Way, and Sulki Chung. 2003. Substantiation and recidivism. *Child Maltreatment* 8 (4): 248–60.

Drake, Brett, and Shanta Pandey. 1996. Understanding the relationship between neighborhood poverty and specific types of child maltreatment. *Child Abuse and Neglect* 20 (11): 1003–18.

Eckenrode, John, Elliot G. Smith, Margaret E. McCarthy, and Michael Dineen. 2014. Income inequality and child maltreatment in the United States. *Pediatrics* 133 (3): 454–61.

Ettinger de Cuba, Stephanie, Mariana Chilton, Allison Bovell-Ammon, Molly Knowles, Sharon M. Coleman, Maureen M. Black, John T. Cook, Diana Becker Cutts, Patrick H. Casey, and Timothy C.

Heeren, et al. 2019. Loss of SNAP is associated with food insecurity and poor health in working families with young children. *Health Affairs* 38 (5): 765–73.

Feely, Megan, Kerri M. Raissian, William Schneider, and Lindsey Rose Bullinger. 2021. The social welfare policy landscape and child protective services: Opportunities for and barriers to creating systems synergy. *The ANNALS of the American Academy of Political and Social Science* (this volume).

Font, Sarah A., and Kathryn Maguire-Jack. 2021. The scope, nature, and causes of child abuse and neglect. *The ANNALS of the American Academy of Political and Social Science* (this volume).

Fox, Ashley M., and Wenhui Feng. 2019. The effect of administrative burden on state safety-net participation: Evidence from SNAP, TANF and Medicaid. Presented at Association for Public Policy Analysis and Management, 41st Annual Fall Conference, Denver, CO.

Gelles, Richard. 1992. Poverty and violence toward children. *American Behavioral Scientist* 35 (3): 258.

Gil, David. 1970. *Violence against children: Physical child abuse in the United States*. Cambridge, MA: Harvard University Press.

Giovannoni, Jeanne M., and Andrew Billingsley. 1970. Child neglect among the poor: A study of parental adequacy in families of three ethnic groups. *Child Welfare* 49:196–204.

Harden, Brenda Jones, Cassandra Simons, Michelle Johnson-Motoyama, and Richard Barth. 2021. The child maltreatment prevention landscape: Where are we now, and where should we go? *The ANNALS of the American Academy of Political and Social Science* (this volume).

Haskins, Ron. 2021. Child welfare financing: What do we fund, how, and what could be improved? *The ANNALS of the American Academy of Political and Social Science* (this volume).

Herd, Pamela, and Donald P. Moynihan. 2018. *Administrative burden: Policymaking by other means*. New York, NY: Russell Sage Foundation.

Hindley, Nick, Paul Ramchandani, and David Jones. 2006. Risk factors for recurrence of maltreatment: A systematic review. *Archives of Disease in Childhood* 91 (9): 744–52.

Hughes, Chris. 1 May 2020. Why Americans need a guaranteed income. *New York Times*.

Institute of Medicine (IOM) and National Research Council (NRC). 2014. *New directions in child abuse and neglect research*. Washington DC: The National Academies Press.

Jackson, Barbara, Kelsey Tourek, and Becky Skoglund. 2019. *Community Well-Being | Community Response: 2018–2019 evaluation report*. Lincoln, NE: Munroe-Meyer Institute, University of Nebraska Medical Center.

Jedwab, Merav, Donna Harrington, and Howard Dubowitz. 2017. Predictors of substantiated re-reports in a sample of children with initial unsubstantiated reports. *Child Abuse and Neglect* 69:232–41.

Johnson-Motoyama, M., E. Putnam-Hornstein, A. J. Dettlaff, K. Zhao, M. Finno-Velasquez, and B. Needell. 2015. Disparities in reported and substantiated infant maltreatment by maternal Hispanic origin and nativity: A birth cohort study. *Maternal and Child Health Journal* 19:958–68.

Kim, Hyunil, Christopher Wildeman, Melissa Jonson-Reid, and Brett Drake. 2017. Lifetime prevalence of investigating child maltreatment among U.S. children. *American Journal of Public Health* 107:274–80.

Lee, Bong J., Kristen S. Slack, and Dana A. Lewis. 2004. Are welfare sanctions working as intended? Employment, continued welfare receipt, and material hardship among TANF recipient families. *Social Service Review* 78 (3): 370–403.

Lindo, Jason M., Jessamyn Schaller, and Benjamin Hansen. 2013. Economic conditions and child abuse. NBER Working Paper 18994, National Bureau of Economics Research, Cambridge, MA. Available from https://doi.org/10.3386/w18994.

Maguire-Jack, Kathryn. 2014. Multilevel investigation into the community context of child maltreatment. *Journal of Aggression, Maltreatment and Trauma* 23 (3): 229–48.

Maguire-Jack, Kathryn, and Jessica Bowers. 2014. Marathon county community response: Voluntary services for families screened out of child protective services. *Child Welfare* 93 (5): 65–82.

Maguire-Jack, Kathryn, Kristen S. Slack, and Lawrence M. Berger. 2014. Wisconsin's Community Response Program for families that have been reported for child maltreatment. *Child Welfare* 92 (4): 95–121.

Maternal, Infant, and Early Childhood Home Visiting Technical Assistance Coordinating Center (MIECHV TACC). July 2015. MIECHV issue brief on family enrollment and engagement. Washington, DC: MIECHV TACC. Available from https://mchb.hrsa.gov/sites/default/files/mchb/MaternalChild-HealthInitiatives/HomeVisiting/tafiles/enrollmentandengagement.pdf.

McDaniel, Marla, and Kristen S. Slack. 2005. Major life events and the risk of a child maltreatment inves-
    tigation. *Children and Youth Services Review* 27 (2): 171–95.
Merritt, Darcey. 2021. How do families experience and interact with CPS? *The ANNALS of the American
    Academy of Political and Social Science* (this volume).
Myers, John E. B. 2004. *A history of child protection in America*. Bloomington, IN: Xlibris Corp.
National Academies of Sciences, Engineering, and Medicine. 2019. *A roadmap to reducing child poverty*.
    Washington, DC: National Academies Press.
Paxson, Christina, and Jane Waldfogel. 2002. Work, welfare, and child maltreatment. *Journal of Labor
    Economics* 20 (3): 435–74.
Pelton, Leroy H. 1978. Child abuse and neglect: The myth of classlessness. *American Journal of
    Orthopsychiatry* 48:608–17.
Pelton, Leroy H. 1981. *The social context of child abuse and neglect*. New York, NY: Human Sciences
    Press.
Pelton, Leroy H. 1994. The role of material factors in child abuse and neglect. In *Protecting children from
    abuse and neglect*, eds. G. B. Melton and F. D. Barry, 131–81. New York, NY: Guilford Press.
Pelton, Leroy H. 2005. *Frames of justice: Implications for social policy*. New Brunswick, NJ: Transaction
    Publishers.
Pelton, Leroy H. 2015. The continuing role of material factors in child maltreatment and placement. *Child
    Abuse and Neglect* 41:30–39.
Pelton, Leroy H. 2016. Separating coercion from provision in child welfare. *Child Abuse and Neglect*
    51:427–34.
Peterson, Cora, Curtis Florence, and Joanne Klevens. 2018. The economic burden of child maltreatment
    in the United States, 2015. *Child Abuse and Neglect* 86:178–83.
Quadagno, Jill. 1990. Race, class and gender in the U.S. welfare state: Nixon's failed Family Assistance
    Plan. *American Sociological Review* 55:11–28.
Radel, Laura, Melinda Baldwin, Gilbert Crouse, Robin Ghertner, and Annette Waters. 7 March 2018.
    Substance use, the opioid epidemic, and the child welfare system: Key findings from a mixed methods
    study. ASPE Research Brief. Washington, DC: Office of the Assistant Secretary for Planning and
    Evaluation, U.S. Department of Health and Human Services. Available from https://aspe.hhs.gov/sys-
    tem/files/pdf/258836/SubstanceUseChildWelfareOverview.pdf.
Raissian, Kerri M., and Lindsey R. Bullinger. 2017. Money matters: Does the minimum wage affect child
    maltreatment rates? *Children and Youth Services Review* 72:60–70.
Roygardner, Debangshu, Kelli N. Hughes, and Vincent J. Palusci. 2021. Leveraging family and community
    strengths to reduce child maltreatment. *The ANNALS of the American Academy of Political and Social
    Science* (this volume).
Schneider, William, Jane Waldfogel, and Jeanne Brooks-Gunn. 2017. The Great Recession and risk for
    child abuse and neglect. *Children and Youth Services Review* 72:71–81.
Sedlak, Andrea, and David Broadhurst. 1996. *Third National Incidence Study of Child Abuse and Neglect*.
    Washington, DC: U.S. Department of Health & Human Services.
Sedlak, Andrea J., Jane Mettenburg, Monica Basena, Ian Petta, Karla McPherson, Angela Greene, and
    Spencer Li. 2010. *Fourth National Incidence Study of Child Abuse and Neglect (NIS-4): Report to
    Congress*. Washington, DC: U.S. Department of Health & Human Services, Administration for
    Children and Families.
Slack, Kristen S., Lawrence M. Berger, J. Michael Collins, Aaron Reilly, and Emma K. Monahan. 2020.
    *Project GAIN (Getting Access to Income Now): Intent-to-treat findings at 12- and 24-months post
    randomization*. Report to the Wisconsin Child Abuse and Prevention Board and Casey Family
    Programs. Madison, WI: University of Wisconsin–Madison, Institute for Research on Poverty.
Slack, Kristen S., Lawrence M. Berger, Kimberly DuMont, Mi Youn Yang, Susan Erharhd-Dietzel, and
    Jane Holl. 2011. Predicting child neglect of young children: A comparison of three samples. *Children
    and Youth Services Review* 33:1354–63.
Slack, Kristen S., Lawrence M. Berger, and Jennifer L. Noyes. 2017. Introduction to the special issue on
    the economic causes and consequences of child maltreatment. *Children and Youth Services Review*
    72:1–4.

Slack, Kristen S., Jane L. Holl, Bong Joo Lee, Marla McDaniel, Lisa Altenbernd, and Amy B. Stevens. 2003. Child protective intervention in the context of welfare reform: The effects of work and welfare on maltreatment reports. *Journal of Policy Analysis and Management* 22 (4): 517–36.

Slack, Kristen S., Jane L. Holl, Marla McDaniel, Joan Yoo, and Kerry Bolger. 2004. Understanding the risks of child neglect: An exploration of poverty and parenting characteristics. *Child Maltreatment* 9 (4): 395.

Slack, Kristen S., Bomi Kim, Mi-Youn Yang, and Lawrence M. Berger. 2014. The economic safety net for low-income families with young children. *Children and Youth Services Review* 46:213–19.

Slack, Kristen S., Bong Joo Lee, and Lawrence M. Berger. 2007. Do welfare sanctions increase child protection system involvement? A cautious answer. *Social Service Review* 81 (2): 207–28.

Stewart, Nikita. 9 June 2020. Child abuse cases drop 51 percent; Authorities are very worried. *New York Times*.

Testa, Mark F., and David Kelly. 2021. The evolution of federal child welfare policy through the Family First Prevention Services Act of 2018: Opportunities, barriers, and unintended consequences. *The ANNALS of the American Academy of Political and Social Science* (this volume).

U.S. Department of Health & Human Services. 2019. Trends in foster care and adoption: FY 2009–FY 2018. Washington, DC: U.S. Department of Health & Human Services Available from https://www.acf.hhs.gov/sites/default/files/cb/trends_fostercare_adoption_09thru18.pdf.

U.S. Department of Health & Human Services, Administration for Children and Families, Administration on Children, Youth and Families, Children's Bureau. 2020. *Child maltreatment 2018*. Available from https://www.acf.hhs.gov/cb/resource/child-maltreatment-2018.

Waldfogel, Jane. 1998. *The future of child protection*. Cambridge, MA: Harvard University Press.

Welch, Morgan, and Ron Haskins. 2020. What COVID-19 means for America's child welfare system. Report. Brookings Institution. Available from https://www.brookings.edu/research/what-covid-19-means-for-americas-child-welfare-system/?preview_id=799522.

Wildeman, Christopher, Natalia Emanuel, John M. Leventhal, Emily Putnam-Hornstein, Jane Waldfogel, and Hedwig Lee. 2014. The prevalence of confirmed maltreatment among U.S. children, 2004–2011. *JAMA Pediatrics* 168 (8): 706–13.

Wildeman, Christopher, and Peter Fallesen. 2017. The effect of lowering welfare payment ceilings on children's risk of out-of-home placement. *Children and Youth Services Review* 72:82–90.

Wolock, Isabel, and Bernard Horowitz. 1979. Child maltreatment and material deprivation among AFDC-recipient families. *Social Service Review* 53 (2): 175–94.

Wu, Chi-Fang, and Mary K. Eamon. 2010. Need for and barriers to accessing public benefits among low-income families with children. *Children and Youth Services Review* 32 (1): 58–66.

How Do Families Experience and Interact with CPS?

By
DARCEY H. MERRITT

The lived experiences of child protective services (CPS)–involved parents is rarely considered from a social justice perspective. Parents and children endure the oversight of the child welfare system in myriad ways, and these experiences usually vary based on race, ethnicity, and socioeconomic status. This article explores how CPS interactions affect family dynamics and well-being and how family members view their experiences with CPS, including their sense of autonomy and empowerment. I focus on the inherent power dynamics between CPS workers and parents, race and ethnicity, and family. I highlight the perspectives of parents and their intended (rather than unintentional) parental behaviors (e.g., providing healthy food choices) to understand ways in which their socioecological contexts impact the well-being of their children. I report results of a pilot study designed to enhance the voices of parents in the literature and provide recommendations for policy and practice that inform innovative solutions to better support CPS-involved families.

Keywords: child welfare system; parents' perspectives; child protective services processes; minority child; welfare families; low-income child

Research has documented few accounts of the child welfare system from the perspectives of families involved in the system. Child protective services (CPS) is the "front-end" of the child welfare system, where reports of abuse and neglect are processed, maltreatment investigations occur, and decisions about opening an ongoing case are made. CPS is inherently coercive, as family participation is usually compulsory or, at best, strongly encouraged, with the

Darcey H. Merritt is an associate professor at NYU Silver School of Social Work. She studies parenting in socioeconomic context, considering the impact of working memory on parental decision-making. She provides empirical and meaningful knowledge to bolster the well-being of children and families, through contributing their voices to the discussion of child maltreatment prevention methods.

Correspondence: Darcey.merritt@nyu.edu

DOI: 10.1177/0002716220979520

explicit or implicit threat of significant consequences, including removal of one's child from the home. Given the high stakes for CPS-involved families, we must understand their experiences with this system and the ways in which they view it as helpful or harmful. Yet very little in the literature has explored how families view their CPS experiences and how their interactions with CPS impact their family dynamics, well-being, and sense of autonomy and empowerment.

This article highlights the experiences of families and discusses the ways in which schools work with the child welfare system to initiate families' involvement with CPS, sometimes in ways that can be detrimental to family well-being. I describe and discuss the process of interacting with CPS, with attention to the inherent power dynamics between CPS workers and parents, race and ethnicity, and family context. Family context has great variation, a sampling of which includes family composition (e.g., number of children, parents), family member relationships, safe home environments, resource rich learning materials in the home, pervasive food insecurities, substance use, and emotional/mental health challenges or strengths.

I present a nuanced approach to understanding the experiences of these families, an approach that considers parental intentions and perspectives. I present results of a pilot study specifically designed to assess parental perspectives regarding CPS involvement to bolster their lived experiences and add their voices to the literature. Finally, I discuss future steps and recommendations for policy and practice in an effort to move the conversation forward and adopt innovative solutions that better support CPS-involved families, considering their often-challenging circumstances.

The Impact of CPS

The United States has a storied history of discrimination, which continues to manifest in structurally oppressive systems, including in many of our social and human service agencies. Despite good intentions to protect children from harm, the child welfare system is not an exception (Kriz and Skivenes 2011; Mixon-Mitchell and Hanna 2017). Most parents consider their families to be sacredly private and immune from oversight and intrusive judgment. But CPS services are based on protocols designed by those in positions of power and privilege who have not likely been subjected to authoritative involvement in their families and may not have considered the impact of CPS on traditionally vulnerable populations, such as those who have repeatedly suffered from disenfranchisement, racism, and other forms of oppression. CPS services are inherently accusatorial, as they are primarily initiated as a result of judgments about parenting efforts and practices, made by authorities outside of family systems, such as educational personnel (21 percent) and law professionals (19 percent) (U.S. Department of Health & Human Services [USDHHS] 2020). Child welfare professionals have the power to deem parenting appropriate or inappropriate, guided by state statutes and system policies, but such judgements come with implicit biases at all levels of service design and delivery (Kriz and Skivenes 2011; Mixon-Mitchell and Hanna 2017; Roberts 2014; Wells, Merritt, and Briggs 2009).

Black families and other families of color have long histories of oppressive and discriminatory oversight across multiple social welfare and human service systems (Pager and Shepherd 2008; Rothstein 2017; Seabrook and Wyatt-Nichol 2016; Wise 2010). In the child welfare system, racial disparities occur at every decision point (Miller et al. 2013; Roberts 2014): abuse and neglect reporting (Ards et al. 2003), investigation and maltreatment substantiation (Rolock and Testa 2005), and foster care placement decisions and case closures (Miller et al. 2013). Research has documented racial disproportionality in the child welfare system, defined as the overrepresentation of children or families from a particular racial group relative to their representation in the general population (Boyd 2014; Cooper 2013; Dettlaff and Rycraft 2008; Dettlaff et al. 2011; Drake and Jonson-Reid 2011; Font, Berger, and Slack 2012; George and Lee 2005; R. Hill 2005; Fluke et al. 2011; Roberts 2014; Kokaliari, Roy, and Taylor 2019; Mixon-Mitchell and Hanna 2017). I discuss theories of the root causes of this disproportionality later in this article, and Detlaff and Boyd (this volume) discuss them as well. Scholars have rarely considered the child welfare system from a social justice perspective (Brooks and Roberts 2002; Edwards 2016; Roberts 2014), which has resulted in a general inattention to the stigmatizing impact on marginalized families and communities that comes with disproportionate system oversight. Further, scholars have rarely considered the link between families' lived experiences of child welfare system oversight (Fong 2019) and associated parental behaviors and decisions.

I posit that parental choices that occur in the context of child welfare system involvement are inextricably linked to deeply rooted feelings related to the judgment inherent in system oversight, and compounded by the threat of potentially devastating consequences, including child removal. I argue that we must consider a family's past experiences of oppression, often stemming from racism and discrimination, in our approach to engaging with families where child safety may be a concern. Every child and parent who becomes involved with CPS is subjected to varying levels of stress and trauma stemming from the inherently intrusive nature of the system. The impact of CPS is exacerbated if children have to be removed from their families of origin and placed in care. CPS has put in place various services for families in attempts to protect children from harm. Some families feel overburdened and negatively affected by system oversight, while others feel supported in their efforts to improve their parenting when the child welfare system enters their lives; others have both experiences (Merritt and Ludeke 2020).

We must also consider the impact of CPS involvement in terms of families' socioeconomic contexts. Research must acknowledge ways in which parental behaviors are impacted by their positionality in society. Those with higher levels of educational attainment, better employment opportunities, and greater earning power are also better positioned to make choices that significantly reduce or even eliminate child maltreatment risk or reduce their risk of surveillance by and adverse interactions with authorities. Parents with sufficient resources are typically able to secure suitable housing and benefit from better-resourced school districts, higher-quality childcare options, and safer neighborhoods. Families that are typically involved with CPS are socially and economically disadvantaged and have far fewer high-quality options across each of these domains (Chaudry and Wimer 2016; Fong 2019; Kang et al. 2019; Landers, Carrese, and Spath 2019).

Both endogenous and exogenous barriers influence parenting quality. Some examples of endogenous challenges to parenting quality are personal characteristics, such as age, marital status, gender identification, and mental health issues. Examples of exogenous challenges in this context refer to poverty, dangerous neighborhoods, underemployment and unemployment, and so on. We must understand the emotional impact of navigating the child welfare system in the face of these barriers, which differ across families, and the varying strategies that parents employ to exercise resilience. The pilot study highlighted in this article seeks to understand the lived experiences of families as they interface with CPS. While provision of child welfare supports and services could be seen as a positive manner of intervening in families to protect children, there are dynamics at play in many families, based on historical experiences with oppressive systems, that, in turn, impact parental perceptions of the system and its ability to support their autonomy and empowerment.

Schools Weaponizing CPS

Child maltreatment practitioners, policy-makers, and scholars need to be mindful of the overlapping impact of the child welfare system and the education system in terms of outcomes for children and in the context of the power dynamics in both systems that are particularly problematic for historically disenfranchised families and communities. Families lacking socioeconomic privilege and resources and those less empowered and socialized to self-advocate for autonomy are also often the ones subjected to outside surveillance from multiple systems. As I discuss, families are first brought to the attention of child welfare agencies when parenting is identified as questionable, neglectful, or abusive by someone external to this system. Most children over the age of three spend the majority of their waking hours during the school year in childcare and school settings where they are under the direct supervision of teachers, nurses, and counselors. Child behaviors in schools typically manifest from normative to troubling, the latter often perceived as flags that can prompt queries into the home environment. However, as I describe, the child welfare and educational systems often work in concert to perpetuate the stigma experienced by economically disadvantaged and marginalized families.

To understand the impact of CPS oversight on families, we must consider the role of educational system oversight and system collaboration practices with child welfare (Garstka et al. 2014). The education system is a key source of reports of child maltreatment. Teachers and other education professionals are mandated reporters from which 20.5 percent of all reports originate (not including 0.6

percent among child daycare providers) (USDHHS 2020), but compared to many other types of professionals, they have the most consistent access to children, placing them in a particularly unique position of power. Unfortunately, an unintended consequence of such oversight is the propensity for school systems to unintentionally, or sometimes even intentionally, weaponize CPS against families, given that teachers risk both moral and professional negative consequences if they fail to exercise extreme caution in their assessments of potential child maltreatment among their students. Further, teachers are not infallible to racial bias.

Mandated child maltreatment referral protocols can also be affected by aspects of the education system that overlap with the medical system, sometimes stemming from system pressures on parents, rather than autonomous parental choice. Examples of such pressurized decisions include health issues (Jackson, Cheater, and Reid 2008), medication compliance (Naylor et al. 2007), and adherence to special education designations (Hibel, Farkas, and Morgan 2010), oftentimes in response to challenging classroom behaviors. Oversight by child welfare workers and accompanying educator/counselor assessments often result in children being deemed in need of medication to mitigate the presenting problematic behaviors displayed in school settings. Parents in families that have experienced various forms of oppression, trauma, and economic stress may feel coerced by the high stakes of family disruption if they are noncompliant with service plans imposed by the education system, including medication interventions. As a result, some parents may reluctantly agree to medicate their children, which may, in turn, contribute to the disproportional use of psychiatric medication with CPS-involved children (Alavi and Calleja 2012; Barnett et al. 2016; McKay 2007; Walsh and Mattingly 2012).

Special education designations (K. Hill 2013), which are often based on a deficit-focus approach to assessment, can also play a role in further stigmatizing and marginalizing parents and children already dealing with other familial and environmental stressors. Teachers may identify a child with disturbing classroom behaviors, inattention, and an inability to focus as needing special education services, yet the child's distressed household environment and familial socioeconomic position may be the catalyst for disruptive classroom behaviors (e.g., a lack of nutritional meals at home, a distressed environment due to domestic violence), and not a reflection of her academic skills or abilities.

To the extent that the child welfare system and oversight by CPS workers creates additional stress and even trauma for a family, family management roles in the context of the parent/child dyad may be adversely affected. Education system mandates that challenge the relationships between parents and their child's teachers may similarly affect family dynamics. Parents may fear scrutiny from their children's teachers when they send their children to school with meager lunches, tattered clothing, or scrapes and bruises that were not the result of intentional abuse. These daily concerns may play out in stress levels and everyday interactions between children and their parents. There is a salient fear of judgment from educational authorities as parents raise their children in the context of persistent experiences of oppression and marginalization. In addition to concerns about potential erroneous allegations of physical abuse and neglect, parents may also experience a sense of diminished control over educational decisions for their children, particularly when caseworkers and/or teachers make recommendations that a parent feels pressured to implement (e.g., adhering to individualized education plans or IEPs). Essentially, when interacting with CPS, aspects of parental choice and control are scrutinized and can be diminished by both the child welfare and education systems. There are justifiable cases when children are truly in danger of harm, warranting a CPS report from schools, followed by an investigation. However, among some marginalized families, schools can be weaponized to carry out family surveillance directly leading to child welfare system oversight and ongoing involvement.

The CPS Process

The typical pathway to CPS involvement begins with a report alleging one or more types of child abuse and neglect (see, also, Berger and Slack, this volume for additional discussion of the CPS process). These reports can originate from a number of sources. Most reports originate from school professionals and legal authorities, followed by social services (10.7 percent) and medical professionals (10.5 percent) (USDHSS 2020). However, neighbors and family members can also make reports to CPS, and individuals can report to CPS anonymously. Mandated reporters or people who are required by law to report instances of suspected child maltreatment to CPS trigger an investigation by a CPS worker who visits the family and makes a determination about the presenting factors involved with the allegation. Depending on whether cases are "screened out" or "screened in," the CPS worker makes a designation to indicate or substantiate child maltreatment (Child Welfare Information Gateway 2013, 2019), and potentially open a case for ongoing services.

There are a host of adjudications that a caseworker can make, based on their perceived level of risk for continued or future harm to a child (Child Welfare Information Gateway 2019). Some children may be placed in temporary foster or kinship care while parents adhere to particular interventions (e.g., family therapy, substance use treatment, and behavioral management programs). Families screened out following a maltreatment report or whose report does not result in an open case are sometimes referred to community-based programs (e.g., after-school programs, parent support groups, youth diversion programs). Other dispositions include placement of a family case in an alternative or differential response track, which allows for a less intrusive level of involvement with families whose children have been deemed to be at low or moderate risk for future harm (Fluke et al. 2019; Hughes et al. 2013). In these cases, next steps typically include voluntary acceptance of CPS services contracted to community agencies, based on specific familial needs. Slack and Berger (this volume) present a more detailed discussion of the adoption of such alternative responses by child welfare systems, which are intended to mitigate the risk of children entering the child welfare system or being removed from their families.

Once a family has an ongoing case opened within the child welfare system, CPS develops a case plan that incorporates child, parent, and family goals. A family-specific menu of services is then put into place with regular system oversight to assess progress. County-level child welfare agencies provide direct services to families or may contract with private child welfare agencies to provide intensive and frequent service delivery. Examples of services, inclusive of community-based resources, include home visiting, agency provided parent-child therapy, and other family support services (e.g., nutrition classes, family management techniques). Caseworkers visit families as often as needed according to the case plan (i.e., weekly, monthly). After a designated period of time, families are assessed to determine if there is an ongoing level of risk for harm that warrants continued, or sometimes elevated, involvement in CPS services.

Power Dynamics

Considerable power dynamics are inherent in the experiences of CPS-involved families, stemming from the imbalance between those in positions of judgment and parents under scrutiny (Bundy-Fazioli, Briar-Lawson, and Hardiman 2008). Families with histories of diminished control over their lives and family management choices are particularly susceptible to the added trauma of CPS oversight, which may exacerbate tensions in stressed familial circumstances. Such histories are directly related to prior CPS involvement, in addition to experiences with other systems characterized by oversight and surveillance, such as the criminal justice and welfare systems (Chamberlain et al. 2019; McLoyd 1990; Merritt and Ludeke 2020). Such oversight may result in strained parent-child relationships, in part due to the enormous stakes of threatened family disruption. Living under conditions where one experiences a diminished locus of control and lack of power not only affects the emotional well-being and functioning of parents, but it can also transfer distress intergenerationally to children, even affecting children's coping mechanisms. Children may feel uncertain about the primary role of their parents when other authority figures seem to be guiding the family system. Parents have an acute awareness of negative assumptions imposed upon them based on their positionality in society, which is further bolstered by ongoing and increasingly salient outward racism and discrimination experienced during their CPS involvement (Franklin, Boyd-Franklyn, and Kelly 2008). Families endure the institutional racism inherent in CPS in varied ways, but CPS involvement perpetuates trauma because these families cannot escape the discriminatory protocols that those with power and authority execute. An example of these processes relates to the likelihood of CPS involvement for Black children despite their white counterparts exhibiting similar issues (Franklin, Boyd-Franklyn, and Kelly 2008). Such experiences can have an extremely negative impact on family cohesion and perceptions of safety in the home while interfacing with CPS (Wells, Merritt, and Briggs 2009).

We must strengthen the relationships between parents and caseworkers in the context of these unbalanced power dynamics and histories of oppressive systems involvement (Cheng and Lo 2020). Child welfare workers should consider their efforts as partnering with parents in a helping capacity, rather than mandating compliance in the face of threats and without acknowledging the diverse contexts (including socioeconomics) in which families live. This kind of approach would allow for a shared power dynamic, rather than embracing the notion that practitioners have power over parents and subsequent family management (Dumbrill 2006; Smith 2008). Services are too often designed and implemented from a deficit lens rather than from a strength-based perspective (Kemp et al. 2014; Walsh and Canavan 2014). For instance, a service plan may require that a parent enhance the learning environment at home, but the assessment of a substandard learning environment is based on more privileged perceptions of what an adequate learning environment looks like, perhaps overlooking the innovative opportunities that families with fewer resources create to help their children learn. Service plans in tandem with educational childcare settings should encourage parental engagement in home learning environments and strive toward helping parents with resources, such as books and educational activities, and with creating a calm environment suitable for learning.

Family Characteristics and Lived Experiences of CPS Involvement

People of color

Those among the lower socioeconomic strata of society and people of color suffer a host of inequities inherent in systemic and structural oppression as they navigate human services organizations and medical and educational settings. These experiences are directly related to their histories of diminished access to knowledge, power, and optimal resources. Families involved with CPS are under near-constant inspection, and parental behaviors and decisions are regularly questioned. Such judgment and behavioral mandates from authorities can negatively impact the dynamics of family functioning (Berger and Font 2015; Merritt and Ludeke 2020; Roberts 2002; Roberts 2014).

CPS-involved families are already vulnerable in large part due to their demographic characteristics and disadvantaged status in both power and socioeconomics. This population disproportionately comprises families of color (Fluke et al. 2010, 2003; R. Hill 2006; Kim, Chenot, and Ji 2011; Lanier et al. 2014; Putnam-Hornstein et al. 2013; Stoltzfus 2005; Wulczyn and Lery 2007; Klein and Merritt 2014); are typically less educated; and lack financial resources and optimal, safe, and healthy living environments (Berger 2004; Berger and Slack, this volume; Fong 2017; Kang et al. 2019; Nam, Meezan, and Danziger 2006). Recent accounts of CPS-involved families indicate that Blacks are substantially overrepresented (20.6 percent), whites are underrepresented (44.5 percent), and Hispanic children (22.6 percent) make up almost the same percentage of maltreatment victims as Hispanic children in the general population (Blacks, 13.7 percent; whites, 50.3 percent; Hispanic, 13.7 percent) (USDHHS 2020). The fundamental causes of racial/ethnic disproportionality in the child welfare system has been widely debated (Boyd 2014; Fluke et al. 2003; Font, Berger, and Slack 2012; Sedlak and Schultz 2005; also see, in particular, Detlaff and Boyd, this volume).

Research has theorized two prominent perspectives—the "Bias Model" and the "Risk Model." These models present competing explanations for racial disproportionality in CPS involvement (Drake et al. 2011). The Bias Model suggests that racial bias manifests from those who report and investigate maltreatment and results in the overrepresentation of Blacks and other minorities in the child welfare system. Thus, overrepresentation is not an indication that minorities mistreat their children more often and not to the extent noted by their disproportionate involvement with child protection services (Klein and Merritt 2014). Conversely, the Risk Model suggests that Blacks and other minority groups do in fact maltreat their children at higher rates than others due to a number of personal and community-level risk factors. Pervasive challenges, such as unemployment and poverty, are associated with inadequate supports and resources and diminished service access, which would otherwise mitigate the impact of parenting stress and reduce maltreatment risk. Both models have evidentiary support; however, research has acknowledged the Risk Model more often as the explanation for this overrepresentation in CPS (see Detlaff and Boyd, this volume; Drake et al. 2011). I posit that both models are at play for those involved in CPS and vary widely according to nuanced circumstances. As noted, the child welfare system is one of a number of oppressive systems rooted in structural discrimination and, as such, racial bias plays a role in the ways in which CPS makes and executes programmatic decisions (Wells, Merritt, and Briggs 2009). This structurally supported bias poses the real risk of maltreatment for our most vulnerable populations.

CPS-involved families and children endure judgment from mandated referring authorities and caseworkers charged with investigating maltreatment allegations. According to the Bias Model, a salient outcome of this excessive scrutiny is that professionals and community members may pathologize and label parenting behaviors by minority parents as abusive and neglectful, and these actions may reflect explicit or implicit racial biases in their decision-making (Klein and Merritt 2014). That parents experience oversight in such a context, dispensed by authorities with the power to disrupt families, is both disturbing and consequential for autonomous parental decision-making (Merritt and Snyder 2015). Enduring constant surveillance while raising a family under suboptimal societal conditions is unsettling for these parents and exacerbates the challenges they already experience while trying to properly care for children.

Ecological contexts

CPS-involved families should always be understood in the ecological contexts in which they live and function (see Freisthler, Merritt, and LaScala 2006). These families typically live in environments that mirror historically oppressive structural systems associated with membership in minority populations and those living in impoverished conditions (Coulton et al. 2007). A host of studies have highlighted the association with and impact of neighborhood characteristics on

CPS-involved families across different races/ethnicities (Freisthler, Merritt, and LaScala 2006; Klein and Merritt 2014; Freisthler, Bruce, and Needell 2007; Kohl, Jonson-Reid, and Drake 2009; Korbin et al. 1998; Merritt 2009). Neighborhood structure plays a significant role in parenting and family functioning (Abner 2014; Coulton et al. 2007; Merritt 2009). Communities experience varying levels of social service oversight and police presence, which have been linked to increased maltreatment referrals and actual rates of maltreatment (Klein and Merritt 2014). One of the more relied-upon neighborhood-level explanations for racial disproportionality in the child welfare system is social disorganization theory (Sampson 2001; Shaw and McKay 1969; Wilson 1987, 1996), which suggests that structural changes in the United States since the 1970s have contributed to urban neighborhood organization and precipitated a clustering of social problems, including child maltreatment (Klein and Merritt 2014). Essentially, the theory suggests that community (dis)organization results in fewer social controls, and shared goals and norms, such as a commitment to child safety.

Characteristics of impoverished communities—those considered socially disorganized—have a differential impact on racial groups, such that the idea of racial heterogeneity is nuanced according to the neighborhood makeup. For instance, research on the impact of neighborhood poverty and racial composition has identified a "differential sensitivity" concerning the risk of being referred to CPS for child maltreatment, noting that living in poor communities was a larger risk for white children and living in more affluent communities was a risk factor for Black children (being "out of place") (Drake and Pandy 2006; Klein and Merritt 2014; Wulcyn et al. 2013), yet some have deemed this a minor contributing factor to being reported to CPS (Drake, Lee, and Jonson-Reid 2009).

Poverty and child maltreatment types

The lived experiences of CPS-involved families cannot be disentangled from poverty. Family functioning and dynamics are strained for myriad reasons related to financial stressors (Levine and Chase-Lansdale 2000; Liu and Merritt 2018; Taylor et al. 2017; Neppl, Senia, and Donnellan 2016). These circumstances are highly influential on parental behaviors and result in deleterious outcomes, such as failing to properly care for children due to a dearth of needed resources, persistent psychological distress, and strained family dynamics. Families in poverty are likely more vulnerable to injustices related to system oversight. They suffer a host of inequities inherent in systemic and structural oppression as they navigate all types of human services organizations (Abner 2014). Both children and parents in these families have been subjected to varying levels of chronic trauma based on their socioeconomic backgrounds and experiences with oversight systems. Poverty, particularly extreme poverty, can be conceptualized as a form of trauma (Garo, Allen-Handy, and Lewis 2018; Hudson 2016), which can lead to poor functioning and suboptimal behavioral choices. Poverty impacts working memory, cognitive appraisal, and decision-making (Blair and Raver 2016; Mani et al. 2013; Noble et al. 2012; Toth et al. 2011), yet the design and implementation of CPS are not grounded in this science.

involved with CPS, I conducted a pilot study to assess parents' perceptions of system oversight based on one's race/ethnicity and socioeconomic status.[1] This study specifically aimed to (1) understand contextual fears and perceptions among marginalized women related to CPS oversight and parenting roles, (2) identify parent-driven remedies to address fears associated with child-rearing practices to enhance child welfare service delivery, and (3) assess thematic parental fears as predictors of specific types of child maltreatment.

Child-rearing practices vary greatly based on parents' fears and concerns. These fears stem from challenging environmental circumstances; lack of access to resources; and deeply rooted, unjust social stratification norms. Moreover, community characteristics shape parents' expectations of children in their attempts to instill the necessary skills for survival in those environments. Efforts to decrease the prevalence of child maltreatment must consider the challenges placed on parenting in impoverished communities, accompanying parental fears, and experiences with systemically oppressive oversight systems.

This study presents new knowledge about the relationship between child-rearing practices and parents' experiences with child welfare agency oversight, primarily among Black and Latinx parents receiving child maltreatment preventive services. An underlying goal of this inquiry was to identify links and pathways between parenting intentions and parents' decision-making in context. Relying on the theoretical underpinnings of the Family Stress Model (Conger, Conger, and Martin 2010), minority stress theory, the Amplified Disadvantage Model (Roche and Leventhal 2009), and critical race theory (Crenshaw et al. 1996), I gathered information on the perceived impact of parental fears on child-rearing decisions according to socioeconomic status and child welfare service variation to identify thematic parental fears as predictors of specific types of child maltreatment.

Utilizing an exploratory phenomenological approach, the study focused on the lived experiences with and parental perceptions of CPS oversight as related to parenting decisions and child-rearing practices. A New York–based agency contracted by the Administration of Children's Services (ACS) to provide services to families at risk for child maltreatment granted approval to access families participating in general preventive services. The criteria for inclusion were that respondents needed to be actively receiving in-home services from the agency. I selected sample participants through purposive, nonprobability sampling techniques and recruited them through agency outreach. I conducted seventeen in-depth, face-to-face, semistructured interviews with primarily Black and Latinx, New York City–based agency mothers lasting approximately 45–60 minutes. The interviews were audio recorded and transcribed verbatim. I obtained informed consent from participants and provided them with a $30 bank card for participation.

The in-depth interview guide covered perceptions regarding (1) parents' fears and nuanced experiences with both public and private (contracted preventive services) child welfare agency oversight and (2) remedies to reduce or eliminate fears related to parenting behavior. The interview guide allowed for an understanding of how parents' fears in context impact child-rearing practices as families interface with oversight systems. Employing a systematic grounded theory analysis, information garnered from the interviews were open and group coded, allowing for the identification of themes related to parents' fears and concerns based on child welfare oversight.

I queried seventeen respondents, of whom sixteen identified as cis-gender females. The average age of the participants was 33, with the bulk of the sample identifying as Black or African American (64 percent) and 30 percent identifying as Latinx. The mean education level among this group was a GED/high school diploma or less ($M = 2.18$, range 0–5). Only slightly over a third were working full time (35 percent), with nearly half reporting unemployment (47 percent), and most indicating a need for financial help a fair amount of the time (in between sometimes and most of the time) as opposed to barely making ends meet and able to meet all financial needs ($M = 1.47$, range 0–3).

The interview domains centered on attributions for child-rearing practices based on parents' fears. A series of questions included parenting practices related to fears that might result in unwanted experiences with systems (e.g., lack of childcare, nutritional sustenance, dangerous neighborhoods, threats of child removal). Employing a systematic grounded theory analysis, I identified and assessed for nuanced commonalities final themes.

Four subthemes emerged: (1) agency treatment, (2) judgment based on race/ethnicity, (3) perceptions of parenting well/parenting intent, and (4) financial disparities (see Table 1). A primary salient theme that emerged from the qualitative accounts was how parents felt about CPS involvement. Overall, parents felt mistreated and unfairly judged by child welfare agency workers based on their race/ethnicity. They expressed trauma resulting from continued CPS oversight that negatively impacted the child/parent relationship. Parents often noted feeling stigmatized and shamed within their communities for having an open child welfare case. Additionally, parents expressed feeling challenged and perceived as not capable of providing the experiences they felt their children deserved due to racial stereotypes and based on financial challenges. Overall, parents expressed perceptions and feelings of judgment, blame, intimidation, being overwhelmed, afraid (of family disruption), and a loss of control. Some expressed satisfaction with the support from private child welfare workers or a combination of feeling supported and feeling intruded upon because of the oversight.

> I really don't like people coming in and out of my house. It's just like I feel like it's an invasion of privacy. But they, you know, everyone has been very nice. They've helped out in every way possible. Then they've helped me out with resources so I guess it's—I guess one bad experience I guess, I don't know. Something good came out of it or is coming out of it. Just have to wait and see. (Sally, 32)

This quote serves as an example of a mixed and nuanced opinion about CPS involvement. This view was shared by a few of the study respondents. Whereas the bulk of the respondents lamented the requirement of adhering to CPS parenting and family management mandates, at times, they shared appreciation for certain components of the services. Below, I highlight some comments from parents that characterize the four subthemes that I identified when analyzing the data.

TABLE 1
Interview Question Prompts and Emerging Themes

Question Prompts	Themes
Do you feel you've been treated fairly while involved with child welfare agencies?	Agency treatment: *ACS oversight and lack of support/fair treatment*
Do they (caseworkers) treat all people the same regardless of their background?	Judgement based on race/ethnicity
What do you think it means to be a good parent?	Perceptions of parenting well/parental intent
Do you make parenting decisions or discipline your kids based on your income?	Financial disparities: *Financial barriers/ socioeconomic status*

Agency treatment

As an exemplar of how parents experienced agency treatment and in response to the question, "Do they (caseworkers) treat all people the same regardless of their background?" the quote below indicates a mother's perception of predetermined judgment, rather than empathy and support. She expresses feeling wrongly judged based on past case notes and distrusting the motives of the worker.

> You know, they definitely don't make it easy. They don't . . . their perception of whatever they read or whatever case notes they have. They come in with, you know, like treating you a certain type of way. It's like, relax. You don't need to . . . you know, I know I've done wrong. I admitted it and I'm making changes to fix it. They're very judgmental and very like. . . . It's not a support. . . . They make it seem like they're here for support and they want to help but I've questioned it sometimes . . . they dictate what needs to be done and it's just been, it's been a tough road. (Bianca, 28 years old, Latina [Hispanic], one child [male, 10 years old])

Judgment based on race/ethnicity

To assess how parents felt about being judged based on their identified race and ethnicity, I asked, "Do caseworkers treat all people the same regardless of their background?" Bianca further shares concern that she was judged based on a stereotype that parents of color are bad. The stigma of CPS involvement was palpable and perceived as negative. Participants also pointed to a link between being viewed as minority stereotypes and how that played out in CPS involvement.

> I don't know. I don't know. I just think if you're a minority and you have an ACS case, they have a certain perception of you. It's like a stereotype. . . . If you already have an ACS case, they think in their mind, y'all are the worst type of parent.

Olivia, a 35-year-old, African American with six children (ages 9 to 27 years old; the older children are the biological children of Olivia's husband, who is older than she is), expressed a similar perception:

Nope. They don't give a damn. ... Skin means a whole lot. If I was light enough, if I was white enough, bright enough. . . . They'd be a little nicer to me. . . because I'm dark. The word was said [that I] look aggressive. This is how I talk. I can calm this is how I talk. . . . But this comes across as aggressive. If he ain't Black in America, it's a not a good thing to talk this way, but I'm not going to stop being me.

Financial disparities

As I have noted, a large proportion of those interfacing with CPS have a low socioeconomic status, which plays a significant role in these parents' ability to parent effectively, especially given that the majority of children who come to the attention of CPS are deemed to be neglected of sustenance, other basic necessities provisions, and suitable childcare settings. Financial supports and resources are essential to sufficient parenting. Responding to the question, "Do you make parenting decisions or discipline your kids based on your income?" Carla, a 33-year-old, African American mother with a young daughter (age seven), shared her worry about providing basic necessities: "I don't worry about being a parent, like my biggest worry if I did worry it would be like just to be able to provide basically. Just providing for them, giving them what they deserve."

The need to provide basic sustenance was challenging to my participants. Again, Carla shared the perils of living in a low-resourced community and her worry about ensuring that the children in her neighborhood were able to access needed resources and things they would like to have beyond necessities:

> Like because I live in like in a low-income neighborhood where I feel like all the children . . . I mean I'm not singling out one child but I just feel like the children have issues because they don't have the necessities or sometimes they don't have the things that they need or maybe want. . . .
>
> I just feel like if I had given myself the chance to further my education then I think that I could probably provide more or do more for them, definitely, but in the sense as far as emotional like emotionally or physically I don't think, I am who I am so I don't think that would change but as far as just like being able to provide. . .

Perceptions of parenting well/parenting intent

To assess how parents felt about their personal perspectives of parenting well and what they intended to convey and achieve in their parenting behaviors, I asked parents what they "think it means to be a good parent?" Nala, a 28-year-old multiracial mom caring for her sister, the CPS target child, whom she has guardianship over (female, age 18, male to female transition) shared: "To not overstep and to have like a good understanding with your kids and to have a love like not a love like oh I love you, I love you. Like a love that they can feel and they see— like they see it through your actions and what you do when like, how you speak to them."

Carla indicated a concern about ensuring the safety of her child and providing for her ultimate happiness:

Making sure your girls or your children are safe, secure, they have a roof over their head. They have clothing on their back, shoes on their feet. They are happy, they are entertained, and they are going to sports and having different recreational activities. They are reading, do you understand? I just want to raise productive citizens, that's all. (Carla, 33 years old, African American, one child [female, age 7])

Many of the mothers expressed a desire to make sure their children felt an unconditional love that can be depended upon and demonstrated in all ways, including financially providing for their needs and ensuring that they grow up in safe environments and attend good schools.

These findings are just a few among many examples from this study that suggest parents felt mistreated and unfairly judged by child welfare agency workers based on their identifying as Black or brown. To my knowledge, there are no studies documenting white CPS-involved families experiencing stigma based on their race. One might expect, nevertheless, that white families also experience stigma based on their socioeconomic status and suffer trauma stemming from their system involvement. Parents expressed feeling challenged and perceived as not good enough to provide for their children based on racial stereotypes and financial challenges, while also sharing their earnest attempts to provide for their children, often even more than resources allowed. Parents also discussed stigma as a means of further shaming them for receiving CPS supervision in their communities. Child welfare workers are noticeable when they go into communities and public housing comprising primarily people of color. Neighbors are acutely aware of which families are under supervision of CPS. Practitioners and policymakers must consider the perspectives of these parents who are enduring child welfare system oversight as we strive toward providing the most supportive environments for children and their parents.

Some families come to rely on CPS workers for both tangible supports and help with parenting, yet some experience the oversight as a burden that hinders their attempts to parent to the best of their ability, and feel the attention is an intrusion. Asking parents about their experience with such oversight and their preferred contextually safe parenting practices is critical if we are to encourage these parents' self-determination. Contextually safe parenting practices refer to ways in which parents keep their children safe according to specific contexts, such as neighborhood composition, safety level, and quality (e.g., availability and access to services, healthy food resources, child- and family-specific community resources). Results from this study highlight how CPS oversight impacts parents' choices.

Future Steps (Research, Policy, and Practice)

A social justice approach that acknowledges the inherent systemic racism and structural disenfranchisement within the institution of the child welfare system should mandate the inclusion of system-involved parents' perspectives not only as a strategy for system improvement, but also as a means to empower parents. I propose a shift in the narrative, such that we acknowledge the privilege of those who develop and implement policy and practice as well as the structural oppression repeatedly encountered by vulnerable families as they interact with social welfare and human service systems. Research efforts to distinguish intentional neglect from unintentional neglect associated with limited resources and barriers stemming from oppression are critically needed. If child welfare system protocols and policies incorporated concerted efforts to assess parents' intentions as a function of their available resources and histories with structural discrimination and environmental contexts, perhaps there would be far fewer children designated as neglected whose families are, in turn, subjected to stigmatizing CPS oversight. Such a shift would allow for parents' needs to be addressed with less intrusive service options, including facilitating access to financial and concrete supports. Tangible remedies are essential—we must increase financial resources and educational opportunities and relieve childcare demands for families at risk.

Practitioners need to confront white dominance in their critique of parenting behaviors. Further, scholars should apply a phenomenological approach that honors the lived experience of parents in the context of child welfare oversight. The current statutes regarding parental behaviors need to be revisited, such that all behaviors related to poverty are not deemed to be maltreatment. Parents need to be provided with the necessary supports and resources to proactively mitigate circumstances that lead to deprivation of basic sustenance and safety for their children.

Future interventions would be enhanced by acknowledging racial and ethnic disparities of parents involved in the child welfare system, and the histories of systemic oppression they have experienced, by creating a paradigm shift in how we support Black and Latinx parents. Further, we must acknowledge how parents perceive disparities in system oversight and that child-rearing choices are related to socioeconomic disparities and accompanying parenting challenges. Finally, research needs to give attention to parenting choices and child-rearing practices that occur based on parents' perceptions of systems involvement.

Policy revisions that mandate a nonjudgmental approach to supporting families (strategies/implications) are also warranted. For instance, if we arrive at a refined and universal definition of neglect and one that acknowledges the unintentionality of experiencing poverty, then our assessments about parenting will be based on compassion and empathy and will be, thus, less accusatory (see Feely et al., this volume). Our mandated reporting laws date back to the 1960s. A missing underlying link is the difference between intentional and unintentional maltreatment. As I have noted, the CDC does not consider intentionality because the goal is to protect children from the most egregious forms of harm, such as child death, and thus it focuses on potential worst-case scenario outcomes rather than parental intent.

Finally, holistic and strength-based approaches are necessary to provide services from a trauma-informed lens and one that incorporates parental perceptions. A strength-based approach is one in which individuals and families are assessed based on their strengths and positive aspects related to their coping abilities, rather than from a deficit lens, which primarily critiques deficiencies and problems related to resiliency efforts. Racial bias training for educators and other mandated reporters is needed. Practitioners should partner with parents to provide social capital underpinned by strength-based help, trauma-informed consideration of parent/child well-being, and a child-centered approach to family engagement.

Conclusion

Parenting choices are directly related to differences in resource-rich or resource-poor settings, both inside and out of the home, and the choices also result in differential power dynamics between CPS workers and parents. CPS interjects a microscope into all aspects of parenting. If societal and environmental contexts, inclusive of the power dynamics inherent in coercive systems, are considered in parenting assessments, mandated reporters, practitioners, and service providers may be less likely to place blame on well-intentioned parents and more likely to note positive efforts and strive to reduce challenges to desirable parenting.

Parents' lived experiences of CPS involvement have been underassessed and underappreciated and have not been considered in efforts to decrease the prevalence of child maltreatment, particularly neglect. Parental intent is given little consideration in nuanced socioeconomic contexts. An understanding of parental decision-making is required to improve service provision. A renewed effort to support and empower parents and decrease punitive oversight, along with acknowledging the structural oppression inherent in all systems and service efforts, would go a long way in our collective efforts to protect children. We need to understand the context of and history of systemic inequities that certain populations have endured and pay attention to parental choices and child-rearing practices based on this history and these parents' perceptions of systems involvement.

Note

1. Pilot Study Title: Parental Fears and Socio-economic Status: Understanding Child Maltreatment (Funding Sources: NYU, Silver School of Social Work, Seed Grant and New York University Research Challenge Grant).

References

Abner, Kristen. 2014. Dimensions of structural disadvantage: A latent class analysis of a neighborhood measure in child welfare data. *Journal of Social Service Research* 40 (1): 121–34.

Alavi, Zakia, and Nancy G. Calleja. 2012. Understanding the use of psychotropic medications in the child welfare system: Causes, consequences, and proposed solutions. *Child Welfare* 91 (2): 77–94.

Ards, Sheila D., Samuel L. Myers Jr., Allan Malkis, Erin Sugrue, and Li Zhou. 2003. Racial disproportionality in reported and substantiated child abuse and neglect: An examination of systematic bias. *Children and Youth Services Review* 25 (5–6): 375–92.

Barnett, Erin R., Rebecca L. Butcher, Katrin Neubacher, Mary K. Jankowski, William B. Daviss, Kathleen L. Carluzzo, Erica G. Ungarelli, and Cathleen R. Yackley. 2016. Psychotropic medications in child welfare: From federal mandate to direct care. *Children and Youth Services Review* 66:9–17.

Berger, Larry M. 2004. Income, family structure, and child maltreatment risk. *Children and Youth Services Review* 26:725–48.

Berger, Larry M., and Sarah A. Font. 2015. The role of the family and family-centered programs and policies. *The Future of Children* 25 (1): 155–76.

Berger, Lawrence M., and Kristen S. Slack. 2021. The contemporary U.S. child welfare system(s): Overview and key challenges. *The ANNALS of the American Academy of Political and Social Science* (this volume).

Blair, Clancy, and Cybele C. Raver. 2016. Poverty, stress, and brain development: New directions for prevention and intervention. *Academic Pediatrics* 16 (3 Suppl.): S30–S36.

Boyd, Reiko. 2014. African American disproportionality and disparity in child welfare: Toward a comprehensive conceptual framework. *Children and Youth Services Review* 37:15–27.

Brooks, Susan L., and Dorothy E. Roberts. 2002. Social justice and family court reform. *Family Court Review* 40 (4): 453–59.

Bundy-Fazioli, Kimberly, Katharine Briar-Lawson, and Eric R. Hardiman. 2008. A qualitative examination of power between child welfare workers and parents. *British Journal of Social Work* 39 (8): 1447–64.

Chamberlain, Catherine, Graham Gee, Stephen Harfield, Sandra Campbell, Sue Brennan, Yvonne Clark, Fiona Mensah, Kerry Arabena, Helen Herrman, Stephanie Brown, and Healing the Past by Nurturing the Future Group. 2019. Parenting after a history of childhood maltreatment: A scoping review and map of evidence in the perinatal period. *PloS ONE* 14 (3): e0213460. Available from https://doi.org/10.1371/journal.pone.0213460.

Chaudry, Ajay, and Christopher Wimer. 2016. Poverty is not just an indicator: The relationship between income, poverty, and child well-being. *Academic Pediatrics* 16 (3 Suppl.): S23–S29.

Cheng, Tyrone C., and Celia C. Lo. 2020. Collaborative Alliance of Parent and Child Welfare Caseworker. *Child Maltreat* 25 (2): 152–61.

Child Welfare Information Gateway. 2013. *How the child welfare system works*. Washington, DC: Child Welfare Information Gateway. Available from https://www.childwelfare.gov/pubPDFs/cpswork.pdf.

Child Welfare Information Gateway. 2019. *Mandatory reporters of child abuse and neglect*. Washington, DC: Child Welfare Information Gateway. Available from https://www.childwelfare.gov/pubPDFs/manda.pdf.

Conger, Rand D., Katherine J. Conger, and Monica J. Martin. 2010. Socioeconomic status, family processes, and individual development. *Journal of Marriage and the Family* 72 (3): 685–704.

Cooper, Tanya A. 2013. Racial bias in foster care: The national debate. *Marquette Law Review* 97 (2): 215–77.

Coulton, Claudia J., David S. Crampton, Molly Irwin, James C. Spilsbury, and Jill E. Korbin. 2007. How neighborhoods influence child maltreatment: A review of the literature and alternative pathways. *Child Abuse & Neglect* 31 (11–12): 1117–42.

Crenshaw, Kimberlé, Neil Gotanda, Gary Peller, and Kendall Thomas. 1996. *Critical race theory: The key writings that formed the movement*. New York, NY: The New Press.

Dettlaff, Alan J., and Reiko Boyd. 2021. Racial disproportionality and disparities in the child welfare system: Why do they exist, and what can be done to address them? *The ANNALS of the American Academy of Political and Social Science* (this volume).

Dettlaff, Alan J., Stephanie L. Rivaux, Donald J. Baumann, John D. Fluke, Joan R. Rycraft, and Joyce James. 2011. Disentangling substantiation: The influence of race, income, and risk on the substantiation decision in child welfare. *Children and Youth Services Review* 33 (9): 1630–37.

Dettlaff, Alan J., and Joan R. Rycraft. 2008. Deconstructing disproportionality: Views from multiple community stakeholders *Child Welfare* 87 (2): 37–58.

Drake, Brett, Jennifer M. Jolley, Paul Lanier, J. Fluke, Richard P. Barth, and Melissa Jonson- Reid. 2011. Racial bias in child protection? A comparison of competing explanations using national data. *Pediatrics* 127 (3): 471–78.

Drake, Brett, and Melissa Jonson-Reid. 2011. NIS interpretations: Race and the national incidence studies of child abuse and neglect. *Children and Youth Services Review* 33 (1): 16–20.

Drake, Brett, and Melissa Jonson-Reid. 2018. Defining and estimating child maltreatment. In *The APSAC handbook on child maltreatment*, 5th ed., eds. J. Bart Klika and Jon R. Conte, 14–33. Thousand Oaks, CA: Sage Publications.

Drake, Brett, Sang Moo Lee, and Melissa Jonson-Reid. 2009. Race and child maltreatment reporting: Are Blacks overrepresented? *Child Youth Services Review* 31 (3): 309–16.

Drake, Brett, and Shanta Pandy. 1996. Understanding the relationship between neighborhood poverty and specific types of child maltreatment. *Child Abuse and Neglect* 20 (11): 1003–18.

Dumbrill, Gary C. 2006. Parental experience of child protection intervention: A qualitative study. *Child Abuse and Neglect* 30:27–37.

Edwards, Frank. 2016. Saving children, controlling families: Punishment, redistribution and child protection. *American Sociological Review* 81 (3): 1–31.

Erickson, Martha F., Madelyn H. Labella, and Byron Egeland. 2017. Child neglect. In *The APSAC handbook on child maltreatment*, 4th edition, eds. J. Conte and B. Klika. London: Sage Publications.

Feely, Megan, Kerri M. Raissian, William Schneider, and Lindsey Rose Bullinger. 2021. The social welfare policy landscape and child protective services: Opportunities for and barriers to creating systems synergy. *The ANNALS of the American Academy of Political and Social Science* (this volume).

Festinger, Trudy. 1983. *No one ever asked us – A postscript to foster care*. New York, NY: Columbia University Press.

Fluke, John D., Nicole Harlaar, Brett Brown, Kurt Heisler, Lisa Merkel-Holguin, and Adam Darnell. 2019. Differential response and children re-reported to child protective services: County data from the National Child Abuse and Neglect Data System (NCANDS). *Child Maltreatment* 24 (2): 127–36.

Fluke, John D., Brenda Jones-Harden, Molly Jenkins, and Ashleigh Ruehrdanz. 2010. *Research synthesis on child welfare disproportionality and disparities*. Baltimore, MD: Annie E. Casey Foundation. Available from https://www.aecf.org.

Fluke, John D., Brenda Jones-Harden, Molly Jenkins, and Ashleigh Ruehrdanz. 2011. *Disparities and disproportionality in child welfare: Analysis of the research*. Baltimore, MD: Annie E. Casey Foundation.

Fluke, John D., Ying-Ying Yuan, John Hedderson, and Patrick A. Curtis. 2003. Disproportionate representation of race and ethnicity in child maltreatment: Investigation and victimization. *Children and Youth Services Review* 25 (5–6): 359–73.

Fong, Kelley. 2017. Child welfare involvement and contexts of poverty: The role of parental adversities, social networks, and social services. *Children and Youth Services Review* 72:5–13.

Fong, Kelley. 2019. Concealment and constraint: Child protective services fears and poor mothers' institutional engagement. *Social Forces* 97 (4): 1785–1810.

Font, Sarah A., Lawrence M. Berger, and Kristen S. Slack. 2012. Examining racial disproportionality in child protective services case decisions. *Children and Youth Services Review* 34 (11): 2188–2200.

Franklin, Anderson J., Nancy Boyd-Franklyn, and Shalonda Kelly. 2008. Racism and invisibility: Race-related stress, emotional abuse and psychological trauma for people of color. *Journal of Emotional Abuse* 6 (2–3): 9–30.

Freisthler, Bridget, Emily Bruce, and Barbara Needell. 2007. Understanding the geospatial relationship of neighborhood characteristics and rates of maltreatment for Black, Hispanic, and white children. *Social Work* 52 (1): 7–16.

Freisthler, Bridget, Darcey H. Merritt, and Elizabeth LaScala. 2006. Understanding the ecology of child maltreatment: A review of the literature and directions for future research. *Child Maltreatment* 11 (3): 263–80.

Garo, Laurie, Ayana Allen-Handy, and Chance W. Lewis. 2018. Race, poverty, and violence exposure: A critical spatial analysis of African American trauma vulnerability and educational outcomes in Charlotte, North Carolina. *Journal of Negro Education* 87 (3): 246–69.

Garstka, Teri A., Alice Lieberman, Jacklyn Biggs, Betsy Thompson, and Michelle Marie Levy. 2014. Barriers to cross-systems collaboration in child welfare, education, and the courts: Supporting educational well-being of youth in care through systems change. *Journal of Public Child Welfare* 8 (2): 190–211.

George, R. M., and B. L. Lee. 2005. The role of race in foster care placements. In *Race matters in child welfare: The overrepresentation of African American children in the system*, eds. M. Testa and J. Poertner, 173–86. Washington, DC: CWLA Press.

Hibel, Jacob, George Farkas, and Paul L. Morgan. 2010. Who is placed into special education? *Sociology of Education* 83 (4): 312–32.

Hill, Katharine. 2013. Special education experience of older foster youth with disabilities: An analysis of administrative data. *Journal of Public Child Welfare* 7 (5): 520–35.

Hill, Robert B. 2005. The role of race in parental reunification. In *Race matters in child welfare: The overrepresentation of African American children in the system*, eds. M. Testa and J. Poertner, 215–30. Washington, DC: CWLA Press.

Hill, Robert B. 2006. Synthesis on disproportionality in child welfare: An update. Baltimore, MD: Casey—CSSP Alliance for Racial Equity in the Child Welfare System. Available from https://www.aecf.org.

Hudson, Nancy. 2016. The trauma of poverty as social identity. *Journal of Loss & Trauma* 21 (2): 111–23.

Hughes, Ronald C., Judith S. Rycus, Stacey M. Saunders-Adams, Laura K. Hughes, and Kelli N. Hughes. 2013. Issues in differential response. *Research on Social Work Practice* 23 (5): 493–520.

Jackson, Cath, Francine M. Cheater, and Innes Reid. 2008. A systematic review of decision support needs of parents making child health decisions. *Health Expectations: An International Journal of Public Participation in Health Care and Health Policy* 11 (3): 232–51.

Kang, Ji Young, Jennifer Romich, Jennifer L. Hook, JoAnn Lee, and Maureen Marcenko. 2019. Family earnings and transfer income among families involved with child welfare. *Child Welfare* 97 (1): 61–83.

Kemp, Susan P., Maureen O. Marcenko, Sandra J. Lyons, and Jean M. Kruzich. 2014. Strength-based practice and parental engagement in child welfare services: An empirical examination. *Children and Youth Services Review* 47 (Part 1): 27–35.

Kim, Hansung, David Chenot, and Juye Ji. 2011. Racial/ethnic disparity in child welfare systems: A longitudinal study utilizing the Disparity Index (DI). *Children and Youth Services Review* 33:1234–44.

Klein, Sacha, and Darcey H. Merritt. 2014. Neighborhood racial & ethnic diversity as a predictor of child welfare system involvement. *Children and Youth Services Review* 41:95–105.

Kohl, Patricia L., Melissa Jonson-Reid, and Brett Drake. 2009. Time to leave substantiation behind: Findings from a national probability study. *Child Maltreatment* 14 (1): 17–26.

Kokaliari, Effrosyni D., Ann R. Roy, and Joyce Taylor. 2019. African American perspectives on racial disparities in child removals. *Child Abuse and Neglect* 90:139–48.

Korbin, Jill E., Claudia C. Coulton, Sarah Chard, Candis Platt-Houston, and Marilyn Su. 1998. Impoverishment and child maltreatment in African American and European American neighborhoods. *Development and Psychopathology* 10 (2): 215–33.

Kriz, Katrin, and Marit Skivenes. 2011. How child welfare workers view their work with racial and ethnic minority families: The United States in contrast to England and Norway. *Children and Youth Services Review* 33 (10): 1866–74.

Landers, Ashley L., Domenica H. Carrese, and Robin Spath. 2019. A decade in review of trends in social work literature: The link between poverty and child maltreatment in the United States. *Child Welfare* 97 (4): 65–96.

Lanier, Paul, Katie Maguire-Jack, Tova Walsh, Brett Drake, and Grace Hubel. 2014. Race and ethnic differences in early childhood maltreatment in the United States. *Journal of Developmental and Behavioral Pediatrics* 35 (7): 419–26.

Levine, Rebekah, and Lindsay Chase-Lansdale. 2000. Welfare receipt, financial strain, and African American adolescent functioning. *Social Service Review* 74 (3): 380–404. doi:10.1086/516410.

Liu, Y., and Darcey H. Merritt. 2018. Familial financial stress and child internalizing behaviors: The roles of caregivers' maltreating behaviors and social services. *Child Abuse and Neglect* 86:324–35.

Mani, Anandi, Sendhil Mulainathan, Elder Shafir, and Jiaying Zhao. 2013. Poverty impedes cognitive function. *Science* 341, 6149.

McKay, Mary 2007. Forced drugging of children in foster care: Turning child abuse victims into involuntary psychiatric patients. *Journal of Orthomolecular Medicine* 22 (2): 63–74.

McLoyd, Vonnie C. 1990. The impact of economic hardship on Black families and children: Psychological distress, parenting, and socioemotional development. *Child Development* 61 (2): 311–46.

Merritt, Darcey H. 2009. Child abuse potential: Correlates with child maltreatment rates and structural measures of neighborhoods. *Children and Youth Services Review* 31 (8): 927–34.

Merritt, Darcey H., and Rachel Ludeke. 2020. Child welfare oversight, parental fears and trauma induced by racial disparities. Symposium paper accepted for presentation at the annual program meeting of the Society for Social Work Research (SSWR), Washington, DC.

Merritt, Darcey H., and Susan Snyder. 2015. Correlates of optimal behavior among child welfare involved children: Perceived school peer connectedness, activity participation, social skills and peer affiliation. *Journal of Orthopsychiatry* 85 (5): 483–94.

Miller, Keva M., Katharine Cahn, Ben Anderson-Nathe, Angela G. Cause, and Ryan Bender. 2013. Individual and systemic/structural bias in child welfare decision-making: Implications for children and families of color. *Children and Youth Services Review* 35:1634–42.

Mixon-Mitchell, Debra, and Michelle D. Hanna. 2017. Race matters: Child protection and the communication process. *Journal of Ethnic & Cultural Diversity in Social Work* 26:1–16.

Nam, Yunju, William Meezan, and Sandra K. Danziger. 2006. Welfare recipients' involvement with child protective services after welfare reform. *Child Abuse & Neglect* 30:1181–99.

Naylor, Michael W., Christine Davidson, D. Jean Ortega-Piron, Arin Bass, Alice Gutierrez, and Angela Hall. 2007. Psychotropic medication management for youth in state care: Consent, oversight, and policy considerations. *Child Welfare* 86 (5): 175–92.

Neppl, Tricia K., Jennifer M. Senia, and Donnellan M. Brent. 2016. Effects of economic hardship: Testing the family stress model over time. *Journal of Family Psychology* 30 (1).

Noble, Kimberly G., Suzanne M. Houston, Eric Kan, and Elizabeth R. Sowell. 2012. Neural correlates of socioeconomic status in the developing human brain. *Developmental Science* 15 (4): 516–27.

Pager, Devah, and Hana Shepherd. 2008. The sociology of discrimination: Racial discrimination in employment, housing, credit, and consumer markets. *Annual Review of Sociology* 34:181–209.

Proctor, Lauren J., and Howard Dubowitz. 2014. Child neglect: Challenges and controversies. In *Handbook of child maltreatment*, eds. J. Korbin and R. D. Krugman, 27–62. New York, NY: Springer.

Putnam-Hornstein, Emily, Barbara Needell, Bryn King, and Michelle Johnson-Motoyama. 2013. Racial and ethnic disparities: A population-based examination of risk factors for involvement with child protective services. *Child Abuse and Neglect* 37 (1): 33–46.

Rebbe, Rebecca. 2018. What is neglect? State legal definitions in the United States. *Child Maltreatment* 23 (3): 303–15.

Roberts, Dorothy. 2002. *Shattered bonds: The color of child welfare*. New York, NY: Civets Books.

Roberts, Dorothy E. 2014. Child protection as surveillance of African American families. *Journal of Social Welfare and Family Law* 36 (4): 426–37.

Roche, Kathleen M., and Tama Leventhal. 2009. Beyond neighborhood poverty: Family management, neighborhood disorder, and adolescents' early sexual onset. *Journal of Family Psychology* 23 (6): 819–27.

Rolock, Nancy, and Mark Testa. 2005. Indicated child abuse and neglect reports: Is the investigation process racially biased? In *Race matters in child welfare: The overrepresentation of African American children in the system*, eds. M. Testa and J. Poertner, 119–30. Washington, DC: CWLA Press.

Rothstein, Richard. 2017. *The color of law: A forgotten history of how our government segregated America*. New York, NY: Liveright Publishing.

Sampson, Robert J. 2001. How do communities undergird or undermine human development? In *Does it take a village? Community effects on children, adolescents, and families*, eds. A. Booth and A. C. Crouter, 3–26. Mahwah, NJ: Lawrence Erlbaum.

Seabrook, Renita, and Heather Wyatt-Nichol. 2016. The ugly side of America: Institutional oppression and race. *Journal of Public Management & Social Policy* 23 (1): Article 3.

Sedlak, Andrea J., Karla McPherson, and Barnali Das. 2010. *Supplementary analyses of race differences in child maltreatment rates in the NIS-4*. Rockville, MD: Westat, Incorporated.

Sedlak, Andrea J., and D. Schultz. 2005. Racial differences in child protective services investigation of abused and neglected children. In *Race matters in child welfare: The overrepresentation of African American children in the system*, eds. M. Testa and J. Poertner, 47–61.

Shaw, Clifford R., and Henry H. McKay. 1969. *Juvenile delinquency in urban areas: A study of rates of delinquency in relation to differential characteristics of local communities in American cities*. Chicago, IL: University of Chicago Press.

Slack, Kristen S., and Lawrence M. Berger. 2021. Who is and is not served by child protective services systems? Implications for a prevention infrastructure to reduce child maltreatment. *The ANNALS of the American Academy of Political and Social Science* (this volume).

Smith, Brenda D. 2008. Child welfare service plan compliance: Perceptions of parents and caseworkers. *Families in Society* 89 (4): 521–32.

Stoltzfus, Emilie 2005. *Race/ethnicity and child welfare*. Washington, DC: Congressional Research Services.

Taylor, Melanie, Gary Stevens, Kingsley Agho, and Beverley Raphael. 2017. The impacts of household financial stress, resilience, social support, and other adversities on the psychological distress of Western Sydney parents. *International Journal of Population Research* Vol 2017, Article ID 6310683.

Toth, Sheree L., Erin Pickreign, Fred A. Rogosch, Rochelle Caplan, and Dante Cicchetti. 2011. Illogical thinking and thought disorder in maltreated children. *Journal of American Academy of Child and Adolescent Psychiatry* 50 (7): 659–68.

U.S. Department of Health & Human Services, Administration for Children and Families, Administration on Children, Youth and Families, Children's Bureau. 2020. *Child maltreatment 2018*. Washington, DC: U.S. Department of Health & Human Services.

Walsh, Trish, and John Canavan. 2014. Strengths-based practice in child welfare. *Child Care in Practice* 20 (1): 1–6.

Walsh, Wendy A., and Marybeth J. Mattingly. 2012. Psychotropic medication use among children in the child welfare system. Issue Brief 59. Durham, NH: The Carsey Institute.

Wells, Susan J., Lani M. Merritt, and Harold E. Briggs. 2009. Bias, racism, and evidence-based practice: The case for more focused development of the child welfare evidence base. *Children and Youth Services Review* 31 (11): 1160–71.

Wilson, William Julius. 1987. *The truly disadvantaged: The inner city, the underclass, and public policy*. Chicago, IL: University of Chicago Press.

Wilson, William Julius. 1996. *When work disappears*. New York, NY: Vintage Books.

Wise, Tim 2010. *Colorblind: The rise of post-racial politics and the retreat from racial equity*. San Francisco, CA: City Lights Books.

Wulczyn, Fred, Robert Gibbons, Lonnie Snowden, and Bridgette Lery. 2013. Poverty, social disadvantage, and the Black/white placement gap. *Children and Youth Services Review* 35:65–74.

Wulczyn, Fred, and Bridgette Lery. 2007. *Racial disparity in foster care admissions*. Chicago, IL: Chapin Hall Center for Children.

Zuravin, Susan J. 2001. Issues pertinent to defining child neglect. In *The CPS response to child neglect: An administrators guide to theory, policy, program design and case practice*, eds. T. D. Morton and B. Salovitz. Duluth, GA: National Resource Center on Child Maltreatment.

Foster Care in a Life Course Perspective

By
FRED WULCZYN

To understand what placement outside of one's home means to the young people involved, we must understand foster care from a life course perspective. I analyze young people's experiences in foster care from this perspective, accounting for when foster care happens, how long it lasts, and what happens when foster care placements end. I show that the population of children coming into foster care is younger and less urban than it was 20 years ago. I also show reliable measures of exposure to foster care over the life course. Children who enter care early in life are the children who spend the largest proportion of their childhood in foster care—a fact that rarely weighs on the policymaking process. We know very little about state and local variation in foster care placement rates, not to mention the influence of social services, the courts, foster parents, and caseworkers over foster children, so I close by arguing investment in research should be a clear policy priority.

Keywords: foster care; life course; urban; rural; developmental effects; permanency

In the United States, there is no one foster care system. The federal government sets guidelines that states follow, but policies from the federal level grant states broad discretion over their state's policy. As a consequence, state policy varies tremendously (see Berger and Slack, this volume). Two recent examples, pertaining to adoption (Vesneski 2011) and congregate care (Wulczyn, Martinez, and Weiss 2015), illustrate the point clearly. The number of state fast track provisions, which are thought to influence how quickly children move through

Fred Wulczyn is a senior research fellow at Chapin Hall at the University of Chicago, where he directs the Center for State Child Welfare Data. He holds an academic appointment as professor (part time) at the University of Chicago's School of Social Service Administration. He is a member of the American Academy of Social Work and Social Welfare.

Correspondence: fwulczyn@chapinhall.org or fwulczyn@uchicago.edu

DOI: 10.1177/0002716220976535

the system to adoption, varies between eight (the federal minimum) and twenty-seven. The provisions differ in the population of children targeted and their reason for being in care. However, the evidence suggests that those policy differences likely have little, if any, impact on adoption rates.

State policy is equally variable for congregate care (Wulczyn, Huhr, and McClanahan 2018). Of the twenty states I reviewed, about half had policies requiring the use of an assessment prior to placing a young person in congregate care; in the remaining states, I found no reference to an assessment requirement. Some states require certain staffing ratios in facilities as a matter of policy, but others do not. Even licensure policies vary between states to a significant degree. In fact, whether the policies are those that govern maltreatment reporting, guardianship, access to services, or any other policy area affecting the child welfare system, between-state policy variation is substantial.

Nevertheless, there are important continuities that characterize how young people experience foster care in the United States (Wulczyn et al. 2005). To see those continuities, I apply a life course perspective to the basic questions that start most policy and practice discussions: When do children tend to enter care? How long do they stay? and What happens to them when they leave? The life course perspective is a body of inquiry that spans social science disciplines (Elder 1998). The life course "refers to the interweave of age-graded trajectories such as work, careers and family pathways, that are subject to changing conditions and future options, and to short-term transitions ranging from leaving school to retirement" (Elder 1994, 5). Life course research stresses the timing, sequence, and duration of events over the life course.

Following the life course perspective, life events join to form trajectories. Trajectories are defined as patterns in the timing, duration, spacing, and order of events (Elder 1998); trajectories have a normative structure that shapes the narrative connecting institutional structures to life course patterns. *Placement* trajectories are made up of entries, exits, and changes in placement laid out in temporal order, with time measured as age laid on top of time measured with a calendar. The result is a placement trajectory tied to the normative, ontogenetic development of the child, nested within a social, institutional, and historical context. Most critically, *when* something happens is often more important than *whether* it happens. For example, the effects of exposure to adverse experiences during certain developmental periods may be largely inconsequential, developmentally speaking, because of when they happened.

To locate foster care placement within the life course perspective, it is important to understand when placement first happens, how long placement lasts, what happens when children leave care, and whether child age is associated with how such questions are best answered. To illustrate this point, I rely on the multistate Foster Care Data Archive (FCDA), unless otherwise noted.[1] The FCDA is a research database built from the data states collect about children in their legal custody and organized with life course theory in mind. The FCDA includes information pertaining to when a child entered care, the number of placements they experienced, when they left care and why, and whether they returned to care.

Foster Care in the Context of Childhood

The link between when a child enters care for the first time and the impact that foster care has on the child's life course outcomes is perhaps the most important reason why a life course perspective is important. Practitioners, policy-makers, advocates, and social scientists all agree that exposure to foster care has an impact on how well children will do going forward. However, the evidence as to whether placement is a protective factor or a risk factor vis-á-vis outcomes later in life is anything but clear. Compared to similar children who were not placed in foster care, one study found that former foster children exhibited higher rates of delinquency in adolescence (Doyle 2013). However, Gross (2020) found that foster care placement reduced future maltreatment, increased school attendance, and improved math scores (Gross 2020). For youth making the transition to adulthood from foster care, the path forward is difficult whether one is looking at education, housing, or employment (Courtney et al. 2018.; Font et al. 2018). Yet other studies suggest that when compared with youth who were reunified with their birth families, similar youth who aged out of foster care had significantly higher odds of graduating from high school and comparable earnings from employment (Font et al. 2018).

Collectively, these are important studies but not because they examine the link between foster care and life course outcomes. Rather, embedded in each question lies a more fundamental question: What does it mean to be a former foster child? A substantial portion of the literature has focused on youth transitioning to adulthood from foster care and rightly so. However, the population of former foster children is far more diverse than young people who leave care on the cusp of adulthood. Six months spent in foster care at age 16 is substantially different than six months spent in foster care at age 5 in terms of preplacement experiences, postplacement experiences, and the potential impact foster care *could* have on life course outcomes net all the other factors that influence what happens in a person's life.

Rather than isolate one group of children exposed to foster care from another, the life course perspective necessitates an integrated perspective that sees foster care within the context of childhood in its entirety. To reinforce this sort of comprehensive view, I have developed two views of placement relative to childhood. The first considers the likelihood a child will enter placement and spend the rest of what remains of their childhood in care. In this instance I have limited our view of the data to children who stayed in her or his first foster care spell (i.e., were never discharged). I ask, given the age at admission, what fraction of those children reach age 18 still in their first placement spell, notwithstanding placement changes that may have taken place?

The second question expands the view of foster care and childhood by asking, when all the days in care are added up (this includes non–first placement spells), what fraction of a child's total childhood (through age 18) was spent in placement? For example, a child admitted to care for 1 year as a 2-year-old who comes back to care for 1 year as a 12-year-old, spent 2 years out of 18 in foster care.

TABLE 1
Percentage of Children Reaching Age 18 before Leaving Foster Care: Children Admitted to Care between 2000 and 2018, First Spells Only

Age at Entry	Year of Entry into Care (Calendar Year)																		
	2000	'01	'02	'03	'04	'05	'06	'07	'08	'09	'10	'11	'12	'13	'14	'15	'16	'17	'18
0	0.2	0.1																	
1	0.5	0.3	0.2																
2	0.5	0.7	0.4	0.2															
3	1.2	0.9	0.8	0.6	0.3														
4	1.3	1.2	1.1	1.0	1.0	0.3													
5	2.0	1.9	1.8	1.4	1.4	1.1	0.7												
6	2.8	2.4	2.3	2.2	2.1	1.5	1.3	0.8											
7	3.7	3.7	3.4	2.9	2.9	2.2	1.8	1.7	0.9										
8	4.7	5.0	4.0	3.5	2.8	3.2	2.1	2.2	2.3	1.2									
9	6.3	6.3	5.5	4.2	5.2	3.8	3.7	3.5	3.2	3.3	1.3								
10	8.2	7.2	7.9	6.7	6.7	5.4	4.7	5.2	4.7	4.8	3.6	2.0							
11	10.7	9.2	9.6	8.5	8.3	6.9	7.0	6.7	7.2	6.0	6.3	6.0	3.1						
12	12.2	11.3	10.7	10.3	11.0	9.7	9.7	9.1	8.4	8.5	8.2	7.8	8.5	4.9					
13	13.2	12.6	12.2	11.9	12.5	11.7	10.9	10.7	12.3	11.1	10.4	12.0	11.3	9.4	5.7				
14	14.4	14.7	13.9	14.3	14.8	14.6	14.4	13.9	14.5	14.4	15.6	14.8	15.5	13.5	14.1	6.9			
15	17.0	18.4	17.8	18.5	17.2	18.5	18.5	17.6	19.0	18.0	19.0	19.8	20.5	21.6	20.5	20.9	13.0		
16	26.9	27.7	29.2	28.3	27.5	28.0	29.5	27.5	28.8	30.4	31.4	31.4	32.8	34.8	33.7	33.0	32.8	19.5	
17	49.2	48.7	52.2	52.8	49.4	51.6	52.8	53.2	55.2	53.3	56.3	55.9	57.5	58.3	61.2	59.8	59.4	59.8	32.2

NOTE: Empty cells are completely censored. No member of the cohort would have reached 18 years given the window of observation. Shaded cells are partially censored in that some members of those cohorts may have reached age 18 but not all members who might one day. The remaining cells all represent fully observed cohorts.

Understandably, children who enter foster care early in life are more likely to spend a greater portion of their childhood in care. That, however, is the point. Children admitted to care early in the life course risk longer exposure to foster care. To the extent that foster care is a risk factor or a protective factor for later life course outcomes, the dose of foster care, measured in terms of onset and duration, is of central importance when questions turn to the impact of foster care on children.

Table 1 answers the first question. Cell values are percentages and correspond to the likelihood that a young person admitted to care at a certain age and in a given year will reach age 18 still in their first placement spell. In essence, these data answer the age-old question, If a child is placed into foster care, what are the chances that he or she will grow up in foster care?

The answer quite plainly is that growing up in foster care is highly unlikely. Viewed in the narrowest of terms, if the question is applied to children who enter care before their first birthday, it almost never happens. In my sample of 16,130 children admitted to care before their first birthday in the year 2000, only 41 of them spent their entire childhood in placement.[2]

Of course, as the age of first entry goes up, so too does the likelihood of staying in care until age 18. Nevertheless, prior to admissions of children at age 13, the risk of staying in foster care until the 18th birthday is below 10 percent, especially among young people admitted during the more recent years (2006 and later). Moreover, the likelihood of reaching age 18 while in the first spell of care has been going down steadily among children of all ages except adolescents who enter care at ages 15, 16, or 17. For those young people, the chances of staying in care have been on the rise when the risk is compared to young people of a similar age admitted in 2000 through 2005.

In summary, based on the totality of children in the sample (1,480,187), there were 74,862 children who entered care and did not leave. That figure is equivalent to 5 percent of the total risk pool. More importantly, the evidence underscores the need to define what we mean when we say, "grow up in foster care." For example, in a paper titled "Outcomes of Children Who Grew Up in Foster Care: Systematic Review," the authors do not define what they mean by the phrase "grew up in foster care" as used in the title (Gypen et al. 2017). According to our figures, 3.6 percent of the 10-year-olds admitted in 2010 reached their 18th birthday in care. Though this is an important figure, and everyone should ask why this happens, the definitional question is important. Can we say these children grew up in foster care, when a larger portion of their childhood was outside of foster care? Moreover, does it matter whether the eight years spent in foster care were from birth through age 7 or from age 10 through 17?

To round out the assessment of life course exposure to foster care, I also consider how much time is spent in foster care as a percentage of total childhood. To do this, for each child in each cohort used to build Table 1, I counted up all the days spent in care across all placement spells and divided those days into the total number of days in childhood (i.e., 365×18). The difficulty with this calculation is that we have but one estimate for children admitted under the age of 1 (the 2000 admission cohort) and 18 estimates for children admitted at age 17 (up to age 18). Thus, the estimates for older children are inherently more stable given the large number of cohorts with complete observations. The number of estimates is important because, as we have seen, judging from the likelihood of reaching age 18 while still in care, the probability of reaching age 18 while still in care has trended downward, at least for some age groups. That means the estimates for younger children are likely biased given that there is not any recent data to offset the experiences of children admitted to care more than two decades ago.

With those caveats in mind, my assessment of foster care as a fraction of childhood is presented in Figure 1. Figure 1 displays the percentage of childhood spent on average in foster care by the members of each age group, provided members of the cohort could have reached age 18 within the observation window.

As expected, older children and youth spend a smaller fraction of their childhood in foster care, given the age at first admission. The youngest children—in

FIGURE 1
Percentage of Childhood Spent in Foster Care: 2000 to 2018 Admission Cohorts

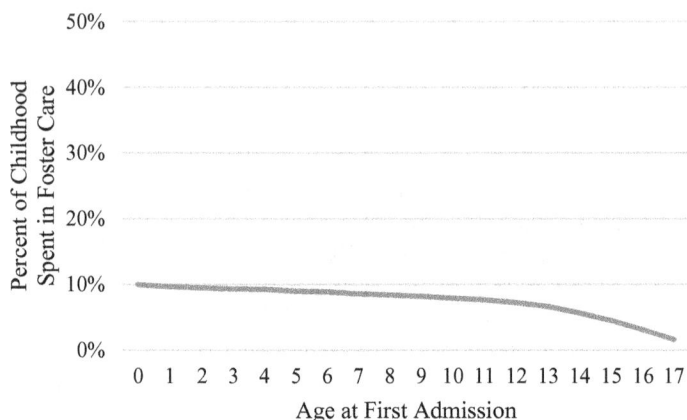

this case children admitted as far back as 2000—spent about 10 percent of their childhood in care, although the analysis does not say specifically when they spent that time in care. Babies spend more time in foster care than children of other ages in large measure because they are more likely to be adopted. They are also the largest group of children in the sample, making up about 22 percent of all first admissions. There are some young people who enter foster care during the midpoint of childhood and remain in placement, but by these estimates, on average, young people between the ages of 10 and 12 will spend about 8 percent of their childhood in foster care. Again, expectations regarding the impact of foster care on life course outcomes have to bear that in mind.

The Changing Face of Foster Care

In this section, I offer a simple overview of admissions to foster care between 2000 and 2018 with the aim of showing that foster care utilization has over the past 20 years shifted dramatically when viewed from a geographic and life course perspective. To do this, I start with the group of fifteen states with data for each of the following years: 2000, 2005, 2010, 2015, and 2018. From this collection of states, I identified each child admitted to care for the first time for the listed years. In total, the evidence presented is based on the unduplicated records of 424,652 children.

From this base of children, I group children into two categories: age at admission and county of placement. Age at placement is further organized into three groups: children who were fewer than 31 days of age at the time of placement, children who were 31 to 365 days old at the time of placement, and children older than 365 days at placement. I refer to these groups as newborns, infants, and older children and youth, respectively. I categorize the counties using the

TABLE 2
Number of First Admissions to Foster Care by Age and Year

Age at Admission	Year of Admission				
	2000	2005	2010	2015	2018
Total	83,091	91,914	81,818	85,243	82,586
Newborns	7,938	10,261	8,097	9,758	10,183
Infants	8,549	10,451	10,353	10,358	9,798
Older children & youth	66,604	71,202	63,368	65,127	62,605
Total	100%	100%	100%	100%	100%
Newborns	10%	11%	10%	11%	12%
Infants	10%	11%	13%	12%	12%
Older children & youth	80%	77%	77%	76%	76%

National Center for Health Statistics' urban/rural classification scheme. That scheme groups counties into six categories: large central metro counties, large fringe metro counties, medium metro counties, small metro counties, micropolitan counties, and noncore counties (Ingram and Franco 2014)

Number of admissions by age

The total number of admissions by age and year is displayed in Table 2. Overall, comparing admissions in 2000 with those in 2018 shows a modest decline, from 83,091 to 82,586, a drop of just 505 children. Between those years, the number of admissions fluctuated. Over the five separate years shown in Table 2, the number of admissions reached a high point of 91,914 in 2005 and a low point in 2010 when there were slightly fewer than 82,000 admissions.

In Table 2, the most important changes in admission patterns are tied to age at admission. Among children between the ages of 1 and 17 when admitted (older children and youth), admissions are down from 66,604 to 62,605. In contrast, the number of newborns and infants admitted increased relative to the year 2000. In 2000, there were 7,938 newborns admitted; in 2018, the number was 10,183. For infants, the change was less pronounced. Nevertheless, the number of infants (children between 31 and 365 days old) admitted in 2018 also exceeded the number admitted in 2000.

Admissions and urbanicity

Along with the changes in the age structure of the population of children entering care between 2000 and 2018, there has been a significant shift away from the large central urban counties. In 2000, 50 percent of all children admitted to foster care for the first time came from the main urban counties in the state or what the National Center for Health Statistics (NCHS) calls the large urban core counties.

TABLE 3
Number of First Admissions to Foster Care by Urbanicity and Year

	Year of Admission				
Urbanicity	2000	2005	2010	2015	2018
Total	83,091	91,914	81,818	85,243	82,586
Large central	41,146	42,437	37,207	36,264	32,254
Large fringe	12,644	14,280	13,132	14,224	13,832
Medium metro	15,294	17,969	16,114	17,562	17,922
Small metro	5,760	6,815	6,141	6,902	7,086
Micropolitan	4,912	6,115	5,532	6,035	6,728
Noncore	3,335	4,298	3,692	4,256	4,764
Total	100%	100%	100%	100%	100%
Large central	50%	46%	45%	43%	39%
Large fringe	15%	16%	16%	17%	17%
Medium metro	18%	20%	20%	21%	22%
Small metro	7%	7%	8%	8%	9%
Micropolitan	6%	7%	7%	7%	8%
Noncore	4%	5%	5%	5%	6%

By 2018, those counties only accounted for 39 percent of all the admissions. On a percentage basis, the most significant increase was in the medium-sized metro counties. In 2000, those counties accounted for 18 percent of the admissions; in 2018 the comparable figure was 22 percent. Though smaller, the proportionate share increased from 2000 to 2018 in the remaining county types.

Age and urbanicity

The combined effects of changing demographics and the shift away from urban areas are displayed in Table 3. In the large central counties, admissions were lower in 2018 than in 2000. Among older children and youth, the change in admissions (−25%) was the most pronounced. In every other area, admissions were higher in 2018 than in 2000, with changes in admissions well in excess of 50 percent for some county groups. For example, in noncore counties, the number of children and youth increased by 31 percent, 66 percent for infants, and 210 percent for newborns.

In the large fringe counties, the number of newborns admitted to care increase by 55 percent (see Table 4). Although small in number, admissions involving infants from micropolitan and noncore counties increased by more than 66 percent. In general, the admission increase was larger as one moves away from the large central urban counties. Within those areas, the largest increases involved the youngest children.

Of course, the shifting age composition and geographic distribution suggests that the racial and ethnic makeup may also be changing. Figure 2 shows the

TABLE 4
Number of First Admissions to Foster Care by Age, Urbanicity and Year

Age and Urbanicity	Year of Admission					Change from 2000–2018
	2000	2005	2010	2015	2018	
Newborns						
Large central	4,584	5,144	3,926	4,438	4,212	–8%
Large fringe	1,080	1,514	1,201	1,560	1,677	55%
Medium metro	1,410	2,074	1,680	1,978	2,154	53%
Small metro	420	713	607	793	874	108%
Micropolitan	287	529	468	660	780	172%
Noncore	157	287	215	329	486	210%
Infants						
Large central	4,362	4,859	4,676	4,461	4,030	–8%
Large fringe	1,292	1,579	1,659	1,763	1,619	25%
Medium metro	1,554	2,066	2,014	2,124	2,016	30%
Small metro	563	820	790	778	816	45%
Micropolitan	473	677	744	719	810	71%
Noncore	305	450	470	513	507	66%
Older children & youth						
Large central	32,200	32,434	28,605	27,365	24,012	–25%
Large fringe	10,272	11,187	10,272	10,901	10,536	3%
Medium metro	12,330	13,829	12,420	13,460	13,752	12%
Small metro	4,777	5,282	4,744	5,331	5,396	13%
Micropolitan	4,152	4,909	4,320	4,656	5,138	24%
Noncore	2,873	3,561	3,007	3,414	3,771	31%

extent to which this is true. Figure 2 displays the percentage change in the number of children admitted to care for the first time in 2018 compared to 2000 by age, race/ethnicity, and urbanicity. Generally, the changes described previously affected Black, Hispanic, and white children and youth similarly. For example, admissions changes were more dramatic as one moves away from the large central urban core counties and toward the nonurban counties (i.e., the micropolitan and noncore counties). However, these changes are especially pronounced for Hispanic and white newborns. Although small in number, the percentage increases were in excess of 150 percent for Hispanic newborns outside the urban core counites. Among whites, the increase in newborn admissions was substantial (+200%) in the most micropolitan and noncore counties.

For Blacks, admissions declined in the large central and large fringe counties and increased in other counties, with the largest increases affecting the very youngest children. For both Hispanics and whites, the largest increase involved newborn children, regardless of the urban character of the county.

FIGURE 2
Percentage Change in the Number of Children Admitted to Care by Race/Ethnicity
and Urbanicity: 2000 and 2018

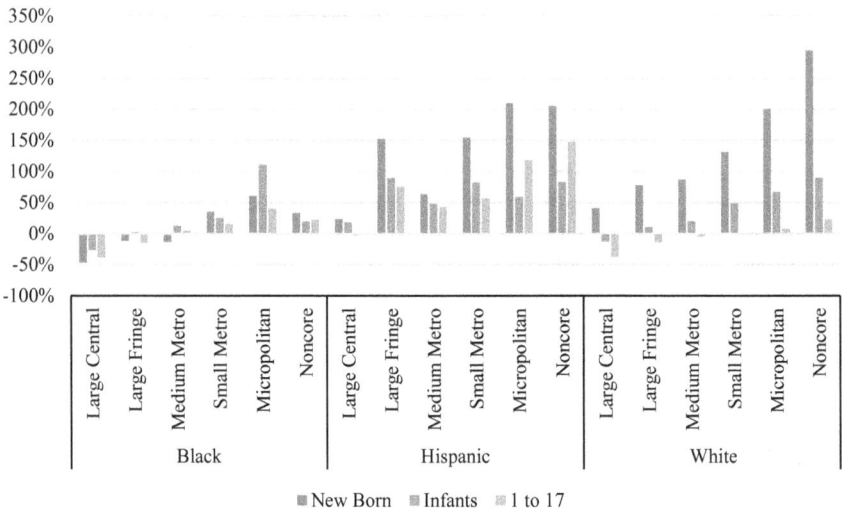

Leaving Foster Care

From a policy and practice perspective, foster care ought to be a temporary solution to the problems that arise when parents are either unable or unwilling to raise their children (Font and Gershoff 2020; Wald 1976). The preference for short stays in foster care is organized around three interrelated themes. First, there is a bedrock assumption that children are better off if they are raised by their natural parents and that parents will, until proven otherwise, act in the best interests of their children. For that reason, parents are granted considerable latitude over raising their children (Wulczyn 2004). Second, the state is reluctant to reach inside the family sphere and abridge the rights of parents because, when it does so, as in the case of foster care, it assumes a subset of parental responsibilities for which it is not particularly well-suited (Bullock et al. 2006). Finally, there is a body of research that shows parent-child separation has (potentially) deleterious effects on children (National Scientific Council on the Developing Child 2013; Ellis, Jackson, and Boyce 2006; Lawrence, Carlson, and Egeland 2006; Wulczyn, Hislop, and Jones Harden 2002).

The desire to raise children within a family and keep placements short falls under the general heading of permanency. Permanency is both a legal construct and a psychological construct. Permanency as a legal construct vests the legal authority to guide the care of the child with a set of adults. Natural parents are the logical first choice, so reunification is the preferred permanency option. When that is not possible, adoption transfers the legal rights and responsibilities of the parents to another set of adults. As a remedy, adoption can only take place after the rights of the parents have been terminated. More recently, in recognition of the diverse nature of family structure and function, the law has expanded to include guardianship as a permanency option (Testa 2004). Typically, guardians are related to the child or are otherwise known to the child. Importantly, guardianship can be established without terminating parental rights (Child Welfare Information Gateway 2019). As a psychological construct, permanency is rooted in the idea that lasting relationships are central to a child's overall sense of well-being (Samuels 2008; Schwartz 1996; Testa 2002).

What are the chances a child will leave foster care?

From a measurement perspective, the desire to keep foster care placements brief translates, through policy and practice, into efforts that are directed at increasing the *chances* a child placed in foster care will leave foster care to one form of permanency or another. Because primacy is given to reunification with parents, we would expect the chances of reunification to be greater than the chances of adoption or guardianship. However, as time passes and the prospects for reunification dwindle, we would expect the chances of adoption and/or guardianship to increase.

To illustrate how the chances of permanency, by type of permanency, shift with passage of time, I use the FCDA to plot the probability of leaving foster care against the passage of time. To do this, the time spent by children in foster care is divided into six-month intervals. At the start of each six-month interval, I count how many children are still in care and how many children leave care during that interval. The result is a conditional probability of leaving foster care given elapsed time. Substantively, the conditional probability of leaving care is more interesting than length of stay, the more conventional measure of how much time children spend in foster care because it captures how the *chances* of leaving care change with the passage of time. Again, because policy and practice are directed at increasing the chances of permanency, it is useful to start with a baseline appreciation for just how likely permanency is in the first place.

Figure 3 provides a general overview of how children leave the placement system, using time and reason for leaving to highlight the major differences. With respect to time, the figure shows distinct patterns that depend on how the child leaves. Each tick mark on the x-axis represents a six-month interval; the y-axis shows the probability that a child in care at the start of the interval will leave care before the start of the next interval. When the graph slopes upward from left to right, it means that leaving placement by that means is increasing with the passage of time; when the graph slopes downward from left to right, it means leaving becomes less likely.

The pattern in Figure 3 adheres closely to expectations insofar as the reunification process is initially high but slows with the passage time. Nevertheless, reunification from care does happen, even after 4.5 years in care. Adoption follows a different path, largely in response to the changes in reunification. Essentially, as the chances of reunification fade, the primary pathway out of the system involves adoption. Adoption rates are initially quite low but rise quickly from 12 months onward until the rate change levels off and begins to decline

FIGURE 3
Probability of Leaving Placement by Time and Reason for Exit

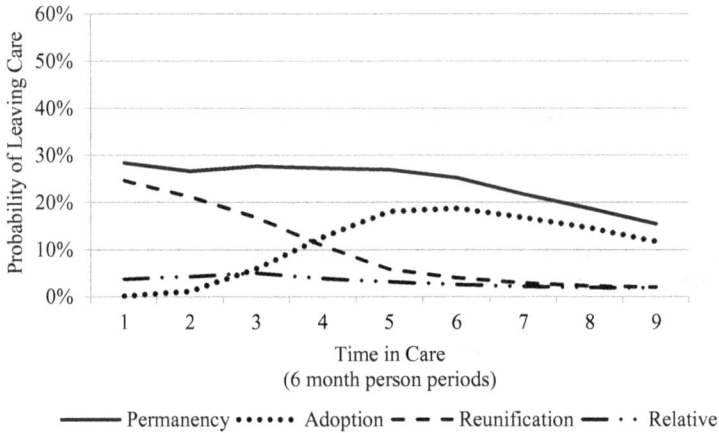

again. That said, the probability that a child still in care 4.5 years later will be adopted remains on average above 10 percent. Exits from guardianship are fairly uncommon. The evidence shows that guardianship exits rise slightly over the first 18 months of care and then subside again. Remembering that this evidence represents what happens in all states, including states that rely more or less on guardianship, the evidence in Figure 3 suggest that guardianship exits account for less than 5 percent of the exits at any given time.

The effect of age, care type, and race/ethnicity on the chances of leaving placement

There are countless ways the details of an individual case influence what happens to a foster child and why. Nevertheless, there are regularities in the experience of foster children that bear a developmental imprint. In this section, with the baseline rates of leaving care in mind, I highlight how age, care type, and race/ethnicity shape our understanding of reunification, adoption, and guardianship. I focus on age because it brings forward the developmental themes that shape what happens and how I interpret what happens. Care type effects are important because placement is the primary service used to shape the life course of foster children during the time they are away from their families. Well-being gains by foster children will only be possible if the quality of the care provided is taken into account. Knowing how placements are used now is one key to making improvements that carry forward into the future. Race and ethnicity are important because of persistent concerns about how much foster care is used in some communities. To improve our understanding of why Blacks experience more foster care, I look closely at adoption and reunification to pinpoint when the experience of Black children diverges from those of white and Hispanic children.

As before, I consider how the probability of leaving changes with the passage of time. Practically speaking, I now divide the evidence that I presented in Figure 1 into distinct groups based on age, care type, and race/ethnicity (see online appendix Figures A1 through A6).

Figure A1 in the online appendix shows how reunification rates differ on the basis of age. Through the first two and half years (person periods 1 through 5), those who entered care as infants have a much lower rate of reunification than those who entered as older children. The gap is largest over the first 12 to 18 months; thereafter the gap closes until months 36 through 54, when the probability of leaving placement to reunification is low and no longer associated with age at placement.

As online appendix Figure A2 shows, exits to adoption follow a different trajectory. Regardless of admission age, adoption is rare in the six months just after placement because the rights of the parents are still front and center. Among children in care at the start of the second six-month interval, the probability of adoption rises but especially so for children who were admitted prior to their first birthday. Among children still in care 18 months after placement, the probability of adoption reaches nearly 20 percent if the child was an infant at admission. For older children, at that point, the probability of adoption is still well below 10 percent. For both groups of children, the rate of change in the adoption process slows starting 30 months after the placement starts. By month 36, the probability of adoption starts to fall. At its peak, 40 percent of the children admitted to foster care as babies will be adopted (provided they were still in care at that point). For older children, the peak reaches just 15 percent. Thus, while the contours of the permanency process resemble the baseline rate of exit, the rates themselves are highly dependent on age at admission.

Figures A3 and A4 in the online appendix show the same evidence for children grouped according to whether they were placed in foster care or congregate care. When looking at reunification, the biggest exit rate differences are observed in the first six months when young people placed in congregate care are much more likely to be reunified than children placed in foster care. Thereafter, the gap closes until roughly three years when the exit rate is no longer linked to care type.

The adoption process is also affected by whether the child is in congregate care or placed with a family. With respect to time, adoption rises with the passage of time, though much less so for young people who spent time in congregate care. Adoption rates among children in foster care rise through the interval of time that starts in month 30. After three years, the rate drops slowly. For children with some time spent in congregate care, the rate of adoption is always low, but it does rise with the passage of time.

Reunification rates for Blacks, Hispanics, and whites are found in online appendix Figure A5. At this level of aggregation, differences in reunification are observed during the first two years of placement. Over the course of the first six months, reunification rates are comparable, regardless of race/ethnicity. A bit more than 20 percent of the children admitted to care will leave placement via reunification during the first six months of placement. Thereafter, the experience of Blacks diverges from what white and Hispanic children experience. White and

Hispanic children are less likely to be reunified as time passes, but the change in the rate of reunification is less pronounced than it is for Blacks. At the start of the second year, the probability of reunification has fallen to 15 percent for whites and 17 percent for Hispanics. The comparable rate for Blacks at that point in a child's placement history falls to 13 percent. Thereafter, starting at the beginning of the third year in care (person period 5), the probability of reunification converges at roughly 5 percent of those still in care, regardless of race/ethnicity. This evidence suggests that disparities in the rate of reunification are, to some extent, dependent on how long after placement one looks. Summaries based on length of stay or the overall likelihood of reunification miss this nuance. More importantly, the opportunity for targeted interventions to address the disparity is missed by public agency leaders and others working to reduce disparity (Wulczyn, Huhr, and McClanahan 2018).

Figure A6 in the online appendix shows the same evidence for adoption. Soon after placement, regardless of a child's race/ethnicity, the probability of adoption is low. After the first six months pass, the probability of adoption rises, although the increase observed for white and Hispanic children is more pronounced. Basically, with the passage of time, whites and Hispanics have comparable adoption rates. For Black children, the adoption rate trajectory follows the familiar shape, but the period-specific rates are lower, especially between the start of year two and year three.

Reason for leaving foster care

In the previous section, I considered how children leave care with respect to the passage of time since admission. Missing from that view is some sense for how likely each pathway out of care is for the young people involved. For example, who is more likely to be reunified, teenagers or infants? In online appendix Figures A7 and A8, I show the exit reason by age at admission for the 2000 and 2005 admission cohorts. I have relied on these older cohorts because the information about their exit reason is more likely to be known (i.e., not censored). I have also added two other exit reasons: reach majority and running away. The former reflects the fact that some young people do not leave care before their 18th birthday, a phenomenon that I have discussed (see Table 1). The latter reason—running away—is an important pathway out of foster care for some young people, but it receives relatively little attention (Dworsky, Wulczyn, and Huang 2018; Wulczyn et al. 2017).

In Figure A7, I show the reason for leaving care set against age at admission. In general, the results speak for themselves. Reunification is the most common reason for leaving care across the age spectrum except for infants (i.e., children under the age of 1 at admission) and 17-year-olds. In the case of infants, adoption is the most common reason for leaving (49 percent); for 17-year-olds, reaching the age of 18 while still in care (42 percent) is slightly more common than the reunification (39 percent).[3]

Adoption is increasingly less likely as the age of admission rises; the likelihoods of running away and reaching the age of majority are increasingly more common as the age of admission rises. In the case of running away and reaching the age of majority while in care, the risk begins to rise among children as young as age five and six. At ages 9, 10, and 11, the risk rises more quickly. The risk of running away peaks at age 18; the risk of reaching the age of majority rises substantially at age 15, a pattern that is consistent with what Table 1 showed.

Figure A8 in the online appendix illustrates how the age effects persist even as the focus of attention shifts to the question of whether Blacks and Hispanics leave care for reasons that differ from those that characterize the ways in which whites leave. Rates of reunification for Blacks are clearly lower. White reunification rates are highest among children below the age of 10; above the age of 10, Hispanics are the young people most likely to leave care because they were reunified.

With that said, for each group, the reunification rates exhibit the customary inverted U-shape. Reunification rates are lowest at the ends of the age spectrum (infants and 17-year-olds), increase sharply among 1-year-olds compared to infants, and then taper off as the age of admission reaches adolescence. Persistent age effects are visible in each of the other graphs within Figure A8. For example, regardless of race and ethnicity, adoption rates are highest among infants, drop significantly among one-year-olds, and then taper off through adolescence. Although there are no significant departures from the age-related patterns, there are differences. For example, one reason reunification rates for younger Blacks are lower is because of the higher rates of relative exits, especially among children who were under the age of 12 when they entered care.

State variation

Up until this point, I have not spent much time addressing variations among states, in part because an understanding of state differences would require a substantial study that cannot be covered adequately here. Nonetheless, because states are granted considerable latitude to shape their own foster care policies inside the federal framework and because little is actually known about the impact state policy variation has on how children experience foster care, it is important to place baseline rates of exit into a state context. It is unfortunate more is not known about variation by state, because this lack of knowledge makes it difficult to anticipate how policy changes will actually affect what happens in a given state. Put another way, policy changes are expected to improve the so-called system, but it is unclear whether, given baseline performance, that expectation is reasonable. To raise the importance of these questions, I compare the baseline rates of exit to reunification, adoption, and relatives in two states.

The state reunification rates are presented in online appendix Figure A9. I selected two states because of the ways in which they differ from each other. For general comparison, I include the average rate of the remaining states in the sample. Profiled in this way, three conclusions seem important. First, given this comparison, the largest differences occur during the first two intervals, which cover the time from admission through the end of the first year in placement. In state A, the rate of reunification is actually lower in the first 6 months than in the second 6-month interval (months 6 through 12). In state B, the initial rate of reunification is considerably higher than the average but drops quickly in subsequent months. By the start of the second year (interval 3), exit rates in the two states mirror each other, although exit rates in state B remain somewhat higher than those in state A, if only slightly. When we compare both states to the average of all states, state A reunification rates are persistently below average across all intervals; children in state B leave more slowly when placements last longer than 18 months.

Adoption

I present adoption rate profiles in online appendix Figure A10. The presentation is the same: the figure depicts evidence for two states as well as the average of the remaining states. The average of the remaining states shows the prototypical or base adoption rate with respect to time. The rate of exit is low initially, accelerates as time passes, and then peaks between 30 and 36 months. Thereafter, adoption slows.

Adoption rates in the two comparison states follow that same profile but with important differences. The point in time when the rate of adoption accelerates differs markedly between the two states. In state A, the inflection point occurs in the second interval, much as it does on average. However, the change in adoption rates from the second interval to the third interval and then the fourth is more pronounced. Of the children in care when those intervals start, the rate of adoption is much higher than it was in the prior interval. In state B, the inflection point does not come until the third interval, and the rate of change is much more gradual. As for when the adoption rate peaks, in state A, the peak comes earlier than average; in state B, the peak is not observed until the end of the fourth year.

Relative exits

Public child welfare agencies often rely on relatives as a discharge resource, although state policies vary with respect to the use of subsidies and the assignment of legal guardianship to relative guardians. Moreover, states differ with respect to the regulations pertaining to licensure and whether children who would otherwise be placed in foster care are instead diverted to live with relatives. Because how children enter care is often associated with how children leave care, diversion policies undoubtedly affect who enters and then leaves placement. Although these are important policy and practice differences, our analysis merely documents whether the pattern of relative exits with respect to time differs at the state level, without regard for the policy context. To accomplish this, I evaluate whether a state's records point to the use of a relative as a discharge resource. In some cases, the state will distinguish between subsidized guardianships and other relative exits. Where that is true, for this analysis, I have grouped all exits to relatives into a single, undifferentiated category. The results are found in online appendix Figure A11.

When compared with Figure 2, which shows the base rate of exit by exit type, the rate at which children leave foster care to live with relatives is well below the rates observed for the other exit reasons. As depicted in Figure A11 in the online appendix, the average rate among all the states in the sample hovers at about 5 percent, with only modest changes with respect to time. More specifically, over the first 18 months, the probability of leaving placement to live with a relative rises from about 3 percent (interval 1) to 5 percent (interval 3), before falling in subsequent intervals. Figure A11 also points to meaningful state effects. In state A, the probability of leaving placement via a relative exit is just below 20 percent in the first six months of care. Thereafter, much like the pattern observed for reunification, the probability falls the longer children remain in care. State B shows a pattern that is more like the average of the other states in that with the passage of time, the probability of leaving placement to live with a relative is essentially unchanged. However, in state B, the probability of a relative exit is persistently lower than average.

Reentry to Care

Within the permanency framework, when a child leaves placement via one of the permanency options (i.e., reunification, guardianship, or adoption), the hope/expectation is that further involvement with the foster care system will not be necessary. This is, in fact, often the case. However, for a nontrivial segment of the population, children do return to foster care (Parolini et al. 2018; Rolock et al. 2018; Wulczyn 1991). Findings from prior research have identified both risk and protective factors associated with reentry. For example, predictors of placement disruption (i.e., moves between homes during a spell of foster care) such as child age, behavioral issues, and placement type (Chamberlain et al. 2006; James 2011; Miller, Randle, and Dolnicar 2018) are also correlated with reentry. Similarly, reentry rates are higher for teenagers (Rolock 2015; Rolock and White 2016; Smith et al. 2006) and, in some cases, for infants (Jones and LaLiberte 2017; Kimberlin, Anthony, and Austin 2009; Shaw 2006). Studies have also identified protective factors, such as marital status, educational level, emotional stress or expressiveness, and expectations that have a positive association with postpermanency stability (Coakley and Berrick 2007; Liao and White 2014; Testa et al. 2015).

For this analysis of reentry, and in keeping with the life course theme, I am interested in highlighting age-specific risks. To do so, I divided the time after the child left care and before they reentered, turned 18, or reached the censor date, into person-periods of six-month duration. As with length of stay, this data structure provides a convenient way to assess the likelihood that someone will return to care given the passage of time. In addition, for each person-period, I recorded the child's age at the start of the period (i.e., the person-period age). The distinction between person-period age and age at exit is important because person-period age allows us to consider life course affects: as a young person approaches adolescence, does the risk of reentry go up even if they left placement long ago?

Baseline hazard rate: Reentry

Figures A10 through A12 in the online appendix pertain to the basic risk of reentry without reference to child characteristics (other than age), placement history, or other factors that might influence whether a young person returns to care. The results are referred to as the baseline hazard rate. In essence, the baseline hazard rate shows how risk changes with the passage of time since discharge. The interpretation of the baseline hazard is straightforward. For each person-period, given a child enters the person-period still at risk of returning to care, how likely is reentry? The shape of the baseline hazard suggests whether the risk is more or less steady with the passage of time, rises, or falls. In addition, if the baseline hazard is relatively flat, the risk of returning to care persists as time passes.

In Figure A12 in the online appendix, I present the baseline hazard for guardianship and reunification separately.[4] In both cases, the risk of reentry is highest soon after discharge. After the first person-period, the risk of reentry declines, regardless of why the young person left care. It is also true that, initially, the risk of reentry is greater for children reunified than it is for children who were placed with guardians. However, among children who have been out of care for four or more years, the risk is roughly the same whether reunified or placed with guardians. While the risk is low, as shown in Figure A12, the risk of reentry persists long after the child first leaves placement. Over the course of childhood, the rate of reentry in this selection of states reaches 27 percent, a figure that is commensurate with federal sources (Children's Bureau 2019). Because the risk persists, I retain a focus on reentry over the course of childhood but pay special attention to the elevated risk close to when the children were first discharged.

In Figure A13 in the online appendix, I show the baseline hazard rates for children who return home by time out of care and age. In this instance, I am interested in whether children younger than one return to care after reunification at rates that are different than those for children older than one. I am interested in the infant subpopulation because, as we have seen, infants make up such a large proportion of children coming into out-of-home care.

When compared alongside the baseline hazard rate for reunification as shown in Figure A12, we see the same basic contour: the risk of reentry is higher initially, tappers off quickly, and then remains persistent but low after four years (person-period 8). That said, the early risk for infants is substantially (15 percent) higher than it is for older children (10 percent). Moreover, the risk for infants remains elevated for roughly two years after reunification.

Figure A14 in the online appendix shows the baseline hazard for children who leave care to live with guardians. In general, the baseline risk of reentry follows the same pattern, but there are three points of distinction worth noting. First, the rate of reentry for children who left care to live with a relative guardian is lower, regardless of age. Second, the baseline risk following an exit to guardianship is greater for infants than it is for older children (Figure A12 also showed this). Finally, the baseline hazard crosses at about two years (person-period 4). What this means is that through two years, the risk of reentry is greater for infants than older children and youth, given a discharge to guardianship. After about two years, the relative risk is greater for older children. It remains elevated as time passes, though there are times when the differences are somewhat smaller (person-periods 14 and 22).

Reentry rates and adolescence

When arrayed by single year of age, the age distribution of the children admitted to care is bimodal (Wulczyn et al. 2005). Typically, the largest group is infants. The second largest group is 15-year-olds, although the peak shifts slightly (i.e., age 14 or 16) by state. It is a pattern that fits what we know about the challenges parents face when raising children. Infants are demanding for obvious reasons; adolescent behavior raises a different, but no less important, set of challenges.

For the most part, studies of reentry have sidestepped the issue of reentry and whether the risk of reentry rises as young people approach adolescence regardless of when they left foster care. Some studies show a link between reentry and adolescence (Rolock and White 2016), but others do not (Jedwab and Shaw 2017; Shaw 2006). In part, the underlying issue has to do with when age is measured. For example, Rolock and White (2016) and Jedwab and Shaw (2017) measured the risk of reentry at the time of discharge from care. Others have measured age as the age at admission (Shaw 2006). The challenge with these approaches is the confound between age and calendar time. As the baseline rates of reentry show, the risk of reentry falls with the passage of time. However, as time passes, a young person moves ever closer to adolescence. Without accommodation, the falling risk of reentry drowns out any increase in the risk associated with adolescence. There is also the issue of reentry on the part of adolescents shortly after they leave care: is there an elevated risk of reentry because they are an adolescent, because the discharge from foster care happened recently, or because of both?

Parolini et al. (2018) solved this problem by using a time-dependent Cox model. The time-dependent model allows for the differentiation of duration dependence (i.e., how long a child has been out of care) and the developmental effect (i.e., elevated risk as adolescence approaches). Here, I have adopted a similar approach to test whether adolescents have an elevated risk of reentry relative to younger children. The results, which are displayed in online appendix Figure A15, show the risk of reentry for children at different ages. As measured, the risk of reentry incorporates age at discharge and time since discharge so that I can assess risk based on age at reentry.

To highlight the risk of reentry among adolescents, I selected children who left foster care before their first birthday (age zero) as the reference group. I then compare the risk of reentry for each other age group (one to three, four to five, and so on) to infants. Compared to infants, lower relative risks are less than 1 (on the y-axis) and higher risks are above 1.

For children who were reunified, the risk of reentry is always lower for children who left care after their first birthday. The risk does rise for children in their adolescence. Again this effect captures the risk of reentry among adolescents who left care recently and those who left some time ago. For young people who left care to live with a guardian, the evidence suggests a rate of reentry that starts to rise among eight- to nine-year-olds. Among 14- to 15-year-olds, the risk of reentry exceeds the risk of reentry reported for infants. In both cases—reunification and guardianship—the risk of reentry is elevated for adolescents.

Conclusion and Implications

"If you've seen one child welfare system in the United States, you have seen one child welfare system." This adage among observers of the U.S. child welfare system is telling of the diversity of what we call the child welfare system and the considerable latitude that the federal government grants states in child welfare (see also Berger and Slack, this volume). As a consequence, how states respond to child maltreatment via the foster care system cannot be neatly characterized. For example, the likelihood that a child will leave foster care within 12 months of placement varies across states from 83 to 28 percent. Reentry rates range from 3 to 28 percent. The federal government routinely updates federal policy and regulations, as do the states. What is missing from these attempts to improve the child welfare system is a sense for how laws passed at the federal level will land given the diverse operating conditions at the state level. For example, is it not possible that regulations targeting permanency rates would have the unintended effect of slowing permanency rates down in the state or states where permanency rates are already comparatively better than in the states where young people are more likely to languish?

To bring additional structure to our understanding of foster care as a response to maltreatment, I imposed a life course perspective onto to the most basic policy questions: When do children first enter care? How long do the stay? How do they leave? and What happens after they leave? Because the life course is an inherently developmental perspective, the imposition of a life course framework asks researchers to consider when something happens and not simply whether it happens. It also requires us to consider childhood in its entirety and place the foster care experience in that context.

Having done so, what do the results tell us? First, foster care tends to play a small role within the context of childhood. The youngest children (under the age of one) at the time of admission are those most likely to encounter foster care, and they are the children for whom the dose of foster care, as a developmental influence, is the largest. Even so, on average, 10 percent of their childhood will be spent in foster care. At the other end of the age spectrum, 15-, 16-, and 17-year-olds are the young people mostly likely to finish what is left of their childhood still in care (through the age of 18). Making the transition to adulthood from the platform of foster care is indeed perilous, but in the grand scheme of things, their time spent in foster care represents a small fraction of their childhood. Ultimately the definition that we attach to what it *means* to have been a foster child has to take these realities into account, especially as the data needed to understand the impact of foster care on life course outcomes become more readily available. Foster care is not a binary experience that did or did not happen.

The timing, sequence, and duration of foster care is critical to how we attach meaning to the experience. That so many spend so little time in care draws attention to questions that consider the need for placement in the first place (see articles by Jones Harden et al., Roygardner et al., Feely et al., and Slack and Berger, this volume).

We do see, even in these simple data, the substantial imprint of what might be called developmentally organized continuities in experience. As shown, the largest single group of children entering care is under the age of one month (12 percent). Importantly, we have seen a substantial increase in that age group in recent years. This is likely due to the influence of the drug (opioid) epidemic, but I think it is important to consider a longer historical horizon. Upward pressure on the foster care caseload dates back to 2000 even as we were witnessing a drop in the number of children entering care nationally. From the data I present here (and it is important to note that not all states are represented), the decline seems connected to what happened in the large urban core counties in contrast to nonurban counties. Rather than see the rising demand as a byproduct of recent changes in substance use, the almost-steady increase in the volume of young people entering care from the nonurban areas suggests a fundamental problem. When Temporary Assistance for Needy Families (TANF) replaced Aid to Families with Dependent Children (AFDC) as the cash assistance program in 1996, there were worries about the impact those changes would have on the child welfare system (Hutson 2001). For the most part, the initial concerns faded as the number of children in out-of-home care started falling post-1996. These data provide evidence that suggest another scenario having to do with a slower erosion of family support systems. That the increase in admissions to foster care is happening where the safety net of support programs is weaker still (Allard 2017) begs a fundamental question. Are the drug epidemic and the rise in foster care placements the problem, or do they represent symptoms of something more pernicious? Does cutting back on safety net programs ultimately weaken families, especially families with very young children, in such a way that it takes a generation or two to observe fully the strain a lack of social support places on marginalized families? (See Feely et al., this volume, for a discussion of how safety net programs could be reoriented to encompass child maltreatment prevention.)

We see other regularities in the evidence that points to what it means to be placed. Babies are the most likely children to be adopted regardless of race and ethnicity. In terms of impact on foster care, no single group of children leaves a larger footprint on the system. The reverse is also true. Viewed through an exposure lens, no group spends more time in foster care than those who come into care during the first year of their life. Yet the attention afforded these youngsters in the system is modest at best. It will be hard to have a significant impact on how much foster care we use in the United States without attending to this group more carefully, especially in the Family First era of federal funding (see articles by Haskins, this volume; Testa and Kelly, this volume). In particular, what are the *cost-effective*, evidence-based interventions that can be deployed in nonurban areas that target families with very young children with the expectation that placement risk will be lowered within 30 days of being born?

I have also shown, albeit in a limited way, the extent to which the placement experience depends on the state where a child lives. Although it is both tempting and important to speculate as to why these profound between-state differences persist, the reality is we know far too little to do more than offer possibilities for where to start the research. For several of the comparisons, the state differences appear to be concentrated early in the placement experience, with the exception of adoption (see, for example, Figures A5, A9, and A11). Much of the policy attention over the past several decades has focused on young people who languish in care, but the evidence presented here suggests that early differences in the placement experience may be as important if not more so. The question is why? Per capita placement rates may play a role in that states with above average placements may have more children who leave quickly; states with lower placement rates may have fewer placement decisions vacated by the courts upon review. There is also the underlying rate of maltreatment and state differences in how maltreatment is defined. All of these possibilities are researchable and knowable given the available data. Doing the research that would uncover the extent to which either possibility is explanatory is itself a fundamental policy choice. If we believe that policy makes a difference, then we should make the necessary funds available so that the field understands whether the evidence sustains those explanations. I suspect, given the results, the policy implications would be as far-reaching as anything we have seen thus far.

There is a host of other potential explanations that warrant further study. To focus on the ends of the continuum, we have seen how urban and rural child welfare systems differ with regard to the secular changes in the demand for foster care. Among other insights, the evidence demonstrates the extent to which state-level trends are a reality shaped by what is happening in each state's urban center. Research is beginning to reveal the between-state differences in outcomes, but the between- *and* within-state variation is largely untouched but for a few exceptions (Maguire-Jack et al. 2015; Wulczyn et al. 2016).

The list of reasons why the within-state variation, in the context of between-state variation, is important is a long one. For example, the courts that adjudicate placement decisions operate, for the most part, at the county level. We know far too little about court operations from a comparative perspective to understand the ways in which courts account for within state variation in outcomes. There is also the question of local ecology. Whether one views ecological variation at county or subcounty levels (Coulton et al. 1995, 2007; Drake and Pandey 1996; Freisthler, Merritt, and LaScala 2006; Lery 2009), the interaction between state policy context and the ecological context is a largely untouched subject. We also have to consider the role of social sector agencies. Over the past couple of decades, public child welfare agencies have moved a significant share of their child welfare services into the hands of the social sector (Blackstone, Buck, and Hakim 2004; Flaherty, Collins-Camargo, and Lee 2008; Government Accountability Office 1997). There has been, however, very little in the way of systematic research that tackles the question of between-provider performance variation in a policy and ecological context (Wulczyn, Orlebeke, and Melamid 2000; Wulczyn, Chen, and Orlebeke 2009). To put it bluntly, the situation in child welfare with respect to outcomes and the delivery of services by social sector agencies is tantamount to studying school outcomes without acknowledging the impact of schools. Much the same could be said of the impact of foster parents and caseworkers. We acknowledge their role as principal agents within the system, but we know too little to understand whether, given the variation at that level of the system, policy will have the intended effect on the quality of services delivered.

Finally, we have witnessed a growing commitment to the evidence-base in child welfare (see articles by Haskins, this volume; Testa and Kelly, this volume). It is a laudable change in focus. However, if the emphasis remains centered on interventions that work, we are likely to encounter disappointment for the evidence of what works represents only a portion of the evidence we need to operate a more effective and efficient foster care system than we have currently (Deaton and Cartwright 2018; Nagin and Sampson 2019). We need a broadened view of the foster care system as a system that affects the lives of children. To achieve that, a research agenda motivated by conceptualization rather than research method is essential. The life course perspective, as one such conceptualization, is a good place to start.

Notes

1. See fcda.chapinhall.org.

2. This example illustrates why life course studies are difficult generally and why estimates of exposure to foster care are especially difficult to generate. To know whether a child grows up in foster care, one has to begin with entry into care 18 years ago. In 2018, that means the earliest cohort with complete observations involves children admitted to care in the year 2000. Because the administrative data systems used by state child welfare agencies are often newer than that, the number of states capable of counting children in this way is relatively few. Now that state systems are more mature, these questions are more easily answered provided the data are organized in a way that allows for a rigorous life course perspective. In this example, I use data for thirteen states.

3. As a point of clarification, some of the states included in the study allow adolescents to extend their stay in foster care past the age of 18. In those cases, reaching the age of 18 is not the same as leaving care at age 18. I show reaching the age of majority with the other exit reasons to highlight how the likelihood of reaching the age of 18 while still in care contrasts with the other ways young people can leave placement, including running away. In addition, given the years of admission included (2000 and 2005), the number of states with extended care was much smaller then, as compared to today. Thus, the 17-year-olds admitted in 2000 and 2005 were more likely to age out in the traditional sense of that phrase.

4. Some children do return to care after having been adopted (Palacios et al. 2018; Rolock 2015). However, states differ with respect to whether it is possible to track adopted children who later return to care. For that reason, I do not address returns to care by children who were adopted. Instead, I refer readers to the cited literature.

References

Allard, Scott W. 2017. *Places in need: The changing geography of poverty.* New York, NY: Russell Sage Foundation.

Berger, Lawrence M., and Kristen S. Slack. 2020. The contemporary U.S. child welfare system(s): Overview and key challenges. *The ANNALS of the American Academy of Political and Social Science* (this volume).

Blackstone, Erwin A., A. J. Buck, and S. Hakim. 2004. Privatizing adoption and foster care: Applying auction and market solutions. *Children and Youth Services Review* 26 (11): 1033–49.

Bullock, Roger, M. E. Courtney, R. Parker, I. Sinclair, and J. Thoburn. 2006. Can the corporate state parent? *Children and Youth Services Review* 28 (11): 1344–58.

Chamberlain, Patricia, J. M. Price, J. B. Reid, J. Landsverk, P. A. Fisher, and M. Stoolmiller. 2006. Who disrupts from placement in foster and kinship care? *Child Abuse & Neglect* 30 (4): 409–24.

Child Welfare Information Gateway. 2019. *Kinship guardianship as a permanency option*. Washington, DC: Child Welfare Information Gateway.

Children's Bureau. 2019. *Reentries into foster care*. Washington, DC: U.S. Department of Health and Human Services.

Coakley, Jennifer F., and J. D. Berrick. 2007. Research review: In a rush to permanency: Preventing adoption disruption. *Child and Family Social Work*. Available from https://doi.org/10.1111/j.1365-2206.2006.00468.x.

Coulton, Claudia J., D. S. Crampton, M. Irwin, J. C. Spilsbury, and J. E. Korbin. 2007. How neighborhoods influence child maltreatment: A review of the literature and alternative pathways. *Child Abuse & Neglect* 31 (11–12): 1117–42.

Coulton, Claudia J., J. E. Korbin, M. Su, and J. Chow. 1995. Community level factors and child maltreatment rates. *Child Development* 66 (5): 1262–76.

Courtney, Mark E., N. J. Okpych, K. Park, J. Harty, H. Feng, A. Torres-Garcia, and S. Sayed. 2018. *Findings from the California Youth Transitions to Adulthood Study (CalYOUTH): Conditions of youth at age* 19, 10–190. Chicago, IL: Chapin Hall at the University of Chicago.

Deaton, Angus, and N. Cartwright. 2018. Reflections on randomized control trials. *Social Science and Medicine* 210:86–90.

Doyle, Joseph J. 2013. Causal effects of foster care: An instrumental-variables approach. *Children and Youth Services Review* 35 (7): 1143–51.

Drake, Brett, and S. Pandey. 1996. Understanding the relationship between neighborhood poverty and specific types of child maltreatment. *Child Abuse & Neglect* 20 (11): 1003–18.

Dworsky, Amy, F. Wulczyn, and L. Huang. 2018. Predictors of running away from out-of-home care: Does county context matter? *Cityscape* 20 (3): 101–16.

Elder, Glen H. 1994. Time, human agency, and social change: Perspectives on the life course. *Social Psychology Quarterly* 57 (1): 4–15.

Elder, Glen H. 1998. The life course as developmental theory. *Child Development* 69 (1): 1–12.

Ellis, Bruce J., J. J. Jackson, and W. T. Boyce. 2006. The stress response systems: Universality and adaptive individual differences. *Developmental Review* 26 (2): 175–212.

Feely, Megan, Kerri M. Raissian, William Schneider, and Lindsey Rose Bullinger. 2020. The social welfare policy landscape and child protective services: Opportunities for and barriers to creating systems synergy. *The ANNALS of the American Academy of Political and Social Science* (this volume).

Flaherty, Chris, C. Collins-Camargo, and E. Lee. 2008. Privatization of child welfare services: Lessons learned from experienced states regarding site readiness assessment and planning. *Children and Youth Services Review* 30 (7): 809–20.

Font, Sarah A., L. M. Berger, M. Cancian, and J. L. Noyes. 2018. Permanency and the educational and economic attainment of former foster children in early adulthood. *American Sociological Review* 83 (4): 716–43.

Font, Sarah A., and E. T. Gershoff. 2020. An introduction to foster care. *Springer Briefs in Psychology*, 1–19. Available from https://doi.org/10.1007/978-3-030-41146-6_1.

Freisthler, Bridge, D. H. Merritt, and E. A. LaScala. 2006. Understanding the ecology of child maltreatment: A review of the literature and directions for future research. *Child Maltreatment* 11 (3): 263–80.

Government Accountability Office (GAO). 1997. *Social service privatization: Expansion poses challenges in ensuring accountability for program results*. Vol. GAO/HEHS-98-6. Washington, DC: GAO.

Gross, Max. 2020. *Temporary stays and persistent gains: The causal effects of foster care*. Available from https://max-gross.github.io/website_documents/max_gross_foster_care.pdf.

Gypen, Laura, J. Vanderfaeillie, S. D. Maeyer, L. Belenger, and F. V. Holen. 2017. Outcomes of children who grew up in foster care: Systematic-review. *Children and Youth Services Review* 76:74–83.

Haskins, Ron. 2020. Child welfare financing: What do we fund, how, and what could be improved? *The ANNALS of the American Academy of Political and Social Science* (this volume).

Hutson, Rutledge Q. 2001. *Red flags: Research raises concerns about the impact of "welfare reform," on child maltreatment*. Washington, DC: Center for Law and Social Policy.

Ingram, Deborah, and S. J. Franco. 2014. 2013 NCHS Urban-Rural Classification Scheme for Counties. *Vital and Health Statistics* 2 (166). Hyattsville, MD: National Center for Health Statistics. Available from https://www.cdc.gov/nchs/data/series/sr_02/sr02_166.pdf.

James, Sigrid. 2011. Why do foster care placements disrupt? An investigation of reasons for placement change in foster care. *Social Service Review* 78 (4): 601–27.

Jedwab, Merav, and T. V. Shaw. 2017. Predictors of reentry into the foster care system: Comparison of children with and without previous removal experience. *Children and Youth Services Review* 82:177–84.

Jones, Annette S., and T. LaLiberte. 2017. Risk and protective factors of foster care reentry: An examination of the literature. *Journal of Public Child Welfare* 11 (4–5): 516–45.

Jones Harden, Brenda, Cassandra Simons, Michelle Johnson-Motoyama, and Richard Barth. 2021. The child maltreatment landscape: Where are we now and where should we go. *The ANNALS of the American Academy of Political and Social Science* (this volume).

Kimberlin, Sara E., E. K. Anthony, and M. J. Austin. 2009. Re-entering foster care: Trends, evidence, and implications. *Children and Youth Services Review* 31 (4): 471–81.

Lawrence, Catherine R., E. A. Carlson, and B. Egeland. 2006. The impact of foster care on development. *Development and Psychopathology* 18 (1): 57–76.

Lery, Bridgett. 2009. Neighborhood structure and foster care entry risk: The role of spatial scale in defining neighborhoods. *Children and Youth Services Review* 31 (3): 331–37.

Liao, Minli, and K. R. White. 2014. Post-permanency service needs, service utilization, and placement discontinuity for kinship versus non-kinship families. *Children and Youth Services Review* 44 (C): 370–78.

Maguire-Jack, Kathryn, P. Lanier, M. Johnson-Motoyama, H. Welch, and M. Dineen. 2015. Geographic variation in racial disparities in child maltreatment: The influence of county poverty and population density. *Child Abuse & Neglect* 47:1–13.

Miller, Leonie, M. Randle, and S. Dolnicar. 2018. Carer factors associated with foster-placement success and breakdown. *British Journal of Social Work* 49 (2): 503–22.

Nagin, Daniel S., and R. J. Sampson. 2019. The real gold standard: Measuring counterfactual worlds that matter most to social science and policy. *Annual Review of Criminology* 2 (1): 123–45.

National Scientific Council on the Developing Child. 2013. The science of neglect: The persistent absence of responsive care disrupts the developing brain. Working Paper 12, Center on the Developing Child, Harvard University, Cambridge, MA.

Palacios, Jesús., N. Rolock, J. Selwyn, and M. Barbosa-Ducharne. 2018. Adoption breakdown: Concept, research, and implications. *Research on Social Work Practice* 29 (2): 130–42.

Parolini, Arno, A. Shlonsky, J. Magruder, A. L. Eastman, F. Wulczyn, and D. Webster. 2018. Age and other risk factors related to reentry to care from kin guardian homes. *Child Abuse & Neglect* 79:315–24.

Rolock, Nancy. 2015. Post-permanency continuity: What happens after adoption and guardianship from foster care? *Journal of Public Child Welfare* 9:155–73.

Rolock, Nancy, and K. White. 2016. Post-permanency discontinuity: A longitudinal examination of outcomes for foster youth after adoption or guardianship. *Children and Youth Services Review* 70:419–27.

Rolock, Nancy, K. R. White, K. Ocasio, L. Zhang, M. J. MacKenzie, and R. Fong. 2018. A comparison of foster care reentry after adoption in two large U.S. states. *Research on Social Work Practice* 29 (2): 153–64.

Roygardner, Debangshu, Kelli N. Hughes, and Vincent J. Palusci. 2021. Leveraging family and community strengths to reduce child maltreatment. *The ANNALS of the American Academy of Political and Social Science* (this volume).

Samuels, Gina. 2008. *A reason, a season, or a lifetime: Relational permanence among young adults with foster care backgrounds*. Chicago, IL: Chapin Hall Center for Children at the University of Chicago.

Schwartz, Meryl. 1996. Reinventing guardianship: Subsidized guardianship, foster care, and child welfare. *NYU Review of Law and Social Change* XXII:441–82.

Shaw, Terry V. 2006. Reentry into the foster care system after reunification. *Children and Youth Services Review* 28 (11): 1375–90.

Slack, Kristen S., and Lawrence Berger. 2021. Who is and is not served by child protective services systems? Implications for a prevention infrastructure to reduce child maltreatment. *The ANNALS of the American Academy of Political and Social Science* (this volume).

Smith, S. L., J. A. Howard, P. C. Garnier, and S. D. Ryan. 2006. Where are we now? A post-ASFA examination of adoption disruption. *Adoption Quarterly* 9 (4): 19–44.

Testa, Mark F. 2002. Kinship care and permanency. *Journal of Social Service Research* 28 (1): 25–43.

Testa, Mark F. 2004. When children cannot return home: Adoption and guardianship. *The Future of Children* 14 (1): 114–29.

Testa, Mark F., and David Kelly. 2020. The evolution of federal child welfare policy through the Family First Prevention Services Act of 2018. *The ANNALS of the American Academy of Political and Social Science* (this volume).

Testa, Mark F., S. M. Snyder, Q. Wu, N. Rolock, and M. Liao. 2015. Adoption and guardianship: A moderated mediation analysis of predictors of post-permanency continuity. *American Journal of Orthopsychiatry* 85 (2): 107–18.

Vesneski, Wiliam. 2011. State law and the termination of parental rights. *Family Court Review* 49 (2): 364–78.

Wald, Michael S. 1976. State intervention on behalf of "neglected" children: Standards for removal of children from their homes, monitoring the status of children in foster care, and termination of parental rights. *Stanford Law Review* 28 (4). Available from https://doi.org/10.2307/1228098.

Wulczyn, Fred. 1991. Caseload dynamics and foster care reentry. *Social Service Review* 65 (1): 133–56.

Wulczyn, Fred. 2004. Family reunification. *The Future of Children* 14 (1): 94–113.

Wulczyn, Fred, L. Alpert, Z. Martinez, and A. Weiss. 2015. *Within and between state variation in the use of congregate care.* Chicago, IL: Chapin Hall.

Wulczyn, Fred, R. Barth, Y.-Y. Yuan, B. Jones Harden, and J. Landsverk. 2005. *Beyond common sense: Child welfare, child well-being, and the evidence for policy reform.* New York, NY: Routledge.

Wulczyn, Fred, L. Chen, and B. Orlebeke. 2009. Evaluating contract agency performance in achieving reunification. *Children and Youth Services Review* 31 (5): 506–12.

Wulczyn, Fred, K. Hislop, and B. Jones Harden. 2002. The placement of infants in foster care. *Infant Mental Health Journal* 23 (5): 454–75.

Wulczyn, Fred, S. Huhr, K. Hislop, L. Chen, B. Orlebeke, J. Haight, L. Alpert, and S. Feldman. 2016. *Lives lived in foster care: Variation in the ways children leave placement.* Chicago, IL: Center for State Child Welfare Data, Chapin Hall, University of Chicago.

Wulczyn, Fred, S. Huhr, and J. McClanahan. 2018. *African American/white disparities in the Tennessee foster care system.* Chicago, IL: Chapin Hall.

Wulczyn, Fred, S. Huhr, F. Schmits, and A. Wilkins. 2017. *Understanding the differences in how adolescents leave foster care.* Chicago, IL: Chapin Hall.

Wulczyn, Fred, B. Orlebeke, and E. Melamid. 2000. Measuring contract agency performance with administrative data. *Child Welfare* 79 (5): 457–74.

Racial Disproportionality and Disparities in the Child Welfare System: Why Do They Exist, and What Can Be Done to Address Them?

By
ALAN J. DETTLAFF
and
REIKO BOYD

Children of color are overrepresented in the child welfare system, and Black children have been most significantly impacted by this racial disproportionality. Racial disproportionality in child welfare exists because of influences that are both external to child welfare systems and part of the child welfare system. We summarize the causes of racial disproportionality, arguing that internal and external causes of disproportional involvement originate from a common underlying factor: structural and institutional racism that is both within child welfare systems and part of society at large. Further, we review options for addressing racial disproportionality, arguing that it needs to be rectified because of the harm it causes Black children and families and that forcible separation of children from their parents can no longer be viewed as an acceptable form of intervention for families in need.

Keywords: racial disproportionality; racial disparities; child welfare; foster care

Research has observed the overrepresentation of children of color in the child welfare system for more than 50 years. Commonly referred to as *racial disproportionality*, this phenomenon describes a condition that exists when the proportion of one group in the child welfare population (i.e., children in foster care) is proportionately larger (overrepresented) or smaller (underrepresented) than the proportion of the same group in the general child population. Overrepresentation in the child welfare system has most significantly occurred for Black children, with national data indicating that Black children represent 23 percent of children in foster care, although they represent

Alan J. Dettlaff is dean and Maconda Brown O'Connor Endowed Dean's Chair at the University of Houston Graduate College of Social Work. His research focuses on examining and addressing issues of structural and institutional racism that contribute to the overrepresentation of children of color in the child welfare system.

Correspondence: ajdettlaff@uh.edu

DOI: 10.1177/0002716220980329

only 14 percent of children in the general population (KIDS Count 2020). This represents a decrease in disproportionality since 2000 when Black children represented 38 percent of children in foster care (Summers, Wood, and Russell 2012). This decrease was realized in part due to national attention to the problem of disproportionality in the early 2000s, which led to a number of state legislative mandates requiring system responses (e.g., Michigan Department of Human Services 2006; Texas Health and Human Services Commission 2006), as well as national philanthropic efforts to assist in these responses (e.g., Casey Family Programs 2009). However, despite decades of efforts to address this, Black children remain overrepresented in foster care at a rate more than 1.6 times their proportion of the general population. While the national dialogue has focused largely on Black children, racial disproportionality has also been observed for Native American and Latinx children, although to a lesser degree and with variation by state.[1]

While racial disproportionality refers to one group's representation in the child welfare system being out of proportion with their representation in the population, racial disparity refers to inequality in group representation in the child welfare system. That is, racial disparity is used to describe inequitable outcomes experienced by one racial group when compared to *another* racial group, while disproportionality compares the proportion of one racial group to the *same* racial group in the general population. Racial disparities can occur at every decision-making point in the child welfare system, beginning with the point of initial report, acceptance of reports for investigation, substantiation of maltreatment, entries into foster care, and exits from care. These decisions are made not only by child welfare caseworkers, but also by supervisors, administrators, judges, and other legal professionals, as well as professionals external to the child welfare system and the general public. At each of these decision-making points, racial disparities occur that disproportionately impact Black children.[2]

Beginning with the point of initial referral, multiple studies demonstrate that Black children are more likely to be reported for suspected maltreatment than White children (e.g., Putnam-Hornstein et al. 2013). Once a report is made, allegations involving Black children are more likely to proceed to investigation than those involving White children (e.g., Fluke et al. 2003). Once accepted, allegations involving Black children are more likely to be substantiated than those involving White children (e.g., Putnam-Hornstein et al. 2013). Following an investigation, Black children are more likely to be removed from their homes and placed into foster care than White children (e.g., Maguire-Jack, Font, and Dillard 2020). Finally, once in care, studies show that Black children are less likely to be reunified with their families and spend a longer time in care than White children (e.g., M. Miller 2008). Over the years, studies have examined factors that explain these disparities and findings have been mixed regarding the role of race, with some studies identifying race as a significant factor at various decision points

Reiko Boyd is an assistant professor at the University of Houston Graduate College of Social Work. Her research focuses on racial disparity and equity in child welfare, Black infant health, transition-age youth, and structural inequality in Black communities.

(e.g., Rivaux et al. 2008), while others have found no significant effect for race when controlling for other factors (e.g., Putnam-Hornstein et al. 2013).

Yet regardless of the reasons disparities occur, racial disproportionality and disparities represent a significant societal problem because of the harm they cause Black children and families. Research consistently demonstrates that, on average, the act of forced separation of children from their parents is a source of significant and lifelong trauma, regardless of how long the separation lasts (e.g., Mitchell and Kuczynski 2009; Sankaran, Church, and Mitchell 2019). Beyond this initial trauma, multiple studies document that children who are removed from their homes are at risk for a host of negative outcomes including low educational attainment, homelessness, unemployment, economic hardship, unplanned pregnancies, mental health disorders, and criminal justice involvement (e.g., Courtney et al. 2011; Pecora et al. 2005). Research has yet to determine whether removal and foster care themselves cause these poor outcomes as opposed to them reflecting a constellation of social and economic disadvantages and traumatic experiences, which may include removal and foster care. Indeed, recent research has shown a potential mitigating effect of foster care on certain negative outcomes (e.g., Font, Berger, and Cancian 2018; Font, Cancian, and Berger 2019). Nonetheless, it is indisputable that, on average, children who spend time in foster care exhibit adverse social, economic, and health-related outcomes throughout the life course.

While these risks exist for all children who experience foster care, we believe they are exacerbated for Black children who are already at risk of experiencing adverse outcomes due to structural and institutional racism and inequality. As a result of the ongoing legacy of racial inequality in America, Black youth are at increased risk of experiencing a host of poor outcomes over the course of their lives including economic hardship, poor health, low educational attainment, teen births, criminal justice involvement, emotional distress, and suicidal ideation (e.g., Hanks, Solomon, and Weller 2018; Hope, Hoggard, and Thomas 2015). For Black youth who experience the trauma of family separation and foster care, we contend that these risks are heightened, resulting in a condition of *compound disadvantage* for youth who are already at increased vulnerability for negative outcomes. As such, for Black youth, foster care as an intervention becomes a source of their ongoing and continued oppression. Even in cases where some form of intervention is necessary to ensure child safety, the negative outcomes associated with foster care can serve to further disadvantage Black youth who must navigate a society characterized by systemic inequality and structural racism. As a result, we believe that foster care as an intervention is fundamentally different than other forms of intervention that are intended to provide support (e.g., Temporary Assistance for Needy Families [TANF], Head Start) in which Black families may also be disproportionately involved.

Although the existence of racial disproportionality and disparities is widely documented, the factors that contribute to these problems have been the subject of debate in recent years. At issue is whether the observed inequities result from differential treatment from child welfare and related systems (e.g., racial bias, underreporting of children of other races), or from differential need among Black families due to their greater likelihood of experiencing poverty and related risks for maltreatment (e.g., neighborhood conditions, family composition). Research supports both of these views, with a large body of research documenting the relationship between poverty and maltreatment (e.g., Kim and Drake 2018).

Findings from the most recent National Incidence Studies of Child Abuse and Neglect (NIS-4) found that children in low-socioeconomic-status households experienced some form of maltreatment at a rate more than five times the rate of other children, and Black children were significantly more likely to live in families with low socioeconomic status (Sedlak et al. 2010). The NIS-4 also documented that Black children were significantly more likely to experience several forms of maltreatment than White children. Yet research also demonstrates the potential role of racial bias in decision-making in child welfare, with multiple studies documenting the persistence of racial inequities even when factors such as poverty and related risks are statistically controlled (e.g., Dettlaff et al. 2011; Rivaux et al. 2008). For example, Rivaux et al. (2008) found that Black children were 77 percent more likely than White children to be removed from their homes following a substantiated maltreatment investigation, even after controlling for factors such as poverty and related risks.

The debate regarding these factors has led to multiple critiques of efforts to address disproportionality, particularly among those who question the role of racial bias given the relationship between poverty and maltreatment (e.g., Bartholet 2009; Drake et al. 2011). As a result, efforts to address disproportionality have stalled, and what has been a problem in child welfare for decades remains unresolved. As such, this debate has served to perpetuate harm to Black children. Not only has this debate hindered efforts to address disproportionality, but it has distracted from the real problem of racism that creates disproportionality, both within child welfare systems and within broader society. Although research clearly documents the relationship between poverty and maltreatment, poverty and disproportionate need are the result of centuries of racism and structural disadvantage that have created the conditions of risk that contribute to maltreatment in Black families. These issues of disproportionate need are then compounded by the pervasive and intrusive involvement of child welfare systems in Black families (Roberts 2002). This article refocuses the understanding of racial disproportionality and disparities on the larger underlying issue of racism that perpetuates and supports the overrepresentation of Black children in the child welfare system, and what needs to be done to address this disproportionality and disparity.

Why Racial Disproportionality and Disparities Exist

In their extensive review and analysis of the research on racial disproportionality and disparities, Fluke et al. (2011) provided four explanations for racial disproportionality and disparities: (1) disproportionate need resulting from poverty and related risks associated with maltreatment; (2) racial bias and discrimination among child welfare staff and mandated reporters, as well as institutional racism in policies and practices of child welfare agencies; (3) child welfare system factors, including a lack of resources to address the needs of families of color; and (4) geographic context, including neighborhood conditions of concentrated poverty and other factors that may contribute to differential rates of maltreatment.

These explanations were similar to prior reviews, including those by Hines et al. (2004) that proposed four interrelated factors: (1) parent and family risks, (2) poverty and community risks, (3) race and class biases in the child welfare system, and (4) the disproportionate impact of child welfare policies on children of color. Barth (2005) also proposed four similar models for explaining disproportionality: (1) differential need resulting from differential risk; (2) racial bias that affects decision-making; (3) placement dynamics that may result in longer lengths of stay; and (4) the multiplicative model, wherein all three factors interact to produce disproportionality. Similarly, findings from a U.S. Government Accountability Office (2007) study examining disproportionality identified three contributing factors: (1) higher rates of poverty among Black families; (2) bias in child welfare systems; and (3) difficulty recruiting adoptive parents and increased reliance on kinship care in cases with Black children, which may result in longer lengths of stay in care.

In this article, we categorize these factors as those that are external to child welfare systems (poverty and related risks, neighborhood conditions) and those that are internal to child welfare systems (racial bias, institutionally racist policies, and placement dynamics). Yet we contend that these factors result from a common underlying factor—structural and institutional racism, both within child welfare systems and society at large. The following section discusses these external and internal factors, focusing on the role of racism in creating and perpetuating risk for maltreatment and child welfare system involvement among Black families.

External Factors: The Role of Racism in Creating and Promoting Risk for Maltreatment

Efforts to understand the pervasive disparities for Black families often apply a rationale in line with explanatory models of disproportionate need, which suggest that Black children and families are more likely to experience many of the risk factors associated with maltreatment (e.g., poverty, parenting stress), thus making them more vulnerable to child welfare system contact (e.g., Barth 2005; Bartholet 2009). Although sufficiently logical, this line of reasoning provides only a partial explanation that begs other critical questions that often remain unaddressed within maltreatment literature: *Why are Black children and families more likely to experience risk factors associated with maltreatment? How have risk factors for maltreatment come to be concentrated among Black families?*

In this section, we address these questions. We focus on the link between racism and risk factors for maltreatment. Recognizing this connection is key to a foundational understanding of why Black families disproportionately experience risk factors associated with child maltreatment and child welfare system involvement. We address the direct role of racism in creating and perpetuating risk for maltreatment through factors external to the child welfare system by discussing (1) historic racism against Black families; (2) the relationship between racism and poverty; (3) the relationship among racism, health, and stress; and (4) the relationship between racism and geographic contexts. We place a primary focus on structural racism and acknowledge that, as with other forms of oppression, racism is not merely a personal ideology based on racial prejudice, but a *system* that involves institutional policies and practices, cultural messages, and individual actions and beliefs (Center for the Study of Social Policy [CSSP] 2019).

Historical overview of racism against Black families

Ahistorical conceptualizations of disproportionality and disparity are fundamentally flawed because they fail to take into account historical events, policies, social dynamics, and economic influences that occurred in the past but continue to shape current determinants of health for Black families. As such, a historical lens must be applied to understand the roots of current racial disparities and the endurance of inequitable outcomes.

Enslavement and dehumanization. Racism against Black families has been a defining characteristic of the United States, predating even the nation's official inception. In 1619, a year prior to the arrival of the Mayflower, a ship arrived at the British colony of Virginia with a cargo of twenty to thirty enslaved Africans (Hannah-Jones 2019). Their arrival marked the initiation of a vicious system of chattel slavery that would last for the next 250 years. As such, generations of Black people were born into slavery, and their enslaved status was passed down to their children. Enslaved people were not recognized as human beings; rather, they were regarded as property that could be bought, sold, traded, and disposed of violently.

As the slave trade became a flourishing economic system, unfounded but socially popular scientific theories were used to decree Black people as less than fully human and thereby rationalize their brutal subjugation. Throughout much of the nineteenth century, scientific racism was promoted through a body of scholarship that focused intently on proving racial inferiority (Eberhardt 2019). Empirical efforts relied on theories asserting that humans originated from multiple sources to proclaim a "natural hierarchy" determined by racial characteristics with White people at the top. Notions of White supremacy and the perceived subhuman status of Black people were legally codified through policies such as the Three-Fifths Compromise, which counted an enslaved Black person as three-fifths of a human and reflected the ideology that Black people were both property and less than human (DeGruy 2005).

Forced family separation. The domestic slave trade institutionalized the forced separation of Black families. Enslaved people were denied the right to form families and to keep them intact. Ties to parents, siblings, and extended family were not honored by enslavers or the courts. Enslaved people could not marry, and they had no claim to their own children, who could be bought, sold, and traded at their owner's discretion. Historical evidence suggests that the forced separation of children from parents was cruel, widespread, and devastating, with desperate pursuits to reunify lost family members occurring during slavery and beyond (H. Williams 2012).

Overall, slavery, with all its vicious facets, should be understood as a massive historical trauma that continues to shape the lives of children, families, communities, and the systems with which they interact (National Child Traumatic Stress Network 2016). Given that the involuntary removal of children through foster care is not the first form of family separation to disproportionately impact Black families in this country, it should be understood that for Black families, the trauma of involuntary removal can be heightened by the legacy of forced family separation that was integral to slavery.

Laws and policies to maintain White supremacy. Following the Emancipation Proclamation in 1863 and the official abolishment of slavery in 1865, the government enacted a series of laws, policies, and systems to maintain White supremacy and reinforce inequity through the continued subjugation of Black people. Starting in 1865, Black codes were enacted in Southern states to restrict the freedom of Black people, which included vagrancy statutes that imposed penalties and made it a crime for Black people to be unemployed. Through Black codes, many misdemeanors or trivial offenses were treated as felonies, with harsh sentences and fines. Black codes prohibited interracial marriage or cohabitation, restricted the practice of professions outside of menial labor, denied voting rights, controlled where Black people lived, and even included provisions to seize Black children for labor purposes.

Despite the guarantees of equality in the 14th Amendment, White supremacy was protected and reinforced through subsequent Supreme Court decisions and legislation. The landmark *Plessy v. Ferguson* decision in 1896 declared that racial segregation of Black Americans was constitutional. Between 1881 and 1964, the majority of states passed Jim Crow Laws, which mandated "separate but equal" status for Black people, requiring that public schools, public facilities, churches, and restaurants have separate facilities for White and Black people. The most common Jim Crow laws prohibited interracial marriage, mandated that businesses separate customers by race, and protected the rights of business owners to refuse service based on race. Jim Crow Laws were fully backed by the Supreme Court until 1964, when the Civil Rights Act outlawed all discriminatory legislation.

The history of enslavement and dehumanization of Black people, forced family separation, and policies to maintain White supremacy form an inequitable foundation that continues to have an impact on social, legal, and political factors that shape experiences of Black children and families. Evaluating why disparities exist requires connecting these external factors and recognizing the role of racism in creating and promoting disproportionate risk for maltreatment.

Racism and poverty

Current and historic racism continues to negatively impact the economic status of Black families and is a root cause of racial disparities in poverty. Enduring consequences of racism, including residential segregation, discrimination in labor markets, unequal access to quality education, and implicit and explicit biases perpetuate the disproportionate concentration of Black families among the poor. As such, racial disparities in income, employment, educational attainment, home-ownership, and wealth persist and endure across generations (Chetty et al. 2018).

Data consistently document inequitable outcomes for Black households across various measures of poverty and wealth. In 2018, the Black poverty rate (20.8 percent) remained more than twice as high as the White poverty rate (8.1 percent); and the median income was $70,642 for White households, while Black households had a median income of $41,361 (Semega et al. 2019). The Black/White wage gap, which indicates how much less Black workers are paid than White workers, has increased from 20.8 percent in 2008 to 26.7 percent in 2018 (Gould 2019). Beyond income, the residual effects of Jim Crow Laws and systematic exclusion from homeownership have contributed to persistent disparities in wealth. Homeownership is particularly influential on the racial wealth gap, as homeownership helps families to accumulate wealth and take advantage of substantial tax savings. In 2019, less than half of Black families (42 percent) lived in owner-occupied housing, compared to 73 percent of White families (Rudden 2019). Further, approximately one in six Black households spend more than 50 percent of their income on housing, leaving them financially strained and unable to devote resources to their children's education, health care, and other basic needs (Stanford Center on Poverty and Inequality 2017).

The racialized nature of poverty in the United States is a direct consequence of racism, the evidence of which can be traced across decades through formal and informal policies that have intentionally and adversely targeted Black people. Poverty and associated economic hardships are well-established risk factors for child maltreatment. Specifically, maltreatment risk is associated with a variety of indicators of economic hardship, including unemployment, single-parent household structure, food insecurity, difficulty paying for housing, and self-reported economic stress (Institute of Medicine and National Research Council 2014). While the link between poverty and child maltreatment is uncontested, the link between poverty and racism has been relatively unacknowledged in the discourse on etiology of racial disparities in the child welfare system. Applying a historical view that properly accounts for racism is key to accurate contextualization and explanations of these disparities. It provides a basis for understanding that racial disparities attributed to disproportionate need are also fundamentally attributable to racism and its enduring effects.

Racism, health, and stress

Racism is also intricately linked to persistent racial disparities across important indicators of health. According to a meta-analysis focusing on the relationship between reported racism and health outcomes, racism is associated with poorer physical health and poorer mental health, including depression, anxiety, and psychological stress (Paradies et al. 2015). Evidence indicates that socioeconomic factors alone do not account for these disparities. At every level of education and income, Black people have a lower life expectancy at age 25 than do White and Latinx populations (Paradies et al. 2015).

The experience of racial stressors among Black Americans across the life course may contribute to "weathering" or accelerated deterioration in health as a consequence of the cumulative physiologic burden placed on biological systems by repeated experiences with discrimination, stigma, economic adversity, and political marginalization (Geronimus et al. 2006). Researchers have also suggested that chronic experiences of racism and microaggressions can result in "racial battle fatigue," which includes constant anxiety and worry, hypervigilance, elevated heart rate and blood pressure, extreme fatigue, and other physical and psychological symptoms (Soto, Dawson-Andoh, and BeLue 2011). Epidemiologist Sherman James referred to the coping strategies that are needed to survive amid this experience of constant discrimination and oppression as "John Henryism," which is also associated with significant adverse health consequences (James et al. 1992).

Notably, prior research demonstrates a strong link between various forms of parent/family stress and child maltreatment risk (e.g., Slack et al. 2011). For Black families, the experience of stress stemming from enduring racial discrimination may have adverse consequences on parenting and maltreatment risk that go beyond general experiences of stress related to parenting or economic hardship.

Racism, geographic contexts, and structural inequities

More than any other group, Black individuals and families continue to bear the burden of the legacy of racial residential segregation (D. Williams, Lawrence, and Davis 2019). Where one lives is a critical determinant of socioeconomic status, health, and well-being. It determines access to quality schools, job opportunities, safe and affordable housing, nutritious food, exposure to environmental toxins, access to reliable public transit, quality medical care, and longer life expectancy. For Black households, residential segregation has severely restricted access to quality resources and opportunities that have stifled economic mobility.

Throughout most of the twentieth century, federal, state, and local governments defined where Black and White people should live by enforcing racially explicit policies. Racial residential segregation was perpetuated by intentional government action, amounting to segregation by law and public policy. For example, the Federal Housing Authority and Veteran's Administration refused to insure mortgages to Black people in designated "White" neighborhoods and would not insure mortgages for White people in neighborhoods where Black households were present. In addition, federally backed loans were awarded to private builders only if racial restrictions were included in their subdivision deeds (Rothstein 2017). Segregation was also firmly reinforced by local laws that segregated schools, hospitals, hotels, restaurants, and parks. The Civil Rights Act of 1964 and Fair Housing

Act of 1968 were meant as remedies, but the cumulative effect of racially discriminatory policies in the housing market had taken their toll. Black families had been forced into racially segregated high-poverty areas, with inferior infrastructure and institutions, substandard housing, and industrial pollution. As a result, the worst urban context in which White people reside is considerably better than the average context of Black communities (D. Williams, Lawrence, and Davis 2019).

Here, we have reviewed the relationship between racism and factors external to the child welfare system that contribute to racial disproportionality and disparities, including poverty, health and stress, and geographic contexts. Considered together, these external factors demonstrate how racist laws, practices, and policies have concentrated various conditions of risk among Black families. As such, racism can be understood as a common denominator across external factors that explains why Black families may disproportionately experience adverse conditions associated with child maltreatment and child welfare system involvement.

Internal Factors: Racism and Racial Bias in Child Welfare and Related Systems

While racism external to child welfare systems creates the conditions of risk that may lead to maltreatment in Black families, racism within child welfare systems exacerbates and maintains racial inequities. This section reviews the racist origins of the child welfare system, the ways in which racism is institutionalized in child welfare systems, and the role of racial bias in decision-making.

Institutional racism and the child welfare system

The history of the child welfare system, as with the history of most formal structures in the United States, is one that involves the gradual development of a system designed by White people with the goal of maintaining the supremacy of White people. Throughout its history, racism has been embedded in child welfare systems' policies and structures to first exclude Black children from involvement and later to perpetuate oppression against them.

Prior to the mid-1800s, there was little involvement of formal systems in families' lives, as White children were viewed solely as the responsibility of their parents. Black children were the property of their slave owners. The origins of the child welfare system began in 1853, when Charles Loring Brace established the Children's Aid Society as a means of caring for abandoned and orphaned White children living on the streets of New York. While there was some institutional care for White children at that time, Loring Brace believed that these children could help to settle the expanding American West, and through placement in family care, grow into productive adults (O'Connor 2004). This led to the Orphan Train Movement, which resettled more than two hundred thousand White children through the early 1900s. Black children remained largely excluded from child welfare services through the mid-1900s, until a series of policy changes in the 1960s had a significant impact on the involvement of Black children (Bates 2016).

The passage of the Social Security Act in 1935 saw the creation of the Aid to Families with Dependent Children Program (AFDC), which provided states great discretion in eligibility requirements. Policy-makers often designed requirements to maintain racial oppression in the form of "illegitimate child clauses" or other home suitability clauses that allowed states to deny benefits to, or expel, Black families whose homes were viewed as immoral (Bell 1965). As examples, in 1959 the state of Florida removed more than fourteen thousand children from their welfare program, more than 90 percent of whom were Black. The following year, the state of Louisiana expelled twenty-three thousand children from AFDC, the majority of whom were Black, on the grounds of unsuitability (Lawrence-Webb 1997).

These events triggered enough public attention to form the basis of the Flemming Rule, which prohibited states from denying eligibility for AFDC due to unsuitability clauses. However, the law also required that states investigate homes that had been deemed unsuitable and, if determined to be unsafe, either provide income assistance or place children in foster care to ensure their safety. This was followed in 1962 by the Public Welfare Amendments to the Social Security Act, which emphasized removal as an intervention when caseworkers deemed families neglectful. The combination of these policy changes, along with the disproportionate number of Black families that were expelled from AFDC and subsequently deemed unsafe by caseworkers who at the time were predominantly White, led to what we now refer to as racial disproportionality, as the majority of children placed in foster care following implementation of the Flemming Rule were Black.

Since then, the role of child welfare policies and their implementation has continued to disproportionately impact Black children. The Child Abuse Prevention Treatment Act (CAPTA) of 1974 introduced mandatory reporting laws, which resulted in a rapid growth of maltreatment allegations and placement of children in foster care. CAPTA also established mandatory minimum federal definitions of child maltreatment. However, CAPTA allowed states broad discretion to expand on these definitions, resulting in laws that vary widely by state and often reflect current social problems within the context of those states. Over the decades following CAPTA, these definitions were largely influenced by racial narratives including the War on Drugs, "welfare queens," "crack babies," and beliefs about appropriate parenting standards that may reflect a White, middle-class lens.

Beyond specific federal policies, the fundamental principle that governs child welfare decision-making, the "best interests of the child" standard, has repeatedly been challenged due to its potential for bias given its ambiguous definition, which leaves room for substantial subjectivity in application. Legal scholar Tanya Asim Cooper (2014, 107) said of the best interest standard, "Its lack of definitive guidance allows foster care professionals and even judges to substitute their own judgment about what is in a child's best interest and allows unintended biases to permeate decision-making." Even the Supreme Court has acknowledged the potential for bias, stating the best interest standard "is imprecise and open to the subjective values of the judge" (*Lassiter v. Department of Social Services* 1981).

Racial bias and decision-making

Beyond the institutional racism embedded within child welfare systems through its origins and policies, racial biases among child welfare and other professionals further contribute to racial inequity. Multiple studies have shown that race significantly impacts decision-making among professional reporters at the point of initial referral. This evidence is most clear among medical professionals. In their seminal study, Jenny et al. (1999) found that among children seen in a hospital for head injuries, abusive head trauma was significantly more likely to be overlooked by physicians if the child was White. Since then, multiple additional studies have identified racial biases among medical personnel. Lane et al. (2002) found that non-White children with accidental injuries were more than three times as likely than White children to be reported for abuse, even after controlling for income. Hymel et al. (2018) found that non-White children with head injuries were nearly twice as likely to be reported for abusive head trauma than White children with similar injuries. Further studies have found that among children who present with head injuries, Black children are more likely than White children to be referred for full skeletal surveys and more likely to be reported for maltreatment (e.g., Lane et al. 2002; Lindberg et al. 2012). Similar disparities have also been documented among educational personnel (e.g., Krase 2015) and other professional reporters (e.g., Krase 2013). Overall, this body of research demonstrates that not only are Black children overreported, but White children in need of intervention are underreported.[3]

Multiple studies have examined the extent to which racial bias impacts decision-making at various decision points once families are involved in the system by using statistical controls to isolate the role of race. These findings have been conflicting, with some finding that, after controlling for poverty or other socioeconomic measures, race is not a significant explanatory factor (Drake, Lee, and Jonson-Reid 2009; Font, Berger, and Slack 2012). However, others have found that even after adjusting for socioeconomic measures, race remains a significant explanatory variable, suggesting the influence of bias (Dettlaff et al. 2011; M. Miller 2008).[4]

As an example, Rivaux et al. (2008) used data from Texas to examine two related decision points—the decision to provide services to families, and the decision to remove a child from the home in lieu of receiving in-home services. After controlling for both income and risk as defined by CPS caseworkers, results indicated that race was a significant predictor of both decision points. After controlling for income and risk, Black children were 20 percent more likely than White children to be involved in cases in which services were provided and 77 percent more likely than White children to be removed in lieu of receiving in-home services. The inclusion of risk in this study, in addition to income, allowed for an important interpretation to be made regarding the role of race, as decisions to place children in foster care are based largely on the assessment of risk of future maltreatment. By holding both risk and income constant, the emergence of race as a significant predictor indicates that the race of the child influenced the decisions made regarding that child, providing evidence of the role of bias.

As further evidence, results showed that Black families were consistently assessed as having *lower risk* than White families, even though they were more likely to receive services and experience removal. The authors suggest that rather than race directly influencing the assessment of risk, disparities may be better explained by differences in the *decision threshold* caseworkers use when making decisions, suggesting that although Black families were assessed as having lower risk, there was a different threshold for taking action (e.g., removal), and that threshold is lower for taking action on Black families than it is for White families.

In addition to studies that have used statistical analyses to examine the role of race, a large body of qualitative studies has documented the experience of Black families encountering bias in their interactions with child welfare systems (see, for example, Merritt, this volume). These studies have consistently documented Black families' experiences of disrespectful treatment, cultural misunderstandings, harsh judgments of differing parenting styles, and a lack of culturally appropriate services (e.g., Harris and Hackett 2008; K. Miller, Cahn, and Orellana 2012). In studies that have included child welfare and legal professionals, these professionals have consistently affirmed the experiences of Black families, acknowledging the role of racial biases not only in their own decision-making, but also in assessment measures, licensing standards, and interventions to assist families (e.g., Dettlaff and Rycraft 2010).

In sum, the racist origins of the child welfare system have led to decades of policies that contribute to the disproportionate involvement of Black children and families. The harmful effects of these policies are exacerbated by decision-making that may be influenced by racial biases. Although disproportionate need may result from factors external to the child welfare system, once Black children come to the attention of this system, they become involved in a system that institutionally perpetuates and maintains these inequities, resulting in ongoing harm. The following section discusses the actions needed to address this persistent and ongoing problem.

Addressing Racial Disproportionality and Disparities

We previously noted that researchers have documented racial disproportionality and disparities in the child welfare system for more than 50 years. Although research has found substantial reductions in the involvement of Black children (and increases in involvement of White children) over the last two decades, racial disproportionality and disparities persist. We argue that disproportionality and disparities are problems that need to be addressed due to the disproportionate harm that we suggest they cause Black children and families. These persistent inequities perpetuate the oppressive conditions that cause harm to Black children and families as a result of ongoing structural and institutional racism in society.

Over the last several decades, child welfare systems have employed a number of strategies in attempts to address racial disproportionality. These include interventions at both the individual and systems levels. Interventions at the individual level have focused largely on addressing aspects of decision-making to minimize bias, including the use of standardized risk assessments, cultural responsiveness training, and family group decision-making. Standardized risk assessments may reduce bias and inconsistencies by aiding workers in making uniform decisions, and some research has demonstrated that these tools may assist in more accurately predicting risk across racial groups (e.g., Baird and Wagner 2000). However, as we noted previously, research has also demonstrated that decision thresholds for taking action based on risk may differ across racial groups and contribute to disparities (Rivaux et al. 2008). (See Drake and colleagues, this volume, for an extensive discussion of risk assessment strategies.) Different forms of cultural responsiveness training have shown to increase knowledge and understanding of how biases may impact decision-making; however, this has not been specifically linked to differences in outcomes (e.g., O. Miller and Esenstad 2015). Family group decision-making (FGDM), which includes the family and key figures in the child's life in planning for services at key decision points, may assist in reducing disparities by giving voice to perspectives that extend beyond the individual caseworker. Although findings on the effectiveness of FGDM in reducing disproportionality are mixed, a small number of studies have found that FGDM may lead to shorter stays in care and increased reunifications for Black children (e.g., Sheets et al. 2009).

Interventions at the agency-systemic level include agency leadership, community partnerships, and improvements to kinship and adoption. Research has shown that in jurisdictions that have successfully reduced disproportionality, agency leadership was an essential aspect of this by identifying disproportionality as a problem and setting a commitment to address it (O. Miller and Esenstad 2015). Research has also demonstrated that meaningful agency-community partnerships, including the use of satellite offices, can improve culturally responsive service delivery, which may be associated with reductions in disproportionality (e.g., Lemon, D'Andrade, and Austin 2008). Finally, expanding the use of informal kinship care and subsidized guardianships to facilitate exits from foster care to relatives may improve permanency for Black children (e.g., Testa 2002).

However, despite these efforts and the progress that has been made, attention to disproportionality and disparities has waned in recent years, and what has been observed as a problem for five decades is now viewed by many as an acceptable status quo. This has resulted largely from the ongoing debate in child welfare about the causes of disproportionality. Those who argue that disproportionate need is the primary cause of disproportionality largely argue that racism and bias in child welfare systems is not a significant factor and have been critical of efforts to address disproportionality through cultural responsiveness training or other efforts to address bias. These arguments that frame disproportionate need as the predominant driver of disproportionality have led child welfare systems to function as if the causes of disproportionality occur outside their systems, and as a result, racial disproportionality is to be expected, which may result in a failure to take action to address it.

We argue that racism, both internal and external to child welfare systems, is the underlying cause of disproportionality and disparities therein. Yet to what extent is racism also the cause of current complacency toward addressing these problems? To what extent does racism drive the current narrative that accepts inequity as the status quo? Dr. Ibram Kendi (2019, 17–18) defines racism as "a marriage of racist policies and racist ideas that produces and normalizes racist inequities." The child welfare system was founded on the *racist idea* that White children are superior to Black children and, over the last century, this *racist idea* formed the basis of *racist policies* that have governed the child welfare system to produce and normalize the *racist inequities* that continue to exist today. We believe this normalization is found in the narratives that claim racial disproportionality is to be expected due to "disproportionate need." Yet racial inequities should never be accepted as a status quo, neither in society nor in the child welfare system.

So, what should be done to address ongoing racial disproportionality and disparities? Can a system that began with a racist intent evolve into a system that achieves racial equity? Or does a new framework need to be considered that reimagines the child welfare system as a fundamentally different system than the one that exists today? Antiracism is a practice that opposes institutional and systemic policies and practices that produce and maintain racial inequity. Applying an antiracist framework to child welfare begins by acknowledging that racial disproportionality and disparities are maintained through the policies of the system, as well as the broader society, in which they exist. Kendi defines racist policies as those policies that produce and maintain racial inequity, while antiracist policies are those that produce and maintain racial equity. In this definition, "policy" is used broadly to include all "written and unwritten laws, rules, procedures, processes, regulations, and guidelines that govern people" (2019, 18). All policies either produce racial inequity or they produce racial equity. Applying an antiracist framework to child welfare acknowledges the racist origins of child welfare policies and practices, identifies the ways in which current policies and practices produce and maintain inequity, and re-creates those policies and practices—both within child welfare systems and in the larger societal context—in a way that is designed to achieve racial equity.

Thus, an antiracist framework is not one of reform, it is one of re-creation. This section began with a review of interventions that have been used in attempts to address racial disproportionality and disparities. Yet it is clear that these strategies are not sufficient. Decades of work have been done, yet racial inequities that harm Black children and families remain. An antiracist framework calls for an end to the policies and practices that continue to produce these inequities. Within the child welfare system, those policies and practices are those that support the involuntary separation and removal of children from their families of origin. The elimination of racial disproportionality and disparities, and the harm they cause, will only be achieved when the forcible separation of children from their parents is no longer viewed as an acceptable form of intervention for families in need. The harm that results from this intervention, and the families that are destroyed as a result, fundamentally distinguishes foster care and the child welfare system from any other system or means of helping vulnerable families. This harm will only be stopped through the elimination of foster care as an intervention and a fundamental reimagining of the meaning of the welfare of children.

Decades of child welfare policy have created the child welfare system that exists today, and as such, ending foster care as an intervention is a long-term strategy that will require gradual steps. However, we believe this needs to be a necessary goal, and actions need to be taken to move toward that goal. This can begin with the following actions.

Enhance the economic safety net for families in need

The economic safety net consists of various programs intended to alleviate poverty among families with low income (e.g., TANF; Supplemental Nutrition Assistance Program [SNAP]; Head Start; Special Supplemental Nutrition Program for Women, Infants, and Children [WIC]; Earned Income Tax Credit [EITC]; childcare and housing subsidies; and so on). Mounting evidence points to clear connections between safety net policies and child maltreatment prevention. Restrictions on safety net policies (e.g., reductions in welfare benefits, lifetime welfare limits, and sanctions) can contribute to increased maltreatment risk and involvement with CPS (Slack, Lee, and Berger 2007), while policies that increase subsidies or continue eligibility (e.g., increased income via the EITC, additional child support) can decrease this (Berger et al. 2017; Cancian, Yang, and Slack 2013). Safety net policies provide existing infrastructures that target the most economically vulnerable families. Using these avenues to invest economic and material support can disrupt cycles of instability and circumvent the need for child welfare system intervention. In addition to safety net programs, targeting family-centered work policies such as paid leave (i.e., parental leave and sick leave), livable wages, and consistent and flexible work schedules can also strengthen household financial security and reduce risks that may lead to child welfare intervention.

Fund robust public health approaches to child maltreatment prevention

Child maltreatment is increasingly acknowledged as a costly public health problem. Yet to what extent are public health approaches reflected in the current service infrastructure of the child welfare system? The funding and implementation of public health approaches to maltreatment prevention (see articles by Jones Harden and colleagues, this volume; and Roygardner, Hughes, and Palusci, this volume) have lagged despite consensus that maltreatment prevention cannot occur by intervening only after maltreatment allegations are reported to CPS. To move from rhetoric to action, we must place greater emphasis on public health approaches that center the needs of families and include primary prevention services outside the child welfare system to provide help before maltreatment occurs. Public health approaches also include universal, non–means tested services that are delivered to entire communities and provide a wide continuum of activities that extend beyond direct services to include neighborhood activities that engage parents, public policies, and institutions that support families, and public education efforts to change social norms and behavior (Zimmerman and

Mercy 2010). Policies that apply a public health lens to maltreatment prevention are needed to replace foster care as a primary intervention and to shift from the reliance on interventions that target individual behavior change to those that intervene on social determinants of health.

Raise the threshold that must be met before removal is authorized and build structures to enforce this

Although involuntary removal is supposed to occur only in cases where there is an imminent danger of serious harm, children are often removed in cases that do not meet this standard (Khan 2019; Pelton 2015). In addition to being subject to bias, decisions to remove can be subjective and reactionary, as can be seen in evidence that documents increased rates of removals following high-profile child deaths (e.g., Kramer 2018). Studies have documented that removal decisions are often based on fear of liability rather than best interests of children, with case-workers describing removals as the "safe decision" over family preservation (e.g., Dettlaff and Rycraft 2008). State statutes require that child welfare agencies engage in "reasonable efforts" to prevent placement of children in foster care. What constitutes reasonable efforts is not defined in federal law and is only vaguely defined in state statutes, yet at a minimum this should include demonstrating that caseworkers explored all other options to ensure child safety, and removal is the only available option to protect a child from imminent and serious harm. However, reasonable efforts are rarely enforced. Policies should be developed to strengthen the enforcement of "reasonable efforts" and provide greater oversight to removal decision-making to ensure only the most severe cases result in involuntary removal.

Trust Black communities to care for Black children

When Black children and families were excluded from the child welfare system during its origins, Black communities developed means of supporting each other and aiding families in need. Can we envision a society in which family and community members are once again first responders to families in crisis rather than government officials? We can move toward this way of responding by expanding the use of and eliminating barriers to informal kinship care. Informal kinship care refers to situations in which parents voluntarily place their children with kin without formal involvement of the child welfare system. In these situations, kin are not required to be licensed or approved according to agency regulations. However, these regulations are often still used to eliminate potential kin providers, even in informal arrangements. To facilitate expansion, child welfare systems should develop policies to eliminate barriers to these placements not directly related to child safety (e.g., nonviolent criminal histories, space requirements). Child welfare systems should also expand the definition of "kin" to include fictive kin (i.e., nonrelated caregivers with close family ties), which currently exists in only twenty-eight states (Child Welfare Information Gateway

2018). While expanding informal kinship care lessens family regulation and oversight by child welfare systems, it also results in a loss of financial support from child welfare systems that comes with formal kin caregiving relationships. As a result, we need policies that provide material supports for informal kin arrangements, whether from child welfare systems or from expansions in existing safety net programs, such as food and clothing allowances, or from expansions in existing safety net programs, such as TANF, SNAP, and children's health insurance.

Conclusion

Placement in foster care disproportionately harms Black children and families through disproportionate rates of removal and the resulting adverse outcomes associated with foster care. Although child welfare reforms have occurred over decades, they have focused largely on system improvements, while the fundamental intervention of forcible involuntary separation has remained unchanged. Eliminating the racial inequities that exist in the child welfare system, as in society at large, will require bold steps that reimagine our understanding of child welfare and child well-being. Envisioning a future where racial disproportionality and disparities no longer exist requires reimagining how society responds to children and families in need. Envisioning a future where racial disproportionality and disparities no longer exist requires envisioning a future where families are strengthened and supported, rather than surveilled and separated. After decades of attempts to address the harm the child welfare system causes to Black children and families, it is now time to acknowledge that child welfare is not a broken system, but rather a system that needs to be broken.

Notes

1. Overrepresentation has been observed among Native American children, who represent approximately 2 percent of children in foster care although they represent only 1 percent of the general child population. Latinx children are underrepresented at the national level, although overrepresentation exists in certain states. As the body of research on disproportionality, as well as debates concerning the appropriate response, has focused primarily on Black children, this article addresses racial disproportionality and disparities among Black children.

2. It is important to note that estimates of disparities may differ considerably when raw differences between groups are considered, as opposed to adjusted differences, which, for example, represent differences between groups conditional on factors such as income, family structure, parental education, and others. We argue that racial disparities in the child welfare system are of concern whether they are robust to such adjustment given that the differences in underlying factors that may lead to such disparities are, themselves, symptoms of historical and contemporary structural inequalities and systemic and institutional racism.

3. This phenomenon has been documented in other systems as well, such that Black youth are twice as likely to be arrested than White youth although self-reported offenses are comparable (e.g., Lauritsen 2005), and Black youth are more likely to be suspended from school compared to White youth who engage in similar behaviors (e.g., Shollenberger 2015). Research on racial disparities has been much more extensive in these systems with much research supporting the role of racial bias in contributing to these

disparities. While not directly comparable to child welfare systems, the pattern of disparities and consistency of findings across systems are of note.

4. It is important to note that many factors related to methodological differences in this body of work—samples, geography, analytic strategy—may explain differences in these findings. It is also important to note that this body of work is relatively small compared to the work that has been done on racial disparities in some other disciplines. Much further research is needed in child welfare to better understand these disparities.

References

Baird, Christopher, and Dennis Wagner. 2000. The relative validity of actuarial and consensus-based risk assessment systems. *Children and Youth Services Review* 22:839–71.

Barth, Richard. 2005. Child welfare and race: Models of disproportionality. In *Race matters in child welfare*, eds. Dennette Derezotes, John Poertner, and Mark Testa, 25–46. Washington, DC: Child Welfare League of America Press.

Bartholet, Elizabeth. 2009. The racial disproportionality movement in child welfare: False facts and dangerous directions. *Arizona Law Review* 51:871–932.

Bates, Julia. 2016. The role of race in legitimizing institutionalization: A comparative analysis of early child welfare intiatives in the United States. *Journal of the History of Childhood and Youth* 9:15–28.

Bell, Winifred. 1965. *Aid to dependent children*. New York, NY: Columbia University Press.

Berger, Lawrence, Sarah Font, Kristen Slack, and Jane Waldfogel. 2017. Income and child maltreatment in unmarried families: Evidence from the Earned Income Tax Credit. *Review of Economics of the Household* 15:1345–72.

Cancian, Maria, Mi-Youn Yang, and Kristen Slack. 2013. The effect of additional child support income on the risk of child maltreatment. *Social Service Review* 87:417–37.

Casey Family Programs. 2009. *Breakthrough series collaborative: Reducing racial disproportionality and disparate outcomes for children and families of color in the child welfare system*. Washington, DC: Casey Family Programs.

Center for the Study of Social Policy. 2019. *Key equity terms and concepts*. Washington, DC: Center for the Study of Social Policy. Available from www.cssp.org.

Chetty, Raj, Nathaniel Hendren, Maggie Jones, and Sonya Porter. 2018. *Race and economic opportunity in the United States: An intergenerational perspective*. Cambridge, MA: National Bureau of Economic Research.

Child Welfare Information Gateway. 2018. *Placement of children with relatives*. Washington, DC: U.S. Department of Health and Human Services, Children's Bureau.

Cooper, Tanya A. 2014. Commentary on chapter 2. In *Civil rights in American law, history, and politics*, ed. Austin Sarat, 64–112. New York, NY: Cambridge University Press.

Courtney, Mark, Amy Dworsky, Adam Brown, Colleen Cary, Kara Love, and Vanessa Vorhies. 2011. *Midwest evaluation of the adult functioning of former foster youth: Outcomes at ages 26*. Chicago, IL: Chapin Hall.

DeGruy, Joy. 2005. *Post traumatic slave syndrome: America's legacy of enduring injury and healing*. Milwaukie, OR: Uptone Press.

Dettlaff, Alan, Stephanie Rivaux, Donald Baumann, John Fluke, Joan Rycraft, and Joyce James. 2011. Disentangling substantiation: The influence of race, income, and risk on the substantiation decision in child welfare. *Children and Youth Services Review* 33:1630–37.

Dettlaff, Alan, and Joan Rycraft. 2008. Deconstructing disproportionality: Views from multiple community stakeholders. *Child Welfare* 87:37–58.

Dettlaff, Alan, and Joan Rycraft. 2010. Factors contributing to disproportionality in the child welfare system: Views from the legal community. *Social Work* 55:213–24.

Drake, Brett, Jennifer Jolley, Paul Lanier, John Fluke, Richard Barth, and Melissa Jonson-Reid. 2011. Racial bias in child protection? A comparison of competing explanations using national data. *Pediatrics* 127:471–78.

Drake, Brett, Melissa Jonson-Reid, María Gandarilla Ocampo, Maria Morrison, and Daji Dvalishvil. 2021. A practical framework for considering the use of predictive risk modeling in child welfare. *The ANNALS of the American Academy of Political and Social Science* (this volume).

Drake, Brett, Sang Moo Lee, and Melissa Jonson-Reid. 2009. Race and child maltreatment reporting: Are Blacks overrepresented? *Children and Youth Services Review* 31:309–16.

Eberhardt, Jennifer. 2019. *Biased: Uncovering the hidden prejudice that shapes what we see, think, and do*. New York, NY: Viking.

Fluke, John, Brenda Jones Harden, Molly Jenkins, and Ashleigh Ruehrdanz. 2011. *Disparities and disproportionality in child welfare: Analysis of the research*. Washington, DC: Center for the Study of Social Policy.

Fluke, John, Ying-Ying Yuan, John Hedderson, and Patrick Curtis. 2003. Disproportionate representation of race and ethnicity in child maltreatment: Investigation and victimization. *Children and Youth Services Review* 25:359–73.

Font, Sarah, Lawrence Berger, and Maria Cancian. 2018. Permanency and the educational and economic attainment of former foster children in emerging adulthood. *American Sociological Review* 83:716–43.

Font, Sarah, Lawrence Berger, and Kristen Slack. 2012. Examining racial disproportionality in child protective services case decisions. *Children and Youth Services Review* 34:2188–2200.

Font, Sarah, Maria Cancian, and Lawrence Berger. 2019. Prevalence and risk factors for early motherhood among low-income, maltreated, and foster youth. *Demography* 56:261–84.

Geronimus, Arline, Margaret Hicken, Danya Keene, and John Bound. 2006. "Weathering" and age patterns of allostatic load scores among Blacks and Whites in the United States. *American Journal of Public Health* 96:826–33.

Gould, Elise. 2019. *State of working America wages 2018*. Washington, DC: Economic Policy Institute.

Hanks, Angela, Danyelle Solomon, and Christian Weller. 2018. *Systemic inequality: How America's structural racism helped create the Black-White wealth gap*. Washington, DC: Center for American Progress.

Hannah-Jones, Nikole. 2019. 1619 Project. *New York Times Magazine*.

Harden, Brenda Jones, Cassandra Simons, Michelle Johnson-Motoyama, and Richard Barth. 2021. The child maltreatment prevention landscape: Where are we now, and where should we go? *The ANNALS of the American Academy of Political and Social Science* (this volume).

Harris, Marian, and Wanda Hackett. 2008. Decision points in child welfare: An action research model to address disproportionality. *Children and Youth Services Review* 30:199–215.

Hines, Alice, Kathy Lemon, Paige Wyatt, and Joan Merdinger. 2004. Factors related to the disproportionate involvement of children of color in the child welfare system: A review and emerging themes. *Children and Youth Services Review* 26:507–27.

Hope, Elan, Lori Hoggard, and Alvin Thomas. 2015. Emerging into adulthood in the face of racial discrimination: Physiological, psychological, and sociopolitical consequences for African American youth. *Translational Issues in Psychological Science* 1:342–51.

Hymel, Kent, Antoinette Laskey, Kathryn Crowell, Ming Wang, Veronica Armijo-Garcia, Terra Frazier, Kelly Tieves, Robin Foster, and Kerri Weeks. 2018. Racial and ethnic disparities and bias in the evaluation and reporting of abusive head trauma. *Journal of Pediatrics* 198:137–43.

Institute of Medicine and National Research Council. 2014. *New directions in child abuse and neglect research*. Washington, DC: The National Academies Press.

James, Sherman, Nora Keenan, David Strogatz, Steven Browning, and Joanne Garrett. 1992. Socioeconomic status, John Henryism, and blood pressure in Black adults: The Pitt County study. *American Journal of Epidemiology* 135:59–67.

Jenny, Carole, Kent Hymel, Alene Ritzen, Steven Reinert, and Thomas Hay. 1999. Analysis of missed cases of abusive head trauma. *Journal of the American Medical Association* 282:621–26.

Kendi, Ibram. 2019. *How to be an antiracist*. New York, NY: One World.

Khan, Yasmeen. 2019. *Family separations in our midst*. Available from https://www.wnyc.org/story/child-removals-emergency-powers/.

KIDS Count. 2020. *Black children continue to be disproportionately represented in foster care*. Available from https://datacenter.kidscount.org/.

Kim, Hyuil, and Brett Drake. 2018. Child maltreatment risk as a function of poverty and race/ethnicity in the USA. *International Journal of Epidemiology* 47:780–87.

Kramer, Abigail. 2018. *Child welfare surge continues: Family court cases, emergency child removals remain up*. New York, NY: New School Center for New York City Affairs.

Krase, Kathryn. 2013. Difference in racially disproportionate reporting of child maltreatment across report sources. *Jouranl of Public Child Welfare* 7:351–69.

Krase, Kathryn. 2015. Child maltreatment reporting by educational personnel: Implications for racial disproportionality in the child welfare system. *Children & Schools* 37:89–99.

Lane, Wendy, David Rubin, Ragin Monteith, and Cindy Christian. 2002. Racial differences in the evaluation of pediatric fractures for physical abuse. *Journal of the American Medical Association* 288:1603–9.

Lassiter v. Department of Social Services, 452 U.S. 18 (1981).

Lauritsen, Janet. 2005. Racial and ethnic difference in juvenile offending. In *Our children, their children*, eds. Darnell Hawkins and Kimberly Kempf-Leonard, 83–104. Chicago, IL: University of Chicago Press.

Lawrence-Webb, Claudia. 1997. African American children in the modern child welfare system: A legacy of the Flemming rule. *Child Welfare* 76:9–30.

Lemon, Kathy, Amy D'Andrade, and Michael Austin. 2008. Understanding and addressing racial/ethnic disparities in the front end of the child welfare system. *Journal of Evidence-Based Social Work* 5:9–30.

Lindberg, Daniel, Robert Shapiro, Antoinette Laskey, Daniel Pallin, Emily Blood, and Rachel Berger. 2012. Prevalence of abusive injuries in siblings and household contacts of physically abused children. *Pediatrics* 130:193–201.

Maguire-Jack, Kathryn, Sarah Font, and Rebecca Dillard. 2020. Child protective services decision-making: The role of children's race and county factors.*American Journal of Orthopsychiatry* 90:48–62.

Merritt, Darcey. 2021. How do families experience and interact with CPS? *The ANNALS of the American Academy of Political and Social Science* (this volume).

Michigan Department of Human Services. 2006. *Equity: Moving toward better outcomes for all of Michigan's children*. Lansing, MI: Michigan Department of Human Services.

Miller, Keva, Katherine Cahn, and E. Roberto Orellana. 2012. Dynamics that contribute to racial disproportionality and disparity: Perspectives from child welfare professionals, community partners, and families. *Children and Youth Services Review* 34:2201–7.

Miller, Marna. 2008. *Racial disproportionality in Washington State's child welfare system*. Olympia, WA: Washington State Institute for Public Policy.

Miller, Oronde, and Amelia Esenstad. 2015. *Strategies to reduce racially disparate outcomes in child welfare*. Washington, DC: Center for the Study of Social Policy.

Mitchell, Monique, and Leon Kuczynski. 2009. Does anyone know what is going on? Examining children's lived experience of the transition into foster care. *Children and Youth Services Review* 32:437–44.

National Child Traumatic Stress Network. 2016. *Racial injustice and trauma: African Americans in the U.S.* Washington DC: National Child Traumatic Stress Network.

O'Connor, Stephen. 2004. *Orphan trains: The story of Charles Loring Brace and the children he saved and failed*. Chicago, IL: University of Chicago Press.

Paradies, Yin, Jehonathan Ben, Nida Denson, Amanuel Elias, Naomi Priest, Alex Pieterse, Arpana Gupta, Margaret Kelaher, and Gilbert Gee. 2015. Racism as a determinant of health: A systematic review and meta-analysis.*PloS One* 10(9).

Pecora, Peter, Ronald Kessler, Jason Williams, Kirk O'Brien, A. Chris Downs, Diana English, and James White, et al. 2005. *Improving family foster care: Findings from the Northwest Foster Care Alumni Study*. Seattle, WA: Casey Family Programs.

Pelton, Leroy. 2015. The continuing role of material factors in child maltreatment and placement. *Child Abuse & Neglect* 41:30–39.

Putnam-Hornstein, Emily, Barbara Needell, Bryn King, and Michelle Johnson-Motoyama. 2013. Racial and ethnic disparities: A population-based examination of risk factors for involvement with child protective services. *Child Abuse & Neglect* 37:33–46.

Rivaux, Stephanie, Joyce James, Kim Wittenstrom, Donald Baumann, Janess Sheets, Judith Henry, and Victoria Jeffries. 2008. The intersection of race, poverty, and risk: Understanding the decision to provide services to clients and to remove children. *Child Welfare* 87:151–68.

Roberts, Dorothy. 2002. *Shattered bonds: The color of child welfare*. New York, NY: Civitas.

Rothstein, Richard. 2017.*The color of law: A forgotten history of how our government segregated America*. New York, NY: Liveright Publishing.

Roygardner, Debangshu, Kelli N. Hughes, and Vincent J. Palusci. 2021. Leveraging family and community strengths to reduce child maltreatment. *The ANNALS of the American Academy of Political and Social Science* (this volume).

Rudden, Jennifer. 2019. *Homeownership rate in the U.S. 2019, by ethnicity.* Available from www.statista .com.

Sankaran, Vivek, Christopher Church, and Monique Mitchell. 2019. A cure worse than the disease? The impact of removal on children and their families. *Marquette Law Review* 102:1163–94.

Sedlak, Andrea, Jane Mettenburg, Monica Basena, Ian Petta, Karla McPherson, Angela Greene, and Spencer Li. 2010. *Fourth National Incidence Study of Child Abuse and Neglect (NIS–4).* Washington, DC: Department of Health and Human Services, Administration for Children and Families.

Semega, Jessica, Melissa Kollar, John Creamer, and Abinash Mohanty. 2019. *Current population reports, P60-266, income and poverty in the United States: 2018.* Washington, DC: U.S. Government Printing Office.

Sheets, Janess, Kim Wittenstrom, Rowena Fong, Joyce James, Michale Tecci, Doanld Baumann, and Carolyne Rodriguez. 2009. Evidence-based practice in family group decision-making for Anglo, African American and Hispanic families. *Children and Youth Services Review* 31:1187–91.

Shollenberger, Tracey. 2015. Racial disparities in school suspension and subsequent outcomes. In *Closing the school discipline gap*, ed. Daniel Losen, 31–43. New York, NY: Teachers College Press.

Slack, Kristen, Lawrence Berger, Kimberly DuMont, Mi-Youn Yang, Bomi Kim, Susan Ehrhard-Dietzel, and Jane Holl. 2011. Risk and protective factors for child neglect during early childhood: A cross-study comparison. *Children and Youth Services Review* 33:1354–63.

Slack, Kristen, Bong Joo Lee, and Lawrence Berger. 2007. Do welfare sanctions increase child protective services involvement? A cautious answer. *Social Service Review* 81:207–28.

Soto, José, Nana Dawson-Andoh, and Rhonda BeLue. 2011. The relationship between perceived discrimination and generalized anxiety disorder among African Americans, Afro Caribbeans, and non-Hispanic Whites. *Journal of Anxiety Disorders* 25:258–65.

Stanford Center on Poverty and Inequality. 2017. *State of the union: The poverty and inequality report.* Stanford, CA: Stanford Center on Poverty and Inequality.

Summers, Alicia, Steve Wood, and Jesse Russell. 2012. *Disproportionality rates for children of color in foster care.* Reno, NV: National Council of Juvenile and Family Court Judges.

Testa, Mark. 2002. Subsidized guardianship: Testing an idea whose time has finally come. *Social Work Research* 26:145–58.

Texas Health and Human Services Commission. 2006. *Disproportionality in child protective services: Statewide reform effort begins with examination of the problem.* Austin, TX: Texas Health and Human Services Commission.

U.S. Government Accountability Office. 2007. *Black children in foster care: Additional HHS assistance needed to help states reduce the proportion in care.* Washington, DC: U.S. Government Accountability Office.

Williams, David, Jourdyn Lawrence, and Brigette Davis. 2019. Racism and health: evidence and needed research. *Annual Review of Public Health* 40:105–12.

Williams, Heather. 2012. *Help me to find my people: The African American search for family lost in slavery.* Chapel Hill, NC: University of North Carolina Press.

Zimmerman, Francie, and James Mercy. 2010. A better start: Child maltreatment prevention as a public health priority. *Zero to Three* 30:4–10.

STATEMENT OF OWNERSHIP, MANAGEMENT, AND CIRCULATION
P.S. Form 3526 Facsimile

TITLE: THE ANNALS OF THE AMERICAN ACADEMY OF POLITICAL AND SOCIAL SCIENCE
USPS PUB. #: 026-060

DATE OF FILING: OCTOBER 1, 2020

FREQUENCY OF ISSUE: Bi-monthly
NO. OF ISSUES ANNUALLY: 6
ANNUAL SUBSCRIPTION PRICE: Institution $1,232.00
                                                                Individual $134.00

PUBLISHER ADDRESS: 2455 Teller Road, Thousand Oaks, CA 91320
CONTACT PERSON: Graeme Doswell, Head of Global Circulation
TELEPHONE: (805) 499-0721

HEADQUARTERS ADDRESS: 2455 Teller Road, Thousand Oaks, CA 91320

PUBLISHER: SAGE Publications Inc., 2455 Teller Road, Thousand Oaks, CA 91320
EDITOR:
Thomas A. Kecskemethy, 202 S. 36th Street, Philadelphia, PA 19104

10. OWNER: The American Academy of Political and Social Science
202 S. 36th Street, Philadelphia, PA 19104-3806

11. KNOWN BONDHOLDERS, ETC.
None

12. NONPROFIT PURPOSE, FUNCTION, STATUS:
Has Not Changed During Preceding 12 Months

13. PUBLICATION NAME: THE ANNALS OF THE AMERICAN ACADEMY OF POLITICAL AND SOCIAL SCIENCE

14. ISSUE DATE FOR CIRCULATION DATA BELOW: MAY 2020

15. EXTENT & NATURE OF CIRCULATION:

	AVG. NO. COPIES EACH ISSUE DURING PRECEDING 12 MONTHS	ACT. NO. COPIES OF SINGLE ISSUE PUB. NEAREST TO FILING DATE
TOTAL NO. COPIES	454	420
PAID CIRCULATION		
1. PAID/REQUESTED OUTSIDE-CO, ETC	308	289
2. PAID IN-COUNTY SUBSCRIPTIONS	0	0
3. SALES THROUGH DEALERS, ETC.	11	4
4. OTHER CLASSES MAILED USPS	0	0
TOTAL PAID CIRCULATION	319	293
FREE DISTRIBUTION BY MAIL		
1. OUTSIDE-COUNTY AS ON 3541	16	14
2. IN-COUNTY AS STATED ON 3541	0	0
3. OTHER CLASSES MAILED USPS	0	0
FREE DISTRIBUTION OTHER	0	0
TOTAL FREE DISTRIBUTION	16	14
TOTAL DISTRIBUTION	335	307
COPIES NOT DISTRIBUTED		
1. OFFICE USE, ETC.	119	113
2. RETURN FROM NEWS AGENTS	0	0
TOTAL	454	420
PERCENT PAID CIRCULATION	95%	95%

16. THIS STATEMENT OF OWNERSHIP WILL BE PRINTED IN THE NOVEMBER 2020 ISSUE OF THIS PUBLICATION.

17. I CERTIFY THAT ALL INFORMATION FURNISHED ON THIS FORM IS TRUE AND COMPLETE.
I UNDERSTAND THAT ANYONE WHO FURNISHES FALSE OR MISLEADING INFORMATION ON
THIS FORM OR WHO OMITS MATERIAL OR INFORMATION REQUESTED ON THE FORM MAY
BE SUBJECT TO CRIMINAL SANCTIONS (INCLUDING FINES AND IMPRISONMENT) AND/OR
CIVIL SANCTIONS (INCLUDING MULTIPLE DAMAGES AND CIVIL PENALTIES).

Graeme Doswell

Graeme Doswell   Date: 08/10/2020
Head of Business Solutions & System Operations
SAGE Publications, Inc.

In compliance with GPSR, should you have any concerns about the safety of this product, please advise: International Associates Auditing & Certification Limited The Black Church, St Mary's Place, Dublin 7, D07 P4AX Ireland EUAR@ie.ia-net.com

www.ingramcontent.com/pod-product-compliance
Lightning Source LLC
Chambersburg PA
CBHW060313030426
42336CB00011B/1029